CIVIL PROCEDURE FOR ALL STATES

CAROLINA ACADEMIC PRESS
Context and Practice Series
Michael Hunter Schwartz
Series Editor

Contracts
A Context and Practice Casebook
Michael Hunter Schwartz and Denise Riebe

Civil Procedure for All States
A Context and Practice Casebook
Benjamin V. Madison, III

CIVIL PROCEDURE FOR ALL STATES

A Context and Practice Casebook

Benjamin V. Madison, III

CAROLINA ACADEMIC PRESS

Durham, North Carolina

ISBN 978-1-59460-510-9
LCCN 2010924058

Carolina Academic Press
700 Kent Street
Durham, North Carolina 27701
Telephone (919) 489-7486
Fax (919) 493-5668
www.cap-press.com

Printed in the United States of America

To my wife, Judy; my sons, Daniel, Andrew, and Stephen;
and my daughters, Mary and Eliza

Contents

Table of Principal Cases

Series Editor's Preface

Welcome to a new type of casebook. Designed by leading experts in law school teaching and learning, Context and Practice casebooks assist law professors and their students to work together to learn, minimize stress, and prepare for the rigors and joys of practicing law. **Student learning and preparation for law practice are the guiding ethics of these books.**

Why would we depart from the tried and true? Why have we abandoned the legal education model by which we were trained? Because legal education can and must improve.

In Spring 2007, the Carnegie Foundation published *Educating Lawyers: Preparation for the Practice of Law* and the Clinical Legal Education Association published *Best Practices for Legal Education*. Both works reflect in-depth efforts to assess the effectiveness of modern legal education, and both conclude that legal education, as presently practiced, falls quite short of what it can and should be. Both works criticize law professors' rigid adherence to a single teaching technique, the inadequacies of law school assessment mechanisms, and the dearth of law school instruction aimed at teaching law practice skills and inculcating professional values. Finally, the authors of both books express concern that legal education may be harming law students. Recent studies show that law students, in comparison to all other graduate students, have the highest levels of depression, anxiety and substance abuse.

The problems with traditional law school instruction begin with the textbooks law teachers use. Law professors cannot implement *Educating Lawyers* and *Best Practices* using texts designed for the traditional model of legal education. Moreover, even though our understanding of how people learn has grown exponentially in the past 100 years, no law school text to date even purports to have been designed with educational research in mind.

The Context and Practice Series is an effort to offer a genuine alternative. Grounded in learning theory and instructional design and written with *Educating Lawyers* and *Best Practices* in mind, Context and Practice casebooks make it easy for law professors to change.

I welcome reactions, criticisms, and suggestions; my e-mail address is michael.schwartz@washburn.edu. Knowing the author(s) of these books, I know they, too, would appreciate your input; we share a common commitment to student learning. In fact, students, if your professor cares enough about your learning to have adopted this book, I bet s/he would welcome your input, too!

Professor Michael Hunter Schwartz, Series Designer and Editor
Co-Director, Institute for Law Teaching and Learning
Associate Dean for Faculty and Academic Development

Preface and Acknowledgments

Although federal civil procedure casebooks abound, the few casebooks on state civil procedure are state-specific, useful for teaching only in one state. Most states have no casebook at all. I know because I have repeatedly looked without success in the state in which I teach for a casebook that would enhance my teaching of state civil procedure. Professors teaching state civil procedure often must cobble together teaching materials from various sources. Thus, the need for a state civil procedure casebook has existed, in most states, for a long time.

After a period of reflection and study, I reached an interesting conclusion about federal and state procedures. I examined my litigation experience at a law firm that practiced nationwide. I also reviewed the few surveys comparing federal procedures to state procedures and extensively researched the procedural law of a cross-section of states. The culmination of this reflection and research convinced me of two general realities—(1) that procedures throughout various states are far more alike than different, and (2) that many states follow federal practice, though the form of federal practice may be from an earlier time that has since changed in modern federal courts. These realizations nudged me in the direction of writing a casebook that could be used to teach civil procedure in all fifty states and the District of Columbia (DC). But how could a casebook incorporate the law of all fifty states and DC in the traditional model of a casebook, dependent on cases, statutes, etc.?

Two influential studies answered my question. In Spring 2007, the Carnegie Foundation's *Educating Lawyers*[1] and Roy Stuckey's *Best Practices for Legal Education*[2] offered significant insights into the need for changes in law teaching. Both reports concluded that law school teaching in general and casebooks in particular were deficient. The studies urged less emphasis on the traditional case-based method. Instead the studies recommended a number of changes, three of which were most significant in writing this casebook. First, the studies demonstrate the value of moving from a case-based orientation to a problem-solving one in which students can apply legal principles to real-life problems. Second, the studies emphasize the need for exercises that help students develop the skills actually employed in law practice. Third, the Carnegie and Stuckey studies stress at length that law schools must encourage students to develop a sense of professional identity. Law professors are charged with mentoring their students so that, before they leave law school, the students have defined their values and know where they will draw the line in practice so as not to compromise those values.

Around this time, I was fortunate enough to speak with Professor Michael Hunter Schwartz, the creator of the Context and Practice Casebook series and Series Editor. I found that Professor Schwartz and other law teaching experts felt, as did I, that the Carnegie and Stuckey studies called for a new type of teaching materials. Because of the

---

1. WILLIAM M. SULLIVAN, ET AL., EDUCATING LAWYERS: PREPARATION FOR THE PROFESSION OF LAW (2007).
2. ROY STUCKEY, ET AL., BEST PRACTICES FOR LEGAL EDUCATION (2007).

shift in paradigm of the effective casebook, the Context and Practice Casebook Series opened the door for me to write a casebook "for all states." Instead of excerpting cases from every state, this book describes the law in general and then explains variations on procedural doctrines. Cases are excerpted where representative of an important doctrine, but they are used far less than in traditional casebooks. To provide students with an appreciation for different approaches to a given procedural rule or doctrine, this book relies heavily on appendices. There are almost thirty appendices. Each appendix has three columns—the left column for states in the majority, the middle column for states forming a significant minority, and the right column for states that do not conform to either the majority or significant minority approach. In the text under the columns, the appendix explains the rule or doctrine in all of the approaches.

The discussion of applicable law is merely the foundation for the heart of each chapter. Follow-Up Questions offer a warm-up to ensure students grasp the applicable law. Every chapter then offers numerous "Practice Problems" and "Professional Identity Questions." These implement precisely what the Carnegie and Stuckey reports recommended. The Practice Problems offer true-to-life hypothetical fact patterns that give students the opportunity to apply the law to a set of facts and reach a conclusion. Interspersed throughout are exercises that require students to practice skills required in law practice. For example, the student may be asked to conduct a client interview or to prepare a memorandum to a senior partner analyzing the statute of limitations. Other examples of exercises include drafting pleadings and discovery; developing a discovery plan to marshal evidence necessary to survive summary judgment; drafting jury instructions; and virtually every task a litigator would have to perform in getting a case through trial and post-trial motions.

The professional identity questions woven throughout every chapter place students in many situations that test a lawyer's integrity. By considering how she would handle the situation, a student learns that the American Bar Association Model Rules of Professional Conduct may decide some questions for her—*i.e.*, no matter how uncomfortable she feels, she is bound to follow a course of action mandated by the Rules. However, these questions also illustrate the broad range of situations in which the Model Rules do not give a clear answer. Here in particular a student must define what her values are and, in light of those values, decide where she will draw the line in practice. These questions are not intended to dictate a strict value system. However, the questions do require the student to look within—and to find the moral values by which she will live. The message of Carnegie's study in particular is that lawyers who act in conflict with their values—out of some mistaken sense of having to do everything that may in any way arguably benefit a client—pay a heavy price. The goal is that, by the end of the course, students will have a better sense of what *they* value and how acting consistently with their internal values will likely bring greater fulfillment in law practice.

Acknowledgments

I first and foremost acknowledge my wife, Judy, whose support for this book took countless forms. Often she had to handle extra responsibilities with our children while I worked on researching and writing this book. At other times, she read and offered both substantive and editorial comments. As a lawyer and excellent writer, she was well-equipped to do so.

I thank Michael Hunter Schwartz for his vision in seeing the need for change in legal education and for developing the idea of, and model for, the Context and Practice Casebook Series. Mike offered excellent suggestions for integrating the Carnegie recommendations into this book. His Contracts casebook, the first in the Context and Practice Series, was a valuable model for me throughout the writing of my book. Many of the teaching methods woven into this book — ranging from graphics as visual learning tools, to practical exercises and group exercises, are the product of techniques I have learned from Mike, either in working with him before, in observing them in his Contracts casebook (the first published in the Context and Practice Series), or in his editing of this book. I am a far better teacher as a result of having worked with him on prior projects and on this book.

I also thank Gerry Hess, the Series Consultant. Because Gerry is both an expert in legal pedagogy and in civil procedure, his comments on each chapter were helpful in many ways but two in particular. First, he encouraged me to develop professional identity questions for every chapter. Gerry understands that civil litigation is an area rife with challenges for lawyers. Without his emphasis on the unique opportunity that civil procedure offers for integrating teaching on professional identity, this crucial piece of the book would be nowhere near as thorough as it turned out to be. Moreover, Gerry's knowledge of procedure allowed him to point out subtle, but important, issues. I know the book is far better as a result of his contributions.

The research necessary to determine the procedural rules and doctrines of fifty states and DC required a massive research effort from assistants. The help of the students who served as research assistants, as well as our Research Librarian Bill Magee, was invaluable. The research assistants included Anna Adams, Nate Buttars, Tim Downing, Miranda Dunning, Courtney Fogarty, John Kanaga, Analise Lang, Autumn Leva, Nathan McGrath, Michael Pallai, Andrew Porter, Matt Tapp, and Lauren Savory. Autumn Leva was the one assistant who worked on this book from its inception and for whom I will forever be grateful. My permanent professional assistant, Carol Dick, has also helped on this project from the start by formatting, copying drafts endlessly, and organizing "team" meetings of my assistants. These are but some of the ways she selflessly offered assistance. I owe her my gratitude.

Dean Jeff Brauch, Associate Dean Doug Cook, and Associate Dean Jim Murphy have supported my development as a teacher since I joined Regent's faculty. Without that development, I would not have recognized the opportunity offered by the Carnegie and Stuckey studies and by the Context and Practice Series. Other colleagues, including our Dean of Students Natt Gantt, Professor Eric Degroff, and Kathleen McKee share my interest in teaching and learning. Our discussions of their work have helped me to appreciate pedagogy as an art in which a professor should continually improve. Professor McKee and I both teach state civil procedure and have had many discussions of how to teach the course. I am sure that such discussions have seamlessly found their way into examples and exercises in this book. Dr. Edgar MacDonald is another with whom I have discussed both the subject of effective writing and the process of publishing a book. His encouragement helped more than he likely realizes. Finally, I thank Professor Doug Rendleman for his advice and support both in teaching and publishing. As the author of many widely used casebooks, his suggestions were invaluable.

Finally, I found the Carolina Academic Press team on this project to be one of the most professional and responsive groups with whom I have worked. They included Linda Lacy, Tim Colton, Kelly Miller, and Martha Hopper.

CIVIL PROCEDURE FOR
ALL STATES

Chapter 1

Introduction

The procedures of state civil judicial systems are far more alike than different. Wherever one litigates, the same step-by-step decision-making process comes into play. At some point in their careers, lawyers realize that their effectiveness in handling cases depends on their ability to make these decisions. Unfortunately, most lawyers only come to this realization after many years in practice. Trial and error, usually at the client's expense, is the typical method by which lawyers realize this crucial lesson. Ultimately, clients suffer from this education on the job. Clients pay for a lawyer's failure to make sound judgments—and not just with inflated fees. Too often poor results in a case are due to the lawyer's failure, not to the merits of the client's case.

One of the most unique features of this book is the degree to which it exposes the thought processes of a lawyer at each stage of the litigation. As this chapter explains further below, the book is organized around a Master Problem in which the student takes on the role of a new associate working on a lawsuit. The chapters progress through the typical stages of a civil suit. The first section of each chapter engages the thought processes and decisions typical of experienced lawyers. The chapter then goes on to discuss the applicable law, provide practice problems, and suggest learning tools before presenting the student with written assignments in which she must apply what she has learned to the Master Problem.

The other unique feature of this book is the degree to which it highlights the value judgments that arise at each stage of a case. Lawyers regularly face questions that test whether they will remain true to their values. Some of these judgments may seem bigger than others. Over the course of the book, as the value judgments progress, the larger lesson is that the consequences of one's decisions cannot be avoided. Lawyers who ignore their values do so at their own peril.

Over the past decade, compelling studies have demonstrated the effect on a lawyer's self-image when disconnecting her decisions from her principles. This research shows convincingly that, over time, lawyers who ignore their values in deciding legal matters develop at best, a poor self-image, and at worst, "self-loathing."[1] Moreover, the stakes are not solely whether a lawyer has a professional reputation of which she can be proud. The question more often comes down to whether, over time, the lawyer can live with herself. Those who ignore their principles are more likely to be unhappy.[2] Such lawyers suffer de-

---

1. The words of one study author are telling: "The lawyer who suppresses moral scrutiny ... fall[s] prey to a kind of self-loathing that those with integrity can resist." Reed Elizabeth Loder, *Integrity and Epistemic Passion*, 77 Notre Dame L. Rev. 841, 876 (2002).

2. *See, e.g.,* Patrick J. Shiltz, *On Being a Happy, Healthy, and Ethical Member of an Unhappy, Unhealthy, and Unethical Profession*, 52 Vand. L. Rev. 871, 906–19 (1999) (discussing the link between lawyers' decisions that lack a connection to principles, and how this relates to lawyer unhappiness and unhealthiness). For an excellent book on the manner in which lawyers can develop an integrated approach to the practice of law leads to satisfaction, see Michael Schutt, Redeeming Law (2007).

pression, get divorced at a high rate, and fall prey to substance abuse.[3] Too often "law practice" is the easy target offered as the reason for lawyers' unhappiness. In reality the problem is not law practice, but rather the way in which one practices law, and whether one maintains one's value system.

The professional identity questions interwoven throughout this book challenge a false assumption that many litigators have made for too long. That assumption is this: the supposed obligation to zealously represent one's client can override one's conscience and one's obligations as a lawyer to the judicial system. For many years now, the American Bar Association Model Rules of Professional Responsibility has eschewed the duty of "zealous" representation in favor of a duty "to act with reasonable diligence and promptness in representing the client."[4] As one commentator astutely notes, "[O]ne of the leading causes of the decline of professionalism is the probable misconception by many lawyers that former Canon 7's duty of zealous representation remains a requirement in the ABA Model Rules of Professional Conduct."[5] In reality, the ABA Model Rules — which have been adopted in at least 42 states — have removed "zeal" from its previously lofty position.[6]

The reason this book emphasizes the need for students — now, not later — to begin forming professional identities is that doing so will likely determine the extent to which the students as lawyers not only enjoy practice, but also represent their clients well. Committing to the values that guide your decision-making offers a reward you may at first not appreciate fully. Intentionally made and no longer recent enough to justify confusion, the change in the Model Rules deemphasizing "zealous" advocacy has empowered students to be the kind of lawyers they want to be. Lawyers no longer need follow the notion that they, to satisfy some conception of what a "zealous" advocate is, must override their sense of decency and right conduct to gain every possible advantage for a client. If they do, the consequences of doing so will likely be those suggested above — unhappiness, perhaps even self-loathing, and a lack of respect for themselves and their profession.

This book represents a bridge from law school to law practice. It develops the step-by-step decision-making of an effective, principled lawyer by challenging the student to put herself in the role of a young attorney making the decisions. To that end, each chap-

---

3. *See id.* at 872–81 (exploring higher than average rates among lawyers of depression, anxiety, substance abuse, divorce, and suicide); *see also* Carole J. Buckner, *Ethical Issues Arising from Lawyer Impairment*, 49-Jan. ORANGE COUNTY LAW 42, 42 (2007) ("While about ten percent of the population at large suffers substance abuse problems, substance abuse among lawyers is 50% higher."); Blane Workie, *Chemical Dependence and the Legal Profession: Should Addiction to Drugs and Alcohol Ward Off Heavy Discipline?*, 9 GEO. J. LEGAL ETHICS 1357 (1996) ("The alcoholism rate among lawyers is more than twice the rate of the general population.... The American Bar Association estimates that forty to sixty percent of attorney discipline cases involve substance abuse problems.").

4. *See* ANNOTATED MODEL RULES OF PROFESSIONAL CONDUCT 25–26 (3d ed. 1996) (specifically recognizing that "Rule 1.3 substitutes reasonable diligence and promptness for zeal").

5. *See* Allen K. Harris, *The Professionalism Crisis — the 'Z' Words and Other Rambo Tactics: The Conference of Chief Justice's Solutions*, 53 S.C. L. REV. 549, 568 (2002).

6. *See id.* Comment 1 to Rule 1.3 still includes a reference to "zeal in advocacy" but places the phrase in the context of explanations that make clear that the lawyer has the ability to exercise independent judgment, or "professional discretion in determining the means by which a matter may be pursued." AMERICAN BAR ASSOCIATION ANNOTATED MODEL RULES OF PROFESSIONAL CONDUCT RULE 1.3, comment 1 (6the ed. 2007). The comment further states that the lawyer is not obliged to "press for every advantage," that doing so should not include "offensive tactics," and that the lawyer must treat all persons in the legal process "with courtesy and respect." *See id.*

ter in the book follows the same progression. That progression is depicted in the following chart:

Table 1-1

Subheading A
Introduction to chapter explaining where in the litigation process the Master Problem stands
Subheading B
Tasks and decision-making process at this stage of litigation
Subheading C
Discussion of applicable law — followed by: (1) follow-up questions challenging students not only (a) to synthesize topics covered, but also (b) to consider decisions that will affect their professional identity and value judgments; and (2) practice problems on which students can practice written analysis of the pertinent legal issues
Subheading D
Suggested tools for students to reinforce topics covered in the chapter, typically with suggested visual learning, active learning, or other learning methods
Subheading E
Written Assignments, based on the Master Problem, at end of each chapter

As shown above, each chapter begins with Subheading A, which gives the status of the Master Problem in that chapter and asks the student to assume the role of an associate handling the Master Problem at that point. Under Subheading B, the second section of each chapter describes where in the litigation process the Master Problem stands and highlights the tasks and decision-making process of an effective litigator at that stage of litigation. The goal here is to take the student inside the mind of an experienced lawyer — to consider matters and ask questions that effective lawyers consider and ask habitually. Although students are often excellent at analyzing hypothetical fact patterns as they leave law school and enter practice, many if not most fail to appreciate the art of handling a case. If they integrate the lessons of this book, they should be far better prepared to recognize the decisions they need to make — decisions that, for many lawyers, take years of practice to learn.

The third section of each chapter, Subheading C, provides a summary of the applicable law, including majority and minority positions among jurisdictions. Few surveys of the approaches of states to the major procedural rules and doctrines exist. In this "Applicable Law" section of each chapter, the description of majority and minority rules among the states represents the result of independent research of the current law of those states. Prior surveys, such as John Oakley and Arthur Coon's excellent 1986 survey comparing the degree to which states replicated the Federal Rules of Civil Procedure[7] took a different approach from the survey represented in the appendices to this book. Building on the 1960 survey by Charles Alan Wright,[8] the authors of the 1986 survey sought to distinguish states in which the procedural systems were such that "there [was] 'but one procedure for state and federal courts' "[9]—which the authors called "federal replicas," from those states that varied from the Federal Rules.[10] The authors of the 1986 survey referred to the variations in a variety of categories seeking to classify the states' *procedural systems as a whole*.[11] For instance, the state system could have adopted the approach of many of the Federal Rules of Civil Procedure but still have procedural areas that depart from the federal approach. If so, such a state would often in the 1986 survey have been classified not as a federal replica, but rather as a variation on the Federal Rules.[12]

Professor Oakley and Mr. Coon's 1986 survey, like Professor Wright's 1960 survey, provided invaluable information about the degree to which the Federal Rules of Civil Procedure had been adopted in various states, and the degree to which variations existed. The survey represented in the appendices in this book takes a different tack. It does not seek to compare states' procedural systems *as a whole* to the Federal Rules. Rather, each appendix concentrates on a procedural rule or doctrine and provides three columns—the far-left column for the majority rule among states, the middle column if a significant minority rule exists, and the right column for states that take unique approaches (called "Nonconforming"). Furthermore, each appendix explains below the columns the criteria for determining whether a state fits the majority approach. In many cases, the criteria represent the essence of the approach of a Federal Rule of Civil Procedure. Many of the majority rules described in a given appendix coincide with the essential elements of the applicable Federal Rule of Civil Procedure. The Oakley/Coon 1986 survey did not classify a state as a Federal Rule of Civil Procedure state unless a number of criteria in that state's system had been satisfied. The approach here differs by focusing on the procedural rule or doctrine. Thus, a state may not follow the Federal Rules of Civil Procedure in parts of its system other than the rule addressed in a given appendix. However, if that state follows the essential aspects of the Federal Rule of Civil Procedure in question, then the state typically is classified as one that is consistent with the Federal Rule—often representing the majority approach among states. After identifying the criteria for the majority rule, the appendix then describes the significant minority rule or rules. The appendices serve primarily to allow students, first, to determine the majority approach on a given procedure and, second, to identify whether the state in which the student intends to practice follows the majority rule, a minority rule, or a nonconforming approach.

---

7. *See* John B. Oakley & Arthur F. Coon, *The Federal Rules in State Courts: A Survey of State Court Systems of Civil Procedure*, 61 WASH. L. REV. 1367 (1986).

8. *See id.* at 1367 (citing 1 W. BARRONG & A. HOLTZOFF, FEDERAL PRACTICE & PROCEDURE §§ 9.1–9.53 (Wright ed. 1960)).

9. *See id.* at 1372 (citing 1 W. BARRONG & A. HOLTZOFF, FEDERAL PRACTICE & PROCEDURE §§ 9 (Wright ed. 1960)).

10. *See id.* at 1373–76.

11. *See id.* at 1372–76.

12. *See id.* at 1374–1427.

Two points bear emphasis here. First, note that the measure for identification of a state's approach on a particular procedural rule or doctrine is whether it "follows the essential aspects of the Federal Rule of Civil Procedure in question." Unlike the Oakley/Coon 1986 survey, a state's adherence systemically is not the focus in this book. This book focuses on specific procedural rules, and whether those conform to majority rules — rules that are often based on the given Federal Rule of Civil Procedure in question. Thus, a state under the Oakley/Coon 1986 survey criteria that would not be considered a "Federal Rule" state, may well be one classified under the majority rule here, a rule that follows the essence of the Federal Rule in question. Lest there be any confusion about what was considered the "essential aspects" of a given Federal Rule of Civil Procedure, the textual part of each appendix explains those aspects considered essential. Thus, a state rule or statute may not be worded identically to a Federal Rule, or may have additional provisions beyond those in the Federal Rule. So long as the state approach contained those criteria identified as the essence of the Federal Rule, however, the state approach was considered consistent with the Federal Rule.

Second, the survey has revealed an interesting phenomenon that one of the 1986 survey authors found in a follow-up article to the 1986 survey. In 2003, John Oakley published an article following up on the 1986 Survey.[13] As Professor Oakley described his "new and briefer study," his follow-up analysis focused on "the degree to which [states that had been identified in 1986 as substantially conforming to the Federal Rules of Civil Procedure] have continued to conform to the Federal Rule as amended over the past two decades."[14] The 2003 survey focused on thirteen amendments to the Federal Rules of Civil Procedure since the 1986 survey and the degree to which states had followed those amendments.[15] Professor Oakley found that states had markedly "reversed" their tendency to follow the Federal Rules approach based on most of them not having adopted the post-1986 amendments.[16] One must clarify, however, just what Professor Oakley meant by a reversal in the tendency to follow the Federal Rules of Civil Procedure. The tendency Professor Oakley confirmed was that states had not enacted amendments to state rules that would ensure continued conformity to the Federal Rules of Civil Procedure.[17] Thus, state systems, since 1986, come to a point of less conformity to the Federal Rules than at the time of the Oakley/Coon survey.[18] The important qualification for this book is that the state procedures in many of these states were still ones that in essential respects followed the Federal Rules of Civil Procedure. Thus, the majority rule reflected in one of the almost thirty appendices to this book often reflects the approach of a Federal Rule, even though states have not widely embraced an amendment to the Federal Rule.

Interwoven throughout Subsection C in each chapter are three other components designed to help students integrate the procedural doctrine(s) covered there. First,

---

13. *See* John B. Oakley, *A Fresh Look at the Federal Rules in State Court*, 3 Nev. L. J. 354 (2003).
14. *See id.* at 354.
15. *See id.* at 350–60.
16. *See id.* at 355.
17. *See id.* at 359–87.
18. *See id.*

"Follow-Up Questions," seek to reinforce the material covered by asking questions to force students to reflect on the materials. Second, every chapter includes many hypothetical but life-like factual situations, called "Practice Problems," for which the procedural law discussed is essential in analyzing and reaching a conclusion. These do not typically specify the law of a particular state, but rather ask the student to determine the law of the state in which she plans to practice and apply that law to resolve the problem.

"Professional Identity Questions"[19] constitute the third category of teaching tools interwoven throughout Subsection C of each chapter. These questions invite students to engage the tough decisions that lawyers have to make. A reality that some young lawyers find hard to face is that in practice they will experience a conflict of values. The book thus encourages the student to begin deciding now, rather than after it is too late, what professional identity the lawyer wants—or, to put it in more colloquial terms, "what kind of lawyer she wants to be." In every generation, those who seek the truth about human nature, life's challenges, and the pursuit of happiness—have concluded that, ultimately, our choices determine our character. In one of his classic works, *Nichomachean Ethics*, Aristotle put it well:

> Thus, in one word, states of character arise out of like activities. This is why the activities we exhibit must be of a certain kind; it is because the states of character correspond to the differences between [various kinds of activities]. *It makes no small difference, then, whether we form habits of one kind or of another from our very youth; it makes a very great difference, or rather all the difference.*[20]

A seasoned and ethical lawyer would offer similar advice to a law student or new attorney. One should develop the habit of paying attention to one's values, in the handling of a case, and it will bear great dividends. The habit will foster strength of character that pays off when the lawyer finds herself in the crucible, with the heat rising, and pressures testing her commitment to her values. Someone who does not form habits that lead her to base decisions on principles, rather than expediency or urgency, will almost surely end up a casualty on the heap of unhappy lawyers. The symptoms of such unhappiness abound in modern law practice.[21] A lawyer's decisions inevitably result in consequences beyond a particular case. These consequences include not only the lawyer's professional reputation in the legal community, but also the lawyer's own self-concept. Will she make decisions that make her uncomfortable living in her own skin? Or will she set certain standards to govern her decision-making that reflect the value system she has integrated into her professional identity? Her habitual decisions will likely determine whether she has a reasonably healthy way of life.

Subheading D represents the fourth section of each chapter. There, students are often challenged to synthesize the steps in a particular phase of the case into a flow chart or analytical framework representing the progression of steps required for a thorough, sound

---

19. The phrase "professional identity" or "professional identity formation" may be found throughout the following recent, influential publications, Roy Stuckey, et al., Best Practices for Legal Education (2007), *available at* http://cleaweb.org/documents/bestpractices/best_practices-full.pdf; and William M. Sullivan, et al., Educating Lawyers: Preparation for the Profession of Law 56–60, 75–78 (2007).

20. Aristotle, Nicomachean Ethics, Book I, section 2 (350 B.C.).

21. *See supra* notes 2 & 3, and accompanying text from this chapter.

analysis. The aim is to explain methods by which students can learn the material through self-directed learning tools. In this way, students can not only reinforce their understanding of a chapter's content and analysis, but also practice using their analytical skills in the way they will most often display after law school—first on the bar exam, and then in practice.

The fifth section of each chapter, Subheading E, includes Written Assignments. Each of these is based on the Master Problem. In these assignments, students must engage in decision-making and display skills that lawyers routinely face handling cases. These exercises range from providing a written memorandum to a senior partner on the potential choices for a particular phase of the case, to drafting pleadings or motions at another stage, to developing a discovery plan. By the end of each chapter, a student should be equipped to perform every written assignment.

Master Problem

Following is the Master Problem that will serve as a platform for each chapter. As the chapters proceed, you (as an associate in the law firm of Dogood, Befayre, and Prosper, P.C.) will develop more facts—the way a lawyer does in real life. Here, however, are the facts with which you start:

Your client is an elderly widow, Sally Wilreiz. Sally is experiencing a run of bad luck and has a number of problems to discuss. First, Sneaky Sam, a stock broker at the investment firm of Wheeler Dealer, Inc., handled her investments. Sam absconded with funds, and many investments made through him are now worthless. Because Sam has disappeared, Sally is interested in whether she can sue Wheeler Dealer, for whom Sam worked.

Second, Sally, who owns a several-acre parcel of land in the City of Arcadia, is upset about a fence on her property. Her brother, a licensed surveyor, had surveyed the boundaries of her property over twenty years earlier when he was visiting from his home in South Africa. At some point since then, the adjoining landowner put up a fence along the back of her lot. Sally became aware of the fence only recently. On his first visit since the surveying work years ago, her brother was walking in the back yard while smoking his pipe and discovered the fence. He asked his sister whether she realized that the fence along the back of her yard was three yards within her property line.

Furthermore, Sally had a porch added to her home twelve years ago. While Sally was walking across the porch one day (six months before she came to see you), a roof panel fell on her foot. It hurt badly enough for her to have an X-ray, which showed a broken bone in her foot. As a result, she wore a walking boot for two months. She called the porch contractor, who referred her to the supplier of the roof panels. Sally related that the supplier said something about a "statute of repose" because the porch had been completed well over ten years ago.

As if these troubles were not enough, Sally recently was in an accident resulting from a large pothole on the highway. The hole was on the border between the municipality of Arcadia and the State of Illyria. (Arcadia is a municipal corporation within the State of Illyria.) The municipality is responsible for the highway within its borders, and the State for that part outside. Neither the municipality nor the State is prompt at repairing road hazards. What began as a large pothole had grown as time passed so that, by the time of the accident, even a car could fall into it.

Sally owned a 2008 Stallion convertible manufactured by HorsePower, Inc. that she had bought recently from a dealer in an adjoining state. On February 2, 2009, Sally was driving the Stallion, at the posted speed limit through the municipality of Arcadia on her way to another location outside of Arcadia. She had never driven on this particular road before. Hitting the pothole on Route 3 at the border of Arcadia and Illyria, Sally's car fell into the hole on the end within Illyria's territorial boundary—a hole that was approximately thirty-one inches deep. Her car flipped because one side entered the hole first and upset the car's balance. One of the features that led HorsePower, Inc. to claim the Stallion was the safest convertible on the road was its roll bar, a metal rod that ran up the car's sides and across the top even when the convertible's top was retracted. When Sally's car turned over, however, the roll bar crumbled. She sustained serious injuries: lacerations to her face (requiring sixty stitches and plastic surgery), a concussion, broken bones, and partial paralysis. She was in the hospital over six months. Moreover, her Stallion was totaled.

Summary of Chapter Topics and Broader Policies Underlying Procedure That Tie These Topics Together

The chapters that follow will show how Sally Wilreiz's case, in typical fashion, would present a series of decisions for you as the attorney. Before the book continues with Sally's case, however, the remainder of this chapter will address two subjects. First, it will give an overview of Chapters 2–12. Those chapters will cover litigation topics in the order in which they typically arise in a civil action. Second, the remainder of this chapter discusses the broader principles underlying the procedural system. If one views the system in pieces, the tendency is to miss the way in which the different parts fit together. One might liken the phenomenon to staring closely at one piece of a mosaic. Only when one stands back and observes the whole may one see the big picture. At times, seeing the big picture will help one at a specific phase in a case. Thus, the discussion is not an academic one, but an eminently practical one.

Summary of Remaining Chapters

The topics of Chapters 2–12 follow the progress of a case in the order in which the topics arise in a typical suit. The following timeline depicts these topics and is correlated to the chapters:

Diagram 1-1

Cause of Action (events leading to suit)
Prefiling Matters to Consider; Choice of Forum [Chs. 2–3]
Π and Δ Decide on Offensive Pleadings & Joinder (of claims & parties); Filing Suit; Service [Chs. 4–5]
Motions, Responsive Pleadings; Default; Voluntary & Involuntary Dismissals [Chs. 6–7]
Discovery Phase (developing proof to establish claims & learning about the adversary's case) [Ch. 8]
Right to Jury Trial; Pretrial Motions & Practice [Ch. 9]
Final Pretrial Conference & Other Events within Last Month before Trial [Ch. 10]
Procedure at Trial [Ch. 11]
Post-Trial Motions & Calculating the Date of Final Judgment to Know Key Deadlines Such as for Notice of Appeal [Ch. 12]

The text presumes that no one should, during the actual representation of a client, have her first experience in determining statutes of limitation, in choosing a forum, or in pleading a case. This book's initial chapters provide the tools for avoiding that prospect. After learning the facts of a case, any competent plaintiff's lawyer must engage in a thorough initial analysis. Entitled "Essential Steps in Initial Case Handling," Chapter 2 outlines the critical steps of that analysis from the author's viewpoint. Obviously, the plaintiff's attorney must identify all claims that can be brought for the client. But the analysis includes less obvious steps such as determining whether any of the claims require notice to the defendant prior to filing suit (*e.g.*, as in a Tort Claims Act suit against a State). Chapter 2 concludes with a method to determine the deadline, under statutes of limitation, for every claim in the case. The result will be that cases are brought with notice, where necessary, and no later than the *earliest* limitation period for a claim. Otherwise, the client may lose at least one claim, and perhaps others.

Entitled "Choosing the Forum," Chapter 3 addresses the question of the court in which the plaintiff can and should file suit. The chapter thus discusses subject matter jurisdiction, personal jurisdiction, and venue. When the attorney has identified the courts that would satisfy all three of these important considerations, she may intelligently discuss strategy with the client. Assuming the client has alternatives, together they can choose which court strategically favors the client.

Chapter 4, "Pleading the Case and Joinder of Claims and Parties," deals with the offensive (also called aggressive) pleadings that a plaintiff must file to plead claims. The chapter explains the general rules on pleading and gives practical advice on avoiding nitpicking motions or other challenges by the defendant to the pleadings. The chapter also addresses joinder of claims and parties. The chapter further recognizes that not only the plaintiff, but also the defendant (via counterclaims, cross-claims, or third-party claims) may need to follow the rules set forth in this chapter. Finally, the chapter address a number of miscellaneous but important pleading issues such as the necessary basis counsel must have—legally and factually—to plead claims (also known as avoiding "Rule 11" sanctions), how to deal with persons under a legal disability, and related issues.

Chapter 5, "Service of Process," explains the requirements for serving a party under the applicable service of process provisions. Because so many different types of defendants may be sued, the chapter addresses a variety of approaches depending on the type of defendant. Serving an in-state individual, for instance, will be far different from serving an in-state corporation. Needless to say, serving an in-state corporation will differ greatly from serving an out-of-state corporation in most cases. And so on.

Entitled "The Defendant Strikes Back," Chapter 6 addresses the array of defensive responses to a party's offensive pleading. Here, the text takes the viewpoint of a young associate who must consider how best to protect her client once sued. As in the initial chapters, Chapter 6 stresses that the attorney needs to become educated sooner rather than later on the law related to the claims in the suit, and the defenses to these claims. Too many attorneys fall into robotic lawyering—reflexively filing pleadings without first developing a plan for defending a case. The best plan may include a heavy assault of initial motions and other defensive pleadings, or it may simply involve filing an answer with affirmative defenses. The latter approach would rely more on the discovery phase of the case to develop the client's defense. The author's point is that the strategy needs to be determined at the outset, with the client's consent, and carried out intentionally.

Chapter 7, "Defaults, Limbo, and Pretrial Dismissals," discusses what happens when a defendant fails to respond in a timely manner and goes into default. In most jurisdictions one may obtain relief from default if she offers a good reason for the default *and* does so promptly. The effect of default is dramatic, and often lawyers do not offer good reasons or do so quickly enough to obtain relief from default. A well-informed lawyer may, nevertheless, still protect her client's interest—even after the client is held in default—by contesting the amount of damages entered. Thus, an understanding of the ground rules for default is essential.

Chapter 8, "Discovery: The Battle for Information" deals with the normal process of discovery in a case. The chapter emphasizes the strategic value of approaching discovery so as to prepare one's case thoroughly but with the least expense. Often overlooked, methods for gathering evidence outside of the formal discovery process take up the first part of the chapter. Further exercises help the student see the value of performing research early in a case and allowing that information to shape the discovery strategy. Because the discovery phase is the lengthiest (and most expensive) one in a case, the author offers suggestions for reducing the amount of discovery and the cost to one's client.

Entitled "The Right to Jury Trial and Summary Judgment," Chapter 9 first discusses the right to a jury trial under state constitutions or statutes. The student will practice determining when a jury trial is available and how to protect the right to a jury trial when both legal and equitable claims are involved. After gleaning an appreciation for the importance of a jury trial, students are then better prepared to study summary judgment, which ends the case without a jury trial.

Chapter 10, "The Last Month before Trial," deals with the pretrial phase—typically the last 30 days before trial. The pretrial phase offers many opportunities to streamline a case. These include, in general, preparation for the final pretrial conference, and in particular identification of witnesses and exhibits, motions to exclude evidence, and proposed jury instructions. This chapter also discusses methods for valuing a case, as well as the related subjects of mediation and settlement.

"At Trial," Chapter 11, handles the stages of a typical trial. The emphasis is on procedures rather than trial advocacy methods. For example, the chapter will discuss the rules of selecting a jury, but not the different approaches to questioning jurors that trial advocacy texts would include. Needless to say, this chapter features a discussion of the importance of motions that should be made during and at the close of trial. The chapter highlights procedural issues to which a litigator should be attuned at trial.

Chapter 12 is called "Post-Trial Motions and Knowing the Deadline for Appeal." Many lawyers fail to recognize the traps inherent in getting post-trial motions heard and preserving one's right to appeal. This chapter deals with the knotty questions of when a final judgment has been entered. By appreciating the crucial deadlines triggered at this stage of a case, one may avoid this trap-laden stage of the litigation process.

Principles Underlying the Procedural System

This book concentrates on the step-by-step progress of a case, and the lawyer's strategic decision-making at each step. There is more to procedure, however, than what first meets the eye. The system, and its rules and doctrines, rest on deep, fundamental principles. Many never appreciate these principles. At best, most law students (and, indeed, lawyers) see the system as a random series of rules that somehow must be understood to avoid malpractice. If one recognizes the broader purposes of the procedure system that serve the needs of society, she will be more likely to enjoy the process of taking part in the system. As shown in the chart under the summary of chapters section, the stages of a civil action set forth above provide one version of the "big picture." Another way to see the system from the broad perspective is to consider the underlying policies which tie together the various rules and doctrines that arise at different points in a case.

What are the deep, transcendent principles underlying the system? At its core, two principles underlie the system. First is the reality that human beings are flawed and will make errors. As our Constitution's Framers knew, we need institutional protections to protect us from each other. What James Madison said about the need for governmental checks and balances in the following excerpt from Federalist No. 51 may as easily be said about our nation's judicial system.

> If men were angels, no government would be necessary. If angels were to govern men, neither external nor internal controls on government would be necessary. In framing a government which is to be administered by men over men, the great difficulty lies in this: You must first enable the government to control the governed; and in the next place, oblige it to control itself....[22]

---

22. JAMES MADISON, THE FEDERALIST No. 51, 262 (Buccaneer Books 1992).

Some of the "checks" in our procedural system are, indeed, constitutional checks. The jury is a check on judges. The due process requirements of sufficient contacts with a state in order to be sued there under personal jurisdiction principles represent another constitutional check on the governmental exercise of authority. Other checks and balances in the judicial system are less celebrated, but still important. The most obvious of these is the right to appeal, and thereby, check a trial court's power. And yet there are innumerable other such instances in the judicial system in which parties are able to rely on procedural rules and doctrines to avoid unfair treatment.

One might say that procedural rules and doctrines help to "protect us from ourselves." After all the system is, like our Constitution, one that accepts the reality that, without procedural mechanisms, any system run by human beings will inevitably fall short of providing impartial justice. It recognizes that human beings, even the best, have biases, prejudices, and other character traits that can affect the impartial administration of justice. Although procedure cannot possibly offset the human factor in all of its manifestations, it can do a pretty good job of ensuring that most litigants get a fair opportunity to have their claims heard or, if sued, a fair chance to defend.

The second deep-rooted principle of the American judicial system is the flip-side of the one just discussed. It is the notion that all persons are equal in dignity and, thus, deserve equal justice under the law. Intuitively, we know that justice hinges on our embracing such equality. Thus, we create a procedural system that in a variety of ways promotes the values of dispensing justice impartially. Parties have the opportunity, in cases in which the jury right applies, to choose a jury by the same terms as the other side. Then a jury of one's peers decides the dispute, not a single judge. Indeed, the standard for summary judgment (or judgments as a matter of law at trial or after verdict) pays credence to this notion. A judge can decide the case as a matter of law only if she determines that fair-minded, reasonable jurors cannot disagree on the evidence. If the judge oversteps her bounds, and substitutes her judgment, the appellate process tells her she was wrong. And, ultimately, the cases that deserve their day in court get their day in court.

The problem arises when lawyers are not aware of the procedures that allow them to "check" the human factor in litigation, and to seek impartial justice for their client. That should be motivation enough for a lawyer to learn procedure—and learn it well. As most experienced judges and lawyers know, a lawyer who knows the procedural system well is a formidable adversary. You need not wait until practice to develop the skills of such an adversary. If a new lawyer makes the decision-making process outlined in this book a habitual part of case-handling, the odds are that the lawyer's client will not be the one disadvantaged by a procedural matter. To the contrary, the client will more likely end up in a position of strength by following the proper procedures. If odds play out according to form, your opponent will then end up at a disadvantage. At the least, a lawyer who follows the steps outlined in this book should get cases with merit to a decision on the merits. She may not win every case on the merits; few lawyers do. However, she will have done her job to get the case to a decision, or if appropriate, to advise the client at an earlier stage to settle. The key here is that the lawyer will intelligently handle the case. Over time, clients (and other lawyers) will realize that a lawyer who handles cases intelligently is a lawyer worth retaining.

Chapter 2

Essential Steps in Initial Case Handling

A. Sally's Case at This Stage of Litigation Process

You have passed the bar exam and were recently hired by a regionally respected law firm, Dogood, Befayre, and Prosper, P.C. Congratulations! The firm primarily handles business clients. However, the group occasionally represents friends or family of its attorneys. Your supervising attorney is out of town for a while. He has an appointment next week with a client who is also a close family friend. An urgent matter has arisen for the client, and your supervisor has advised her to meet with you to review the issue.

Your supervisor hands you a memorandum which contains facts in the Master Problem—"Sally's Case," set forth in Chapter 1. He tells you he's sure this case will give you some opportunities to "cut your teeth."

At the end of the memorandum, you notice a few of his handwritten notes. He had written: "(1) get accident report; (2) get any contract Sally had with Sam or Wheeler Dealer, Inc.; (3) determine whether Sally was incapacitated for any amount of time, either from the concussion or due to age (such that the statute of limitations may be tolled); (4) figure out when the fence was placed along the back line of Sally's lot; and (5) determine when car manufacturer sold the car either to distributor or to dealer."

B. Tasks and Decision-Making at This Stage of a Case

Diagram 2-1 illustrates where, in the stages of a case timeline, you now find yourself.

Imagine how overwhelmed you might feel after reading his memo. What task should be tackled first? Where should you start? Your "worries" are not unfounded: most new lawyers have no idea which issues must be addressed at the outset of a case, and law schools have done a notoriously poor job of preparing students to deal with real-life situations. Another attorney in your firm recommends that you go to your local bar association's library to see if they have resources to guide new attorneys. You find *From Law School to Law Practice*, a book that offers a wide range of advice—including how to pre-

Diagram 2-1

Cause of Action (events leading to suit)
Prefiling Matters to Consider; Choice of Forum [Chs. 2–3]
Π and Δ Decide on Offensive Pleadings & Joinder (of claims & parties); Filing Suit; Service [Chs. 4–5]
Motions, Responsive Pleadings; Default; Voluntary & Involuntary Dismissals [Chs. 6–7]
Discovery Phase (developing proof to establish claims & learning about the adversary's case) [Ch. 8]
Right to Jury Trial; Pretrial Motions & Practice [Ch. 9]
Final Pretrial Conference & Other Events within Last Month before Trial [Ch. 10]
Procedure at Trial [Ch. 11]
Post-Trial Motions & Calculating the Date of Final Judgment to Know Key Deadlines Such as for Notice of Appeal [Ch. 12]

pare for your first client meeting.[1] Next, you run a computer search for relevant articles, and David Armstrong's "A View from the Other Side of the Fence"[2] catches your eye. This piece was written by a former lawyer who is now a businessman and offers excellent advice on how to properly prepare for (and conduct) meetings with clients.

The resources suggest that you start by gathering as much information as possible about the facts of your case. You spring into action. First, you call Sally and ask her to send any paperwork in her possession that is related to the events mentioned in the memo, especially any contracts she has with Wheeler Dealer, Inc. You inform Sally that you are sending her, via courier, a release form for her to sign that will allow you to speak with her health care providers.

Within a few days, you have a bunch of unorganized documents and many medical bills on your desk. Among them you discover a contract between Sally and Wheeler Dealer dated January 2, 2005. The contract binds both parties to arbitration of any disputes regarding the management of Sally's investments by Wheeler Dealer, Inc., or by its brokers.

You send an employee of your firm, Frankie Find-it, to Sally's property with instructions to locate any signs on the fence at the rear of the lot in order to identify the fence company that placed it there. Frankie finds a sign that identifies the fence company; you call the company and determine that the fence was placed in 1988.

---

1. Suzanne B. O'Neill & Catherine Gerhauser Sparkman, From Law School to Law Practice (2008). This book is an American Law Institute/American Bar Association publication and is a worthwhile investment for new attorneys. It can be ordered at www.ali-aba.org.

2. David K. Armstrong, *A View from the Other Side of the Fence*, 16 Utah B.J. 14 (2003).

You also have Frankie go by Sally's house to pick up all paperwork related to the purchase and maintenance of the 2008 Stallion. When you review the papers, you see that they actually include documentation showing that HorsePower, Inc. sold the car directly to the dealer from which Sally bought it only a month before she did so. The sale from HorsePower to the dealer occurred on July 3, 2008, and Sally's purchase from the dealer was on August 3, 2008. The records show Sally followed all maintenance requirements on the car since she bought it.

A discussion with Sally's neurologist is the next logical step, although the doctor will only convey medical information after Sally has signed a valid "Release of Information" form. The neurologist relates Sally's diagnosis as pre-senile (early) dementia. Sally has exhibited typical signs of this condition, with alternating intervals of impairment and lucidity. Over the last few years, the neurologist has noted brief gaps in Sally's ability to manage her affairs.

You have an upcoming appointment with Sally and will need to assess her lucidity at that point in time. The neurologist provides several questions that would constitute an "unofficial" mental status examination (one typical question would involve Sally's comprehension and interpretation of that day's world events).

Your next line of inquiry concerns the concussion that Sally sustained in the collision. The neurologist was Sally's attending physician during the entire six-month hospitalization. The concussion had left Sally in a state of semi-consciousness, a type of low-grade coma. The doctor plainly states that the brain injury definitely incapacitated Sally during the six-month hospital stay. Eventually, Sally returned to her pre-accident, baseline level of cognitive function, and the neurologist released her from the hospital. The doctor recommended that Sally arrange for a relative or trusted friend to serve as a power of attorney ("POA") during those intervals when Sally was not lucid. A POA is a legal document by which an individual appoints another person or party to handle his or her legal affairs. Physicians generally recommend that patients with fluctuating mental capabilities appoint a POA as soon as the diagnosis is made, and during a lucid interval. Otherwise, a patient may deteriorate mentally and a POA can only then be secured through legal channels — a process which can take days or weeks.

Finally, you obtain the accident report from the police department. It is reprinted in Figure 2-1.

You try to anticipate any questions Sally might have during your meeting so that you are prepared to answer them. Some questions to consider: (1) whether Sally can file suit against Wheeler Dealer, Inc.; (2) whether Sally can "do anything" about the neighbor's fence; (3) whether she can sue the supplier of the roof that was affixed to her porch years earlier; (4) whether she has to give notice to a defendant on any of her claims; and (5) what are the statute of limitations periods on each of her claims?

In your research at the local bar association, and in your law school's Professional Ethics course, you have probably encountered the issue of conflicts of interest. When confronted with a prospective client, a lawyer must confirm that no conflicts of interest exist between a prospective client and the defendant(s). You e-mail your supervising attorney to ensure that this has been addressed, and he responds that he did not have a chance to check for conflicts of interest before he left town. You have the paralegal at your firm who is in charge of client records run a computer check on Sam, Wheeler Dealer, Inc., Sally's neighbor, the roof panel supplier, the City, the State, and HorsePower, Inc. You need to determine whether any of them are past or current clients of your firm. If your firm has represented any of the parties on a matter in the past that is unrelated to Sally's case, then you should be able to represent Sally. However, if any of the parties are current clients of your firm

Figure 2-1

Local Traffic Crash Report
Arcadia Division of Police

Local Report Number _12345_

Report Taken	☐ Headquarters ☒ Substation	Total Number of Vehicles and Pedestrians Involved *ONE*		Combined Vehicle and Property Loss (Account for the total of all vehicles and property damaged) ☒ Over $150 ☐ Under $150

In City Of Arcadia Court State of Illyria | • Within corporate limits of Arcadia (if not, file with correct agency) | Date of Crash M 02 D 02 Y 2009 | Day WEDNESDAY | Time 11:00 AM/PM

Crash Occurred On ROUTE 3 | Other Streets/Roads in Vicinity ARCADIA / CENTRAL BORDER ON RT. 3

Misc.

A Unit No. 1 | No. Of Occupants 1 | Operating ☒ Parked ☐ Driverless ☐ Non-Contact ☐ | Insurance Co. Or Agent GORGE YOU INSURANCE CO.

Driver - Pedestrian Name (Last, First, MI) WILREIZ, SALLY | Address (No., Street, State, Zip Code) 612 THOMAS MORE LN. ARCADIA, ILLYRIA 112233

Phone No. 999-111-2222 | Birth Date M 02 D 02 Y 1949 | Age 60 | Sex F | State Illyria | Drivers License No. XYZ-64321 | Occupation PROFESSOR

Owner (If Same As Driver, Write Same) Same | Address | Phone

Veh. Year 2008 | Make HorsePower, Inc | Model Stallion Conv. | Color Red | Style | State Illyria | License Plate No. SAL-TH-GAL | Towing Service Joe's Towing | Veh/Ped Dir From To

Circle Damage Areas | Damage Severity ☐ Non-Functional ☐ Functional ☒ Disabling | Damage Scale ☐ None ☐ Light ☐ Moderate ☒ Heavy | Vehicle Disposition ☐ Driven Away ☐ Remained At Scene ☒ Towed | Fire ☒ No Fire ☐ Fire Due To Crash ☐ Other Fire | 9 Top / 10 Undercar / 11 Load / 12 Trailer

B Unit No. | No. Of Occupants | Operating ☐ Parked ☐ Driverless ☐ Non-Contact ☐ | Insurance Co. Or Agent

Driver - Pedestrian Name (Last, First, MI) | Address (No., Street, State, Zip Code)

Phone No. | Birth Date M D Y | Age | Sex | State | Drivers License No. | Occupation

Owner (If Same As Driver, Write Same) | Address | Phone

Veh. Year | Make | Model | Color | Style | State | License Plate No. | Towing Service | Veh/Ped Dir From To

Circle Damage Areas | Damage Severity ☐ Non-Functional ☐ Functional ☐ Disabling | Damage Scale ☐ None ☐ Light ☐ Moderate ☐ Heavy | Vehicle Disposition ☐ Driven Away ☐ Remained At Scene ☐ Towed | Fire ☐ No Fire ☐ Fire Due To Crash ☐ Other Fire

C From Unit No. | Name (Last, First, MI) Wilreiz, Sally | Birth Date M 02 D 02 Y 1949 | Age 60 | Position A B C D E F
| | Address Same address as above | Phone 799-111-2222 | Sex F

D From Unit No. | Name (Last, First, MI) | Birth Date M D Y | Age
| | Address | Phone | Sex

E From Unit No. | Name (Last, First, MI) | Birth Date M D Y | Age
| | Address | Phone | Sex

P-PEDESTRIAN

F From Unit No. | Name (Last, First, MI) | Birth Date M D Y | Age
| | Address | Phone | Sex

Restraints: A B C D E F

G From Unit No. | Name (Last, First, MI) | Birth Date M D Y | Age
| | Address | Phone | Sex

1 Not Used / 2 None Available / 3 Lap Belt Used / 4 Lap/Shoulder Belt Used / 5 Shoulder Belt Used / 6 Child Safety Seat / 7 Air Bag Used / 8 Use Not Reported

H From Unit No. | Name (Last, First, MI) | Birth Date M D Y | Age
| | Address | Phone | Sex

Ejection: A B C D E F

I From Unit No. | Name (Last, First, MI) | Birth Date M D Y | Age
| | Address | Phone | Sex

1 Not Ejected / 2 Partial / 3 Total / 4 Trapped Inside Vehicle

Date Report Filed M D Y | Desk Officer's Name & Badge #

S-36.133 (Revised 7/2000)

Driver - Pedestrian - Vehicle Section

Occupant Section

[Continued on next page.]

(even if the matter is unrelated to Sally's case), you would need to have written consent of all affected parties before undertaking representation. You must also decide whether it is ethically sound to represent Sally, regardless of having procured written consent. Fortunately, none of the potential defendants has ever been represented by your firm. You may now represent Sally confidently, knowing this issue has been properly addressed.

You return to the list you created while reviewing the resources you found at the local bar and see "written engagement letter"—a letter that specifies the terms of the representation,

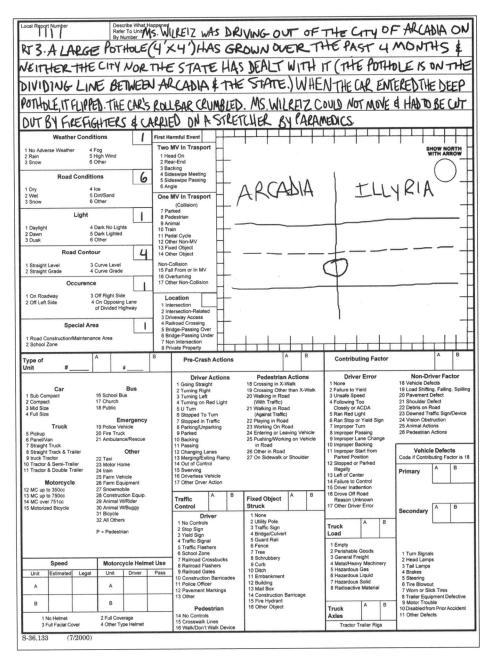

signed by the client. *See, e.g.*, Model Rules of Prof'l Conduct R. 1.2 (2007) (providing general rules on scope of representation). The professional assistant to your supervisor gives you a template for engagement letters. You use that template to develop the letter shown in Figure 2-2.

Before your meeting with Sally, you have the engagement letter delivered to her. Having learned of Sally's potential cognitive challenges, you wisely suggest that she bring a trusted friend or family member to your meeting—if possible, whoever she has named as her power of attorney. It is important that Sally "has capacity" when signing the engagement contract so that it is a valid (binding) contract. For that reason, you should

Figure 2-2

✗ example of acceptable fee agreements under course content

DOGOOD, BEFAYRE & PROSPER, P.C.
[DATE]

Re: Engagement Agreement between Sally and Dogood, Befayre & Prosper, P.C.

Dear Sally:

should be more specific

You have asked that we serve as counsel for you re: the above referenced matter. I am submitting this letter to you to serve as the written agreement for our firm's engagement to provide legal services concerning the matter. We look forward to serving as counsel in this engagement.

should identify scope. ex. ONLY through trial, not appeal

You will be our client in this engagement. I will be responsible for the engagement on behalf of our firm. The scope of this engagement will be limited to the provision of legal services for the Matter described above. Our fees for the engagement will be based upon an hourly rate of $350 per hour for any partner's time spent handling your various claims, $175 per hour for any associate's time, and $75 per hour for a paralegal's time.* In addition, we will bill for or request direct payment for disbursements or expenses that we incur, including any long-distance telephone charges, delivery charges, photocopy or reproduction costs, computerized legal research charges, filing fees, and travel expenses, if any. Payment is due upon receipt of our monthly statements. *→ needs a time frame for turning in fees*

→ specify travel expenses

Upon the signing of this agreement, you agree to deposit with Dogood, Befayre, and Prosper, P.C. the sum of $5,000.00 as a retainer against which we will bill to and collect from for expenses incurred. After the initial deposit is expended you will be billed as expenses are incurred.

explicitly reassure client that you are working on their case (but don't lie)

If you have any questions concerning the terms of our engagement or if you ever have questions about our charges, please contact me at your convenience to discuss the matter. Our engagement as counsel will begin upon our receipt of a signed copy of this agreement (by fax, mail, or hand). Thank you for choosing us as counsel. We look forward to a good and productive relationship.

Sincerely,

Ben Befayre, Esq., Partner
For Dogood, Befayre & Prosper, P.C.

I hereby agree to the terms of this engagement:
_____ [Client's signature]
_____ [Date signed]
_____ Witness
_____ Witness

* Because you work at a firm that primarily represents business clients, the firm more likely bills by the hour than by contingent fee. If the engagement agreement were to substitute a contingent fee component (usually providing for approximately one-third of any settlement or recovery), that would replace the part of this agreement that mentions hourly rates.

request whoever has power of attorney over Sally's legal affairs to sign the engagement contract as well. Normally, an engagement letter need not reflect witnesses to a client's signature. However, when a client has potential capacity issues, counsel ought to do everything possible to ensure any agreement will be upheld. You add two lines for witness signatures to the standard engagement letter (as shown above). You make a note that you must inform Sally that neither Dogood, Befayre, & Prosper, P.C. nor any lawyer in the firm will have any attorney-client relationship with her until the engagement letter is signed and witnessed.

You have done pretty well so far. You are learning that handling a lawsuit can be quite complicated. Once again, you consult your "checklist." At this point, some preliminary legal research is in order. You note that you need to research the elements of all potential claims under the substantive law, and (1) whether subject matter jurisdiction exists for all claims; (2) whether any pre-suit notice requirements apply to a particular claim such that the client could not bring suit without giving notice; and (3) how to apply the applicable statute of limitations analysis to each claim. You spend the better part of your weekend researching these issues and discover that you have some information that may be unfavorable to Sally's case. The information you find, coupled with Sally's questionable mental capacity, makes you uncomfortable.

Pay close attention when you feel uncomfortable. This feeling often means you are facing a value judgment, even if you may not be fully aware of the question yet. A reality that some young lawyers find hard to face is that her own inexperience is presenting a conflict of values. As a young lawyer, one will often unconsciously be tempted to sacrifice the interests of your client to remove the feeling of being uncomfortable. One has to pay close attention to bring the issue to consciousness so that you can avoid inadvertently sacrificing your client's best interests. When lawyers are new to practicing law, for instance, they want to appear competent and in control. They also are trying to impress their senior colleagues and try to do so through their dealings with the client. In the process, they often make the mistake of failing to communicate to their client *all* of the information that is relevant to a particular case — particularly information that is unfavorable to a case. As a result, important matters often go unspoken between the lawyer and client. If you consult your value system and ask what you, if you were the client, would want to know, you will likely determine that you should discuss *all* information with your client. To make informed decisions, clients need to hear everything — unfavorable and favorable — just as the lawyer needs to hear everything from the client. Candor is a sound rule of thumb when dealing with clients. As a lawyer gains experience, she learns that clients not only can handle both favorable and unfavorable facts, but that they actually appreciate candor.

When you meet with Sally, you will thus want to deliver the unfavorable news to her regarding some of her potential claims. The first piece of unfavorable news is that your initial research has led you to believe that the claim over the fence is probably time-barred. If you are forthright with Sally, you must tell her the chances of pursuing the issue of the fence are minimal. The second piece of unfavorable news deals with the injury to her foot due to the porch panel. You have confirmed that construction on Sally's porch was completed twelve years earlier. The statute of repose in your jurisdiction (like many) prohibits claims against suppliers providing materials used to improve real property that are brought anytime after ten years from the date the improvement was completed. Thus, the statute of repose will almost certainly bar her claim for personal injuries to her foot.

The final piece of potentially unfavorable news relates to her dispute with the broker-age house, although this news is not completely unfavorable. You anticipate that Sally might be surprised when you explain to her that the arbitration clause in her contract with Wheeler Dealer, Inc. may prevent her from arguing her claim in a court of law. In-stead, she will have to pursue that claim in arbitration, and your firm's partners recommend that such a matter be referred to a law firm they trust with expertise in securities claims.[3] Even if the claim against Wheeler Dealer had not been covered by the arbitration agreement, your firm recognizes that securities law is a highly specialized area of the law. If one does not practice a highly specialized area of the law regularly, the lawyer/firm should evaluate her/its competence to handle the claim. Fortunately, the partners in Sally's firm seem well aware of the cases both that their firm can handle and those they should not.

In short, you need to spell out for Sally the entire truth about potential claims, re-gardless of whether or not you think she will be disappointed. Clients need to hear the truth, even if the truth is not "good news." To illustrate: if the client is unaware that some of her claims are not viable, she could waste substantial time and money on her case, building expectations beyond what the law firm can actually deliver. The result will be a disappointed client and a law firm that has promised more than it can deliver.

Perhaps the most sensitive part of your discussions with Sally will be when you ad-dress the issue of her mental capacity. You recall from your research that you should dis-cuss with your client all of the issues that are significant to the case, regardless of whether the issues are "uncomfortable" to discuss. You conclude that the capacity issue is signifi-cant to Sally's case for two reasons. First, you must confirm Sally's capacity at the time she signs the engagement letter, or the contract will not be binding. Second, Sally's ca-pacity could be significant to your statute of limitations analysis. You have learned that "tolling"—or, in lay-person's terms, "postponing"—the statute of limitations will de-pend on periods of time when Sally can claim that she lacked mental capacity. You recall the guidance you received from the neurologist and contemplate how you will approach the subject of her mental capacity during the meeting. You resolve to choose your words carefully. Perhaps you will lead with this: "Please recognize that I would not discuss the subject of your mental capacity if it were not significant to your legal representation."

Additionally, you must ascertain all of Sally's *potential* claims. If you are able to rule out claims she is unlikely to prevail on, you can deliver the more favorable news about claims that might have merit. You will also communicate to Sally that the first step in any case is to research the claim(s) she would like to pursue. You plan to explain the steps that Mr. Be-fayre and you will have to take in advocating her claims. You also plan to explain to Sally that (prior to proceeding with her case) you must confirm the statutory and case-law require-ments in order to verify that she is able to prove each element of her claim(s). You realize the most time sensitive issue is that the time for filing each claim be identified immedi-ately—to avoid the claims being barred by statutes of limitation. To do so, you would have to let Sally know that you cannot determine these time periods until you are made aware of

---

3. Alternative Dispute Resolution, such as binding arbitration, voluntary mediation, or the like, is a topic beyond the scope of this book. Many of the same strategic and decision-making questions addressed throughout this book, however, would apply to one arbitrating a claim. In Chapter 10, see pages 231–50, an extended discussion on valuing a case, mediation, and settlement deals with many of the issues one would group under the Alternative Dispute Resolution banner. However, arbitration is unique enough that it deserves a book itself rather than trying to discuss it in the context of book on civil pretrial and trial practice.

all claims in her case, all potential defendants, and then research the applicable law. Indeed, you tell her that some claims may require notice to a party even prior to bringing the claim.

After getting the engagement letter signed and witnessed, you set up another meeting in a couple of weeks. You promise that, at that time, you will be able to answer the above questions more fully and that Mr. Befayre and you will begin preparing papers to file on her behalf.

Ensuring Protection of Privileges

If Sally shows up at the client meeting with her daughter who has power of attorney to handle Sally's affairs, what other questions might arise? Consider issues you have probably encountered in first-year Civil Procedure, Evidence, or some other course, namely, the attorney-client privilege and the work-product doctrine. Legal advice and other communication (oral or written) between attorney and client ranks among the most protected information in the practice of law. The attorney-client privilege protects such communications and generally makes them immune from discovery. However, the privilege can be waived if a third party is present during attorney-client discourse. Some questions to consider include the following:

1. Would an elderly client's daughter appointed through a power of attorney to conduct the client's legal affairs be sufficiently associated with the client so as to avoid waiver? The answer is probably yes. However, you must research the matter to make sure.

2. What if the attorney takes written notes of the interview and learns valuable information about the case, and this is reflected in her notes? Ordinarily these would qualify for protection from disclosure under the work-product doctrine.

3. Again, would the presence of Sally's daughter somehow constitute a waiver? A careful attorney would ensure no possibility of waiver existed.

You've made it through the initial client meeting. You are gratified when Sally tells you that she has never met a young lawyer whose demeanor is so professional. At that point, you are pleased that you had researched client counseling and laid a preparatory foundation prior to the meeting. You realize, however, that your work for Sally is just beginning. You must now aggressively begin your legal research, outlining not only the substantive elements of the claims, but also identifying pre-suit notice requirements and the statutes of limitation for each claim. You realize that you should investigate any rules on calculation of deadlines, either in statutes or state rules.

C. Overview of Applicable Law

Calculating Deadlines, Pre-Suit Notice of Claims, and Statutes of Limitation

During your meeting with Sally, you explained that your first research priority will include determining the statutes of limitation ("SOL") for each viable claim, and also identifying those claims which require provision of notice prior to filing suit. You realize that deadline calculations will be required for limitations analysis and for pre-suit notices. How does one determine the start date for counting a specified period? How does one know the latest date on which an SOL or notice deadline falls? You discover a discussion in one treatise on "statutes of repose," and recall that one defendant (the roof panel supplier) mentioned this. You resolve to research your state's statute of repose to confirm the initial opinion that you gave Sally—that the repose statute would bar her claim against the supplier.

Your questions raise the subject of how to calculate deadlines in court proceedings. Many refer to this as "judicial counting" to distinguish it from ordinary counting. It is wise to give judicial counting a separate label because it is decidedly different from ordinary counting. As your research reveals, calculating judicial deadlines requires one to ignore the date an event occurred (*e.g.*, an accident date). "Day 1" of the applicable notice or limitations deadline applies on the day *after the event*. Failure to master these fundamental rules of counting can result in, at worst, dismissal of a case, and at best, missing a deadline that might prejudice your client.

How to Calculate Deadlines ("Judicial Counting")

Every state has a statutory or court rule on counting. Appendix 2-1 (identifying states' approaches as generally consistent with Federal Rule of Civil Procedure 6); 86 C.J.S. *Time* § 30 (2008); *see, e.g.*, N.Y. C.P.L.R. § 203 (McKinney 2008); 5 Ill. Comp. Stat. 70/1.10-.11 (2008); Cal. Civ. Proc. Code §§ 12–13 (West 2008). *See generally* N.J. Marini, *Inclusion or Exclusion of First and Last Day for Purposes of Statute of Limitations*, 20 A.L.R. 2d 1249 (1951) (a detailed analysis on computation of time).[4] Following is a composite of numerous state statutes addressing computation of time,[5] all of which take the same approach:

Model Computation of Time Statute

1. When a statute or rule of court requires that an act be performed in a prescribed amount of time after any event or judgment, the day on which the event or judgment occurred shall not be counted against the time allowed.

---

4. Case deadlines in federal court are governed by Federal Rule of Civil Procedure 6.
5. *See* Am. Jur. 2d *Time* §§ 15–22, 26–29 (2009) (collecting authorities from states throughout the United States); Fed. R. Civ. P. 6 (federal rule typifies the same approach as applied by states).

2. When a statute or rule of court specifies a maximum period of time in which a legal action may be brought and the last day of that period falls on a Saturday, Sunday, legal holiday, or day or part of a day on which the clerk's office is closed as authorized by statute, the action may be brought on the next day that is not a Saturday, Sunday, legal holiday, or day or part of a day on which the clerk's office is closed as authorized by a statute.

3. "Month" means a calendar month and "year" means a calendar year.

To decipher such a statute, you would do well to read the entire statute to establish an overview of its content. Next, the legislation should be deconstructed piece by piece to ascertain the terms used and the meaning of each provision. Finally, you should consider the interrelationship between segments of the statute and apply them to the factual situation at hand.

As the following section will show, one should recognize the difference between calculating deadlines expressed (1) in terms of "days," and (2) in terms of "years" or "months."

Following an Expert's Cognitive Processes in Reading a General Time Calculation Statute

The following material is meant to convey how an expert in statutory interpretation would proceed, providing you with a peek into the mental steps that an experienced attorney takes without even realizing it. Take note of this process: after this section, you will be asked to perform your own calculations for different deadlines.

Let's say our expert attorney reads the computation statutes noted above. Even if she has read the statute before, she will resist the temptation to take shortcuts. Perhaps the legislature has changed the general statute on calculating deadlines since the last time she reviewed it. After reading the provisions in their entirety, our attorney goes back to the beginning and analyzes each segment of the statute.

Calculation of Deadlines Expressed in Days

The seasoned lawyer would be careful to read the first part of the statute and, before trying to calculate deadlines expressed in terms of "years" or "months," to first understand deadlines expressed in terms of "days." She observes that Subsection A refers to "when a statute or rule of court requires that an act be performed in a prescribed amount of time after any event or judgment...." She notes that this language simply means that the statute governs any jurisdictional *statutes* or *court rules* that require action after the occurrence of an event or judgment. She does not have to be reminded that there are hundreds of statutes and court rules in most jurisdictions that fall under this general calculation-of-deadlines statute.

As our seasoned attorney proceeds to the next statutory section, she recognizes the phrase "requires that an *act* be performed in a prescribed amount of time." Our expert is not confused by the odd choice of the word "act" in this context. Although a novice might expect an "act" to be a physical action by a person, our wise lawyer knows better. If asked to articulate her thinking, she would say that the use of the word "act" is the state legislature's way of defining a legally significant event. What kind of "act" would be a legally significant event? Our expert lawyer knows the answer, but if asked she would explain: "The act referred to here is, generally speaking, whatever act the statute or rule requires a party in litigation to do." She would also clarify that: "The act would be the filing of a pleading in court, serving a notice or pleading on a potential defendant (if the suit has not yet been filed), or an actual defendant (if the suit has been filed)." She would next observe that the statute refers to an act that must be performed within a "prescribed amount of time." The expert knows that this is just an alternative way of saying that the "act" — whether filing, pleading, or other action — has a deadline.

Our expert would then consider the next portion of the statute which provides: "the day on which the event or judgment occurred shall not be counted against the time allowed." She takes note that the Federal Rules and every state court system in which she has litigated have a similar provision. The provision is fundamental to calculating judicial deadlines. She knows that when calculating a deadline, you do not count the day that the event in question occurred (*e.g.*, final judgment, event giving rise to cause of action, etc.). Instead, the clock starts ticking the day after the event in question occurred.

Now, let's assume that our expert has a specific deadline to calculate. She determines that in the applicable jurisdiction the deadline for a notice of appeal from a final judgment order must be filed within 30 days[6] after the trial court enters its order. How would you interpret a specific calculation rule in accordance with the general calculation statute, so as to correctly ascertain the all-important deadline for filing the notice of appeal? First, the expert attorney would know that the calculation provision governs this deadline. If asked, she would reply, "It applies because the rule specifies an 'act' to be done (*i.e.*, filing notice of appeal) within a prescribed amount of time. That's exactly what the general calculation statute says it will cover." Thus the expert applies the section of the general calculation statute which provides that: "[T]he day on which the event or judgment occurred shall not be counted against the time allowed." She knows that she must count a deadline 30 days from the date of judgment; "Day 1" will be the day *after* the judgment. The expert knows better than to count the date of judgment as "Day 1" because doing so would directly contradict provisions of the general calculation statute. As an additional precaution, our expert checks to see whether the last day is a Saturday, Sunday, or legal holiday. This can be critical because the general calculation statute specifies that when a deadline falls on a Saturday, Sunday, or legal holiday, that deadline will "carry over" to the next business day. The expert handily analyzes each of the steps without really thinking about them as a segment-by-segment process because the analysis has become second nature. However, at one point she was a novice and had to navigate each individual step.

You can now apply the same approach to a concrete example of calculating a deadline for filing a notice of appeal. Assume a final judgment is entered on May 1, 2009 and that your state's deadline for filing notice of appeal is 30 days from entry of a final judgment. The general calculation statute mandates that the date of an event or judgment shall not be counted. The May 1 date of judgment will not count, and the notice of appeal deadline will be 30 days after May 1, or May 31. You must next determine whether May 31 falls on a Saturday, Sunday, or legal holiday. Figure 2-3 is a May calendar for reference:

---

6. *The Bluebook* calls for numerals to be spelled out. However, this casebook spells numbers when referring to months or years, but retains numerals when referring to days, so as to remind the reader of the distinction between them in judicial counting.

Figure 2-3

May **2009**						
SUNDAY	MONDAY	TUESDAY	WEDNESDAY	THURSDAY	FRIDAY	SATURDAY
					judgment 1 *entered* →	*Day* 2 *1*
3	4	5	6	7	8	9
10	11	12	13	14	15	16
17	18	19	20	21	22	23
24	25	26	27	28	29	30
Day 30 → 31	*Moved b/c of sunday*					

The expert's interpretation of the calculation statute as applied to a 30-day notice of appeal deadline proves to be valuable. By following that guidance, you begin counting the 30 day interval on May 2, the day after final judgment. This interpretation is consistent with Federal Rule of Civil Procedure 6—and a majority of states. *See* Appendix 2-1 (nearly all of states follow Fed. R. Civ. P. 6 approach to calculating deadlines). It is immaterial that May 2 falls on a Saturday because the expert is concerned only about Saturdays, Sundays, and legal holidays *at the end of the period.* By counting from May 2, you follow our expert's approach and initially conclude that 30 days from that date is Sunday, May 31; because that day *is* at the end of the calculated interval, you know from the example that you carry over the deadline to the next business day. When the last day of a time period in question falls on a weekend or legal holiday, the Federal Rule and state rules as well, dictate that the next business day that is not a weekend or holiday will be the due date. See Appendix 2-1 (note that states vary in their definitions of legal holidays and one would need to check the appropriate state statute or rule to determine whether a day is categorized as such). You suspect that Monday, June 1, is not a holiday, but you still must check your jurisdiction's statute or rule defining legal holidays. After eliminating that possibility, you conclude that June 1, 2009, is indeed the last day for filing a notice of appeal from the final May 1 judgment order.

Calculation of Deadlines Expressed in Terms of "Years" or "Months"

Our seasoned lawyer would then tell us that the calculation of deadlines expressed in terms of days, such as the above example, will be different from the method for calculating deadlines in terms of "years" or "months." She draws our attention to paragraph 3, which she says is uniformly followed, that provides that deadlines expressed in terms of years (like statutes of limitations) will be treated as "calendar years." She says it is very important to understand that concept. She offers, as an example, that a statute may provide that: "[A]ny claim for personal injuries arising from the negligence of another shall be brought within two years from the date on which the person is injured." For such a calculation, she explains that "calendar year" is a term of art. One must take the date in question of the event or "act" in whatever year it occurred and then count however many years are appropriate to the exact same date. For instance, under the two-year statute of limitations, an accident that occurred on January 14, 2009 would—by using the calendar year method—take one forward two years to January 14, 2011.

Some might say this approach is inconsistent with the first paragraph of the calculation statute—the requirement of not counting the day of the event or act. Why, they might ask, should one not start counting on January 15, 2009 and have the two year statute of limitations deadline be January 15, 2011? Our expert would say these folks are not the first to ask that question and she has two responses. First, she says, "Let's say an accident happened on January 1 of a given year. If one counts the days in that year, one will see that December 31 is the 364th day. Thus, January 1 would be one year from the date in question. And if one counts another year, then January 1 of the next year would be two years from the accident." Of course, January 1 is a holiday, and she notes that every jurisdiction recognizes that, if a deadline (including a statute of limitation deadline) falls on a weekend or legal holiday, one carries forward to the next day that is not a weekend or holiday. But here the point is that counting years really is not inconsistent with the language about "not counting" the day of the event or act. She points to a court's helpful explanation of the same:

> The statement that the period "began to run" on the day of the relevant event is not inconsistent with [Federal Rule of Civil Procedure 6]'s exclusion of the day of the event from counting-the rule does not purport to determine when a period begins to run, but merely to aid in the counting of days. If one considers October 19, 1994 to be "0" (i.e., not included in the counting), October 20 to be "1," and so forth, the 365th day is October 19, 1995....[7]

Second, our expert lawyer would further say that, of course, if there were a leap year in the period in question, that would throw things off. "*That*, she would emphasize, is exactly why the "calendar year" approach is so important. It asks you to simply take the date of the event or act in a given year and find that same day in the year that corresponds to the number of years the statute of limitations provides. The same concept applies to "calendar months." For example, if a statute of limitations states a deadline of nine *months* and the date of the event was January 2, 2009, you would count nine months and then find the corresponding date in that month. Therefore, in that case, the statute of limitations would run out on October 2, 2009. Our experienced lawyer notes that the "calendar year" and "calendar month" concepts can be thought of as *modifying* the not-count-the-day-of-event/act rule if that helps one in performing such calculations. As she notes, the calendar year and calendar month calculations are designed to avoid problems that would be created by leap years falling within a given period, or months that have more or less than 30 days in a several month period. As she notes, it is really a way to make it easier on you to calculate the deadline with certainty.

The expert says that a case that was particularly helpful to her in understanding several concepts related to calculation of deadlines was *Medina v. Lopez-Roman*, 49 S.W. 393 (Tex. App. 2000). Following is that case:

---

7. *Meriweather v. City of Memphis*, 107 F.3d 396, 399 (6th Cir. 1997).

Medina v. Lopez-Roman

49 S.W.3d 393 (Tex. App. 2000)

MARILYN ABOUSSIE, Chief Justice.

Appellant Christopher Medina brought ... [medical malpractice] ... claims and various [other] claims against appellees, Dr. Stuart Crane and Dr. H. Lopez-Roman (collectively, "the doctors").... The district court rendered summary judgment in favor of the doctors on all claims. In this consolidated appeal, Medina challenges both orders. We will reverse and remand.

FACTUAL BACKGROUND

On December 3, 1993, fifteen-year-old Christopher Medina was admitted to Williams House, a residential treatment center in Lometa, Texas, for the purposes of conducting a mental health evaluation and determining the most appropriate residential or foster care placement for him. Williams House staff approached Dr. Stuart Crane, who was leaving Williams House after working with some of the children, and explained that Medina had left his prescription medications behind. A staff member asked Dr. Crane to write a prescription for Medina; Dr. Crane wrote Medina a prescription for Ritalin and Tegretol.

Approximately two to three weeks after Medina entered Williams House, staff members brought Medina to the Metroplex Pavilion in Lampasas, Texas, for a screening to determine whether Medina required psychiatric treatment on an inpatient basis. Dr. Crane, who was working at the Metroplex Pavilion that day, evaluated Medina and spoke with Williams House staff, ultimately determining that Medina could remain at Williams House and be seen on an outpatient basis.

On March 3, 1994, Medina fell on his head while at Williams House and injured his neck. Staff members drove him to the emergency room at Rollinsbrook Medical Center in Lampasas, where he was treated by Dr. Lopez-Roman. When Medina arrived, he complained of dizziness and pain in his neck, and commented that he was unable to move his upper extremities. Dr. Lopez-Roman performed a physical examination of Medina and ordered cervical spine X-rays, a blood count, and a blood chemistry test. Because no radiologist was on staff that evening, Dr. Lopez-Roman viewed the X-rays himself but found nothing abnormal. Throughout the approximately two-hour period Medina was in the emergency room, Dr. Lopez-Roman's examinations revealed various findings; for example, at one point Medina did not respond to painful stimuli, but he later complained that the IV needle being inserted into his arm was painful. Medina complained that he could not move his arms, but he later moved his hands and legs. Because of Medina's fluctuating symptoms and psychological history, Dr. Lopez-Roman asked hospital staff to contact Medina's psychiatrist. Hospital staff paged Dr. Crane, who soon called Dr. Lopez-Roman.

Dr. Lopez-Roman asked Dr. Crane whether it was possible that Medina might "somatize," i.e., express physical symptoms because of emotional factors. Dr. Crane informed Dr. Lopez-Roman that there was a possibility of somatization with Medina, considering his history of developmental disorder and mild retardation. Based on his examination of Medina and consultation with Dr. Crane, Dr. Lopez-Roman noted that he believed Medina was exhibiting psychosomatic symptoms, not spinal-cord injuries. Dr. Lopez-Roman discharged Medina from the emergency room later that same evening.

Medina returned to Williams House where he spent the night. The following morning, Williams House staff transported Medina to Austin, Texas, to be returned to the custody of Arturo Escajeda, a caseworker with the Texas Department of Protective and

Regulatory Services. Because Medina was still complaining about pain, Escajeda demanded that Medina be transported to a local hospital where he was diagnosed with a broken neck. Medina subsequently underwent surgery to fuse his C-1 and C-2 vertebrae and began ongoing physical rehabilitation.

On May 13, 1994, Medina sent a statutory pre-suit notice letter, as required under [the applicable Texas statute], to Dr. Lopez-Roman, asserting a health care liability claim relating to the injury he sustained March 3, 1994 and threatening to file suit.... Medina brought suit against Dr. Lopez-Roman in December of 1994 but later filed a non-suit. On April 3, 1996, Medina turned eighteen. On October 15, 1996, Medina sent a statutory pre-suit notice letter to Dr. Crane alleging that Dr. Crane failed, among other things, to properly diagnose Medina and provide accurate information to Dr. Lopez-Roman on March 3, 1994. On October 31, 1996, Medina sent a second pre-suit notice letter to Dr. Lopez-Roman. Medina filed suit against both doctors on April 3, 1998, his twentieth birthday. Medina requested service of citation simultaneously with the filing of his suit, but Dr. Lopez-Roman was not served until October 6, 1998.

Both doctors filed motions for summary judgment on the basis that the applicable period of limitations had expired and Medina's claims were therefore barred.... On October 27, 1999, the district court rendered a summary judgment in favor of the doctors on Medina's ... medical malpractice claims....

....

Medina's first four points of error all concern the applicable limitations period for his [health care] claims. Medina contends that the district court erred in granting summary judgment on the ground that his ... claims were barred by limitations. The statute of limitations for health care liability claims is [two years].

[B]oth doctors contend that Medina's claims are ... barred because the period of limitations expired one day before Medina filed suit. The doctors acknowledge that the limitations period was tolled until April 3, 1996, the day Medina turned eighteen. However, the doctors argue that because the two-year period began to run on April 3, 1996, it expired on midnight of April 2, 1998, a "full two years later." ...

We find untenable the doctors' method for calculating when the limitations period expired. Instead, we apply the more logical computation method whereby one looks at the calendar day that a minor attains majority and then uses the corresponding date two years later. The Supreme Court adopted our holding in *Pitcock v. Johns*, 326 S.W.2d 563 (Tex. Civ. App. 1959) (writ ref'd), in which this Court engaged in a detailed analysis of the proper method of calculating a statutorily-dictated period of time and reasoned as follows:

> Where "month," as employed in a statute, judicial proceeding, or contract, means calendar month, a period of a month or months is to be computed not by counting days, but by looking at the calendar, and it runs from a given day in one month to a day of the corresponding number in the next or specified succeeding month ... that is, if it begins on the 5th of January, it would end on the 5th of February, although thirty-one days would elapse. If it begins on the 5th of February, it would end on the 5th of March, although but twenty-eight days have elapsed, leap year being excepted. Or if it begins on the 5th of February during leap year, it would end on the 5th of March, although twenty-nine days elapse. If it begins on the 5th of June, it would end on the 5th of July, although thirty days had elapsed.

Id. at 565–66.... Thus, under *Pitcock,* a calendar month runs from the date of the event to the same date in the next month or succeeding month, depending upon the date of the limitations period....

The same rule applies to computing periods of limitation based on years. The term "year" is defined as a calendar year. Tex. Gov't Code Ann. § 312.011 (18) (West 1998). Thus, using the measure of a calendar year, we look to the date upon which the event occurred and then look at the calendar to find the same date, two years later, to determine the expiration of the statute of limitations....

....

The events giving rise to Medina's alleged cause of action occurred in March of 1994, at a time when he was younger than eighteen years of age and therefore, in the eyes of the law, under a legal disability.... [T]he two-year limitations period for his cause of action did not commence running until his eighteenth birthday when his legal disability was removed.... Medina turned eighteen on April 3, 1996 [April 3, 1996 would be legally characterized as the "accrual date" for the plaintiff's claims—*i.e.,* the date on which the statute of limitations began to run. If the plaintiff were an adult, the accrual date on his claims would have been earlier but, because he was an infant, the claims could not "accrue" by law until he became an adult upon turning eighteen years old]. Medina's right to enforce his claim against Dr. Crane and Dr. Lopez-Roman thus arose the first instant of April 3, 1996, and existed during the whole of that day. Applying the computation method discussed above, Medina had until two calendar years later, April 3, 1998, to file suit....

....

We accordingly reverse the summary judgment orders and remand the cause to the district court for further proceedings.

Follow-Up Questions

1. This case explains the way in which courts, throughout the nation, calculate "calendar month" and "calendar year" deadlines as well as a plaintiff's status change from infant to adult. *See* 74 Am. Jur. 2d § 7 (2009). In this example, however, the defendants conceded that the plaintiff's claims did not start (accrue) until he turned eighteen, on April 3, 1996. Nevertheless the defendants maintained that the plaintiff's claim was barred by the statute of limitations. What was their argument? How did the court's reliance upon the calendar-year approach lead the court to its conclusion?

2. Is this court's approach to calendar months and years consistent with the concept of excluding the day of the event—a rule also followed in Texas?[8] If so, how is it consistent? By counting from a particular date (month/day) in one year, to the same month/day in another year, does one exclude the starting day in the initial year?

---

8. The following is the rule on judicial counting from the Texas Rules of Civil Procedure:
   In computing any period of time prescribed or allowed by these rules, by order of court, or by any applicable statute, the day of the act, event, or default after which the designated period of time begins to run is not to be included. The last day of the period so computed is to be included, unless it is a Saturday, Sunday or legal holiday, in which event the period runs until the end of the next day which is not a Saturday, Sunday or legal holiday....
Tex. R. Civ. P. 4.

3. In the Master Problem, Sally Wilreiz's automobile accident occurred on February 2, 2009. Using the general calculation method outlined above, and the explanation of calendar years by the Texas Court of Appeals in *Medina*, what would be the last date on which she could file suit for negligence leading to personal injuries if the governing statute was a two-year rule?

4. Assume that during today's commute to school you were rear-ended by an inattentive driver. Determine the statute of limitations for a personal injury claim in your current jurisdiction. Next, review the appropriate calendars and determine the day and year that represent the last day on which you could file suit against the driver. What if the last day falls on Memorial Day? In that case, what would be the deadline for filing suit?

Professional Identity Questions

1. Some lawyers do not file suit until the very end of the limitations period, for differing reasons. Many will say that a plaintiff's injuries will not fully "mature" for a period of time; the delay will provide their clients an opportunity to present all potential injuries to the fact-finder. Sometimes the lawyer is simply too busy handling other cases to bother with a case until the limitations deadline looms. Do you consider either of these reasons legitimate? Would you delay filing suit based upon either argument? Would doing so create anxiety for you, especially as your case load grows over time?

2. If you develop the habit of filing on the final day of a limitations period, what risks do you take? How is this likely to affect your reputation in the legal community? If another attorney otherwise considers you a fine lawyer, but knows you are a chronic "last-minute filer," might that colleague choose to refer a case to another lawyer who habitually files before limitations deadlines? If you learned that a case would have been referred to you except for the referring lawyer's concern about your being a "deadline flirter," how would you feel on learning that?

3. If you miscalculated a limitations period, and your client's case was dismissed based on the statute of limitations, would you tell your client that your miscalculation led to the dismissal? Some lawyers do not tell their clients the truth. Perhaps rationalizing that the case would not have worked out for the client anyway, these lawyers offer other grounds on which the case lacked merit. How would you characterize such explanations? What, in your human experience, might explain lawyers' avoiding the truth and offering such explanations that may avoid their being held accountable? Over time, do you believe the effect of misleading clients will become a burden the lawyer must bear? Might there be a connection between carrying such burdens—especially if accumulated from a number of instances over time that internally the lawyer knows to be wrong—and the higher incidence of substance abuse among lawyers as compared to the general population (*see* Ch. 1, notes 1 & 2)?

Practice Problems

Practice Problem 2-1

On January 15, 2006, Doug Defendant slammed into Polly Plaintiff while she was stopped at a red light. On Thursday, January 15, 2008, Polly filed a suit seeking recovery for personal injuries resulting from Doug's negligence. The applicable statute of limitations is two years after the event causing the injuries. Doug asserts that Polly's suit is barred by the statute of limitations. Is Polly's suit time-barred? Which parts of the Model Computation of Time statute apply to this scenario? Why must one also consider the calendar year calculation to answer this question?

Practice Problem 2-2

A civil jury trial goes to verdict and the court enters a final judgment of $1 million for plaintiff against the defendant on April 3, 2009. The applicable state Supreme Court Rule requires that notice of appeal be filed within 30 days (the rule doesn't say "month," but says 30 days) from the date judgment is entered. Defendant files her notice of appeal on May 4, 2009. Plaintiff moves to dismiss the appeal on grounds that the notice is untimely. Failure to file a timely notice of appeal is jurisdictional. Should the court grant the motion to dismiss the appeal?

Notice to the government!

Pre-Suit Notice of Certain Claims

You have already recognized that an attorney must research requirements for pre-suit notice to a defendant prior to filing a claim. As the Texas case (excerpted above) demonstrates, pre-suit notice of malpractice claims against health care providers is not unusual. In many states, this requirement also applies to negligence (or other tort) claims against municipalities. *See, e.g.,* James L. Isham, *Insufficiency of Notice of Claim Against Municipality as Regards Statement of Place Where Accident Occurred*, 69 A.L.R. 4th 484 (1989). Moreover, tort claims against a state or against the federal government[9] will face much the same hurdle under the applicable Tort Claims Act. *See* 57 Am. Jur. 2d *Municipal, County, School & State Tort Liability* § 12 (2009) (explaining knowledge or notice of danger, with specific reference to highways, streets, and bridges); 8 Am. Jur. *Trials* § 635 (2009). Sovereign immunity would ordinarily bar suits against a state, but Tort Claims Acts represent instances in which the sovereign waives its immunity up to a specified dollar cap. *See* 57 Am. Jur. 2d *Municipal, County, School & State Tort Liability* § 12 (2009).

---

9. A claim against the United States is one of the few claims within the *exclusive* jurisdiction of the federal courts. 28 U.S.C. § 1346 (United States as a defendant). Thus, such a claim could not be filed in state court. Nevertheless, state courts have concurrent jurisdiction over most claims deriving from federal law. As a result in most cases lawyers can combine state and federal claims in a suit filed in state court. Of course, defendants can in appropriate circumstances remove cases from state court to federal court. *See* 28 U.S.C. §§ 1441–1446 (2009).

These pre-suit requirements will not always be referred to as "notice" requirements. Sometimes they will instead be provisions that require presentation of a claim to a non-judicial body for consideration before one can file suit. *See generally* J. James Frazier & Mike Moore, *Complaint as Satisfying Requirement of Notice of Claim Upon States, Municipalities, and Other Political Subdivisions* 45 A.L.R. 5th 109 (1997). Such procedures are routinely called "exhaustion of remedies." *See id.* § 5. They present the same difficulties, however, as pre-suit notice. If one does not present the claim to the required non-judicial body before filing suit, the defendant can move to dismiss the case for failure to exhaust remedies. In short, one needs to research not only terms such as "pre-filing notice" or "pre-suit notice," but also "exhaustion of remedies," "right to sue," and any other similar phrase that could unearth pre-suit requirements necessary to address before bring a lawsuit. Often a lawyer would do well to consult treatises in the state and find a discussion of all pre-suit requirements, if they are discussed in one place, or search out a separate discussion of pre-suit requirements if addressed in a separate part of a treatise.

Follow-Up Questions

1. What is the difference between pre-suit notice and filing suit? Research the law of the state in which you intend to practice and determine how you can typically satisfy applicable pre-suit notice requirements? Will doing so ordinarily involve filing documents with the court?

2. In every case that lands on your desk, how can you remember to research whether the law applicable to the claim (or defendant in question) will require pre-suit notice as a prerequisite to filing a complaint? What is the risk if you have not developed a system for recognizing such claims?

3. Are there certain types of cases or defendants in which pre-suit notice is usually necessary?

Professional Identity Questions

1. What habits in case handling can you develop to (1) know of any deadlines for giving notice prior to filing suit, and (2) to avoid missing such deadlines? If you create procedures to ensure you are aware of and meet your client's deadlines, how do you think that will affect your view of yourself as a lawyer? How do you believe doing so will affect the view others in the legal community, along with clients, have of you as a professional?

2. Do you find it intimidating that you must consider such issues in every case? If so, consider a client's desire to hire a lawyer who has a reputation for thoroughness. How would you define a conscientious lawyer? If you were a client, would you expect a lawyer to know and abide by any deadlines required to protect the client's claim? Does the possibility of developing a reputation as a thorough, conscientious lawyer help motivate you to develop systems that will ensure you remain aware of key deadlines?

Practice Problems

Practice Problem 2-3

The State of Olympia has a state park that features, at its center, a statue of King Neptune, the mythical "Master of the Sea." On June 1, 2008, part of the triton (the large, three-pronged pitch-fork that Neptune carries) separated from the statue and fell on a tourist. Laura Little suffered a gash in her arm that required thirty stitches. The injury also causes her to experience on-going pain from nerve damage. A police officer from Olympia happened to be in the area when the incident occurred. In his accident report, he wrote: On June 1, 2008, at King Neptune Park, part of King Neptune's triton "fell" and injured Laura Little. In accordance with City policy, the police officer filed the accident report before the end of his shift, and a copy was sent to the State Attorney General. On February 1, 2010, Laura Little filed a lawsuit seeking damages for negligence in failure to maintain safe conditions at the park. The City filed a responsive pleading requesting that the court dismiss the suit on the grounds that Laura failed to give notice to the City as required by statute.

In the state in which you intend to practice, research whether a State Tort Claims Act exists and, if so, (1) what is the deadline, if any, for providing notice to the State of the potential claim; and (2) whether the notice provided here through the police officer would be sufficient. If such notice as was given here would not be sufficient, what does your State Tort Claims Act require in terms of notice to the State — including the manner of notice, to whom notice must be given, and the form in which notice must be given?

Practice Problem 2-4

The City of Arcadia has a sidewalk that in which one of the panels of concrete shifted so that it stuck ten inches into the air. Persons walking along the sidewalk had to consciously step over this area or risk tripping. Some tripped and fell but were not seriously injured. Unfortunately, Pauline Plaintiff tripped and fell face down. She broke both arms as she tried to "break" her fall by putting her arms down. In addition, she suffered severe lacerations to her face. Her cognitive ability, however was not affected by the accident. After staying in the hospital, and then returning home, she called the City Manager and told him off for having such a hazard as this condition.

Research the law of the State in which you intend to practice and determine what, if any, pre-suit notice someone like Pauline would have to give to a City in the State prior to filing suit. If there is such a requirement, what is the deadline for giving such notice? Would Pauline's telephone call to the City Manager suffice or would the notice have to be in writing? To whom would it have to be delivered and in what manner?

Practice Problem 2-5

Cal Contractor enters into a construction contract with the Municipality of Olympia to build an addition onto the City's elementary school. Cal timely performs his obligations under the contract. Olympia fails to pay Cal by the date set forth in the contract despite Cal's repeated demands. Cal is not sure what remedies are available to him, so he seeks your advice on the matter. Con-

[handwritten margin notes: — set out Nature of specific item 1245; — verify by affidavit 1245; — No action against cty. until Claim presented to gov. body 1248]

sider exhaustion of remedies accomplished by presenting the claim to the governing body of the municipality; if this is an option, determine the requirements and deadlines. Explain how you would advise Cal to pursue available remedies.

Statute of Limitations

Once you have identified all potential claims, you must determine the date each claim must be filed to ensure timeliness. Often, attorneys assume that the statute of limitations analysis involves solely knowing time periods for particular types of claims. Such attorneys are surprised to discover the complexity of the limitations analysis. The following discussion shows that you must engage in a multi-step analysis to determine the limitations deadline for *each* claim that is brought against *each* defendant.

Determining the Claims

The first step in any statute of limitations analysis is determining the claims for which you need to know the various limitations period. You must segregate each claim on which your client can sue and analyze the statute of limitations for that claim independently from any other claim.

Determining the Limitations Period Applicable to a Claim/Defendant

The second step of any statute of limitations analysis is to determine the period of time allocated by law for a particular kind of claim. Typically, claims vary in length depending on the type of claim. Each state sets its own statute of limitations period for particular types of claims (*i.e.*, property, contract, tort, equitable, etc.). *See* 4 AM. JUR. *Trials* §441 (2009). In many states, the statute of limitations for personal injury actions is two years, while the statute of limitations for property damage is five years. *See, e.g.*, VA. CODE ANN. §8.01-243(A)-(B) (2009). For examples of other statutes of limitation, compare CAL. CIV. PROC. CODE §§335–349.2 (2009) (two year statute of limitations period for actions other than the recovery of real property), with CAL. CIV. PROC. CODE §§315–330 (2009) (five year statute of limitations period for claims seeking recovery of real property); *see also* N.Y. C.P.L.R. §§212(a) (2009) (setting the statute of limitations period to recover real property at ten years); *id.* §214(a) (setting the statute of limitations period at two years and six months for medical malpractice claims).

In many states, shorter limitation periods apply for intentional torts (*e.g.*, one year), somewhat longer (*e.g.*, two to three-year periods) for negligence claims, while a plaintiff may have several years to bring a contract claim, and even longer in many states (*e.g.*, five or more years) for property claims. *See generally* 4 AM. JUR. Trials §441 Appendix (2009). States vary, however, in the length of time prescribed for a particular kind of action. Thus, an attorney must be careful to check her state's limitations period for each claim in a case.

③ Accrual Issues

Determining the "accrual" date of a claim is the third step in the analysis. The accrual date is the point at which the claim comes into existence. As a general example, most tort actions accrue when the injury occurs and a contract action usually accrues when the breach occurs. The traditional rule starts the accrual of a limitations period upon the occurrence of the wrong. 51 AM. JUR. 2d *Limitations of Actions* § 148 (2009); 4 AM. JUR. *Trials* 441 §6 (2009). Breach of contract tends to fit within the general rule. When a contracting party fails to abide by the terms of the contract, the wrong has occurred. 51 AM. JUR. 2d *Limitations of Actions* § 169 (2009) (explaining that the interval within which a lawsuit must be filed generally begins to run at the time the contract is breached, rather than when actual damages are sustained). Likewise, a claim for property damage generally accrues when the property damage occurs. *Id.* § 151. However, tort actions may not fit within the general rule, depending on whether the "occurrence of the wrong" happens at the same time as the injury. In a typical car accident, occurrence of the wrong occurs simultaneously with the injury. In other instances, the negligent act or omission occurred prior to the injury. Even in instances in which the negligence and the injury are separate in time, however, personal injury claims like Sally's often accrue when the injury occurs rather than on some prior date such as when City and State workers neglected to repair the road.

Another frequent scenario is when a negligent act or omission occurs but the plaintiff is not aware of the injury caused by the negligence. To deal with such cases, the "discovery" rule has become a widely accepted accrual principle in many states. *Id.* § 179 (stating that under the discovery rule the accrual of a cause of action occurs at the time the plaintiff either "discovered or reasonably should have discovered" the existence of the basis for her claim); *see also* 4 AM. JUR. *Trials* 441 § 17 (2009) (explaining that the discovery of injury test is open to judicial interpretation but that the most well reasoned cases hold that the injury has occurred "[w]hen the plaintiff is definitely aware of an injury which may form the basis for litigation.").

In claims of fraud, for instance, it makes sense to say that a claim arises when the defrauded party learns of the fraud. 4 AM. JUR. *Trials* 441 § 10 (2009) (confirming that, in cases of fraud, the majority of jurisdictions have accepted the view that the interval for filing suit begins at the time such fraud is discovered or by the exercise of due diligence, should have been discovered by the plaintiff). To insist that the statute of limitations on a fraud claim was running even though the plaintiff was unaware of the fraud would indeed represent a cruel system. For instance, Sally could have a fraud claim against Wheeler Dealer based on the events described in the Master Problem. In most states, Sally's claim would accrue when Sally learned (or in some jurisdictions when she "should have been aware") of the fraud.

④ Tolling Issues

In a limitations analysis, the fourth step is to determine any basis for tolling that, if applicable, will interrupt the limitations period. "Tolling" refers to suspending or stopping the running of a statute of limitations; it is analogous to a clock stopping, and then restarting. 51 AM. JUR. 2d *Limitation of Actions* §§ 169–71, 174 (2009) (explaining that limitation laws usually include exceptions such as a party's incapacitation and stating that the statute of limitations can be tolled if a claimant was prevented in some extraordinary way from bringing her cause of action).

If a plaintiff is under eighteen years old, for instance, most states will classify her as an infant. In this respect, the Texas appellate decision in *Medina v. Lopez-Roman* (*see supra* pages 29–31) is also representative of every other state. As an infant, one lacks capacity to sue during the period of this "disability." 4 AM. JUR. *Trials* § 24 (2009). Almost every state will allow for tolling of the time during which the infant lacks capacity, and will begin the limitations period on the day she becomes "of age." *See also* N.Y. C.P.L.R. § 208 (2009) (providing that the time within which to bring the cause of action is extended to within three years of the time the disability ceases). *See generally* 51 AM. JUR. 2d *Limitation of Actions* § 224 (explaining that many states have statutes providing that the action is tolled until the infant reaches the age of majority or is extended for a period of time thereafter). Similar rules apply to persons who lack capacity for one reason or another, such as an individual involuntarily committed to a mental health facility. 4 AM. JUR. *Trials* § 24 (2009) (explaining that mental incapacity is recognized by statute as a basis for tolling statutes of limitation). *But see* 51 AM. JUR. 2d *Limitations of Actions* § 230 (2009) (explaining the majority rule that mental disability is a narrow exception: for purposes of tolling a statute of limitations, a mental disability "must be of such a nature as to show that the plaintiff is unable to manage his or her business affairs or estate, or to comprehend his or her legal rights or liabilities."). Until a person is formally released, the time of institutionalization will usually be tolled. 51 AM. JUR. 2d *Limitations of Actions* § 203 (2009) (stating that most states have statutory provisions providing a time period following the removal of the mental disability during which a plaintiff can assert his claim).

State law will specify what is required to show lack of capacity. A statute may provide for tolling of the limitations period during a hospital stay resulting from an accident. Assuming such a statute exists in her jurisdiction, Sally could argue that the limitations period was tolled during her six month hospitalization due to the concussion she sustained from the accident. On the other hand, she would have difficulty relying solely on a doctor's opinion that she has experienced intermittent periods of lucidity, followed by periods of time in which she lacks cognitive ability. If the doctor cannot specify dates on which Sally was incapacitated (or if the state in question requires a court order finding her to have become incapacitated), Sally could have difficulty relying on the effects of early dementia to toll statutes of limitation.

Medical malpractice cases involve very complex limitations analyses. Obvious malpractice events, such as amputation of the wrong limb, present little difficulty. The complexity arises, for instance, in a case where the doctor failed to diagnose at a time when— if done accurately—the plaintiff would have avoided great pain, suffering, and trouble. As an example, consider the scenario of a patient who goes to a doctor for examination of a mole. The physician might take a biopsy or simply examine the lesion. Any physician with ordinary knowledge and skill should recognize signs of a mole likely to develop into a dangerous skin cancer. If the treating physician recognizes the risk, and removes the mole, the patient would have no risk of developing skin cancer later. However, if the doctor failed to diagnose the dangerous condition, failed to remove the mole (or have another do so), and informed the patient not to worry, she has been negligent. Later, the mole becomes cancerous and metastasizes; the patient is then forced to deal with chemotherapy and, even if remission occurs, the patient endures a threat of recurrence for the remainder of her life. When does the statute of limitations accrue on such a claim? Did it begin when the physician failed to diagnose the mole as a dangerous condition—meaning that the limitations would likely have run on the plaintiff's claim? Or later, when the patient learns of the misdiagnosis? Courts have taken different approaches. Some require medical testimony of the date on which a misdiagnosed medical condition became a deleterious health issue. *See* AM. JUR. *Trials* 441 §§ 34–35 (2009). Others lean toward the bright-line test of when a patient learns of the misdiagnosis. *See, e.g.,* VA. CODE ANN.

§§ 8.01–249 (2009) (specifying that accrual of the cause of action in a medical malpractice case involving breast implantation surgery occurs when the injury is discovered and
that the discovery of the injury occurs when "[t]he fact of the injury and its causal connection to the implantation is first communicated to the person by a physician").

Moreover, if the health care professional does anything to hide from the patient information
that would expose the misdiagnosis, the statute of limitations often will be tolled. *See,
e.g.,* 51 Am. Jur. 2d *Limitation of Actions* § 185.

The Final Step: Calculating the Limitation Deadline in Light of the Above Rules

The fifth and final step involves putting everything together and calculating the latest
date upon which suit can be filed in light of the principles enumerated above. As previously noted, different claims will usually not only have different limitations periods, but
different accrual dates. Thus, the variety of deadlines in a case often ends up being a stag-
gered set of dates. For instance, a personal injury claim can accrue two years after an accident. Yet, the same plaintiff may have a breach of contract claim that accrued before or
after that date, depending on when the other party to the contract breached. In addition,
a fraud claim would have its own accrual date depending on when the fraud became
known (or should have become known). Finally, a claim for violation of property rights
also would have its own independent accrual rules and time period.

Follow-Up Questions

1. What would be the logical series of questions so that you cover each of the analytical steps in a statutes of limitations analysis? Ensure that it is comprehensive and would address all questions, such as accrual rule(s) that may
   apply to a statute of limitations. Also ensure that your written analysis does
   the same for tolling principles. For example, how would tolling (if applicable) affect your conclusions regarding the statute of limitations period governing the relevant claim?

2. If a client has multiple claims against a party (or parties) arising from the
   same transaction or occurrence, would it be most prudent to file within the
   shortest statute of limitations and add all claims on which one has a good
   faith basis to file suit?

3. Is it likely that the accrual rule for each type of claim will be different? How
   would that affect your analysis of the limitations of your client's claims? What
   is the accrual date for Sally's personal injury claim? For her breach of contract claim against the investment firm, Wheeler Dealer? For any fraud claim?
   For her claim for trespass as it pertains to the fence? For her negligence claims
   against the City, the State, and the vehicle manufacturer?

4. Different states have a variety of methods for incapacity determinations. If
   your state requires a judicial finding of incapacity, how will you know when
   someone has been declared "incapacitated"? Can you ask the fact-finder for
   a declaration of incapacity to avail your client of tolling principles? Would
   you do so by putting that issue in the pleadings and having it resolved as a matter of fact at trial?

5. If your state requires that incapacity determinations must be established as an issue of fact by the court and you still have time to file suit without relying on tolling, do you see any advantages to going forward with an incapacitation hearing?

Professional Identity Questions

1. Assume your state does not require a formal finding of incapacity in order to trigger tolling, but rather describes certain symptoms that must be confirmed by the fact-finder. Assume further that you conclude that, without tolling of the statute of limitations, your client's claim will be time-barred. After explaining the reality that the client's case is time-barred absent tolling, how would you feel describing the symptoms required to demonstrate incapacity to your client, and mentioning that only if the client had some such symptoms establishing incapacity could she toll the limitations period—even if you had no indication from the client that such symptoms might have existed? Would that constitute "coaching" your client by informing her that the viability of her claim may depend on her personal testimony or manifestation of certain symptoms?

2. If a client presented to you a contract claim that you could tell immediately was barred by the statute of limitations, would you feel uncomfortable filing suit for breach of contract on the theory that the statute of limitations is a defense and, if the defendant does not think to raise it, that is the defendant's problem?

3. Assume you are in a state that follows the discovery rule for fraud claims. You have already brought suit on the fraud claim and are preparing your client to be deposed by defendant's counsel. In preparation, your client tells you that she suspected on a given date that the potential defendant had misrepresented to her a fact on which she relied to her detriment and then suffered damages. If that date is the accrual date, the statute of limitations will be barred. How would you feel suggesting to the client that, if she chose a later date on which she was "more certain" that the defendant had misrepresented the fact, then she would weaken the defendant's statute of limitations argument?

Practice Problems

Practice Problem 2-6

On May 1, 2009, Harry Harried was driving to work and was predictably late. As a result, he was speeding. Whenever Harry approached intersections, he would accelerate to avoid stopping. At one intersection the traffic signal turned yellow at least 100 yards before he "gunned it." Carrie Careful, celebrating her seventeenth birthday, saw her traffic signal turn green, and she entered the intersection. She even looked in both directions before proceeding, but a tree blocked her view of Harry's approach. As Carrie entered the intersection, Harry's car collided with Carrie's car and Carrie was badly injured.

According to her physician, the full extent of her injuries (and the likelihood of permanent damage) may not be known for several years. At present, she has

constant neck pain and partial paralysis of one leg. On May 15, 2009, Carrie retains you as her attorney. She asks at your meeting what is the latest date on
which she could file suit against Harry. Research the law of the state in which
you plan to practice and determine the applicable statute of limitations as well
as the date on which Carrie would have to file suit.

Practice Problem 2-7

The drivers' side door of Paul Plaintiff's automobile was struck on January 1,
2004, by Dan Defendant. Dan had ignored a red light, and the resulting collision seriously injured Paul. Paul died from those injuries on December 1, 2005.
An executor was certified to handle Paul's estate and on November 30, 2007,
filed a wrongful death action against Dan Defendant. Analyze the statute of limitations for a wrongful-death claim in the state in which you plan to practice.
Be sure to examine any provision on tolling of the statute of limitations on the
death of a person with a claim because that may be crucial to the executor's ability to sue. Also, research whether any provision allows an executor some period
of time in which to bring claims on behalf of an estate.

Practice Problem 2-8

Robin, age 38, felt a lump in one of her breasts and on December 1, 2005, she
visited Dr. Dan, who was supposed to be a specialist in breast cancer. Dr. Dan
took a biopsy of the lump. Two weeks later, Dr. Dan reported the results to Robin
as "benign." He told her it was "probably a cyst" and that she should come back an-
nually, which she did. Over time, the lump increased in size. Robin expressed concern over the growth of the lump. Privately, Dr. Dan himself had some concern
that perhaps he should have more closely examined a biopsy on Robin's first visit.
He did review that biopsy again and his examination left him concerned, but he
did not share this concern with Robin. At the time of her last visit to Dr. Dan. in
December 2008, Robin began to doubt Dr. Dan's competence. On December 1, 2009,
Robin went to Dr. Kim, whom she had been assured was the best local breast cancer specialist. Dr. Kim requested biopsy records from Robin's first visit to Dr. Dan.
As soon as he looked at them, he noted that the pathology report indicated a condition called "ductal carcinoma in situ." This condition is much less serious if
treated promptly because the cancerous cells are localized and, if removed, the
person has little or no risk of developing cancer again. Dr. Kim advised Robin that
if the lump had been removed earlier, she would not have had any problem. However, in the interval since Dr. Dan misdiagnosed Robin, the cancer had spread.
Dr. Kim advised Robin that she would require not only a mastectomy, but also
chemotherapy because of the spread of the disease. He also advised her that her
life expectancy was now greatly reduced. Robin sues Dr. Dan, who raises the statute
of limitations as a defense, claiming that she is asserting negligence over events
that occurred in 2005. First, determine whether you are in a jurisdiction that requires pre-suit notice prior to filing suit on a malpractice claim against a health
care professional? Second, given the law of the state in which you practice, what
arguments can Robin offer against Dr. Dan's statute of limitations defense?

Practice Problem 2-9

On April 10, 2005, Dot Gale purchased a new Tornado auto from Wizard
Motors, a car dealership in the County of Oz. (Wizard Motors had itself bought
the Tornado exactly one month before from Major Motors Corp.) Dot drove the

car very little, but on occasion she did visit a lovely lady named Glenda who lived East of Oz. On December 27, 2006, Dot was driving to see Glenda, when the right front wheel of the auto came off, causing the car to wreck, and seriously injure Dot. Indeed, she was in a coma for eight months and had to stay in the hospital until she regained consciousness. In the interim, the car was towed back to Oz where it was determined that the front wheel had come off because of a defect in the front wheel assembly attributable to the fault of the manufacturer.

On March 2, 2009, Dot commenced an action at law against both Wizard Motors and Major Motors Corp., the manufacturer of the Tornado, to recover property damages and damages for personal injuries. The complaint alleged the foregoing facts and recited that both the property damage and Dot's injuries had been proximately caused by not only the defendant's negligence but also by the breach of defendants' implied warranty of merchantability. The defendants asserted the defense of a statute of limitations to each claim for damages. Research the applicable law of the state in which you plan to practice and explain how the court should rule on a statute of limitations defense as to each claim.

Practice Problem 2-10

Mr. and Mrs. Piggot were looking for a home in Magical Forest Subdivision in the State of Illyria. Tired of working in the media world with the endless push to sensationalize events, Wolf Blitzer had become a real estate agent. The Piggots retained him as their agent. They looked at a number of homes. The Piggots particularly liked a home on the edge of the subdivision. They were concerned, however, about the property adjacent to the subdivision. (The lot in which they were interested abutted this outside property.) Specifically, they inquired about the allowable uses of the property. On February 2, 2003, Wolf told them in response to their queries that the land adjacent to the lot was zoned for residential use. In fact, the land was zoned for industrial use, and Wolf knew it. The Piggots bought the lot. Four years later (March 2007) a company began to build a factory on the adjacent property. The Piggots were outraged. They talked to the manager of the company and told him the land was zoned for residential purposes only. He responded that they were mistaken because the land had been zoned for industrial purposes for over a decade. The Piggots then confirmed as much with the local zoning authority. They come to you in February 2009 and ask whether they have a fraud claim against Wolf and whether they would still be able to bring it. Research the law of the state in which you plan to practice to determine the answer to the Piggots' question.

Practice Problem 2-11

The Piggots decided to remain on the lot described in the preceding Practice Problem. It took a year for the factory to be completed, but by the end of 2004 it was ready for operation. Once it began operating, it emitted a putrid odor as a result of the manufacturing process for the paper products it produced. After a year of putting up with the smell, the Piggots were fed up. They organized other subdivision owners to picket outside the factory on the public sidewalks. They took turns carrying signs that said things like "THIS FACTORY STINKS," "THIS COMPANY'S BUSINESS SMELLS," and "RUINING THE ENVIRON-MENT—ALL FOR THE LOVE OF MONEY." After years of picketing, and media attention from some of Wolf Blitzer's former colleagues, the business's sales started to decline noticeably. The manager of the plant, Tim Burr, was infuri-

trespass

property damage

ated at the picketing. On July 15, 2009, he left the plant, went to the Piggots' property, and saw the picketing signs leaning on outdoor furniture on their lawn. Tim pulled a sledge hammer out of his trunk, walked over to the signs, and smashed them to bits. In the process, he broke the furniture against which the signs were leaning. The Piggots saw him as he finished and was leaving.

On August 1, 2009, the Piggots come to you about bringing suit against the company and Mr. Burr. They ask if they have a nuisance claim against the company that owns the plant due to the smell. If so, would they still have time to bring the suit? As to Mr. Burr, they ask whether they have claims for trespass on their property and for damage to their signs and furniture. Under the law of the state in which you plan to practice, by what date would these claims have to be brought?

① Nuisance — 5 years   ② Property damages — 5 years   ③ Trespass — 5 years

Statutes of Repose Analysis

Repose statutes do not follow the same analysis as a statute of limitations. The lawyer who fails to spot the applicability of a statute of repose and assumes that the ordinary rules of limitations analysis apply can end up with a barred claim. Statutes of repose are different from statutes of limitation because, if applicable, the date on which the limitations period begins to run will be a "date certain"—typically, the completion date of a building for which materials have been provided. *See* Jay M. Zitter, *Validity and Construction of Statute Terminating Right of Action for Product-Caused Injury at Fixed Period After Manufacture, Sale, or Delivery of Product*, 30 A.L.R. 5th (1995). Thus, if part of a ceiling later falls and injures someone, the date for a claim against those protected by the statute of repose (*e.g.*, the supplier of ceiling materials) begins *not* when the injury occurred (as is typical of statutes of limitation analysis). Instead, the clock on the statute of repose had been running ever since the completion of the building. As a result, statutes of repose provide even more finality than statutes of limitation. Typically, statutes of repose apply to those who participate in building structures, including general contractors, subcontractors, and suppliers of materials used in buildings or other improvements to real property. *Id.*

If applicable, a statute of repose ensures a definite period of time during which suits may be brought arising from materials used in improvements to real property, such as materials incorporated into buildings, pools, or the like. Thus, the usual accrual limitations analysis will not apply. Again, it bears repeating: if someone is injured due to alleged negligence of a party who supplied materials involved in an improvement covered by a statute of repose, the claim *does not accrue upon injury*. Instead, the statute of repose *will have been running already*—from the completion of construction of the improvement—and thus often bars the plaintiff's claim. *See, e.g.*, CALVIN W. CORMAN, LIMITATION OF ACTIONS § 5.1.7 (1991). Moreover, normal tolling principles typical of limitations analysis are inapplicable. Even if a plaintiff is incapacitated, the statute of repose will bar a claim when the time period after completion of construction has run. *Id.* ("unlike statutes of limitation, statutes of repose have not been tolled because of a … litigant's defective capacity.").

The most litigated issues in cases involving the statute of repose relate to whether the material provided by the defendant is the kind of item covered by a statute of repose. As suggested above, materials incorporated as part of improvements to real property generally fall within the protection of the statute of repose. *See* 63B AM. JUR. 2d *Products Liability*

§ 1633 (2009). However, many states' statutes of repose except from their protection equipment or machinery that is not incorporated by design (*e.g.*, not in the architectural drawings) in the improvement. *See id.* For example, courts have held that equipment in a plant or in piping at a refinery is outside the statute's protection. *See id.*

Before giving up on a client's claim in a case that may appear to be governed by the statute of repose, the resourceful lawyer will research the law of her state and determine whether the materials at issue could fall outside the statute.

Follow-Up Questions

1. How would you explain to a client the difference between a statute of limitations and the statute of repose?

2. In determining whether something is covered by your state's statute of repose, what experts could help you argue for or against the inclusion of the item within the statute of repose?

Professional Identity Question

Assume that a plaintiff is rendered a quadriplegic by a wall collapsing on her after the time allowed by the applicable statute of repose has run. Your client is the supplier of the dry wall that fell on the plaintiff. After meeting your client, you realize that he is not sophisticated about the law and is not aware of the statute of repose. Indeed, he assumes that he will have to face the lawsuit. Personally, however, you find it repulsive that a statute such as this would result in a quadriplegic's suit being dismissed. Would you advise your client of the defense? If not, would you be committing malpractice?

Practice Problems

Practice Problem 2-12

A general contractor builds a hotel for hotel owner. As part of its project, the contractor hires an electrical company to install an electrical panel with circuit breakers in the building. The electrical company does so. Subsequently, more than fifteen years after completion of the building, a maintenance person employed by the hotel is seriously injured when the electrical panel malfunctions and shocks him (though he followed instructions for changing breakers). The maintenance person sues the electrical panel box supplier, who raises the statute of repose as a defense. Research the law of your jurisdiction and determine how the court should rule.

Practice Problem 2-13

You represent an employee at a plant. You learn that a conveyor belt had been installed at the time of the plant's construction eleven years ago. Recently, your client lost part of her hand when it was caught in the conveyor belt. The conveyor had "slats" of open space at regular intervals. The belt failed to stop immediately, as it is supposed to do when any object extends between the "slats." Your client explained that she slipped and put her hand down to catch herself, unfortunately on the conveyor belt. You sue the conveyor belt manufacturer. The company raises the statute of repose as a defense. How should the court rule?

If equipment, statute of repose does not apply, so can sue within 5 year limit

D. Methods to Reinforce and Integrate Topics Covered in This Chapter

You might represent the five steps of a statute of limitations analysis in a flow chart. The following is the beginning of a possible flow chart.

A statute of limitations analysis always has five steps. Although each step (*e.g.*, tolling) may not apply in any given case, you should take each step in the analysis to avoid missing an issue. The steps follow:

Diagram 2-2

```
┌─────────────────────────────────────────┐
│  What are all potential claims in the    │
│  case?                                   │
└─────────────────────────────────────────┘
                    │
                    ▼
┌─────────────────────────────────────────────────────────┐
│  What does your jurisdiction provide as the time period  │
│  for bringing each of the claims above (e.g., two years  │
│  for personal injury, five years for property damage)?   │
└─────────────────────────────────────────────────────────┘
                    │
                    ▼
┌─────────────────────────────────────────────────────────┐
│  What is the "accrual date" for the claim in question,   │
│  i.e., when the clock starts ticking on each claim?      │
└─────────────────────────────────────────────────────────┘
                    │
                    ▼
┌────────────────────────────────┐        ┌──────────────────────────┐
│  Is there any basis for         │───────▶│  Infant?                 │
│  "tolling" so that time during  │        └──────────────────────────┘
│  which the limitations period   │        ┌──────────────────────────┐
│  otherwise would be counted     │───────▶│  Incapacitated Person?   │
│  should be taken out of the     │        └──────────────────────────┘
│  time calculation?              │        ┌──────────────────────────┐
│                                 │───────▶│  Incarcerated Person?    │
└────────────────────────────────┘        └──────────────────────────┘
                    │                      ┌──────────────────────────┐
                    ▼                      │  Person declared          │
┌────────────────────────────────┐───────▶│  incapacitated by Court   │
│  In light of each of the steps  │        │  or Institution?          │
│  above, what is the last date   │        └──────────────────────────┘
│  on which each claim can be      │        ┌──────────────────────────┐
│  brought?                        │───────▶│  Person in Armed Forces? │
└────────────────────────────────┘        └──────────────────────────┘
```

E. Written Assignments

Following are suggested written assignments, based on the Master Problem, which should help reinforce further the topics and analysis covered in this chapter.

1. Make a chart of all statutes of limitation applicable in the state in which you will practice. Put the briefest statutes of limitation on the left and progress to the longer statutes of limitation on the right. Do you notice any trends, such as having tort limitations periods generally shorter than contract limitations periods, or having both of those categories shorter than damage to property or other property-related claims (*e.g.*, ejectment of a "squatter" on one's property)?

2. For the Master Problem, research the law of the state in which you plan to practice and determine whether Sally has to give pre-suit notice to (1) the City of Arcadia, (2) the State of Illyria, and/or (3) HorsePower, Inc. If she has to give such notice as to any of these defendants, prepare a sample notice such as you would provide to the defendant, including everything required by the applicable law in your state and addressing the notice to the person or persons required by your state's law.

3. Review all facts you know at this point on the Master Problem. Assume Sally came in to see you on January 15, 2010, a little less than a year after the accident. Research the law of the state in which you plan to practice and determine the statute of limitations for all claims Sally can bring against (1) the City of Arcadia, (2) the State of Illyria, and (3) HorsePower, Inc. Be sure to work through each step in the statute of limitations analysis outlined in this chapter. Then identify the deadline for the claim that has the earliest limitations deadline. Would you file suit on all claims by that deadline? If not, what risks do you run by filing suit on one claim and waiting on others?

Chapter 3

Choosing the Forum: Subject Matter Jurisdiction, Personal Jurisdiction, and Venue

A. Sally's Case at This Stage of Litigation Process

After you explain to Sally and her daughter that any claims are now barred against the roof panel supplier and against the neighbor over his fence, they are understandably disappointed but not overly so. In addition, they accept your firm's recommendation to have another firm that specializes in securities law handle the claim against Wheeler Dealer, Inc. Nevertheless, Sally tells you that she does not know of another lawyer she trusts more than Mr. Befayre, and that she wants both of you to handle her suit against the City of Arcadia, the State of Illyria, and HorsePower, Inc. She asks you to take all steps necessary to pursue claims for compensation against these defendants. You have already determined that the claims against these three defendants are not time-barred. Now you must determine where Sally may file the lawsuit. To do so, you must analyze subject matter jurisdiction, personal jurisdiction, and venue.

B. Tasks and Decision-Making at This Stage of a Case

The point at which you now find yourself in the timeline of a case is set forth in Diagram 3-1.

Choosing the court in which to file suit in is a process filled with strategic decision making. In some jurisdictions, juries typically award higher money damages than in other jurisdictions. Given a choice, a plaintiff in a case like Sally's would (of course) want to file in a jurisdiction that habitually awards higher damages awards. Other strategic considerations include the reputation and tendencies of a court's judges. In most courts, you cannot choose the judge who will handle a case. Instead, the judge is usually assigned (often by a random method of assignments) at the time of filing. Thus, you have to evaluate all judges on a court. Even if the case is one like Sally's that qualifies for a jury trial, the

Diagram 3-1

Cause of Action (events leading to suit)
Prefiling Matters to Consider; Choice of Forum [Chs. 2–3]
Π and Δ Decide on Offensive Pleadings & Joinder (of claims & parties); Filing Suit; Service [Chs. 4–5]
Motions, Responsive Pleadings; Default; Voluntary & Involuntary Dismissals [Chs. 6–7]
Discovery Phase (developing proof to establish claims & learning about the adversary's case) [Ch. 8]
Right to Jury Trial; Pretrial Motions & Practice [Ch. 9]
Final Pretrial Conference & Other Events within Last Month before Trial [Ch. 10]
Procedure at Trial [Ch. 11]
Post-Trial Motions & Calculating the Date of Final Judgment to Know Key Deadlines Such as for Notice of Appeal [Ch. 12]

judge's rulings on pretrial and trial matters can influence the verdict. The speed with which a particular court moves cases to trial and resolves them represents another factor to consider. In general, plaintiffs are better served by courts that take cases to trial sooner rather than later.

Potential Issues in Deciding Where to Sue

Deciding where to file a lawsuit is rich with learning opportunities. After you learn the issues involved, you will be able to envision your decision-making process as a practicing attorney. At this stage, the lawyer must help the client choose between competing alternative courts in which to file suit, at times based on factors that may justifiably make you uneasy.

Not all "forum shopping" is illegitimate. In the first year of law school, students will undoubtedly hear the phrase "forum shopping" in discussions of the *Erie* doctrine — that malleable doctrine designed to maintain state rules of decision in diversity cases filed in federal court. However, based on the famous decision of *Erie Railroad Co. v. Tompkins*, 304 U.S. 64 (1938), and its progeny, the Court's opinions are not necessarily aligned against forum shopping *per se*. Instead, the Court seeks to avoid allowing parties to gain an unfair advantage by filing in federal court and to reserve the benefit of the impartial forum for parties who qualify for diversity jurisdiction. *See Hanna v. Plummer*, 380 U.S.

460 (1965). In other words, the *Erie* doctrine avoids forum shopping that undermines principles of federalism, not *all* forum shopping.

Lawyers should explain to clients the advantages and disadvantages of filing suit in alternative courts. Lawyers are entitled to discuss the potential courts in which a suit may be filed and weigh the strategic options with one's client. In providing such advice, an attorney can face difficult questions—questions that test her professional identity. As such, lawyers should consider these questions *before* addressing the issues with her client. Better for the lawyer to decide ahead of time what kind of professional identity she will have, and how she will respond to an issue of forum selection implicating the attorney's value system, than to allow a strong-willed client to pressure the attorney into a decision inconsistent with her values. For example, how will you respond if your client asks you about the racial composition of juries in the alternative jurisdictions in which suit can be filed? In *Batson v. Kentucky*, 476 U.S. 79 (1986), the Supreme Court held that litigants who exercise peremptory strikes based on the race of jury members violate the Constitution. Would you tell your client that you believe it is inappropriate to consider race as part of the forum selection process? Is there a context in which you feel it is appropriate to discuss racial composition of juries? If you resolve that under no circumstances do you believe it to be an inappropriate subject to discuss, is there a way to express your opinion to your client without suggesting that your client is a racist for even asking the question? Or, do you believe your client *should* be confronted for asking a question along these lines? How can you confront someone about a delicate issue such as this, but do so in a civil manner?

Although perhaps less emotionally charged, discussions with a client about judges on various courts are also ones that implicate a lawyer's principles. Lawyers are obliged to not denigrate the judicial system. Will you criticize judges or offer specific personality characterizations of judges to your client? If you do, will you consider how to describe the composition of a court, or particular judges, without denigrating that court, the judges, or the judicial system? Can you discuss the compositions of courts by prefacing your discussion with a well thought-out description of the legal system as one that attempts to provide justice but which, as a result of human vulnerabilities, can never do so perfectly?

C. Overview of Applicable Law

Subject Matter Jurisdiction

As in federal court, a state court that lacks subject matter jurisdiction over a case cannot enter a valid judgment. "The principle of subject matter jurisdiction relates to a court's inherent authority to deal with the case or matter before it." *Bosworth v. Whitmore*, 37 Cal. Rptr. 3d 560, 568 (Cal. Dist. Ct. App. 2006). In other words, a judgment is void if the state court deciding the case lacked the authority to hear it. The issue of subject matter jurisdiction arises far more frequently in federal courts than in state courts. The reason is simple: the scope of federal jurisdiction is much narrower than that of the jurisdiction bestowed on state courts. Article III of the United States Constitution authorizes federal courts to hear cases that fall under only nine categories, many of which rarely arise. Conversely, state courts typically have a court of general jurisdiction that hears most categories of civil cases. Although the "names" of courts of general jurisdiction vary among the states — such as superior courts in California,[1] district courts in New York,[2] and circuit courts in Virginia[3] — these courts handle most of the judicial business of the states at the trial court level. In most states, the courts of general jurisdiction yield jurisdiction to courts that handle specialized claims, such as claims dealing with juveniles, child custody, or business litigation.[4]

Courts of general jurisdiction usually have a minimum dollar threshold that must be met to file a lawsuit. 20 Am. Jur. 2d *Courts* § 15 (2009). For that reason, almost every state has courts — sometimes called "small claims courts"[5] — that hear the cases below the dollar threshold required to enter the "main" court of general jurisdiction.[6]

The breadth of jurisdiction of state courts of general jurisdiction means that few cases are beyond their authority to decide. For instance, in the Master Problem, in most states, Plaintiff Sally Wilreiz would have little trouble suing for the auto accident in a state court of general jurisdiction, assuming she gave proper notice to the City and to the State in those states that require pre-suit notice. Sally is suing for a substantial amount of money and her lawsuit involves a variety of claims against several defendants: the City, the State (or its appropriate agency), and the vehicle manufacturer HorsePower, Inc. When subject matter jurisdiction is an issue, the limits are usually obvious, either because the type of case (*e.g.*, juvenile matters) or the amount at issue (*e.g.*, no more than a few thousand dollars) is clear. Although it is not completely irrelevant, the question of subject matter jurisdiction is far more straightforward in state practice than in federal practice.

One area in which subject matter jurisdiction *can* impede a state court suit involves cases in which an employee is injured on the job. In virtually every state, employers pay workers' compensation insurance to cover medical expense of employees' injured while on the job. In return, the employer enjoys a legal "bar" to lawsuits against the employer in most cases. Typically, the exclusive way in which employees can pursue compensation is by relying on workers' compensation. If they have a dispute about an award, states have workers' compensation commissions that resolve such disputes. An employee that seeks to bypass this system and bring her claim in a court of general jurisdiction before pursuing the workers' compensation mechanisms, will face the workers' compensation bar — a bar that will usually lead to dismissal of the suit. By setting up specialized commissions to resolve the claims, the state is essentially assigning subject matter jurisdiction to those commissions. Your state may, indeed, have commission in other areas in which a claim must first be brought through a specialized system. Although courts of general jurisdiction may have an appellate role in a given state's system, they could lack subject matter jurisdiction to hear cases in the first instance if cases are assigned to commissions or specialized courts.

---

1. *See, e.g.,* Guide to California Law, California Court System, http://www.weblocator.com/attorney/ca/law/c02.html (last visited Aug. 17, 2009).

2. *See, e.g.,* National Center for State Courts, New York, http://www.ncsconline.org/WC/Publications/ProSe/Directory Entries/NY.htm (last visited Aug. 17, 2009).

3. National Center for State Courts, Small Claims Courts, http://www.ncsconline.org/wc/CourTopics/ResourceGuide.asp?topic=SmaCla (last visited Aug. 17, 2009).

4. *See* National Center for State Courts, Specialty Courts Report, http://www.ncsconline.org/wc/CourTopics/overview.asp?topic=SpecCt (last visited Aug. 17, 2009).

5. For an example of the requirements, procedures, and general provisions of Connecticut's small claims courts, see http://www.jud.state.ct.us/faq/smallclaims (last visited Aug. 17, 2009).

6. *See* National Center for State Courts, Small Claims Overview, http://www.ncsconline.org (last visited Aug. 17, 2009).

Follow-Up Questions

1. In your jurisdiction, what are the criteria that must be met in order to file a lawsuit in the court of general jurisdiction?

2. Does your jurisdiction have specialized courts in which certain types of cases, (regardless of the relief requested or dollar amount) must be filed? An example in some states would be Family Courts in which any matter related to domestic relations, including claims arising from separations, divorce, or custody, must be resolved.

3. Assume the following facts. Your client is employed by a construction company. While he was helping guide steel beams suspended from a crane, the crane contacted high-voltage power lines, conducting the electricity into his arms and seriously injuring him. Can you sue your client's employer? Why or why not? Can you sue the utility company if the power lines were not at the height that is recommended by the National Electrical Safety Code (the widely accepted standard for recommended heights of power lines)? Is there a difference between bringing a lawsuit against the employer versus bringing a lawsuit against the utility company such that you could sue the utility company in a court of general jurisdiction? Explain the difference if one exists.

Professional Identity Question

Some jurisdictions have "lower" courts that can hear reasonably large damage claims (*e.g.*, $50,000), while its courts of general jurisdiction are reserved for claims that involve higher amounts. Assume that this is one of the first lawsuits you have ever filed. You want to file suit in the lower court because you find it less intimidating than the court of general jurisdiction. Your client has significant enough damages to potentially qualify for an award of more than $50,000. Would you allow your anxiety to influence where you file suit and the amount of damages you request? If you considered the matter in light of your values, what decision would you recommend to the client in terms of where to sue? Would that advice — as informed by your value system — lead you to focus on the client's interests, despite your personal preference? What safeguards might you implement to prevent yourself from rationalizing decisions based on your personal interests? Will you seek a mentor — an experienced lawyer whom you respect and with whom you can discuss matters in accordance with your principles? Would the development of such safeguards, and finding a mentor on whom you can rely, likely serve to help you maintain your professional identity?

Practice Problems

Practice Problem 3-1

Cal Contractor would like to file a lawsuit for breach of contract against Dan Deadbeat seeking $2,000 for unpaid work he performed on Dan Deadbeat's home.

Cal files his claim for breach of contract in the court of general jurisdiction for the state in which you plan to practice. In the state in which you plan to practice, are suits of claims in this amount reserved to courts other than courts of general jurisdiction? If so, can Dan assert a lack of subject matter jurisdiction?

Practice Problem 3-2

Willie Worker is injured while working on the job for Pork Products Plant, Inc. in Florence, South Carolina. Willie brings suit in a court of general jurisdiction in the City of Florence, South Carolina, against Pork Products, Inc. for his injuries. However, South Carolina, like most states, assigns original jurisdiction to hearings on claims by employees against employers for injuries on the job to workers' compensation commissions. Thus, what defense should Pork Products Plant, Inc. raise to Willie's suit?

Personal Jurisdiction

Unlike subject matter jurisdiction, the issues of personal jurisdiction and venue arise regularly in state litigation. Therefore, the rest of this chapter will concentrate on these topics.

The issue of personal jurisdiction arises when a defendant does not reside in the state. All analyses of personal jurisdiction over a nonresident raise two overarching questions. First, does a state statute (typically called a "long arm statute") authorize the exercise of personal jurisdiction over the suit? If the answer to this question is "no," the analysis has to stop there. A court cannot exercise personal jurisdiction if the state statute authorizing jurisdiction over nonresidents itself has not been satisfied. Even if a state's long arm statute has been satisfied, the inquiry continues. The forum court's exercise of jurisdiction over nonresidents must comport with the U.S. Constitution's Due Process Clause. In other words, the requirements for establishing personal jurisdiction over a nonresident are conjunctive. The plaintiff must show both (1) that the forum state's long arm statute authorizes jurisdiction, and (2) exercise of personal jurisdiction is consistent with the Due Process Clause.

Statutory Analysis (Long Arm Statutes)

As explained at the outset, analyses of personal jurisdiction should begin with the simple question of whether the statute of the state in which the suit is brought authorizes the exercise of jurisdiction over a nonresident. Long arm statutes fall into three categories. The first type of long arm statute, the "traditional to-the-limits-of-due-process," authorizes state courts to exercise jurisdiction to the full extent that the due process clause permits. *See, e.g.,* CAL. CIV. PROC. CODE § 410.10 (2009) ("A court of this state may exercise jurisdiction on any basis not inconsistent with the Constitution of this state or of the United States."); *see also* Appendix 3-1, left column (identifying states with this kind of long arm statute).

The second type of long arm statute is a variation of the "to the limits of Due Process" long-arm statute. These states' statutes include long arm statutes that enumerate various categories of conduct that will subject the nonresident to personal jurisdiction. They then add a catch-all provision that permits exercise of personal jurisdiction over the nonresident for any other conduct that would reach to the limits of the Due Process Clause. *See* Appendix 3-1, middle column. Effectively, these statutes operate in the same fashion as the first category because they allow any conduct, even if not enumerated, to satisfy the long-arm statute so long as it satisfies the Due Process Clause. The third category of statutes are true "enumerated long-arm statutes." These statutes permit state courts to exercise jurisdiction over a nonresident if certain criteria — enumerated in the statute — are met. *See* Appendix 3-1, right column. They do not, however, have the catch-all to-the-limits-of-due-process provision that statutes in the second category contain. Common provisions in enumerated long arm statutes include conducting business in the forum state, committing a tortious injury in the forum, owning property in the forum, and other similar contacts with the forum. *See* 4 CHARLES ALAN WRIGHT & AUTHUR R. MILLER, FEDERAL PRACTICE & PROCEDURE § 1068 (2009); *see also* Appendix 3-1, right column (identifying states with this kind of long arm statute). For purposes of personal jurisdiction, the long arm requirement generally applies to federal courts in the same way as state courts, except in rare cases.[7] Federal Rule of Civil Procedure 4(k) provides that federal district courts can exercise personal jurisdiction to the extent permitted by the statutes of the state in which the federal court sits.

Constitutional (Due Process) Analysis

Even if the plaintiff satisfies a state's long arm statute, she also must satisfy the United States Constitution. The reason is simple: even if a long arm statute authorizes the exercise of personal jurisdiction, such exercise may infringe due process principles. Therefore, you must also ask whether the exercise of jurisdiction over a nonresident of a state comports with the Due Process Clause of the Constitution.

Threshold Questions

Most due process analyses require you to engage in the minimum contacts test of *International Shoe Co. v. Washington*, 326 U.S. 310 (1945), and its progeny. However, before performing the minimum contacts analysis, certain threshold inquiries should be addressed. Additional grounds for establishing personal jurisdiction over a defendant may exist, and the astute lawyer will discover them if she asks a few simple questions. Out of habit, an attorney ought to consider these grounds first. If any exist, you can avoid the effort (and expense) required to research, brief, and argue minimum contacts as the basis for personal jurisdiction. Why do analytical handstands when you can show a simpler basis for personal jurisdiction that comports with the principles of due process?

Consent

An important threshold question is whether the defendant has consented to jurisdiction. A defendant may consent to jurisdiction either expressly or impliedly. For example, a defendant expressly consents to a forum's exercise of personal jurisdiction when it enters into a contract in which the defendant consents to litigation in the forum through

---

7. FED. R. CIV. P. 4(k)(1) (providing that service on a party "is effective to establish jurisdiction over the person of a defendant ... who could be subjected to the jurisdiction of a court of general jurisdiction in the state in which the district court is located."). In cases where a federal statute has authorized nationwide service of process, a defendant may be sued anywhere in the United States, as long as the exercise of jurisdiction would be constitutional in the forum chosen. *See id.* 4(k)(2). Because such statutes are few, the state long arm analysis is typically a necessary step in the analysis of whether a federal court has personal jurisdiction.

a "forum selection" clause. *See* 4 WRIGHT & MILLER, FEDERAL PRACTICE & PROCEDURE § 1062. A defendant may also consent to jurisdiction in the forum by appointing a registered agent for purposes of accepting service of process. *See id.* § 1064 ("Generally, a company's registration under a state's appointment statute amounts to a consent to be sued in the courts of the state and a waiver of objections to the assertion of personal jurisdiction over the corporation."). Implied consent arises from failing to raise personal jurisdiction as a defense or actively engaging in litigation in the forum. *See id.* § 1062.

[margin note: narrower/lesser more since 2014]

← *General Jurisdiction over Corporations*

Assume, for purposes of this section, that the plaintiff cannot establish a nonresident's consent to personal jurisdiction in the forum state. If possible, plaintiff's counsel should still seek to avoid the challenges (and vagaries) of a minimum contacts analysis. Doing so will require the plaintiff's lawyer to determine whether the nonresident is a corporation or an individual. This section will assume that the nonresident is a corporation and explore general jurisdiction — a concept thought to be limited to corporations. The subsection immediately following this one will outline the analysis of points to consider, before engaging the minimum contacts analysis, if the defendant is an individual.

[margin note: modified by Daimler Chrysler]

Even if the claim(s) in the case arise from activities outside the forum state, a court may exercise jurisdiction over a corporate defendant if the plaintiff shows a substantial connection between the corporation and the forum. *See Helicópteros Nacionales de Colombia, S.A. v. Hall,* 466 U.S. 408 (1984); *Perkins v. Benguet Consol. Mining Co.,* 342 U.S. 437 (1952). Under *Helicópteros* and *Perkins,* plaintiffs can sue corporations that own property interests, employ substantial personnel, or do extensive business in a state — *even if the events that are being litigated occurred outside of the forum.* For instance, most plaintiffs could sue ExxonMobil in any U.S. state regardless of where the claim arose, because the company has property and substantial employees in almost every state. The same is not true for most companies. Here, you must recognize that general jurisdiction differs from the specific jurisdiction of *International Shoe.* Specific jurisdiction exists only if the plaintiff's claims arise from its jurisdictional contacts with the forum. Thus, you usually must perform a minimum contacts analysis. However, before turning to that fertile area of law routinely tilled by the U.S. Supreme Court, the wise lawyer will check to see whether a corporate defendant's connections with a forum could support general jurisdiction. If the corporation owns property in the forum (even if only as a tenant occupying office space) and employs persons who live and work in the forum, the chances of general jurisdiction exist. The more property the corporation owns and/or controls in the forum, and the more employees who live and work for it year round in the forum, the better the chances of general jurisdiction. *See generally* 4 C. WRIGHT & A. MILLER, FEDERAL PRACTICE & PROCEDURE § 1067.5 (2009).

An Individual's Domicile or Service on an Individual within State Boundaries

If the plaintiff is seeking jurisdiction over an individual defendant, she ought to consider doctrines different from but analogous to general jurisdiction. Even if the plaintiff's claim does not arise from an individual's jurisdictional connections to a state, two categories of jurisdiction permit the plaintiff to sue an individual defendant in a forum: (1) personal jurisdiction based on the individual's domicile status in a forum; and (2) "transient jurisdiction," or service of the individual while within the territorial boundaries of the forum.

Domicile

An individual has long been subject to personal jurisdiction in courts of the state in which she is domiciled. A plaintiff may sue an individual defendant in the state in which she is domiciled for events that occurred outside the state. *See Milliken v. Meyer*, 311 U.S. 457 (1940). The rationale here seems to be two-fold. First, if one is domiciled in a state, she has to have a reasonably strong connection to that state. Second, this jurisdictional basis assures a plaintiff that she can — if in no other state in the Union — at least sue the individual in one state.

Transient Jurisdiction

Likewise, although the question was not definitively answered when it came before the Supreme Court, at least four justices concluded that "transient jurisdiction" may be established over an individual defendant when she is served within a state's territorial boundaries while the action is pending. *See Burnham v. Superior Court*, 405 U.S. 604 (1990). According to Justice Scalia's opinion, which was joined by three other justices in *Burnham,* the length of time the defendant is within the forum's boundaries is irrelevant, as is the "reason" the defendant is within the forum's boundaries. The Court held that service on an individual within a state's boundaries has always passed constitutional muster. *Id.* at 610–20. Thus, by definition, Justice Scalia and the justices who joined him concluded that "[t]he short of the matter is that jurisdiction based on physical presence alone constitutes due process because it is one of the continuing traditions of our legal system that define the due process standard of 'traditional notions of fair play and substantial justice.'" *Id.* at 619. However, Justice Scalia was careful to distinguish service on a corporate officer within a state's boundary, and refused to consider it as having the same effect as in-state service on an individual. *See id.* at 610 n.1.

In an opinion authored by Justice Brennan, four justices in *Burnham* concluded that a minimum contacts analysis — not historical practice — determined whether personal jurisdiction was appropriate. "By visiting the forum State, a transient defendant actually "avail[s] himself ... of significant benefits provided by the State. His health and safety are guaranteed by the State's police, fire, and emergency medical services; he is free to travel on the State's roads and waterways; he likely enjoys the fruits of the State's economy as well." *Id.* at 637–39. Thus, even though Mr. Burnham had been to California only on this particular occasion and, even then, was there for a brief period, Justice Brennan concluded that the minimum contacts analysis justified exercise of personal jurisdiction. *Id.* Justice Stevens refused to join either Justice Scalia's or Justice Brennan's opinions, but concurred in the result finding personal jurisdiction over Mr. Burnham in California. *Id.* at 640. Although they differ on the theory that justifies jurisdiction, therefore, the Court seems comfortable recognizing that service of an individual within the territorial boundaries of a forum will satisfy due process.

If a plaintiff is suing an individual and cannot establish personal jurisdiction over the defendant by either "domicile," or "transient jurisdiction," then the plaintiff must establish jurisdiction over the defendant through the defendant's "minimum contacts" with the forum. The same requirement of satisfying the minimum contacts test applies to the exercise of jurisdiction over a person as it does to a plaintiff suing a non-resident corporation over which the plaintiff cannot establish general jurisdiction. *See Kulko v. Cal. Super. Ct.*, 436 U.S. 84 (1978). Accordingly, we thus now turn to the most common due process analysis — the "minimum contacts" analysis.

Specific Jurisdiction: The "Minimum Contacts" Analysis

The hallmark of the "minimum contacts" analysis is that the claim must always arise from the defendant's jurisdictional contacts. *See* 4 WRIGHT & MILLER, FEDERAL PRACTICE & PROCEDURE § 1067.1. When performing a "minimum contacts" analysis, often called a "specific jurisdiction" analysis, the plaintiff must demonstrate the existence of personal jurisdiction under the holding of *International Shoe* and its progeny. To establish personal jurisdiction over the defendant, the claim(s) in the suit must arise from the defendant's contacts with the forum.

For example, in *International Shoe*, the State of Washington's claim against International Shoe Company grew out of the company's failure to pay unemployment taxes based on salespersons' work in that state. *Int'l Shoe Co.*, 326 U.S. at 313–14. The Court was willing to require less than the extensive contacts necessary to establish general jurisdiction. *See id.* at 318–20. The contacts the defendant had with the forum consisted of less than 20 salespersons who, over a few years, had accounted for under $40,000 in sales. Yet, the Court held that the defendant had been engaging in purposeful conduct in the State of Washington for which it should reasonably have anticipated being hauled into court there. *Id.* at 320.

In later cases, the Court refined its analysis to clarify more fully the nature of contacts necessary to establish personal jurisdiction. These cases flesh out the meaning of "minimum contacts." *World-Wide Volkswagen Corp. v. Woodson*, 444 U.S. 286 (1980), exemplifies the evolution of the minimum contacts analysis. There, the question was whether an Oklahoma court had personal jurisdiction over a New York car dealer and a distributor that distributed solely to New York, New Jersey, and Connecticut. The Court considered whether the defendants, based on their actions before the suit, could have anticipated being sued in Oklahoma. *See id.* at 297–98. If so, the defendants could have structured their conduct differently. (Examples of "structuring conduct differently" include procuring insurance to cover possible litigation expenses or curtailing activities that put one at risk for being sued). However, the Court could find no basis for which the two defendants could have properly anticipated being hauled into court in Oklahoma. Their business focused on activities in the northeastern U.S., and they did not advertise anywhere near Oklahoma. This case is an extreme example, due to the notable lack of contacts with the forum. Yet, *World-Wide Volkswagen* was significant because the Court highlighted the critical question in the minimum contacts analysis: *Before the suit is filed*, would a reasonable defendant in the position of the defendant in question have anticipated being sued in the forum and taken actions in light of its pre-suit conduct? "[T]he foreseeability that is critical to due process analysis ... is that the defendant's conduct and connection with the forum State are such that he should reasonably anticipate being hauled into court there." *Id.* at 297. Thus, *World Wide Volkswagen* began to put "meat" on the skeleton outlined in *International Shoe*. Afterward, the Court decided a number of other cases that are essentially applications of *International Shoe* and *World Wide Volkswagen* to specific factual contexts. The overall analysis varies somewhat depending on whether the claim is a tort claim, contract claim, or other type of claim.

Before addressing the variety of factual contexts that may require special attention, a chart summarizing the stages of the personal jurisdiction analysis should help to demonstrate where in the analysis these specific factual contexts come into play. Diagram 3-2 is a suggested means of proceeding through the steps in determining whether a forum court can exercise personal jurisdiction over a nonresident.

Fleshing Out Specific Jurisdiction in Various Factual Contexts

The "Contexts in Which to Analogize" contained as part of Question 2 of Diagram 3-2 *infra* at page 58 illustrate a possible series of questions you can ask in performing a personal jurisdiction analysis. Although the following discussion will refer to such "analogous contexts," this phrase is not something derived from language in cases. Instead, it recognizes two main points of the minimum contacts analysis. First, the overarching principles of the minimum contacts analysis, and the policies underlying those principles, are fully included in the *International Shoe* and *World-Wide Volkswagen* cases. Second, the progeny of those two seminal cases may be viewed as branches off the same tree trunk. However, the Court in each of these later cases is applying the principles outlined in *International Shoe* and *World Wide Volkswagen* in different scenarios that typically lead to questions applicable to a specific factual setting. Thus, for purposes of organization, they are treated as contexts that are analogous to *International Shoe* and *World Wide Volkswagen*. Hence the phrase "analogous contexts" in Diagram 3-2. In short, these cases provide a frame of reference for you to compare the facts of your case to the application of the minimum contacts analysis in leading decisions. For each factual scenario in these decisions, you should know the specific criteria involved, such as the four factors discussed below in "The Contract Context." In addition, each analogous context illustrates the manner in which the policies underlying the minimum contacts analysis play out in particular situations. Although they should not be seen as an artificial restriction on the application of the minimum contacts test, the analogous contexts should provide a framework within which to analyze whether minimum contacts exist.

The Contract Context

Burger King Corp. v. Rudzewicz, 471 U.S. 462 (1985), demonstrates application of the minimum contacts analysis in the context of business negotiations and a contract. In *Burger King*, the defendant, a prospective franchisee from Michigan, had undergone preliminary negotiations with Burger King's regional office, but ended up doing most of the business negotiations with Burger King's Florida headquarters. The parties entered into a franchise agreement with a term of twenty years, and the contract specified that Florida law would govern the contract. Sometime later, Burger King brought a lawsuit against the defendant in Florida for breach of contract. The defendant raised lack of personal jurisdiction as a defense. The Court held that the defendant could be sued in Florida because he had established minimum contacts with the forum and therefore, could reasonably expect to be sued there. In its analysis, the Court noted that factors such as: (1) prior negotiations; (2) anticipated future dealings; (3) terms of the contract; and (4) actual course of dealings, should be evaluated in determining whether the defendant could have reasonably anticipated being sued in the forum state. *Id.* at 479 ("It is these factors — prior negotiations and contemplated future consequences, along with the terms of the contract and the parties' actual course of dealing — that must be evaluated in determining whether the defendant purposefully established minimum contacts within the forum."). The defendant's actions, in light of the factors provided by the Court, showed that the defendant was on notice of the prospect of being sued in Florida. Prior to suit, a reasonable franchisee, contemplating her contacts with the Florida franchisor, should have anticipated

Diagram 3-2

Personal Jurisdiction Flowchart/Analytical Framework

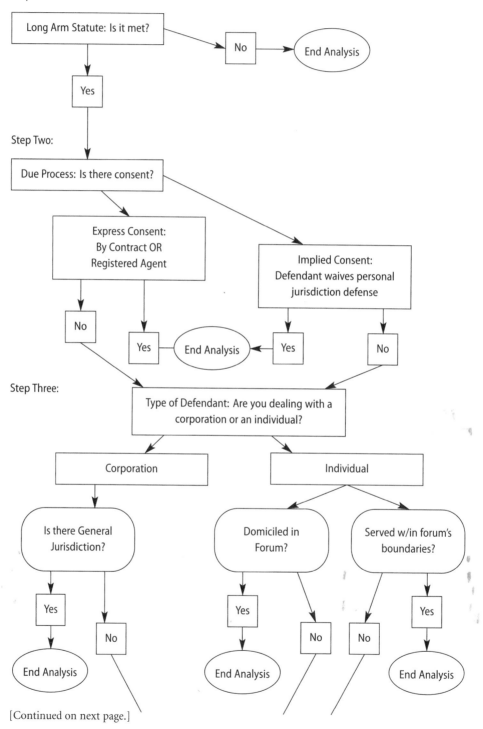

[Continued on next page.]

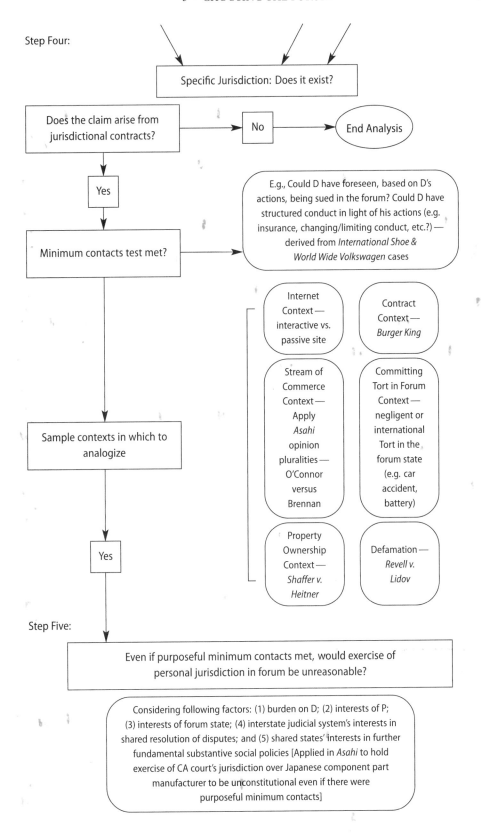

Step Four:

Specific Jurisdiction: Does it exist?

Does the claim arise from jurisdictional contracts? → No → End Analysis

Yes

Minimum contacts test met? → E.g., Could D have foreseen, based on D's actions, being sued in the forum? Could D have structured conduct in light of his actions (e.g. insurance, changing/limiting conduct, etc.?) — derived from *International Shoe & World Wide Volkswagen* cases

Sample contexts in which to analogize

Internet Context — interactive vs. passive site

Contract Context — *Burger King*

Stream of Commerce Context — Apply *Asahi* opinion pluralities — O'Connor versus Brennan

Committing Tort in Forum Context — negligent or international Tort in the forum state (e.g. car accident, battery)

Property Ownership Context — *Shaffer v. Heitner*

Defamation — *Revell v. Lidov*

Yes

Step Five:

Even if purposeful minimum contacts met, would exercise of personal jurisdiction in forum be unreasonable?

Considering following factors: (1) burden on D; (2) interests of P; (3) interests of forum state; (4) interstate judicial system's interests in shared resolution of disputes; and (5) shared states' interests in further fundamental substantive social policies [Applied in *Asahi* to hold exercise of CA court's jurisdiction over Japanese component part manufacturer to be unconstitutional even if there were purposeful minimum contacts] being sued in Florida. *See id.* at 479–81. Personal jurisdiction in the forum was foreseeable and, therefore, the exercise of personal jurisdiction was proper.

The Stream of Commerce Context

So-called "stream of commerce" cases present a more complicated situation. Those cases involve a product originating with a manufacturer and moving—in the most basic context—through commerce via some form of middle-man (usually a wholesale distributor) to a retailer and ultimately to the consumer. The more complicated variety of stream-of-commerce cases occurs when a component part manufacturer supplies the part to a finished product manufacturer, which incorporates the component into the finished product, and after traveling through more and more middle-men, a consumer buys the product. In either form of the stream-of-commerce, the consumer typically is injured and brings a products liability suit against a manufacturer in the consumer's home state. In *Asahi Metal Industry Co. v. Superior Court of California,* 480 U.S. 102 (1987), the suit involved a Japanese component parts manufacturer whose tire valve was included in a valve assembly of an allegedly defective tire. The Court split evenly over the criteria necessary to put a defendant manufacturer on notice that it could be sued in a forum for a product defect. The four-justice opinion authored by Justice O'Connor held that placing the product in commerce, without more, would not give a defendant notice. *Id.* at 108. Instead, her opinion suggested that "additional conduct" such as the following, would be necessary to establish foreseeability: "designing the product for the market in the forum State, advertising in the forum State, establishing channels for providing regular advice to customers in the forum State, or marketing the product through a distributor who has agreed to serve as the sales agent in the forum State." *Id.* at 112 (further stating that "minimum contacts must come about by *an action of the defendant purposefully directed toward the forum State*" and that "the placement of a product into the stream of commerce, without more," is insufficient).

Conversely, the four-justice opinion authored by Justice Brennan would not require the additional factors because a manufacturer that placed its product into the stream of commerce and knew where it was going to be distributed should anticipate being hauled into any forum where the product was sold. *Id.* at 117 (Brennan, J., concurring) (stating that "as long as the defendant is aware that the final product is being marketed in the forum, the possibility of a lawsuit there cannot come as a surprise.").

The test proposed by the opinion of Justice Brennan demands less than that of Justice O'Connor's opinion. Thus, we know this much: if the plaintiff can show that a manufacturer, in light of its conduct, should have foreseen being sued in the forum under Justice O'Connor's suggested "additional conduct" approach, then surely the plaintiff will meet the Justice Brennan test.

Torts Contexts Other Than Stream of Commerce

When stream of commerce is not an issue, tort scenarios are often the easiest in which to establish minimum contacts. If a person commits a negligent act (*e.g.,* causes a car accident) in a state, she ought to expect to be answerable in that state for her negligence. Likewise, someone who commits fraud, an assault or battery, or other tortious conduct within a state can hardly claim to lack notice. The more challenging cases may be those like defamation cases, where the events are triggered out of the forum but have an impact within the forum. In *Calder v. Jones,* 465 U.S. 783 (1984), the Court upheld personal jurisdiction over two Florida residents who participated in defaming the plaintiff in newspapers distributed throughout her home state of California. Since *Calder,* many courts in defamation cases require a showing that (1) the plaintiff was injured by the defamatory statement in the forum, and (2) the defendant knew the plaintiff was located in that forum. *See, e.g., Revell v. Lidov,* 317 F.3d 467 (5th Cir. 2002) (dismissing a defamation cause of action because neither defendant had sufficient minimum contacts with Texas where the plaintiff was a resident, and the defendants were not aware of plaintiff's residence in Texas, thus precluding their knowledge of the place where the effects of the alleged defamation occurred).

The Property Ownership Context

Another analogous context is ownership of property in a forum. *See Shaffer v. Heitner,* 433 U.S. 186 (1977). *Shaffer* did everyone a favor by simplifying jurisdictional analysis in cases involving property ownership as the contact with a forum. Previously, courts would draw distinctions between in personam action, on the one hand, and in rem (and quasi in rem) actions, on the other. Treating property ownership as simply another form of contact that could satisfy the minimum contacts test (as opposed to having to parse the difference between *in rem* and *quasi in rem* jurisdiction) makes a great deal of sense.

In *Shaffer,* the basis for asserting personal jurisdiction over the out-of-state directors was that, by Delaware statute, the situs of their stock was deemed to be in that state. Because such property ownership could not reasonably have put them on notice of being sued in Delaware over a shareholder derivative suit deriving from acts and omissions in Oregon, the Court rejected personal jurisdiction under the minimum contacts test. The Court, however, offered examples of instances where property ownership would put the owner on notice of being sued in the forum. The examples included a suit to foreclose on a defaulted mortgage secured by real property in the forum, or a suit by a person injured on the defendant's property. *See id.* at 207–08.

The Internet Context

The Internet has given a fascinating new twist to personal jurisdiction analyses. One of the first and most influential decisions dealing with the effect of Internet sites on personal jurisdiction is *Zippo Manufacturing Co. v. Zippo Dot Com, Inc.,* 952 F. Supp. 1119 (W.D. Pa. 1997). In *Zippo,* the court introduced a "sliding scale" approach in which the degree of an Internet site's interactivity represents the key factor. Following is oft-quoted language describing this sliding scale:

> At one end of the spectrum are situations where a defendant clearly does business over the Internet. If the defendant enters into contracts with residents of a foreign jurisdiction that involve the knowing and repeated transmission of computer files over the Internet, personal jurisdiction is proper.... At the opposite end are situations where a defendant has simply posted information on an Internet Web site which is accessible to users in foreign jurisdictions. A passive web site that does little more than make information available to those who are interested in it is not grounds for the exercise of personal jurisdiction.... The middle ground is occupied by interactive Web sites where a user can exchange information with the host computer. In these cases, the exercise of jurisdiction is determined by the level of activity and commercial nature of the exchange of information that occurs on the Web site.

Id. at 1124.

Later cases have shown that in virtually every case the Internet component will supplement another factual context (with its own governing precedent for applying the minimum contacts test). For instance, *Revell v. Lidov*, 317 F.3d 467 (5th Cir. 2002), addressed the ability of the plaintiff to establish personal jurisdiction in the plaintiff's home state of Texas, over both an individual who lived in Massachusetts and an incorporated university located in New York. The individual posted allegedly defamatory comments about the plaintiff on a bulletin board hosted on a server maintained by the corporate defendant (actually, a university incorporated under New York law). The district court rejected personal jurisdiction in part because it deemed the Internet bulletin board in question to be "*Zippo*-passive." The United States Court of Appeals for the Fifth Circuit disagreed and held that the Internet bulletin board was "interactive" because "any user of the internet [could] … *send* information to be posted, and *receive* information that others may have posted … [and] participate in an open forum." *Id.* at 472. Accordingly, based on the Internet analysis alone, the Fifth Circuit could have upheld personal jurisdiction. Because the court did not, we see that the Internet context may help courts bolster their conclusion that personal jurisdiction exists *in cases where another factual context applies*. However, for the reasons explored below, when the other factual context does not support personal jurisdiction, the Internet context usually will not overcome the lack of jurisdiction based on other grounds.

The Fifth Circuit in *Revell* recognized that the situation there, as in most cases, hinged not solely on the defendants' use of the Internet. Instead, another context — the context of alleged defamation — allowed the court to apply tests that ultimately decided the question of personal jurisdiction. *Id.* at 472–75. Applying the case law on personal jurisdiction predicated on defamation, the Fifth Circuit held that even though the plaintiff may have been injured in Texas, the defendants lacked any knowledge that the effects of the communications would occur there. *Id.* at 476. In the Fifth Circuit's words, a plaintiff claiming personal jurisdiction based on defamation must not only show injury in the forum but also a defendant's "knowledge of a particular forum to which conduct is directed … [so that such] forum be the focal point of the tortious activity. …" *Id.* at 475–76. Therefore, even though the Fifth Circuit held that the Internet site in question was interactive, it rejected personal jurisdiction based on the case law of the more specific analogous context — *i.e.*, personal jurisdiction cases predicated on alleged defamation.

As *Revell* illustrates, the Internet component to personal jurisdiction analysis almost always is secondary to another more specific analogous context. The question of personal jurisdiction typically will not hinge on the Internet activity. Instead, the Internet activity may enhance personal jurisdiction if the other analogous context supports the exercise of personal jurisdiction. However, as shown in *Revell*, the court may conclude that on the *Zippo* scale the Internet site is interactive but still reject personal jurisdiction based on the other analysis that should apply to the facts (in *Revell*, personal jurisdiction cases arising from defamation). Conversely, a passive Internet site ought not remove the possibility of personal jurisdiction if another context shows that the defendant's actions were such that the defendant could have anticipated suit. For instance, a defendant with significant purposeful conduct (other than Internet activity) in the forum will not be shielded from personal jurisdiction merely because its Internet site is a passive one. Wisely, no court has suggested making the Internet analysis the governing one when, as is almost always true, another factual context (with its own precedent) exists.

The Last Step of the Due Process Analysis: Reasonableness

Regardless of whether you find purposeful minimum contacts, you still have to ask the last question in Diagram 3-2: Would the exercise of personal jurisdiction in the forum be unreasonable? In *Asahi*, the Court disagreed over whether there were purposeful minimum contacts, but a majority agreed that requiring the Japanese defendant to litigate in the United States would be unreasonable in light of due process. *Asahi*, 480 U.S. at 113–14. The Court reiterated the following five factors listed in *World Wide Volkswagen* for courts to consider in determining this reasonableness of the exercise of jurisdiction:

> A court must consider [1] the burden on the defendant, [2] the interests of the forum state, ... [3] the plaintiff's interest in obtaining relief, ... [4] "the interstate judicial system's interest in obtaining the most efficient resolution of controversies; and [5] the shared interest of the several States in furthering fundamentally substantive social policies."

Id. at 113 (quoting *World-Wide Volkswagen*, 444 U.S. at 292) (brackets added); *see also Burger King Corp.*, 471 U.S. 462, 476–77 (1985) (recognizing same five factors).

In *Burger King*, the Court applied these same factors and held it reasonable to exercise personal jurisdiction despite the burden on a Michigan individual forced to litigate in Miami. Conversely, the burden on a Japanese defendant was extreme. *Asahi*, 480 U.S. at 114. As the Court observed, "The unique burdens placed upon one who must defend oneself in a foreign legal system should have significant weight in assessing the reasonableness of stretching the long arm of personal jurisdiction over national borders." *Id.* Moreover, the Court observed that the Japanese defendant had been brought in as a third-party defendant to the claim of the original defendant, a Taiwanese company that manufactured tire assemblies, so that the interests of the State of California in providing a forum were minimal. *Id.* Although less significant, the remaining three factors also counseled against the reasonableness of exercising personal jurisdiction. *Id.* at 114–15.

Follow-Up Questions

1. What type of long arm statute governs in the state in which you plan to practice? If it is one with enumerated categories, what are those categories? Do any of the categories require both satisfaction of certain criteria and additional requirements such as the conduct of substantial business in the jurisdiction?

2. If you intend to practice in a state that has enumerated categories of conduct specified in the long arm statute, has the highest court in the state in which you plan to practice interpreted certain of those enumerated categories as applying more broadly than others?

3. To what extent does your long arm statute contemplate computer and Internet activity as a basis for long arm jurisdiction? Has the highest court of the state in which you plan to practice set forth a test for determining whether such computer/Internet activity is sufficient not only to satisfy the long arm statute but also the Constitution's Due Process Clause?

Professional Identity Questions

1. Assume that one of your clients is having difficulties in dealing with an out-of-state party and wants to sue. If that client asks you whether it could improve its chances of establishing personal jurisdiction over the defendant by leading the out-of-state party to take certain actions (*e.g.*, inviting that party to visit the client's state without intending to accomplish anything other than improve one's chances of obtaining personal jurisdiction over the opponent), how would you respond?

2. If you knew that an out-of-state party had no connection to the state in which you planned to sue, would you feel uncomfortable suing in that state anyway on the theory that the defendant might waive the personal jurisdiction defense?

Practice Problems

Practice Problem 3-3

Ruby Red Slippers, Inc. ("RRS") is a company based in Texafornia. It makes ruby red slippers that have become immensely popular with girls and young ladies. Indeed, the *Wall Street Journal* ran an article recently about how the ruby red slippers have been such a remarkable product because of their "crossover" appeal to girls ranging in ages from toddlers to teenagers. The product had become so popular that it was difficult to go out in public without seeing some girl or young lady wearing sparkling ruby red slippers. Indeed, the success of the product influenced national TV to air *The Wizard of Oz* in prime time.

RRS has done business in virtually every state, but states on the eastern seaboard have been responsible for more sales than any other region. RRS has stations set up in every mall in the state in which you plan to practice and surrounding states. These stations are not permanent, but rather RRS operates mall kiosks. RRS hires employees who dress up as characters from *The Wizard of Oz*—typically the Tin Man, the Scarecrow, and the Cowardly Lion—at these mall kiosks.

Dot attends high school in the state in which you plan to practice. She buys RRS's slippers at a mall kiosk. Then, during the first time that she wore the slippers, the heel unexpectedly fell off the shoe. As a result, Dot fell, hit her head, and went into a coma.

Dot's Aunt Em practices law in the jurisdiction in which you plan to practice. Aunt Em consulted with an expert on shoes, known by plaintiffs' lawyers as the Wizard of Footwear, who confirmed that the shoes were defectively manufactured. The expert advised that the shoe design was such that the heel would easily come off if someone wearing them stepped on uneven surfaces, something that all shoe manufacturers have to anticipate.

Dot was still in a coma at the time Aunt Em filed suit against RRS in the court of general jurisdiction in the state where you plan to practice. RRS timely filed a motion to dismiss for lack of personal jurisdiction. You are the law clerk for Judge Glenda. She asks you to write a memorandum analyzing objectively the issues raised by RRS's motion and her options in ruling. What would you advise Judge Glenda?

Practice Problem 3-4

Beale Yates lived with his wife Bee in the state where you plan to practice. They enjoyed their beautiful home for many years. Beale, however, developed an obsession with computers and stayed on the computer non-stop, experimenting and thinking of ways he could use the Internet for a successful business. Unable to take Beale's obsession any longer, Bee asked him to leave and if he ever felt ready to re-establish a meaningful relationship with her, to return home. Thus, they separated but have not obtained a divorce or annulment. Moving to Texafornia, Beale began to act on his plans for an Internet business. He developed a computer software product called "Doors," which allowed a user to shift from one document to another and then return to the original document without having to "reopen" the document. Beale's new Internet business worked as follows. The product included a computer disk that contained the software for "Doors," including installation and operation software and instructions for operating the software on one's computer, along with licensing materials. Beale advertised this product solely on his Website, www.computerdoors.com, where computer users from any location could connect to the website, complete order and payment information, and request product shipping to the desired destination. The business was a huge success. After a little over a year, it had received orders from every state and had shipped the product for each order. The bulk of the orders came from large states like California and Texas, each of which accounted for more than a thousand orders. Orders from customers in the state in which you plan to practice were more modest — in the range of 30 orders per year. Beale responded to customers by shipping the product to their respective addresses in various states.

Bob Aple, who lives in the state where you plan to practice, ordered the "Doors" software product, and was dissatisfied with it. The software, when installed according to the instructions, led Bob's computer to crash. As a result, Bob's computer files were ruined, and he was forced to replace all hardware and software on his computer at considerable expense. Bob wrote Beale several times demanding immediate payment of $25,000, but Bill did not respond. Bob hired an attorney, who brought an action seeking recovery of his damages. He served Beale through the long arm statute of the state in which you intend to practice. This statute allows courts to exercise jurisdiction over nonresidents who, among other things, entered into contracts with state residents, shipped products into the state that resulted in damages, owned property in the state, or used the Internet so as to do business with persons in the state. Beale timely filed a motion to dismiss for lack of personal jurisdiction over Beale.

For the following questions, you should treat both the defendant Beale and his Internet business as one individual for purposes of analyzing service and personal jurisdiction. (Beale had not incorporated the business, but simply ran it as a sole proprietorship, making the status of the business the equivalent of its sole owner, Beale.)

Should the court sustain Beale's motion to dismiss the action based on lack of personal jurisdiction?

Venue

The question of venue deals with which of the divisional units within a state (often municipalities, counties, boroughs, etc.) represent proper locations for suit to be filed. In the federal system, the question is always which of the 94 federal districts qualifies as a proper venue. In many instances, states are divided into separate federal districts to funnel a case to the forum most convenient to the parties and to the witnesses. The question in state court procedure is analogous. The venue scheme in every state seeks to identify the jurisdictional locales (whatever they may be called) in which it is most convenient for the parties and the witnesses to try the case.

State venue schemes seem to follow a pattern. They tend to identify locales within a state that logically would be the most convenient for parties. *See, e.g.,* H.C. Lind, Annotation, *Construction and Effect of Statutory Provision for Change of Venue for the Promotion of the Convenience of Witnesses and the Ends of Justice,* 74 A.L.R. 2d 16 (1960). An exhaustive survey of state venue statutes showed that the following categories typically determine the venue for a suit:

1. Where events leading to the lawsuit occurred, or where property is located if that is the subject;

2. Where the defendant resides or may be found;

3. Where a corporate defendant does business, has offices, or has an agent or representative;

4. Where a corporate plaintiff does business, has offices, or has an agent or representative; or

5. Where the plaintiff resides.

See id. at 310–15. If venue properly lies in two or more locales, the plaintiff can file suit in any one of these. *See id.*

If the place where suit is filed is not one authorized by the venue statute of the state in which you practice, you will have an objection to venue there. *See* G. SHREVE & P. RAVEN-HANSEN, UNDERSTANDING CIVIL PROCEDURE §6.01 (4th ed. 2009). Be careful to make the objection in a timely fashion because the venue defense often has to be made by such a deadline or be waived. *See id.* ("venue questions are likely to be raised at the outset.") If a party has a basis for arguing that another locale is more convenient to parties or witnesses, then that party can file a motion for a change of venue. *See id* §6.02[2]. The moving party, of course, has the required burden of showing—through sworn affidavits, for example—that convenience of the parties and/or witnesses would be accomplished by moving the venue. *See id.*

A defendant who can show that neither any defendant nor the claims in the suit have anything to do with the state in question can move to dismiss based on forum non conveniens. *See id.* §6.02[1]. One should keep this defense in mind because, although personal jurisdiction may be obtained over some defendants, the forum non conveniens defense could result in dismissal despite such personal jurisdiction. For instance, a plaintiff may be able to establish personal jurisdiction over a defendant, such as through general jurisdiction. A large petroleum company that operates in most states offers a classic example of such a defendant. Because the defendant has such pervasive contacts with the forum, the court can exercise general personal jurisdiction even though the plaintiff's claim case does not arise from any of the defendant's activities in the state. Here, a defendant could rely on the doctrine of forum non conveniens to seek dismissal. To do so, the defendant should point to another forum — *i.e.*, the one where the activities giving rise to the claim arose — as the one that should exercise jurisdiction. *See id.* Unlike a federal court that can transfer a case to a federal court in another state, a state court lacks power beyond the territorial limits of the state borders. Thus, a state court cannot transfer a case to the forum that the defendant has identified as the appropriate forum. However, state statutes or rules may allow dismissal on this basis only if certain conditions are met so that plaintiff does not lose her right to sue. For instance, the statute may require the defendant to agree — in return for granting the motion — not to raise the statute of limitations or similar defenses. *See id.* With such a condition in place, the court can dismiss the case without prejudice and allow the plaintiff to re-file in the appropriate forum. *See id.*

Follow-Up Questions

1. Research the venue statutes of the states in which you plan to practice. Do these statutes give a preference to any locations in selecting venue?

2. What is the deadline for objecting to improper venue, to moving for a change of venue, and for moving to dismiss based on forum non conveniens? If you fail to make such an objection or motion by the specified deadline, is the objection waived?

3. How do the venue statutes of the state in which you plan to practice resolve the question of multiple defendants? If venue is sound in a jurisdiction as to one defendant, but would not support venue for another, does establishing venue as to one defendant allow you to sue in that venue and "drag" other defendants in? If that venue is truly inconvenient to one of these other defendants, does that defendant have the ability to move for a transfer of venue to another district and, if so, what showing must the defendant make to achieve a transfer?

Professional Identity Questions

1. Assume that a defendant has some, but relatively minimal, connection to a venue within the State in which you plan to practice. (The venue statutes of this state allow a defendant to be sued in any venue in which it does business.) In your case, the defendant is a company that does business in many cities and other jurisdictions in the state and happens to do minor business in the city in question. The court in that city, however, is well known for having been the site of some of the highest jury verdicts in the state. Assume further that other venues in the state are clearly ones in which the defendant performs substantial business and are closer to the location of the events over which the suit is brought. In short, your filing suit in any venues other than the city with the reputation for high jury verdicts would make more sense if you were considering the witnesses' and parties' convenience. Should you sue in the city where the defendant does minimal business solely because of the reputation for higher jury verdicts?

2. The senior partner for whom you work tells you that, in his experience, if you file an objection to venue and move to transfer in every case, at least some of the time the plaintiff will "disappear" — *i.e.*, decide that the case is going to be too much trouble if motions are filed at the very beginning. As the senior partner tells you, "Find some way to file a motion to transfer venue and you'll send a signal that you're going to wear that opponent out!" To ensure you get the message, the senior partner instructs you file a motion to transfer venue even if you cannot find a basis for arguing that the change would serve the convenience of parties or witnesses. As he concludes, he wants you to do so "to weed out those plaintiffs who are serious from those who are not." Would you do so? Would doing so be inconsistent with your values? If so, how could you deal with the situation in the law firm, assuming there are other partners to whom you could take your concerns? If you are unable to find an ally in your law firm, could you talk to the client about filing such a motion, advise the client that she could end up paying sanctions, and tell the senior partner (if the client nixes the partner's idea) that the client asked you not to file the motion? Would that be appropriate conduct? What risks do you take by having the client nix the senior partner's instructions? Is it not the client's call, however, in the end whether to incur expenses, and take risks of sanctions, such as the partner's instructions would involve?

Practice Problems

Practice Problem 3-5

Review the facts of Practice Problem 3-3 (*supra* pages 64). Assume the following variation on the facts of that Problem: Instead of buying the shoes while at a mall in the state in which you practice, Dot bought the footwear while visiting her relatives in another state. The accident leading to her coma occurred in that other state as well. Aunt Em files suit against Ruby Red Slippers ("RRS") in the state in which you plan to practice, not the state where Dot bought the slippers and suffered her injury. RRS does business in malls, selling the same kind of footwear Dot bought, throughout both the state in which you intend to practice and the one in which she bought the slippers. RRS filed timely motions to dismiss based on improper venue or, alternatively, to transfer venue to the location where Dot bought the shoes and suffered her injuries. Can the state court in question transfer venue to a court in the state where the accident occurred? Can it nevertheless grant a motion to dismiss based on improper venue and/or forum non conveniens? Should it? If it does, are there protections in the law of your jurisdiction regarding actions that are dismissed in this fashion based on the argument they should be litigated in another state?

Practice Problem 3-6

The venue statutes of most states provide that venue will exist, among other instances, where events giving rise to the suit occurred or where a defendant resides. Paula Plaintiff was injured in an accident on a state highway within the boundaries of the state in which you plan to practice. Two other cars, one driven by Dan Defendant and the other driven by Deb Defendant, were involved in the accident. According to Paula, Dan and Deb were weaving in and out of traffic and otherwise driving recklessly when their cars collided with Paula's vehicle,

causing her to run off the road. Dan lives in the same state as the accident location, but his home is several hundred miles north of the accident location. Deb
also lives in the same state, but her home is a hundred miles southwest of the accident location. Paula's lawyer files suit in locale where Dan lives because it has a
reputation for high verdicts. Dan timely objects to venue. How should the circuit court rule? If either Dan or Deb wishes to move for transfer of venue to the
locale where the accident occurred, what will she need to file as an alternative to
his objection, and who will bear the burden of satisfying the circuit court of
the propriety of the transfer, etc.?

D. Methods to Reinforce and Integrate Topics Covered in This Chapter

Personal jurisdiction and venue analyses lend themselves to a flow chart format. Two
potential flow charts follow below. The first is for venue. Following that is one for personal jurisdiction. You can review the authorities in your state and determine whether
the flow charts are consistent with that law or, if not, how either or both charts need to
be revised.

Chart 3-1

POSSIBLE VENUE FRAMEWORK

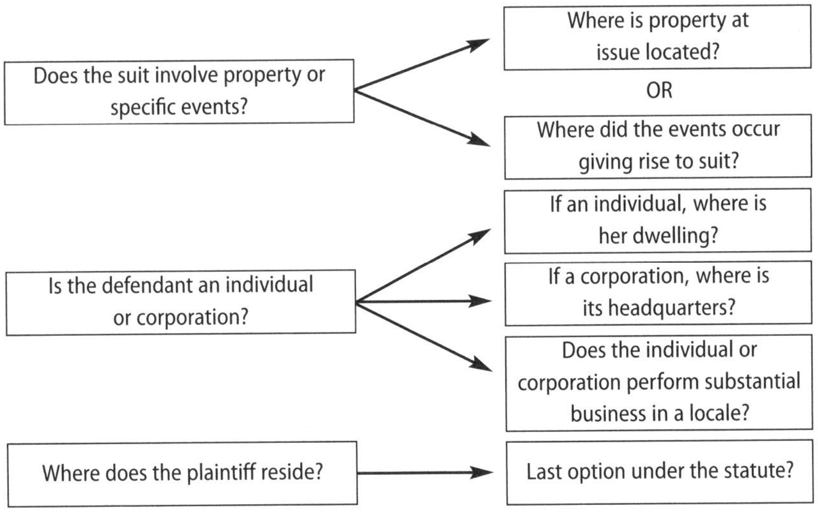

Chart 3-2

PERSONAL JURISDICTION FRAMEWORK

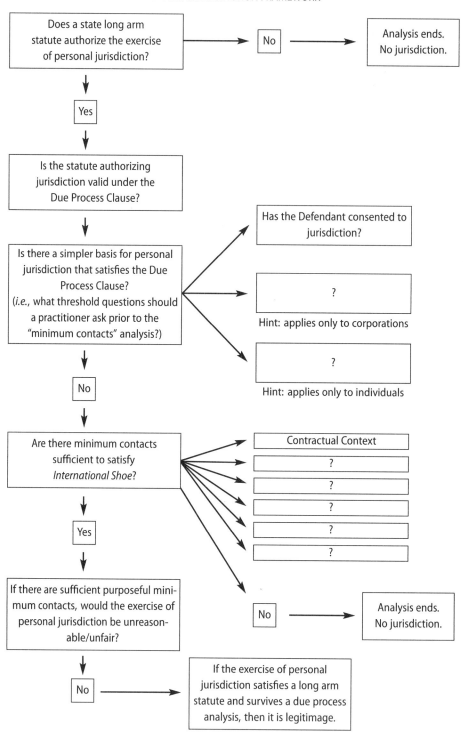

E. Written Assignments

1. In the Master Problem, assume the following additional facts: The defendant vehicle manufacturer: (1) is incorporated in Texafornia (the fifty-second state in the U.S., following Illyria as the fifty-first); (2) has an interactive Website available 24 hours a day that promotes its products and includes as a featured product the Stallion convertible; (3) distributes cars to certain states in the western United States and to other states in the eastern United States; and (4) the distributors supply Stallion convertibles to over 200 dealers around the country including two states that border the State of Illyria. Sally bought the Stallion vehicle at a dealership in one of the states that borders Illyria, the dealership being less than ten miles from the line between Illyria and that state. The manufacturer, moreover, advertises the Stallion in national magazines.

   Mr. Befayre asks you for an objective memorandum analyzing whether HorsePower, Inc., the Stallion's manufacturer, can be sued in the State of Illyria. Specifically, he asks you to identify the provisions of the long arm statute that may apply, your analysis of the strengths and weaknesses of each provision, and to further analyze whether the exercise of jurisdiction would comport with the Due Process Clause.

2. Mr. Befayre also asks you for a separate memorandum on appropriate venues. He asks you to assume, for purposes of argument, that a court in Illyria can exercise personal jurisdiction over the defendant vehicle manufacturer. Your task is to find all venues in which suit could be brought. He tells you to forget federal court because he's satisfied that Sally, a citizen of the State of Illyria, will be suing the (1) City of Arcadia, which is also considered a citizen of Illyria, and (2) the State of Illyria and/or its Department of Transportation (DOT) — all of which will make complete diversity of citizenship impossible. Thus, both Mr. Befayre and you recognize that suing in federal court is not an option. Based on his research, the partner tells you that both the State's headquarters, and the DOT headquarters for the DOT region encompassing Arcadia, are located in the state capital of Illyria, the City of Utopia, which has a court of general jurisdiction called the Circuit Court of the City of Utopia. Assume that the City of Arcadia has a state court of general jurisdiction, the Circuit Court for the City of Arcadia. Mr. Befayre also advises you that, although the State and/or its Department of Transportation are responsible for the section of road with the pothole just outside Arcadia, cases involving any matters occurring on that road are usually filed in the county on "the other side of the pothole" — the county of Devon, whose court of general jurisdiction is the Circuit Court for the County of Devon. Rubbing his head, Mr. Befayre muses that "he's just not sure in the peculiar circumstances of Sally's case whether suit would have to be brought in the circuit courts for Arcadia or Devon." He tells you that juries in these courts tend to be conservative and give lesser verdict amounts to plaintiffs. "Although it may be a stretch," he tells you, he would like to file suit in the Circuit Court for the City of Utopia, where juries are known to deliver much higher verdicts to injured persons than most jurisdictions in the state. Yet he asks you to be objective and let him know whether, if he filed in the City of Utopia, the case would likely get dismissed or moved. If so, he may choose to sue in one of the other venues you identify. Analyze the options for venue, in light of the above facts and guidance, and provide an objective memorandum to Mr. Befayre.

Chapter 4

Pleading the Case and Joinder of Claims and Parties

A. Sally's Case at This Stage of Litigation Process

At this point, you have researched and determined all viable claims, have identified and given notice of any claims that require pre-suit notice, and have determined the date by which Sally must file to satisfy the briefest limitation among all viable claims. Moreover, you have analyzed and decided—with your client's agreement—the court in which to sue. Now, you must roll up your sleeves and start drafting your client's pleadings. Can you join claims against the City, the State, and HorsePower, Inc. in the same complaint? What investigation must you perform before filing suit? Are there allegations that are common to each claim and, if so, where should you put those in the complaint? What must you allege to ensure Sally's complaint is not vulnerable to a motion to dismiss for failure to state a claim? What relief should you request? Should you state in your complaint that Sally demands trial by jury?

B. Tasks and Decision-Making at This Stage of a Case

The phase of litigation where the case now stands is highlighted in Diagram 4-1.

As in the federal system, the initial pleading in state courts will be a complaint. You recall your federal civil procedure professor warning you to take this stage of the case seriously. With the claims Sally has authorized you to pursue, you want to plead them sufficiently so as to avoid the delay in litigation resulting from the defendant's initial motions. By reading updates on the law and attending Continuing Legal Education seminars, you recall some key decisions relating to how you should plead claims. One of the first questions is whether you will need to be specific when pleading Sally's claims. In past decades, a plaintiff's lawyer could plead claims without worrying about factual specificity. Indeed Mr. Befayre is surprised when you tell him that some recent United States Supreme Court decisions interpreting the federal pleading standards seem to suggest that all claims may require more detailed pleading—not just fraud, mistake, or other claims traditionally requiring particularized pleading. He comments that the practice he had developed over the years of including facts to support each element of a claim apparently will now become more useful than ever. He tells you that it is not that hard to add specific facts to

Diagram 4-1

Cause of Action (events leading to suit)
Prefiling Matters to Consider; Choice of Forum [Chs. 2–3]
Π and Δ Decide on Offensive Pleadings & Joinder (of claims & parties); Filing Suit; Service [Chs. 4–5]
Motions, Responsive Pleadings; Default; Voluntary & Involuntary Dismissals [Chs. 6–7]
Discovery Phase (developing proof to establish claims & learning about the adversary's case) [Ch. 8]
Right to Jury Trial; Pretrial Motions & Practice [Ch. 9]
Final Pretrial Conference & Other Events within Last Month before Trial [Ch. 10]
Procedure at Trial [Ch. 11]
Post-Trial Motions & Calculating the Date of Final Judgment to Know Key Deadlines Such as for Notice of Appeal [Ch. 12]

support each element of the claim and, thus, it makes little sense to plead claims without such facts. He asks: "Why risk the time and expense of having a motion to dismiss sustained and then having to file an amended complaint containing facts we could have pled in the first place?"

Mr. Befayre advises you to be alert to potential problem areas, such as the presence of a party who lacks capacity and thus requires special treatment. Moreover, in line with this anticipation of potential problems, he suggests that you anticipate the "offensive" or affirmative claims that defendants might assert back against Sally. He reminds you that defendants can assert their own claims, such as counterclaims, cross-claims, third-party claims, and the like. He says that he has yet to hear any facts that suggest a defendant in this case would have a basis for asserting a claim against Sally. However, he tells you that you can bet the defendants will raise defenses in their answers seeking to avoid or limit liability. He explains that he learned early on that clients accept news of such claims or defenses far better if they have been advised of the potential for them ahead of time. Finally, Mr. Befayre and you discuss the right to a jury trial, and the ease with which a party can waive this valuable right. On the critical matter of jury trial, you agree to confirm the requirements and deadlines necessary to ensure that Sally's right to a trial by jury is fully preserved.

C. Overview of Applicable Law

Requirements for Offensive Pleadings

The guidelines for pleading a complaint are fairly straightforward. The complaint must include a caption indicating the court in which it is filed, the names of the parties, and the addresses of all defendants. The title "COMPLAINT" should go in or directly under the caption, depending on the practice in the court in which you will be filing. Then, after endorsing in bold letters at the top of the caption, "PLAINTIFF DEMANDS TRIAL BY JURY," the rest of the complaint will be devoted to the business of pleading the allegations that will get Sally's suit underway.

On the question of how much detail to include in a complaint, some doubt has arisen recently. Most judges, lawyers, and academics had considered the sufficiency of a complaint to be a matter of settled law. Federal Rule of Civil Procedure 8 — not only the Federal standard but the model for pleading rules in most states — offers the following simple criteria: "A pleading that states a claim for relief must contain ... a short and plain statement of the claim showing the pleader is entitled to relief...." FED. R. CIV. P. 8(a)(2); *see* Appendix 4-1 (showing that most states have adopted the pleading standard of Fed. R. Civ. P. 8). For half a century, the United States Supreme Court's decision in *Conley v. Gibson*, 355 U.S. 41 (1957), guided courts on interpreting Rule 8's modest pleading criteria. The Court's guidance was generous to claimants:

> In appraising the sufficiency of the complaint we follow, of course, the accepted rule that a complaint should not be dismissed for failure to state a claim unless it appears beyond doubt that the plaintiff can prove no set of facts in support of his claim which would entitle him to relief.

Conley, 355 U.S. at 45–46.

Conley went on to elaborate, in a similar vein:

> The respondents also argue that the complaint failed to set forth specific facts to support its general allegation of discrimination and that its dismissal is therefore proper. The decisive answer to this is that *the Federal Rules of Civil Procedure do not require a claimant to set out in detail the facts upon which he bases his claim.* To the contrary, all the Rules require is "a short and plain statement of the claim that will give the defendant fair notice of what plaintiff's claim is and the grounds upon which it rests." The illustrative forms appended to the Rules plainly demonstrate this. Such simplified "notice pleading" is made possible by the liberal opportunity for discovery and the other pretrial procedures established by the Rules to disclose more precisely the basis of both the claim and defense and to define more narrowly the disputed facts and issues....

Id. at 47–48.

In two recent decisions, however, the Supreme Court has raised doubts about whether notice pleading is being replaced by some form of a pleading standard that is more demanding than the "notice" pleading of *Conley*. The first of these decisions, *Bell Atlantic Corp. v. Twombly*, 550 U.S. 544 (2007), was an antitrust action against telephone companies in which the plaintiff alleged a violation of antitrust statutes based on "parallel conduct" — that the companies' business activities shadowed one another. However, the antitrust claim required not only parallel conduct, but also a conspiratorial agreement as a second element. Because the plaintiff did not plead sufficient facts on the second element, the Court affirmed dismissal of the case. *See id.* at 567–70.

In an even more recent decision, *Ashcroft v. Iqbal,* 129 S. Ct. 1937 (2009), the Court has confirmed a philosophical shift that will demand more than notice pleading as set forth in *Conley.* Iqbal, a Pakistani Muslim, was detained in a maximum security facility in New York after the September 11 attacks. Afterward, he brought suit against a number of federal officials, including John Ashcroft, the former Attorney General, and Robert Mueller, the Director of the Federal Bureau of Investigation. According to the complaint, these government officials designated him a person of high interest based on his race, religion, or national origin. The complaint further alleged a policy of detaining persons for such reasons indiscriminately after the 9/11 attacks. The complaint ultimately alleged that the defendants "willfully and maliciously" agreed to subject him to harsh confinement solely due to his race, religion, or national origin. Attorney General Ashcroft and Director Mueller were alleged to be the prime architects of a policy that violated the First and Fifth Amendments. Citing *Twombly,* the Court held the complaint insufficient to state a claim under Rule 8. *Id.* at 1949. The Court observed that "labels," "conclusions," "formulaic recitation of the elements of a cause of action," and "naked assertions" without factual support would not suffice. *Id.* Instead, the Court observed:

> To survive a motion to dismiss, a complaint must contain sufficient factual matter, accepted as true, to "state a claim to relief that is plausible on its face." A claim has facial plausibility when the plaintiff pleads factual content that allows the court to draw the reasonable inference that the defendant is liable for the conduct alleged. The plausibility standard is not akin to a "probability requirement," but it asks for more than a sheer possibility that a defendant has acted unlawfully. Where a complaint pleads facts that are "merely consistent with" a defendant's liability, it "stops short of the line between possibility and plausibility of 'entitlement to relief.'"

Id. (quoting *Twombly,* 550 U.S. at 556–57, 570) (citations omitted).

Some fear that *Twombly* and *Iqbal* harbor a return to the old, pre-1938 "Code" pleading standards that required detailed facts to support a claim. The decisions, however, more likely represent a shift to some point in between Code pleading standard of old and the "anything goes" standard of *Conley.* In these decisions, the Court has sent a message that it interprets Rule 8 as requiring facts, not conclusions, to be pled on each element of each claim. Most good lawyers already followed the practice of identifying the elements of a claim and pleading not just conclusions (*e.g.,* the defendant committed an assault), but also facts to support each element (*e.g.,* the defendant walked up on January 1, 2009, acted as if he was going to punch the plaintiff but stopped within inches of the plaintiff's face). Requiring some facts to support each element of a claim usually is not burdensome.

The decisions in *Twombly* and *Iqbal* are binding solely on federal courts. Even if a jurisdiction adopted as its pleading rules Federal Rule of Civil Procedure 8, nothing requires the jurisdiction—or the courts in that jurisdiction—to interpret the state pleading rule (even if originally modeled on Fed. R. Civ. P. 8) as narrowly as the Supreme Court is beginning to interpret Rule 8. Thus, some jurisdictions may retain the decades old practice of allowing minimal pleadings. The highest courts of some states have followed the Supreme Court's lead, but other courts in states with rules modeled on Federal Rule of Civil Procedure 8 have disagreed.[1]

---

1. *Cf., e.g., Iannacchino v. Ford Motor Co.,* 888 N.E.2d 879, 889–90 (Mass. 2008) (noting a heightened standard for pleading based upon the language used by the Court in *Twombly* to "retire" the "no

Nevertheless, virtually every state, following the standard set forth in Federal Rule of Civil Procedure 9, requires more particularized pleadings for claims of fraud or mistake. *See* Appendix 4-2 (showing that a majority of states have heightened pleading standards for allegations of fraud, mistake, and the like). "In alleging fraud or mistake, a party must state with *particularity* the circumstances constituting fraud or mistake." FED. R. CIV. P. 9(b) (emphasis added); *see also* Barney J. Feinberg, Annotation, *Construction and Application of Provision of Rule 9(b), Federal Rules of Civil Procedure, That Circumstances Constituting Fraud or Mistake Be Stated with Particularity*, 27 A.L.R. FED. 407 (1976).

A useful rule of thumb in pleading a matter requiring particularized pleading is to ask the five "W's": Who?, What?, When?, Where?, and Why? Pleading with particularity, in other words, ought to answer these questions: *Who* was involved in the event(s)? *What* happened in the event(s) and/or by what means? (*e.g.*, in person, by mail, by facsimile, etc.)? *When* did the event(s) in question happen? *Where* did the event(s) occur? *Why* do/does the event/events matter causally? Thus, in pleading a fraud claim, one should include as to all allegedly fraudulent communications or nondisclosures: (1) the names of all parties involved; (2) the precise content of the allegedly fraudulent communications and not only what was communicated—or, in the case of fraudulent nondisclosure, what of significance was not disclosed—but also the means by which the communications occurred (in person, by mail, etc.); (3) the exact date(s) of all such communications/nondisclosures, including date(s) sent and date(s) received; (4) why the communications/nondisclosures led the plaintiff to rely on them (*i.e.*, why the communications were ones reasonably relied on by the person asserting the claim—typically referred to as the "materiality" element); and (5) where the communication(s) happened. *See* Feinberg, *Construction and Application of Provision of Rule 9(b)*, 27 A.L.R. FED. 407 (1976).

Through further research, you learn that the rules for asserting counterclaims, cross-claims, and third-party claims are governed by the same principles of pleading applied to complaints. Again, a defendant should bear in mind the recent decisions requiring more factual specificity in allegations, unless the jurisdiction is one that has rejected the approach of the Supreme Court in *Twombly* and *Iqbal*. Regardless, a defendant must also plead with particularity matters that require particularized pleadings, just as a plaintiff must do. You take note that most states have a compulsory counterclaim rule: If a counterclaim is related to the same transaction or occurrence forming the basis of the plaintiff's complaint, the defendant must plead the counterclaim in the present action or have it barred later. *See infra* pages 88 & Appendix 4-6 (showing that a majority of states have adopted the compulsory counterclaim rule); W. R. Habeeb, Annotation, *Failure to Assert Matter as Counterclaim as Precluding Assertion Thereof in Subsequent Action, Under Federal Rules or Similar State Rules or Statutes*, 22 A.L.R. 2d 621 (1952). Thus, you will research the counterclaim rule in your jurisdiction and contemplate the claims, if any, that defendants could assert against Sally. You recall Mr. Befayre's admonition that clients do not like surprises but, if warned, are easier to deal with.

---

set of facts" pleading standard of *Conley*), *with, e.g., In re Pressure Sensitive Labelstock Antitrust Litig.*, 566 F. Supp. 2d 363, 370 (M.D. Pa. 2008) (rejecting a heightened pleading standard based on Supreme Court's decisions under Federal Rule 8); *Hyland v. Homeservices of Am.*, No. 3:05-CV-612-R, 2007 U.S. Dist. LEXIS 65731, at *4–*5 (W.D. Ky. Aug. 17, 2007) (same).

Requirement for Good Faith Basis in Law and Fact ("Rule 11")

Unlike the pre-suit notices discussed in Chapter 2, a pleading filed in court must pass the filter of that state's version of Federal Rule of Civil Procedure 11. The 1983 amendment to the Federal Rule took a provision that was largely toothless and made it a meaningful standard for measuring court filings. Although ethical standards already in place should have deterred lawyers from filing pleadings with allegations that lacked a good faith basis in fact or law, many lawyers apparently needed the threat of sanctions (as set forth in the 1983 amendments) to cease filing of unsubstantiated and/or frivolous claims. *See* 5A C. WRIGHT & A. MILLER, FEDERAL PRACTICE & PROCEDURE § 1331 (2009) (explaining background and history of Rule 11). Following the 1983 amendments to the Federal Rule, most states enacted versions of the same rule. RESTATEMENT (THIRD) OF THE LAW GOVERNING LAWYERS, reporter's cmt. (b) (codifying states that enacted provisions modeled on Federal Rule 11).

The 1983 amendments to Federal Rule 11, and state provisions following their lead, generally required lawyers to certify that they had made a good faith investigation into the facts alleged and that the allegations were warranted in fact. The other requirement in these rules was that the claims alleged had a good faith basis in law or the extension of existing law. These certifications could be called the "objective" certifications—ones from which courts inferred a reasonable attorney standard to decide whether the lawyer had violated the certification. If so, she would be sanctioned, along with her client. (However, the client would not be sanctioned for certifications concerning a good-faith basis in law on the theory that clients could not know the law.) The 1983 amendments also required the lawyer to certify that she was not filing the pleading for any improper purpose, such as to harass or to delay. This certification was a subjective one, and before imposing sanctions courts would consider whether there were sufficient indicia showing the requisite intent.

Those overseeing the federal system believed that the 1983 amendments, which were designed to reform the pleading system, needed reform themselves. The 1983 amendments, according to this view, had led to a decline in professional relations and to "satellite litigation" over whether Rule 11 sanctions should be imposed, as opposed to litigating the merits of the case. *See* 5A WRIGHT & MILLER, FEDERAL PRACTICE & PROCEDURE § 1331. In 1993, Federal Rule of Civil Procedure 11 was amended to diminish its "bite." For instance, if the pleader does not currently have a basis for particular facts, she can avoid Rule 11 problems by specifically designating them and stating that "after a reasonable opportunity for further investigation or discovery, plaintiff will likely have evidentiary support" for the designated allegation. Even more significantly, the amendments enacted a "safe harbor" provision. Under this provision, one who seeks Rule 11 sanctions must, before filing a motion, give notice to the adversary of the precise matters on which she plans to seek sanctions, and the grounds therefor. The adversary then has 21 days to withdraw the allegations. If the allegations are withdrawn, the court never sees a Rule 11 motion, and the matter is resolved.

The curious situation now is that many, if not most, states have not adopted the 1993 amendments to Federal Rule of Civil Procedure 11. *See* Appendix 4-3 (states rules on sanctions for lack of good faith in pleadings); *see also* John B. Oakley, *A Fresh Look at the Federal Rules in State Courts*, 3 NEV. L. J. 354, 360–81 (2004). Thus, states generally have retained a more stringent version of Rule 11 than the Federal system. *See id.* Needless to say, you should investigate closely the requirements of the state in which you are filing a case. The requirements may be in a rule of court or in a statute. If the state in question follows the 1983 version of Federal Rule 11, the lawyer should remember the ample federal court precedent dealing with motions brought under that version of the Rule. Federal court precedent should be highly persuasive authority in her state, along with the governing decisions of the highest court of that state.

Follow-Up Questions

1. What version of "Rule 11" sanctions for violations of pleading requirements does the state in which you intend to practice follow?

2. Notice that under the 1993 amendments to Rule 11 and to state rules conforming to the 1993 amendments to Rule 11, the plaintiff can allege: "After a reasonable opportunity for further investigation or discovery, the plaintiff will likely have evidentiary support to show [fill in here the factual allegation]." In the state in which you intend to practice, can a plaintiff make such an allegation without having a factual basis at the time of filing the complaint? Assuming that such an allegation will withstand pleading rules and initial motions in your jurisdiction, what would you as plaintiff's counsel want to do early in the case to avoid your opponent's taking advantage of such an allegation? If you were defendant's counsel, what would you do when you see such an allegation?

Professional Identity Question

The senior partner for whom you work tells you that he likes to bring a Rule 11 motion in every case because it often scares the opponent into dropping the case. He asks you to file a Rule 11 motion on behalf of a client even though neither she nor you can identify a specific basis for doing so. He said to just put in the motion that the complaint "lacks a good faith basis in law or fact." Would you file the motion? If not, how would you deal with the senior partner's request? If there were other partners in the firm to whom you could talk about the matter, would you discuss the matter with them? Would you talk to the client about filing such a motion, the potential costs of doing so and the risks of having sanctions imposed for filing a Rule 11 motion without a good faith basis? Would talking with the client be "disloyal" to the senior partner or your firm? Does a lawyer's obligation to her client override such loyalties?

Joinder of Claims

In preparing an offensive pleading, an attorney must consider questions of claim joinder. Most states have enacted statutes or rules that permit a party to join as many claims as she has against an opposing party. *See* Appendix 4-4 (reflecting a majority of states permit joinder of as many claims as a party has against another). The rules and statutes are careful not to refer to "plaintiff" or "defendant," but rather refer to "any party" because they recognize that defendants may bring their own claims to which the general joinder-of-claims provision will apply. Most state provisions on permissive join-der closely follow Federal Rule of Civil Procedure 18. *See* Appendix 4-4. In federal court, the pleader has to worry not only about whether the joined claim satisfies the proce-dural rule in question, but also whether the joined claim is within the jurisdiction of federal courts. In state courts, the analysis is easier — does the rule permit joinder of the claim? In virtually every state, a party may join as many claims as she has against another party, regardless of transactional relatedness. *See* Appendix 4-4. However, some states require transactional relatedness for claims to be joined. *See* Appendix 4-4 (see minority position).

Even if a state's rules label claims as permissive, the careful lawyer will consider that state's law on claim preclusion and issue preclusion.[2] At times a party may bring an initial action asserting certain claims and omitting others. If the attorney considers solely a state's rules on joinder of claims, but does not consult the law of claim and issue preclusion, she may later be surprised to find that these doctrines preclude the asser-tion of a claim. A lawyer may recommend for strategic reasons not to bring the claim in the initial action. She would do well, however, to advise her client that claim or issue preclusion may bar the claim or issue later and leave the ultimate decision to the client.

Likewise, a party can also assert alternative and even inconsistent theories. For in-stance, a widow in Illinois state court sued two defendants for damages arising from the death of her husband in a car accident. *See McCormick v. Kopman*, 161 N.E. 2d 720 (Ill. Ct. App. 1959). She alleged alternative and inconsistent claims: (1) against a tavern under the State's Dram Shop Act, alleging liability of the tavern for serving her husband after he was intoxicated; and (2) against the driver that collided with her husband, alleging that the other driver was negligent and that her husband was not intoxicated. The jury found the other driver liable but not the tavern. The driver moved to set aside the jury verdict based on the inconsistent allegations in the case. The trial court rejected this ar-gument because such allegations are permitted and plaintiff was "uncertain as to what the true facts were." *Id.*

Implicit in the *McCormick* court's holding is an exception to the ability to plead in-consistent facts. Mrs. McCormick was "uncertain" as to what the facts were. If one knows that a set of facts is untrue, alleging them might violate the Rules of Professional Con-duct. *See* MODEL RULES OF PROF'L CONDUCT R. 3.3(a) (2003) (the rule stands for the principle that a lawyer should not knowingly make a false statement of fact or law to a tribunal).

---

2. Claim preclusion (also referred to as "res judicata") and issue preclusion (also referred to as "collateral estoppel") are usually covered thoroughly in first-year civil procedure courses. Thus, this book does not engage them. Professor Richard Freer has an excellent discussion of the preclusion doctrines in one of his many publications. *See* R. FREER, INTRODUCTION TO CIVIL PROCEDURE 509–85 (2006). However, as noted in the text, the careful attorney will consider these doctrines and their ef-fect on unasserted claims. *See infra* page 88 & n.5. (discussing example of how, despite the state's mi-nority approach of not making transactionally related counterclaims compulsory, claim preclusion would likely result in precluding defendant from asserting claim if not asserted in the initial litigation).

Follow-Up Questions

1. In the *Rex v. Hurry* complaint (see *infra* pages 83–86 below), the Plaintiff joins her claims for assault and battery against Defendant Hurry with her negligence claim against the same Defendant. Even though one is a negligence claim and the other two are intentional torts, are these claims appropriately joined under the approach to joinder of such claims in your jurisdiction?

2. Under Federal Rule of Civil Procedure 18, a party can join any claim she has against another party. The policy underlying such a wide-open approach supports the resolution of as many disputes between the same parties as possible in one suit. A broad rule of claim joinder promotes efficiency; otherwise claims between the same parties, with overlapping facts, would be handled in separate cases. Litigants and taxpayers would suffer from such inefficiency. Do the same policies support your jurisdiction's approach to joinder of multiple claims between the same parties?

Joinder of Parties

Joinder of parties typically involves rules similar to, but somewhat different, from joinder of claims. As with the Federal Rules of Civil Procedure, most state civil procedure systems encourage joinder of parties. Typically, the criteria are the same two as set forth in Federal Rule of Civil Procedure 20. These criteria are: (1) that the claims against the parties sought to be joined arise from the same transaction or occurrence, or series of transactions or occurrences; and (2) a common question of law or fact. *See* Appendix 4-5 (showing that a majority of states have rules that mirror the requirements of Fed. R. Civ. P. 20). The policy for broad party joinder mirrors that for broad claim joinder — namely, efficiency. Despite the policy favoring joinder, a plaintiff typically cannot join defendants when the claims against different defendants fail to be transactionally related to each other. 1A C.J.S. *Actions* § 288 (2008). For example, in *Powers v. Cherin*, 249 Va. 43, 452 S.E.2d 666 (1995), the plaintiff suffered injuries in a car accident. After being taken to the hospital, the doctor treating the plaintiff allegedly committed malpractice. In these circumstances, the Virginia Supreme Court held that claims against the driver defendant and the physician defendant were not sufficiently related and, thus, they could not be joined. *Id.* at 37, 452 S.E.2d at 669.

Professional Identity Question

Suppose the law of your jurisdiction is clear — that a claim against defendant Hurry arising from the car accident could not be joined with the claim against defendant Payne (see *Rex. v. Hurry* and Payne fact summary and complaint below). However, you knew that the lawyers who represented these two defendants were inattentive, and thought you might get by with joining the claims. Would you file the joined claims?

Sample Fact Pattern for Examining Requirements of Offensive Pleadings

Suppose in your research, you find the following hypothetical case, *Brad T. Rex. v. Ena Hurry and Dr. Lovey Payne,* and pleadings based on the fact pattern. The sample illustrates requirements and limitations on pleadings, joinder of claims and parties, and other issues on which you now need to become an expert in order to draft Sally's pleadings. The fact pattern, according to the description, serves as the basis for three pleadings—a complaint, a counterclaim, and a third-party complaint.

Facts on Which Pleadings and Questions Are Based

One evening, January 18, 2008, to be precise, Brad T. Rex was riding a motorcycle that he had borrowed from his friend, Harley Davidson. Assume for this fact pattern and the pleadings based on it that motorcycle airbag jackets[3] had by this time become standard equipment purchased as part of the sale of a motorcycle, and Rex was wearing one. The motorcycle airbag jacket in question was manufactured by Kagasaki, Inc., and was supposed to deploy whenever the bike driver was thrown off the bike.

On this sunny, cold day, Rex was driving the motorcycle on a public, single-lane road called Easy Street in the City of Arcadia, State of Illyria at around 4:00 p.m. He was driving between 15 miles per hour (the minimum speed limit) and 35 miles per hour (the maximum speed limit). Rex was proceeding on Easy Street where it intersected with Dangerous Drive (the "Intersection"), and the Intersection was controlled by a stoplight. Rex, the Plaintiff in pleadings below, was traveling west on Easy Street. Other vehicles traveling west on Easy Street proceeded through the Intersection, as did Rex. Although Rex cannot now recall whether he saw a green light, he at least inferred from the other vehicles' entering the Intersection that he "must have" had a green light.

At the same time and on the same day, the Defendant, Ena Hurry, was driving her car north on Dangerous Drive in the right-hand lane of the two lane road. Hurry, late for a hair appointment, was traveling well above the posted speed limit. As she approached the Intersection, she did not pay attention to the traffic light. Instead, Hurry proceeded into the Intersection. Rex and the motorcycle slammed into the side of Hurry's car. The collision catapulted Rex over Hurry's car and he landed on the asphalt. The state-of-the-art motorcycle airbag jacket did not inflate, and Rex sustained serious injuries throughout his body. Rex's injuries required—and will continue to require—medical attention. Additionally, the accident caused significant pain, discomfort, suffering—all of which required him to miss several months working as the head chef of a popular restaurant. Not only was Rex badly injured, but the damage to Davidson's motorcycle was at least $50,000.

As Rex struggled to stand after being tossed to the pavement, and was feeling a bit woozy, Hurry approached Rex in a threatening manner and shoved Rex with both hands. Rex, who had had enough by this time, began to scream at Hurry, calling her "a syphilis-ridden criminal." He pushed her back with such great force that Hurry tumbled to the ground, doing two backward somersaults and landing face-down. Hurry suffered cuts, bruises, and severe pain.

---

3. For a discussion of this safety product, see webBikeWorld at http://www.webbikeworld.com/r2/ airbag-jacket/motorcycle-airbag-jacket.htm (last visited August 17, 2009).

Immediately following the collision, at least one person stopped at the scene of the crash and heard Rex call Hurry "a syphilis-ridden criminal." Hurry neither has syphilis, nor is she a criminal. The witness called for the police and an ambulance.

Rex was taken to the hospital. The attending physician, Dr. Lovey Payne, heard the entire account of the above events, examined Rex, and treated his cuts and bruises, but failed to order a CAT scan to determine whether Rex had suffered a concussion. Rex later developed severe headaches that another physician determined were the result of the concussion. These headaches, the second physician opined, could have been avoided if Rex had been properly treated by limiting his movement for a week. As it is, he will apparently suffer headaches for the indefinite future.

Sample Complaint

PLAINTIFF DEMANDS TRIAL BY JURY[4]

IN THE CIRCUIT COURT FOR THE CITY OF ARCADIA

BRAD T. REX,	)	
	)	
Plaintiff,	)	
	)	
v.	)	Complaint
	)	
ENA HURRY,	)	
	)	Case No. 2008cv10
Defendant,	)	
	)	
Service Address:	)	
123 Speedster Street	)	
Arcadia, Illyria 23456	)	
	)	
and	)	
	)	
LOVEY PAYNE, M.D.,	)	
Service Address:	)	
222 Easy Street	)	
Arcadia, Illyria, 23455	)	
	)	
Defendant.	)	

COMPLAINT

The Plaintiff, Brad T. Rex, by counsel, for his Complaint against defendants, Ena Hurry and Lovey Payne, states as follows:

Parties

1. The Plaintiff, Brad T. Rex, is a citizen of the State of Illyria and the Defendants, Ena Hurry and Lovey Payne, are citizens of the same State.

---

4. A party should always consider whether to demand a jury at the time of the Complaint or Answer. Failing to include a brief demand, such as is illustrated here (or filing a separate pleading with the demand), will result in waiver of the jury right. *See infra* Ch. 9 ("The Right to a Jury Trial") at p. 219.

Facts Common to All Counts

2. On January 18, 2008, the Plaintiff was driving a motorcycle owned by Harley Davidson, who had given the Plaintiff permission to ride the bike for over a month while the Plaintiff's motorcycle (which he had recently wrecked) was in the shop for repairs. The Plaintiff was wearing a state of the art motorcycle airbag jacket manufactured by Kagasaki, Inc. Kagasaki advertised that its motorcycle airbag jacket would inflate whenever the rider was thrown off the bike, thus protecting the rider from serious injury.

3. The Plaintiff was driving Davidson's motorcycle between the minimum speed limit of 15 miles per hour and the maximum speed limit of 35 miles per hour. He was driving during daylight at around 4:00 p.m. on a public, single-lane road called Easy Street in Arcadia, Illyria, which intersects with Dangerous Drive (the "Intersection"). The Intersection is controlled by a traffic light. The Plaintiff, who was traveling west on Easy Street, entered the intersection at the same time as the one or more other vehicles traveling in the same direction as Plaintiff.

4. On the same day and at the same time described in the preceding paragraph, the Defendant Hurry was operating her car on Dangerous Drive in the right-hand lane of the two lanes heading north. Defendant Hurry proceeded through the intersection negligently despite the lack of a green light.

5. The Defendant Hurry, who was traveling at a high rate of speed that exceeded the speed limit, proceeded through the Intersection.

6. The Plaintiff and his motorcycle collided with the side of the Defendant Hurry's car. The Plaintiff was thrown over the car onto the asphalt and received numerous and serious injuries throughout his body, for which he has received — and will continue to receive — medical care. The Plaintiff has experienced pain, suffering, discomfort, and significant loss of income from his job as head chef at a restaurant. The collision and aftermath damaged Davidson's motorcycle in an amount that will likely exceed $50,000 to repair.

7. Rex was wearing a new state-of-the art motorcycle airbag jacket manufactured by Kagasaki, Inc. Kagasaki advertises the jacket as an essential safety device that will inflate immediately when a rider is thrown from a motorcycle and protect the person wearing it from serious trauma. The airbag jacket that Rex was wearing did not inflate when Rex was thrown from the motorcycle.

8. Stunned by these events, the Plaintiff stood up after great effort — only to have the Defendant Hurry approach him in a threatening manner and push him with both of her hands on his shoulders.

Negligence Claim

9. The preceding allegations are hereby restated and incorporated as if set forth here.

10. The Defendant Hurry had a duty at the time of the events to use ordinary care to avoid injury to others and to the property of others.

11. The Defendant Hurry breached her duty to use ordinary care in a variety of ways, including but not limited to driving at an unsafe speed and/or failing to follow the traffic signals at the Intersection.

12. The Defendant Hurry's breach is described in the preceding paragraph.

13. As a proximate result of the Defendant Hurry's breach of her duty, the Plaintiff suffered a concussion, cuts, and bruises; suffered great pain of body and mind; and incurred expenses for medical attention and hospitalization; and has lost income from being unable to work at the restaurant where he is employed as head chef.

Assault

14. The preceding allegations are hereby restated and incorporated as if set forth here.

15. When the Defendant Hurry intentionally approached the Plaintiff after the collision in a physically threatening manner, she created a reasonable apprehension of immediate, offensive bodily contact.

16. The Defendant Hurry had the apparent ability to carry out the threatened offensive bodily contact.

17. The Defendant Hurry's actions constituted an assault for which she is liable to Plaintiff for both compensatory and punitive damages.

Battery

18. The preceding allegations are hereby restated and incorporated as if set forth here.

19. The Defendant Hurry intentionally touched Plaintiff in a manner offensive to a reasonable person.

20. The Defendant Hurry's actions constitute a battery for which she is liable to Plaintiff for both compensatory and punitive damages.

Malpractice

21. The preceding allegations are hereby restated and incorporated as if set forth here.

22. Defendant Payne had a duty to exercise reasonable care consistent with that of a reasonable physician in Arcadia so as to avoid injury to the Plaintiff.

23. Defendant Payne breached his duty to exercise reasonable care consistent with that of a reasonable physician in Arcadia by failing to treat the Plaintiff's concussion at all, much less in a manner consistent with how a reasonable physician in Arcadia would treat a concussion.

24. Defendant Payne's breach of duty set forth above has proximately resulted in, and will continue to result in, injuries and symptoms that are likely to be long-lasting and possibly permanent.

25. Defendant Payne's actions fall below the standard of care for like physicians in the community. The standard of care would have dictated that a physician, encountering a patient like Rex who had been in an accident such as he related to Payne, perform tests to determine whether Rex had suffered a concussion—something that Payne failed to do. The failure of a physician to care for a patient in a manner consistent with the standard of care in the community constitutes malpractice.

26. Rex suffered significant damages resulting not only from the accident, but which were compounded by Payne's failure to diagnose his concussion promptly—something that he should easily have been able to determine with standard tests.

27. Defendant Payne therefore committed malpractice for which he is liable to Plaintiff for compensatory damages.

WHEREFORE, the Plaintiff demands the following relief against the Defendants:

a) compensatory damages in a sum exceeding $1 million, exclusive of interests and costs, the complete amount to be determined at trial;

b) punitive damages in an amount to be determined at trial against Defendant Ena Hurry.

BRAD T. REX

By /s/ Jim Justice

Of Counsel

The Law Offices of Jim Justice, Esq.
111 Liberty Street
Arcadia, Illyria 23464
757-222-3333
jim@justice.com

Counsel for Plaintiff

Follow-Up Questions

1. If the state in which you plan to practice adopts an interpretation of pleading rules similar to that of the Supreme Court's interpretation of Federal Rule of Civil Procedure 8 adopted in *Twombly* and *Iqbal*, would the allegations in the above complaint survive a motion to dismiss? If so, why? If not, why not?

2. Does the above complaint contain any allegation that is either unnecessary or too specific? Is there a danger in an allegation that is more specific than necessary to meet the pleading requirements of one's jurisdiction? If any allegations are overly specific, how would you revise them?

3. Whether explicitly or implicitly, *e.g.*, through case law permitting scant allegations of negligence to survive challenges to the sufficiency of the pleading, does the state in which you intend to practice apply less stringent pleading standards to negligence claims than to other claims? If so, how, if at all, would you revise the above complaint? In the state in which you intend to practice, are there some claims that require more specificity to satisfy pleading requirements than others? If so, what are they and what level of specificity would be necessary to plead the claim so as to satisfy the requirements?

4. Notice that the request for relief seeks not only compensatory damages but also punitive damages. Does the state in which you plan to practice require any particular allegations to warrant punitive damages? If so, what are those allegations and can you make them here? Would you need to engage in further investigation to be able to make the necessary allegations for punitive damages?

Professional Identity Questions

1. In your first meeting with Brad T. Rex, he tells you that he cannot say for sure that he did not have a yellow light as he was entering the intersection. He asks you whether, if that were the case, he would have as strong a case against Ena Hurry. How would you respond? If you told him that he clearly would not, and then he said, "Now that I think about it, I will say that I saw a green light as I entered the intersection." Would you accept Rex's about-face without further questioning or would you probe further? If you believed he was saying the light was green only because of your response to his question, and not because he actually remembered it being green, would you take the case? Or, instead of refusing his case, is there another approach you could take that would allow you not only to maintain your professional standards, but to bring suit for Rex?

2. Assume that, instead of being an individual defendant, Ena Hurry was an employee of a floral business and was delivering flowers at the time of the accident. You sue the business rather than her. Could you interview Ena Hurry and get a statement from her about what happened at the accident? If you happened to learn of a friend of Ena's, could you get an account of the accident by asking that friend to talk about the accident with Ena and then pass on to you what Ena said, without Ena's knowing about your request or the friend's passing on the information?

Practice Problem

Practice Problem 4-1

In meeting with plaintiff Rex, he tells you that he actually did not see a green light but "assumes it was green" because other vehicles entered the intersection immediately before he did. With this background, could you allege that the light was green as Rex entered the intersection? Would you feel uncomfortable making such an allegation?

Defendant's Ability to Assert Offensive Claims and to Join Parties

Plaintiffs are not the only ones who can assert offensive claims. As noted above, rules and statutes are careful not to refer to "plaintiff" or "defendant" but rather refer to "claimant," "responding party," "opposing party," or other such neutral terms. Throughout this chapter, unless the context clearly shows that the terms "plaintiff" and "defendant" are meant to apply only to particular parties, the terms should be understood to be interchangeable in terms of the ability of any party to plead offensive claims, join claims or parties, etc. If a plaintiff has a counterclaim asserted against her, she is a defendant as to the counterclaim. Conversely, if a defendant in the original suit asserts a counterclaim, cross-claim, or third-party claim, she becomes a plaintiff. The rules for pleading a claim are the same for a plaintiff as for a defendant asserting offensive claims. Moreover, the rules for responding to offensive pleadings apply not only to defendants but to any party who has claims asserted against her (*e.g.*, plaintiff, co-defendant, etc.).

In the federal system and in virtually every state system, defendants can assert counterclaims against a plaintiff, cross-claims against co-parties, or third-party claims against third parties who may be liable to the defendant/third-party plaintiff for all or part of the plaintiff's claims. The majority approach is that counterclaims are mandatory if the subject of the counterclaim arises from the same transaction or occurrence as the plaintiff's claim. *See* Appendix 4-6. A minority approach among states provides that counterclaims are not mandatory, even if they arise from the same transaction or occurrence as the main claim. *See id.*[5] In such states, counsel should beware that failing to include a compulsory counterclaim may, if the defendant ends up in later litigation against the same opponent or a party in privity with the opponent, result in claim or issue preclusion barring relitigation of a claim or issue. The reason is that most states, in deciding in a later suit whether a claim was "brought" (and thus barred) in earlier litigation, courts ask whether the party *could have* brought the claim. Clearly, where a defendant's counterclaim arises from the same transaction or occurrence, it would fall within the "could have been brought" category—even though the state in question may not have a compulsory counterclaim rule requiring the claim to be brought in the first suit. *See, e.g.*, note 5 this chapter. For an excellent discussion of claim and issue preclusion as they apply across the country (*i.e.*, in both federal and state courts), see R. Freer, Introduction to Civil Procedure 509–85 (2006).

Permissive counterclaims (by definition), cross-claims, and third-party claims typically are not mandatory. *See* Fed. R. Civ. P. 13(b) ("pleading *may* state as a counterclaim against an opposing party any claim that is not compulsory"); Fed. R. Civ. P. 13(g) ("A pleading *may* state as a cross-claim any claim by one party against a co-party...."); Fed. R. Civ. P. 14(a)(1) ("A defending party *may*, as third party plaintiff, serve a summons and complaint on a nonparty who is or may be liable to it for all or part of the claim against it."); *see also* Appendix 4-6 (showing that a majority of states have permissive counterclaim rules like Federal Rule 13(b)); Appendix 4-6 (showing that a majority of the states have cross-claims rules that permit, but do not require, such claims as does Federal Rule 13(g)); Appendix 4-7 (showing that a majority of states have adopted third-party claims rules such as that in Federal Rule 14). If a party chooses to bring one of these claims, however, the guidelines applicable to pleading claims in a complaint are applicable to claims asserted in these pleadings too. Thus, all of the guidance outlined above for pleading claims in a complaint applies equally to these pleadings.

* * *

---

5. For instance, Virginia gives the defendant the option to bring a counterclaim but does not make it compulsory. *See* Va. Sup. Ct. Rule 3:9(a). However, because Virginia has recently adopted the *Restatement (Second)* approach to defining a claim for purpose of claim preclusion—*i.e.*, whether the claim was brought or could have been brought in a transactionally related proceeding—defendants who choose not to file a counterclaim because the rule makes them permissible, may well find their claim barred not by rule preclusion but by principles of claim preclusion. *See, e.g.*, Va. Sup. Ct. Rule 1:6 (adopting *Restatement (Second)* approach to defining claim for purposes of claim preclusion).

Having reviewed potential claims that someone who has been sued can assert, following are examples of a counterclaim:

[IF PLAINTIFF'S COMPLAINT DID NOT DEMAND TRIAL BY JURY, THE COUNTERCLAIM CAN AND LIKELY SHOULD STATE "DEFENDANT AND COUNTERCLAIM PLAINTIFF DEMANDS TRIAL BY JURY"]

Sample Counterclaim

IN THE CIRCUIT COURT FOR THE CITY OF ARCADIA

BRAD T. REX,	)	
	)	
Plaintiff/Counterclaim Defendant,	)	
	)	
v.	)	Case No. 2008cv10
	)	
ENA HURRY,	)	
	)	
Defendant/Counterclaim Plaintiff.	)	
	)	
and	)	
	)	
LOVEY PAYNE, M.D.,	)	
	)	
Defendant.	)	

COUNTERCLAIM

The Defendant and Counterclaim Plaintiff, Ena Hurry ("Hurry"), by counsel, for her Counterclaim against Plaintiff and Counterclaim Defendant, Brad T. Rex ("Rex"), states as follows:

Facts Common to All Counts

1. On January 18, 2008, Rex was driving a motorcycle and collided with Hurry's vehicle during daylight at around 4:00 p.m. on a public, single-lane road called Easy Street in Arcadia, Illyria, which intersects with Dangerous Drive (the "Intersection").

2. Rex then responded by screaming loudly at Hurry that she was "a syphilis-ridden criminal." He proceeded to push her so hard that she went backwards and did two somersaults, landing face down. As a result of the fall, Hurry suffered cuts, bruises, and severe pain.

3. At least one third-party witness, and possibly others, heard Rex's statement described in the preceding paragraph.

4. Hurry has neither syphilis nor any other communicable diseases. She is not a criminal and has never been convicted of even a traffic offense, much less a more serious crime.

Slander

5. The preceding allegations are hereby restated and incorporated as if set forth here.

6. The words screamed by Rex at Hurry, described above, after the accident represent words that constitute slander per se.

7. The words were published because a third person, and possibly others, heard them.

8. The words are false.

9. These events constitute slander per se for which Hurry is entitled to both compensatory and punitive damages.

Assault

10. The preceding allegations are hereby restated and incorporated as if set forth here.

11. The Plaintiff/Counterclaim Defendant intentionally approached Defendant/Counterclaim Plaintiff after the collision in a physically threatening manner and thereby created a reasonable apprehension of immediate, offensive bodily contact.

12. The Plaintiff/Counterclaim Defendant had the apparent ability to carry out the threatened offensive bodily contact.

13. These actions constitute an assault for which Hurry is entitled to both compensatory and punitive damages.

Battery

14. The preceding allegations are hereby restated and incorporated as if set forth here.

15. The Plaintiff/Counterclaim Defendant intentionally touched Defendant/Counterclaim Plaintiff in a manner offensive to a reasonable person.

16. These actions constitute battery for which Defendant/Counterclaim Plaintiff is entitled to both compensatory and punitive damages.

WHEREFORE, the Defendant/Counterclaim Plaintiff demands the following relief against the Plaintiff/Counterclaim Defendant:

a) compensatory damages of $100,000 or such greater amount as shall be proved at trial;

b) punitive damages in an amount to be determined at trial.

ENA HURRY

By _____

Of Counsel

Dee Fender, Esq.
1000 Liberty Street
Arcadia, VA 23510
757.625.5000
deefender@yahoo.com

Counsel for Ena Hurry

CERTIFICATE OF SERVICE

I, Dee Fender, hereby certify that on this 18th day of December, 2009, I mailed by first-class United States mail this Counterclaim to counsel for Plaintiff and

Counterclaim Defendant, Jim Justice, Esq., 111 Liberty Street, Arcadia, Illyria 23464.

/s/ Dee Fender
_____

Counsel for Defendant

Follow-Up Questions

1. Does the state in which you intend to practice have a compulsory counter-claim rule such as Federal Rule of Civil Procedure 13(a) — the rule that states that a defendant "must" assert by counterclaim "any claim" against the opposing party "arising from the same transaction or occurrence"? If so, is the phrase "same transaction or occurrence" defined by state statute, rule, or case law? Would the claims Hurry included in her counterclaim fall within the same transaction or occurrence according to the criteria in your jurisdiction?

2. Even if the state in which you intend to practice is in the minority of juris-dictions that lack a compulsory counterclaim rule, does the law in your ju-risdiction allow joinder of claims even if they are not transactionally related? What other body of law mentioned in this chapter should you check — law that would point to the effect of failure to include a claim in one suit, if there is later litigation? Before deciding whether to assert the counterclaim, should you discuss such implications with your client?

Professional Identity Question

Suppose you work for a senior partner who tells you that his standard prac-tice is to file a counterclaim in every case. As he further explains, he ensures that the counterclaim is "loaded" with claims. He tells you that he's found that "fat" counterclaims often scare off plaintiffs. He says that if a plaintiff complains and seeks Rule 11 sanctions against him, he just withdraws the claims that he can-not support. Would you follow this approach? If not, how would you deal with the partner's request? What involvement should your client have in this process?

Group Exercise on Dealing with Client Regarding Counterclaims

When sued, some parties try to bring a claim against the plaintiff even when the facts do not support a legitimate claim. Suppose, for instance, that instead of the shoving between Rex and Hurry described above, Rex merely made an obscene gesture at her from a distance and with a car between them so that he could not touch her if he tried. In no jurisdiction would such facts support an assault claim and assume that, in your jurisdiction, more egregious facts than Hurry relates would be required to state an intentional infliction of emotional distress claim. Yet Hurry has a lawyer friend from another state tell her she should have you bring these claims. If Hurry wanted you to bring a battery and intentional infliction of emotional distress claim based on these facts, how would you respond? Could you acknowledge Hurry's frustration but, at the same time, explain to her that asserting the claims would water down her more substantial claims, among other adverse effects, even if the court is unlikely to sanction her. She may not like to hear that she ought not vent her frustration by asserting claims that are, at best, marginal and, at worst, virtually impossible to win. If a party alleges claims that lack a sufficient basis, and bringing such a claim would likely hurt the party and her lawyer's credibility—such tactics can affect rulings throughout the case in subtle ways, and ultimately in the jury's perception of the case.

Break into groups of three. One student should take the role of Hurry, another the role of her attorney, and the third the role of objective observer. Have Hurry request the counterclaim with the particular claims noted above, based on what her lawyer friend told her. Then the student assuming the role of her attorney should explain the reasons that bringing such claims are not advisable. Finally, the objective observer can offer her comments on the exchange. The group can discuss matters such as: (1) how to speak in layperson's terms rather than legalese; (2) the importance of a lawyer's maintaining her composure, maintaining confidence, but not becoming adversarial with her client; and (3) the ways that one's tone, body language, and the like can affect how one party to the conversation comes across to the other. Here, the observer's comments are crucial because she should be observing details such as these. Some persons cannot, unless it is brought to their attention, realize that they come across in ways that may offend a client. Once drawn to a student's attention, the student can try the exercise again and practice modifying her tone, body language, etc.

Joinder may also arise when a defendant becomes a third-party plaintiff by asserting a third-party claim against a person or entity not named in the original suit (third-party defendant). All states include a version of the so-called "impleader rule" set forth in Federal Rule of Civil Procedure Rule 14. *See* Appendix 4-7 (reflecting majority of states with rules similar or identical to Fed. R. Civ. P. 14). Rule 14 permits a party, against whom a claim has been asserted (usually a defendant), within a defined time period, to prepare a third-party complaint against a person or entity that may be liable for all or part of any judgment against the defendant/third-party plaintiff. Third-party claims—usually referred to as "impleader" claims—include *only* claims by a party against whom relief is sought (third-party plaintiff) that a third party (third-party defendant) is or may be liable to original defendant. The third-party defendant is not a party in the litigation until the defendant serves a summons. In both cross-claims and third-party claims, the "is or may be liable" language almost exclusively refers to two types of claims: (1) an indemnity claim, under which the party asserting the claim can assert that the other has a duty to indemnify the claimant; or (2) a contribution claim, in which both parties are typically joint tortfeasors and thus by law obligated to share in any amount recovered against one. *See* 6 C. Wright, A. Miller & M. Kane, Federal Practice & Procedure § 1446 (2009).

Most states' impleader statutes allow, as does Rule 14, the third-party defendant to assert claims against anyone in the litigation against whom she has legitimate claims and to raise defenses that the original defendant/third-party plaintiff may have overlooked. *See id.*; *see also* Appendix 4-7 (reflecting states' adoption of Fed. R. Civ. P. 14, which includes allowing parties to assert claims against the joined party and the joined party to assert claims or defenses). In addition, the impleader provisions generally allow, once a new defendant has been added, any party to assert a claim against that new party. *See id.* Nevertheless, an *impleader claim need not be brought in the suit.* Indeed, a defendant's claim for contribution against other joint tortfeasors or for indemnity from someone with whom he has an indemnity contract (or indemnity implied by law), does not arise until the defendant has been found liable and paid a judgment. Only then will the statute of limitations on the contribution or indemnity claim start ticking. Thus, the impleader rule or statute is a mechanism that gives the defendant a choice. On one hand, she can sue the third party for contribution or indemnity in the initial action and, if found liable, that third-party's liability will be adjudged along with the other parties in the case. On the other hand, she can let the first action run its course and, if she is found liable, then pursue the third party from whom she would then be entitled to contribution (responsible for part of any judgment, usually as a joint tortfeasor) or indemnity (responsible for all of any judgment, usually by contractual agreement or implied-in-law indemnity principles). The second alternative, of course, involves a new suit after the judgment in the first suit has been entered. Although efficiency may favor bringing the third party in for the initial suit, the defendant with potential contribution or impleader claims ought to consider the strategic impact that can have. A third party claim often results in the added party pointing the finger at the defendant/third-party plaintiff. Such an "additional" adversary, particularly one who is well-funded, can make it more difficult for the defendant/third-party plaintiff to defend herself in the main case.

The first complaint in this chapter, *Rex v. Hurry, supra* pages 83–86, provides an example of the attempted joinder by a plaintiff of more than one defendant — Rex sues both Hurry and Dr. Payne. The sample third-party complaint below illustrates how impleader could lead to a new party being added. After the sample third-party complaint, a series of questions will explore both the joinder (in Rex's initial complaint) of defendant Hurry and defendant Payne, and the impleader (in Hurry's Third-Party Complaint) of Kagasaki Motorcycles, Inc.

Sample Third-Party Complaint

IN THE CIRCUIT COURT FOR THE CITY OF ARCADIA

BRAD T. REX,	)
	)
Plaintiff,	)
	)
v.	) Case No. 2008cv10
	)
ENA HURRY,	)
	)
Defendant /Third-Party Plaintiff,	)
v.	)
	)
KAGASAKI, INC.,	)
Service Address:	)
1111 Motorcycle Way	)
Monogelia, Texafornia 98765	)
	)
Third-Party Defendant.	)

THIRD-PARTY COMPLAINT

Pursuant to [insert jurisdiction's impleader rule/statute], Ena Hurry files this Third-Party Complaint against Kagasaki, Inc.

General Facts

1. On January 18, 2008, the Plaintiff was driving a motorcycle owned by a friend, Harley Davidson, who had given the Plaintiff permission to ride the motorcycle for over a month while the Plaintiff's motorcycle was in the shop for repairs. Motorcycle airbag jackets had become available by this point, and Plaintiff was wearing one. The motorcycle airbag jacket in question was manufactured by Kagasaki, Inc., the Third-Party Defendant. The jacket was attached by a pin to the motorcycle and designed so that, whenever the rider was thrown, the pin would detach. The jacket was designed so that, when the pin detached, the jacket would inflate and prevent serious injuries to the person wearing it.

2. The Plaintiff was driving Davidson's motorcycle within the minimum speed limit of 15 miles per hour and the maximum speed limit of 35 miles per hour. He was driving the motorcycle during daylight at around 4:00 p.m. on a public, single-lane road called Easy Street in Illyria, Virginia, which intersects with Dangerous Drive ("The Intersection"). The Intersection is controlled by a traffic light.

3. On the same day and at the same time described in the preceding paragraph, the Defendant Hurry was operating her car on Dangerous Drive in the right hand lane of the two lanes heading north.

4. The Plaintiff and his motorcycle collided with the side of the Defendant Hurry's car. The Plaintiff was thrown over the car onto the asphalt.

5. Plaintiff was wearing a new state-of-the-art motorcycle airbag jacket sold with the motorcycle as standard equipment. The manufacturer of the airbag jacket was Kagasaki, Inc., the Third-Party Defendant. It advertises the jacket as an essential safety device that will inflate immediately when a rider is thrown from a motorcycle and protect him from serious trauma. The motorcycle jacket worn by Plaintiff did not inflate even though he was thrown from the bike and the pin detached from the motorcycle.

Defendant/Third Party Plaintiff's Claim Against Third-Party Defendant

6. Kagasaki, Inc., the Third-Party Defendant, advertises that its motorcycle airbag jacket is the only state-of-the art motorcycle safety device designed to inflate, without any action taken by the rider, whenever the rider is thrown from the bike.

7. According to the Third-Party Defendant, the airbag jacket is designed to prevent the rider from incurring significant injuries during an accident.

8. The airbag jacket did not inflate when Plaintiff was thrown from the bike.

9. Third-Party Defendant has a duty to use ordinary care in the manufacture of its motorcycle airbag jacket, including but not limited to manufacturing the jackets in a manner to prevent bodily injury.

10. Third-Party Defendant breached its duty either by failing to design the airbag jacket so that it would inflate when the rider was ejected and/or by defectively manufacturing this particular jacket so that the air bag jacket did not operate properly.

11. Third-Party Defendant's breach of duty proximately resulted in the injuries to Plaintiff for which he has sued Defendant/Third-Party Plaintiff. Therefore, Third-Party Defendant Kagasaki is a tortfeasor responsible for Plaintiff's injuries.

Contribution

12. Although Defendant/Third-Party Plaintiff has denied liability to the Plaintiff, to the extent that the Defendant/Third-Party Plaintiff is nevertheless held liable to the Plaintiff, then Third-Party Defendant is liable to Defendant/Third-Party Plaintiff for all or part of any judgment entered against for Plaintiff against Defendant/Third-Party Plaintiff.

13. Although Defendant/Third-Party Plaintiff has denied liability to Plaintiff, if she is found to be liable as a tortfeasor to Plaintiff, Third-Party Defendant Kagasaki is a joint tortfeasor jointly and severally responsible for any injuries to Plaintiff, under principles of contribution.

14. The Defendant demands that Third-Party Defendant Kagasaki be ordered to file responsive pleadings pursuant to [state here the jurisdiction's impleader rule or statute].

WHEREFORE, the Third-Party Plaintiff moves the Court to:

a) enter judgment against Kagasaki, Inc., for all or part of any damages awarded to Brad T. Rex to the extent that Ena Hurry is held liable to Brad T. Rex and enter a judgment against Kagasaki for its proportional share of the judgment.

b) award such other costs, prejudgment interests, and other relief as the Court deems appropriate.

ENA HURRY

By /s/ Dee Fender_____

Counsel for Defendant

Dee Fender, Esq.
1000 Liberty Street
Arcadia, Illyria 23464
757.625.5000
deefender@yahoo.com

Counsel for Defendant

CERTIFICATE OF SERVICE

I, Dee Fender, hereby certify that on this 18th day of December, 2009, I mailed appropriate copies of the Third-Party Summons and Complaint to the Secretary of State of Illyria, with all required fees and charges and papers, so as to be sent by the Secretary under applicable law by certified mail to Third-Party Defendant, Kagasaki Motors, Inc. at the address in the caption of this Complaint, and mailed by first-class United States mail this Third-Party Complaint to counsel for Plaintiff, Jim Justice, Esq., 111 Liberty Street, Arcadia, Illyria 23464.

/s/ Dee Fender_____

Counsel for Defendant

Follow-Up Questions

1. Plaintiff Rex's complaint joins not only claims against the same defendant Hurry (negligence, assault, battery), but also joins a malpractice claim against another defendant, Dr. Lovey Payne. Under the rules of the state in which you plan to practice, is the joinder of the claims against these two defendants proper? Why or why not?

2. Assume that you represent a defendant who has a contribution or indemnity claim against a third party. By permitting but not insisting on such a claim, what strategic option does the third-party rule offer such a defendant? What would be reasons to bring such a claim in the initial suit? What would be reasons to wait and, if the defendant is found liable, to bring a separate suit then? As a defendant sued alone, why might you refrain from pursuing a legitimate claim for contribution or indemnity in a third-party action? What might happen in the minds of jury members if multiple defendants start blaming each other?

3. If you represent a defendant in a case in which the plaintiff has joined multiple defendants, or there is a third-party defendant, can you take any steps to minimize the dynamic of defendants' fighting among themselves or pointing at one another? Some defendants, for instance, enter into joint defense agreements by which they may agree to withhold claims against each other, share discovery, develop strategy to defend against a plaintiff's claims uniformly, or otherwise address any number of matters affecting them all. In the state in which you intend to practice, are such agreements permitted and, if so, are they discoverable by the plaintiff?

Practice Problems

Practice Problem 4-2

Assume that you represent a defendant who may be joined with an unsympathetic defendant. In your judgment, your client's association with such a defendant would affect the jury's impression of your client. Even though theoretically juries should view defendants as independent parties, you know from experience that an unsavory defendant can affect the jury's perception of other defendants. Research whether, in the state in which you intend to practice, a defendant can move for severance and separate trials of claims by the plaintiff against more than one defendant who has been joined, either as a codefendant or a third-party defendant. If severance is recognized as a possible way to achieve separate trials, what is the test the court will apply to determine whether to grant such a motion?

Practice Problem 4-3

If a claim against a joined defendant is complex, and trial will be before a jury, jury confusion may justify handling the claims separately. Does the state in which you plan to practice take potential jury confusion into account in the resolution of whether to sever claims against different defendants for separate trials?

Amendments to Plaintiff's or Defendant's Pleadings

Most states follow Federal Rule of Civil Procedure 15 in allowing liberal amendment to pleadings, regardless of whether they are plaintiff's or defendant's pleadings. See Appendix 4-8 (majority of states follow Fed. R. Civ. P. 15's approach). Thus, parties generally have the opportunity to amend as a matter of right before a party has responded to her initial pleading. See Fed. R. Civ. P. 15(a)(1); Appendix 4-8. More often, parties seek leave to amend between the early phase of a case and trial, but still will receive leave in most cases unless the opposing party can show real prejudice. See Fed. R. Civ. P. 15(a)(1); Appendix 4-8. Indeed, amendments at trial are possible to conform the pleadings to the evidence unless, again, the opponent would truly be prejudiced. See Fed. R. Civ. P. 15(b); Appendix 4-8. Needless to say, a party is more likely to be able to show prejudice at trial, or even late in discovery before a trial, on the ground that the party has been unable to prepare for trial in light of the additional pleadings. Thus, counsel seeking leave to amend would be wise to do so well before the close of discovery.

Most states likewise provide that amended pleadings with new claims that arise from the same transaction or occurrence as the original complaint will "relate back" to the filing date or the original complaint for purposes of the statute of limitations. See Appendix 4-8 (majority rule follows Fed. R. Civ. P. 15(c) on relation back).

The Importance of Timely Identifying Parties under a Disability

Before filing suit, an attorney should consider whether any party—her own client or the defendant—happens to qualify as a person under a legal disability. A person under a legal disability can range from a teenager who has not yet reached majority, and thus is an "infant" in the eyes of the law, to someone committed to an institution. The presence of an incapacitated party is important because certain procedural steps will often be required that otherwise would not be. The law of virtually every state offers protections to incapacitated persons. See generally Joan L. O'Sullivan, Role of the Attorney for the Alleged Incapacitated Person, 31 STET. L. REV. 687 (2002). Thus, when suing on behalf of a potentially incapacitated person, the attorney should consider filing suit through a competent representative of such a person. In suits by infants, a common practice is to caption the case as follows: Patty Parent, as Plaintiff and Next Friend/Parent and/or Guardian of Iva Infant, a Minor v. Dan Defendant. Likewise, in representing both a parent and a child, the attorney should have the court appoint a guardian ad litem to protect the infant's interests. 42 AM. JUR. 2d Infants § 161 (2008). Indeed, the attorney could face a conflict of interest if the parent's and child's interests in the litigation diverge. MODEL RULES OF PROF'L CONDUCT R. 1.7 (2003).

Likewise, if representing a potentially incapacitated person, an attorney would be wise to have a competent representative appointed. In some states, the attorney herself can be named as guardian ad litem for the person. See, e.g., Va. Code § 8.01-9 (allowing such a practice). Perhaps more importantly a plaintiff suing a party who arguably is incapacitated should ensure that a proper representative is appointed. If she does not do so, a judgment may end up being challenged on the basis of the failure of the incapacitated person to have such a representative.

D. Methods to Reinforce and Integrate Topics Covered in This Chapter

As this chapter demonstrates, the litigator must remember a number of details at the pleadings stage. Following are some suggested activities to reinforce the topics covered above.

First Suggested Method

A useful way to remember key issues in the pleading stage is to make checklists. Here are some suggestions of items to include in your checklist. (If you include the items below, you should rewrite them in your own words. In that way, you are more likely to "make the reminders your own" and, thus, remember them.) Moreover, research the law of the state in which you plan to practice for any idiosyncrasies, traps, or pitfalls that may not be included below.

- Ensure the pleadings not only meet all requirements for pleading claims, but are sufficiently specific to meet the requirements in your jurisdiction. What types of claims require particularized pleading?

- What investigation factually and/or legally will be required to allege everything in the complaint? Do you want or need to assert an "upon further investigation or discovery" allegation because, at the time of filing, you feel that you lack a sufficient basis to assert the claim? Is that permitted in your state?

- Are you representing a person, or suing a person, who is arguably incapacitated? If so, what steps should you take in light of that?

- What claims will you join in your complaint?

- What parties will you join and what are the requirements for doing so?

- If you represent a defendant, what counterclaims could you make against the plaintiff, and what cross-claims should you consider?

- Does a basis exist for arguing for contribution from a joint tortfeasor, or indemnity from a contracting party or implied indemnity in the law (*e.g.*, an employer held liable for an employee's acts)? Even if such a basis exists, would your client be better off not bringing such a claim initially but only if forced to pay a judgment?

- If representing a defendant in a multiple defendant case, will a joint defense agreement serve your client's interests?

- Is there any party who arguably qualifies under a legal disability? What is the effect of the legal disability, and should you take any action to protect your client's interests?

- Are there any necessary parties to the suit who have not been joined?

- If you represent a nonparty with a claim or defense, should you move for leave to intervene?

- Does your client have a basis for claiming damages other than compensatory damages, such as punitive damages? What factual allegations must you include in your complaint to request punitive damages (*e.g.*, intentional conduct, recklessness)?

- Have you considered whether a jury is in your client's best interests and, if so, demanded a jury within the required deadline?

Second Suggested Method

Another activity will help you appreciate the necessity for "tickler" reminders that, in practice, will often mean the difference between your client's case proceeding and getting dismissed. Almost every e-mail system now has the ability give you an automatic reminder on a date you specify. One of the assignments below is to draft a complaint for Sally. Later, in Chapter 8, you will be covering discovery. If your syllabus indicates the dates that your class will address discovery, set an e-mail reminder to come to you at that time. It should ask you to consider whether to amend your complaint in light of facts learned in discovery.

If for some reason your e-mail does not have a system for reminders, check on the Internet for services that provide reminders. A number of Internet sites offer free event reminder e-mails (for example, the following Internet site http://yourli.st/). First, take the date when you are assigned this reading and pretend that you serve a complaint on that day. Then calculate the date in your jurisdiction when the answer will be due. Put a prompt in your e-mail or Internet reminder that will remind you to file a demand for a jury trial within 10 days of the defendant's answer (assuming 10 days is the deadline in your jurisdiction, as in most, though Federal Rule of Civil Procedure recently made the deadline in federal cases 14 days).

Of course, in practice, you and your colleagues need to develop a system that includes more than one reminder. Backup reminders to you, to your assistant, and ideally to other lawyers are critical. Most malpractice insurers insist on, or will offer a better rate, if such protections are in place. The reason is simple: sometimes lawyers do not pay attention to the first reminder. Perhaps you are in trial or an emergency in your personal life arises. Sooner or later, everyone misses one of these initial reminders, and the follow-ups to oneself and to others usually save that person from missing a deadline.

E. Written Assignments

1. Draft a complaint for Sally Wilreiz against the City of Arcadia, the State of Illyria, and HorsePower, Inc. Include all claims that you can assert against each defendant.

2. Assume for this assignment only that Sally Wilreiz sued only two defendants, the City of Arcadia and the State of Illyria. Draft a third-party complaint on behalf of one or both of these defendants against HorsePower, Inc. alleging negligence in the design and/or manufacture of the vehicle's rollbar that proximately caused injuries for which Sally is suing the City and the State.

Chapter 5

Service of Process

A. Sally's Case at This Stage of Litigation Process

You have decided whom to sue, have chosen a court in which to sue, and have prepared a complaint for Sally. You know that the next step will be to file the complaint and pay a filing fee. However, you have named three different types of defendants in Sally's suit (a/k/a "the Master Problem") — the City of Arcadia, the State of Illyria, and HorsePower, Inc. You are not sure of the steps to take in serving these defendants.

B. Tasks and Decision-Making at This Stage of a Case

Although filing a complaint and serving process are not the most challenging decisions in a case, they are essential to proceeding to a valid judgment. Highlighted in Diagram 5-1 is the point in the litigation process on which this chapter focuses.

Determining service requirements generally hinges on (a) whether the defendant is a state resident, and (b) what type of defendant one is serving (e.g., individual, municipality, corporation). Two of the defendants in the Master Problem, the City and the State, are located within the state in which you plan to practice. (For your purposes, you should assume that the State of Illyria represents the state in which you will be practicing.) You know that you must identify the City and State officials to serve and the methods of service prescribed for such governmental officials. The manufacturer is out-of-state. You can rely on the analysis performed in Chapter 3 to support jurisdiction over HorsePower, Inc., under both your jurisdiction's long arm statute and due process principles. Even though you have cleared these hurdles, you recall that you still have to follow specific steps for serving a nonresident defendant. Along with determining how to serve the governmental officials, you resolve to determine whether you can serve HorsePower, Inc. by following the procedures set forth for serving nonresidents through Illyria's secretary of state, as discussed below.

[handwritten notes:] key points — a. domicile of Δ b. type of Δ

Diagram 5-1

Cause of Action (events leading to suit)
Prefiling Matters to Consider; Choice of Forum [Chs. 2–3]
Π and Δ Decide on Offensive Pleadings & Joinder (of claims & parties); Filing Suit; Service [Chs. 4–5]
Motions, Responsive Pleadings; Default; Voluntary & Involuntary Dismissals [Chs. 6–7]
Discovery Phase (developing proof to establish claims & learning about the adversary's case) [Ch. 8]
Right to Jury Trial; Pretrial Motions & Practice [Ch. 9]
Final Pretrial Conference & Other Events within Last Month before Trial [Ch. 10]
Procedure at Trial [Ch. 11]
Post-Trial Motions & Calculating the Date of Final Judgment to Know Key Deadlines Such as for Notice of Appeal [Ch. 12]

C. Overview of Applicable Law

"Process" and Commencement of Suit

To analyze service of process, you should first define what "process" means. Process includes both a summons and a complaint. For each defendant being served, a plaintiff will need a summons, completed by the court's clerk, attached to a complaint. A summons is a formal document, signed by the clerk, which will look something like the following:

Summons in a Civil Action

_____ COURT FOR THE _____ OF _____

_____	)	
Plaintiff,	)	
	)	
v.	)	Action No. _____
	)	
_____	)	
Defendant.	)	

SUMMONS IN A CIVIL ACTION

To: *(Defendant's name and address)*

A lawsuit has been filed against you.

Within _____ days after service of this summons on you (not counting the day you received it) — or _____ days if you have elected to waive service — you must serve on the plaintiff an answer to the attached complaint or a motion under the Rules of Civil Procedure of _____. The answer or motion must be served on the plaintiff or plaintiff's attorney, whose name and address are: _____.

If you fail to respond, judgment by default will be entered against you for the relief demanded in the complaint. You also must file your answer or motion with the court.

CLERK OF COURT

Date: _____   _____
                                Signature of Clerk or Deputy Clerk

PROOF OF SERVICE

This summons for *(name of individual and title, if any)* _____ was received by me on *(date)* _____.

❑ I personally served the summons on the individual at *(place)* _____ on *(date)* _____; or

❑ I left the summons at the individual's residence or usual place of abode with *(name)* _____, a person of suitable age and discretion who resides there, on *(date)* _____, and mailed a copy to the individual's last known address; or

❑ I served the summons on *(name of individual)* _____, who is designated by law to accept service of process on behalf of *(name of organization)* _____ on *(date)* _____; or

❑ I returned the summons unexecuted because _____; or

❑ Other *(specify)*:

My fees are $_____ for travel and $_____ for services, for a total of $_____.

I declare under penalty of perjury that this information is true.

Date: _____

_____
                    Server's signature

_____
                    Printed name and title

_____
                    Server's address

Additional information regarding attempted service, etc:

_____

_____

A federal civil action commences when the complaint is filed with the court. Many states follow this approach, allowing a suit to commence even without completing service of process. GEOFFREY C. HAZARD, JR., COLIN C. TAIT & WILLIAM A. FLETCHER, PLEADING AND PROCEDURE: STATE AND FEDERAL CASES AND MATERIALS 332 (8th ed. 1999). "An extreme example is California, in which filing the action tolls the statute of limitations, provided service is accomplished within three years." *Id.* Conversely, in other states, "a suit is commenced and the statute of limitations is tolled only when service of process is accomplished." *Id.* Be sure to know the position of your jurisdiction. If you are in one of the minority states where the statute of limitations continues running after filing the complaint until service, your client's case may end up being time-barred if you delay service. You will want to speed up the service of process (*i.e.*, the summons and complaint) if you are practicing in such a jurisdiction.

Follow-Up Questions

1. Does the state in which you plan to practice have a rule or statute specifying the form of process? On the Internet, search for a summons form for your state. Fill in the form with the names of parties from the *Brad Rex v. Ena Hurry* case described *supra* in Chapter 4 at pages 82–86. Print your final product. After you filed the complaint and thus initiated the suit, would you be able to serve this form at that point on your own, if you attached it to a complaint, or would you need the clerk to sign the summons?

2. Does your state consider an action to be commenced upon filing the complaint, regardless of when it is served, or require both filing and service of the summary and complaint for the action to be deemed commenced and the limitations period satisfied?

Professional Identity Questions

If you are in a jurisdiction that allows you to file suit, and then let the suit sit there for a long period (even years) before serving the defendant, do you feel that such conduct truly is "fair play"? Would you consider informing the client that you are simply not comfortable allowing a suit to sit without being served, unless the client had a good reason for delaying service? One can argue that, in an adversarial system, whatever the rules and statutes allow is fair. Lawyers with this view would not think twice about letting the suit sit unserved for as long as they can. Do you believe that the adversarial system justifies taking any advantage in this way, if permitted by the law applicable in your jurisdiction? Or would you sue and wait to serve only if the client had a legitimate reason for waiting to serve? What might be legitimate reasons for delaying service?

The Purpose of Service

Service of process rules derived from American common law "to protect state sovereignty and to assure that the defendant had actual notice of the lawsuit." James Weinstein, *The Federal Common Law Origins of Judicial Jurisdiction: Implications for Modern Doctrine*, 90 VA. L. REV. 169, 173, 195 (2004). The modern approach to service of process tends to be less strict than in the past:

> [T]he trend is away from an overly strict approach, with courts now tending to ignore service irregularities where there was actual notice of suitable tenor and content or where the manner of transmitting and form of notice substantially complied with the prescribed procedure.

GEOFFREY C. HAZARD, JR., COLIN C. TAIT & WILLIAM A. FLETCHER, PLEADING AND PROCEDURE: STATE AND FEDERAL CASES AND MATERIALS 326, 654 (8th ed. 1999).

Nevertheless, the relaxation in manner of service does not mean that you can casually neglect ensuring that a defendant receives actual notice of a suit. In *Mullane v. Central Hanover Bank*, 339 U.S. 306 (1950), the United States Supreme Court underscored a party's constitutional right, under the Fourteenth Amendment's Due Process Clause, to have notice reasonably calculated to reach the party. *Mullane* involved a common trust fund formed pursuant to a New York law that allowed the pooling of funds that were otherwise insufficient for the numerous beneficiaries to afford a trustee. Central Hanover Bank served as the trustee of the common trust in question. Under the applicable New York statute, the trustee sought a hearing to present an accounting that, once approved by the court, would cut off the trustee's liability up to the hearing date. Following the New York statute, the trustee notified beneficiaries of the hearing by the only means required — by advertisement published in a newspaper for four weeks before the hearing.

A beneficiary challenged the constitutionality of the notice by publication. The Court held unconstitutional such notice to those beneficiaries whose addresses the trustee knew. *Id.* at 314–20. Conversely, the Court held constitutional notice by publication to those beneficiaries who could not be identified or whose addresses were unknown. *Id.* at 317–20. In so ruling, the Court issued certain guidelines for constitutional notice:

> An elementary and fundamental precept of due process in any proceeding which is to be accorded finality is notice reasonably calculated, under all the circumstances, to apprise interested parties of the pendency of the action and afford them an opportunity to present their objections....
>
> .... The means employed must be such as one desirous of actually informing the absentee might reasonably adopt to accomplish it. The reasonableness and hence the constitutional validity of any chosen method may be defended on the ground that it is in itself reasonably certain to inform those affected ... or, where conditions do not reasonably permit such notice, that the form chosen is not substantially less likely to bring home notice than other of the feasible and customary substitutes.

Id. at 315. The court specifically approved notice by first class mail as a "feasible and customary" substitute to formal service in notifying those beneficiaries for whom the bank had addresses. *Id.* at 318.

Even though *Mullane* sets the constitutional minimum for notice, states are free to adopt statutes that impose greater requirements on plaintiffs. In those states that require more stringent requirements than *Mullane*, a plaintiff who complies with the more stringent requirements will thus exceed the due process requirements of *Mullane*.

Follow-Up Questions

1. Do you know the addresses of the defendants named in the suit? If so, *Mullane* will allow you to send notice of the suit to them by first class mail. Does your jurisdiction's service requirements typically require *more* than service by first class mail, thus requiring you to go beyond the due process minimum?

2. In what scenarios would service by publication in a newspaper satisfy *Mullane*'s constitutional test? Do your jurisdiction's statutes permit service by publication? If so, in what circumstances and by what means?

Service of Process Requirements

The requirements for service of process typically depends on whether the defendant is an individual, a business entity, or a governmental entity. The following section first discusses service on individuals and then service on entities.

Service of Process on Individuals

In serving individuals, the approach of Federal Rule of Civil Procedure 4 is the one followed by most states. *See* Appendix 5-1 (reflecting majority of states follow Fed. R. Civ. P. 4). A plaintiff may choose to serve a defendant by any of the following means set forth in Rule 4: (1) deliver *personally* a copy of the summons and complaint to "an individual other than an infant or incompetent person," (2) leave copies "at the individual's dwelling house or usual place of abode with some person of suitable age and discretion then residing therein," or (3) deliver a copy "to an agent authorized by appointment or by law to receive service of process." *See* Appendix 5-1; *see also* 62B AM. JUR. 2d *Process* § 183 (2009). With this approach, service under any of the three means is equally valid. Some states "have not only adopted process rules similar to the Federal Rules but have promulgated more expansive or liberal rules," such as those "permit[ing] substituted service of process on an individual at his or her usual place of business." *See* Appendix 5-1; *see also* 62B AM. JUR. 2d *Process* § 183 (2009). Conversely, some states require an attempted service first by one means (typically personal service), and if the first is unsuccessful, then by a second means (*e.g.*, substituted service on person of suitable age at residence). If the second means fails, then such statutes allow for service by a third means, and so forth. *See* Appendix 5-1 (identifying the significant minority approach to service). In other words, such state service statutes insist on a hierarchy: plaintiffs must attempt service methods in a particular order, and one method must be tried before the next can be used. Implicit in the hierarchical statutes is the belief that some forms of service are better than others.

Personal Service: Service by Delivering a Copy of the Summons and of the Complaint to an Individual

"Personal service is the primary method of obtaining jurisdiction over the person of a defendant." 62B Am. Jur. 2d *Process* § 187 (2009). Personal service: (1) "notifies the defendant of the commencement of an action against him or her"; and (2) "provides the ritual that marks the court's assertion of jurisdiction over a lawsuit." *Id.* Personal service can be "waived by consent or agreement." *Id.* Some states have followed the lead of Federal Rule of Civil Procedure 4(d) and permit parties to waive service in return for more time to respond. *See* John B. Oakley, *A Fresh Look at the Federal Rules in State Courts*, 3 Nev. L. J. 354, 361–381 (2003) (some states incorporating waiver include Colorado, Rhode Island, Utah, Vermont, Virginia, and Wyoming). However, most states maintain the original version of Federal Rule of Civil Procedure 4 without the waiver of service component. *See* Appendix 5-1 (majority position on service).

Personal service does not require in-hand delivery. *Id.* § 190. In the following case, a process server confronts a recalcitrant defendant. The Supreme Court of Wyoming applies the rule followed in most jurisdictions.

CRB v. Department of Family Services
974 P.2d 931 (Wyo. 1999)

HILL, Justice.

Appellant CRB appeals from an order of the district court determining paternity and setting child support payments. Appellant challenges the efficacy of the service of process and the service of a notice to appear on his attorney.

We affirm.

. . . .

FACTS

On June 3, 1997, the State of Wyoming, through the DFS (Department of Family Services), filed a Petition to Establish Paternity and Support in the First Judicial District Court. The Petition alleged that CRB was the putative father of the then unborn child of LS. An order was issued by the district court requiring LS and CRB to appear at an informal hearing on August 25, 1997.

At the time, CRB was residing in Lake Charles, Louisiana. Personal service of the summons, petition for paternity and the order to appear at the informal hearing was attempted on July 9, 1997. The process server tried to serve CRB at his apartment, but CRB refused to open the door to accept service. Confronted with the refusal of CRB to open his door, the process server telephoned CRB and, while observing CRB through the apartment window, advised CRB he was being served and the documents were being placed in CRB's mailbox.

Counsel for CRB filed a special appearance on August 6, 1997, for the purpose of contesting personal jurisdiction on the grounds of insufficient serv-

Author's note: Often in sensitive domestic relations and paternity cases, states have procedures by which a party's name may be protected such as here, by using a party's initials, ("CRB" in the caption and case and "LS" mentioned in the first paragraph under "FACTS" below in this case)

ice of process. Neither CRB nor his counsel appeared at the August 25, 1997, informal hearing, and the district court commissioner subsequently issued a report proposing that service of process was sufficient and that the paternity petition be set for hearing.

While the record is not clear, CRB apparently filed a motion to dismiss at some point after the commissioner's report was issued. In response, the district court found that a *prima facie* showing had been made that CRB was subject to the court's jurisdiction and CRB had failed to present facts proving otherwise. The district court, however, gave CRB until September 30, 1997, to file affidavits in support of his contention that there was a lack of jurisdiction. On September 29, 1997, CRB filed an Objection to Jurisdiction along with supporting affidavits. The district court issued a decision letter on October 8, 1997, concluding that, in light of the circumstances, service of process was sufficient. CRB filed a motion for reconsideration on the issue, which was denied by the district court on January 13, 1998.

The paternity petition was then set for hearing and an order requiring CRB to appear was issued on February 10, 1998. The order to appear was served on CRB's counsel on February 27, 1998.

An informal hearing on the paternity petition was held on March 9, 1998, and neither CRB nor his counsel appeared. The district court commissioner issued his report with recommendations on March 12, 1998. The district court issued its Judgment and Order for Paternity and Child Support on April 15, 1998, finding CRB to be the father of the child and setting custody, visitation and child support. CRB takes this appeal from that Judgment and Order.

. . . .

Service of Process

CRB contends that service of process was insufficient under W.R.C.P. 4(d) because the summons and complaint were not delivered either to him personally or to another person over the age of fourteen years residing at his dwelling house or usual place of abode. Additionally, CRB argues that even accepting the District Court's finding that "in hand" delivery is not required so long as the person to be served is in close proximity to the process server, service was still insufficient because the evidence does not conclusively demonstrate that it was CRB who was in the apartment at the time service was attempted.

The requirements for personal service of process over an individual are set forth in W.R.C.P. 4(d)(1) (emphasis added):

(d) *Personal service*—... *Service* shall be made as follows:

(1) Upon an individual other than a person under 14 years of age or an incompetent person, by delivering a copy of the summons and of the complaint to the individual personally, or by leaving copies thereof at the individual's dwelling house or usual place of abode with some person over the age of 14 years then residing therein, or at the defendant's usual place of business with an employee of the defendant then in charge of such place of business, or by delivering a copy of the summons and of the complaint to an agent authorized by appointment or by law to receive service of process[.]

We are confronted with the question of what constitutes delivery of "a copy of the summons and of the complaint to the individual personally" in a situation where the defendant is aware that service is being attempted and seeks to avoid service by refusing to open his door to accept service. While this Court has not directly addressed this issue in this context, other authorities have:

> While personal service of process does not require "in hand" delivery, it should not become a game of wiles and tricks and a defendant should not be able to defeat service simply by refusing to accept the papers or by instructing others to reject service. Even though a defendant refuses physical acceptance of a summons, service is complete if a defendant is in close proximity to a process server under such circumstances that a reasonable person would be convinced that personal service of the summons is being attempted.... A process server may leave the summons outside of the door of a structure, informing the defendant that he is so doing, where the defendant interposes the door between himself and the process server.

62B AM. JUR. 2d *Process*, § 204 (1990) (citations omitted). Several state courts have also held that where the defendant attempts to avoid service by interposing a door between the defendant and the process server, service is sufficient if the summons is left in close proximity to the defendant. The Georgia Court of Appeals, under a statute with language substantially similar to W.R.C.P. 4, held that where service was avoided by refusing to open a door to accept it and the summons was left on the ground outside of the door service was sufficient. *Jacobson v. Garland*, 227 Ga. App. 81, 487 S.E.2d 640 (1997).

It is the duty of a defendant to accept and submit to the service of process when he is aware of the process server's purpose.... It is generally held that if the process server and the defendant are within speaking distance of each other, and such action is taken as to convince a reasonable person that personal service is being attempted, service cannot be avoided by physically refusing to accept the summons.

....

In this instance, CRB refused to open his apartment door to accept service. In response, the process server called CRB while still outside the apartment and informed him that he had papers to serve on him. When CRB continued to refuse to open the door, the process server informed CRB that he would deposit the summons and complaint in CRB's mailbox.

CRB engaged in conduct within the State of Wyoming which carried with it certain potential consequences, including legal obligations.... CRB cannot attempt to evade those obligations by avoiding service of process. The record is clear that CRB knew service was being attempted and he deliberately attempted to avoid that service. Under these circumstances, the process server took appropriate action by informing CRB at that time that he was being served and then leaving the summons and complaint in a location where CRB was likely to find them. The rules governing service of process are intended to give a defendant reasonable notice that an action has been brought.... In this instance, despite the best efforts of CRB, he was given reasonable notice of the action against him and, therefore, service under the circumstances of this case was sufficient.

        ....

CONCLUSION

Service of process on CRB by leaving the summons and complaint in his mailbox was sufficient given that CRB had refused to accept service and CRB was told that the summons and complaint would be left in close proximity to CRB such that he could easily retrieve the documents....

Affirmed.

———————

Service by Leaving a Copy at the Individual's Dwelling or Usual Place of Abode with Someone of Suitable Age and Discretion Who Resides There

"In most jurisdictions, statutes or rules authorize service of process by leaving a copy thereof at the residence, dwelling house, or place of abode, and the like, of the party to be served." 62B Am. Jur. 2d *Process* § 191 (2009). Typically, the process must be left "at the defendant's residence, place of abode, and the like, with some suitable person." *Id.* Such suitable persons include defendant's family members. *Id.* The issues that usually arise when service is effected in this way are two. The first question that frequently arises is what constitutes the defendant's "abode"? The second question often raised is whether the person on whom process was served is "suitable"?

Defining Abode

Statutes and cases refer alternately to "dwelling house," "usual place of abode," or "residence." In this discussion, the term "residence" will encompass these terms. The criteria for identifying a defendant's "residence" derive from a number of factors, including the following:

> [T]he retention of a room and storage of possessions there, the intention to return, the use of that address on official forms such as drivers' licenses and voters' registrations, the use of a telephone listing at that location, a failure to provide the post office with a forwarding address, the receipt of actual notice, and the defendant's ability to present at least some evidence that his or her abode is elsewhere.

Id. § 195. Most courts do agree that "it is the place where the person is living at the particular time when the service is made." *Id.* § 194.

A person's place of employment, under the general rule, does not equate to an individual's residence. Serving a defendant at her business will not suffice unless left with the defendant personally. *Id.* § 203. A person's "dwelling" becomes problematic when she lives in an apartment complex or multiple dwelling unit. In such circumstances, service is not complete if left in a part of the building "in which the party to be served does not actually reside, or does not exercise exclusive dominion and control." *Id.* § 201.

"Person of Suitable Age and Discretion"

Under Federal Rule of Civil Procedure 4 and similar state rules, process served at an individual's residence must be left with a person of suitable age and discretion. 62B AM. JUR. 2d *Process* §208 (2009). The criteria for the suitable-age-and-discretion standard are a factual determination. Usually, a member of defendant's "family," who is at least a teenager, will weigh in favor of suitability if the family member lives at the residence. *Id.* §210. *See, e.g., Trammel v. National Bank of Georgia*, 285 S.E.2d 590, 592 (1981) (finding that twelve-year-old daughter of defendant who resided at place of service with defendant was of "suitable age and discretion" and collecting other cases in which service on teenagers living with defendant upheld). In some states, a person need not be a family member to receive service at an individual's residence if the person receiving service has been residing there. *See* 62B AM. JUR. 2d *Process* §209 (2009) (requirement often focuses on whether the person receiving service has been "residing" at the residence).

"Nail and Mail" Service

Some jurisdictions have so-called "nail and mail" statutes. 62B AM. JUR. 2d *Process* §193 (2009). These statutes permit attaching the summons and complaint to the main door or entrance of the dwelling and, then, mailing the summons and complaint to the same address before continuing any default proceedings. *See, e.g.*, N.Y. C.P.L.R. 308 (2009); VA. CODE ANN. §8.01-296 (2009). "Nail and mail statutes" are used "when it is impossible to serve a party personally or to deliver the process to a person of suitable age and discretion at the party's dwelling or place of abode." VA. CODE ANN. §8.01-296 (2009); *see also id.* §8.01-204.

> Such "nail and mail" service may be used only where personal service cannot be effected by the use of "due diligence." Such a statute requires affixation of the summons to the door of the defendant's residence and then a mailing of the process to the defendant. This should be accomplished by use of a nail, tack, tape, rubber band, or some other device which will ensure adherence....

Id.

Service When a Party Cannot Be Served in Person or at Usual Place of Abode

Service by Mail

Many states allow service by mail when the defendant cannot be served in the more direct ways described in the preceding sections. *See* 62B AM. JUR. 2d *Process* §211 (2009) (service by mail). Also, state long arm statutes for serving nonresidents usually require service by mail through an official in the forum state, such as the secretary of state. *Id.* For mail service to be effective, a certification of such mailing to the court is always required. *Id.*

Service by Publication

All jurisdictions contain provisions for "constructive service of process or notice of the commencement of an action by publication, in place of service of the writ or summons upon the party personally." 62B AM. JUR. 2d *Process* §222 (2009). Only statutes may authorize service by publication. *Id.* Service by publication is an "extraordinary measure" and, therefore, may only be allowed in certain cases due to necessity when no other method of service is able to provide notice. *Id.* Publication statutes must only authorize such service upon residents when personal service

> is impossible or impracticable by reason of the fact that the defendant is a non-resident, or that he or she is absent from the state or not to be found therein, or that the defendant with intent to defraud his or her creditors or to avoid service of process has left the state or is concealing him- or herself within it with a like intent, and that unavailing efforts have been made to ascertain his or her whereabouts.

Id. § 227. Most jurisdictions require filing a motion and a "due diligence" affidavit to begin service by publication. *Id.* §§ 223, 226. The affidavit must contain the pertinent facts forming "the grounds for the issuance of an order directing publication" so that the court has "a factual basis to order service by publication." *Id.* § 224. The affidavit must further state that the defendant's residence is unknown. *Id.* § 227. This affidavit "must set forth facts indicating the serving party made a due diligent effort to locate an opposing party to effect personal service." *Id.*; *see also id.* § 228. If the court deems the affidavit sufficient, it will issue "an order directing publication in a newspaper of the summons and notice and, frequently, by mailing of notice to the defendant." *Id.* § 223. The notice usually runs in a newspaper or other publication circulated widely for several weeks. *Id.* § 235.

Service by Delivering a Copy of Each to an Agent Authorized by Appointment or by Law to Receive Service of Process

Most jurisdictions permit "personal service to be made upon an agent authorized by appointment or by law to receive service of process." 62B Am. Jur. 2d *Process* § 215 (2009); *see also id.* § 216. Agents may be appointed by private contract, by power of attorney, or by law. *Id.* §§ 218–20. An agent appointed by law (constructive agent) means one appointed by state or federal statute, not someone considered an agent under the common law of agency. *Id.* § 220.

Serving Parties Who Are Incapacitated or under a Legal Disability
Infants and Incompetents

"[M]ost" states prescribe a method of service against incompetents, but the Federal Rule of Civil Procedure 4 method for serving an individual may be followed if a state does not. 62B Am. Jur. 2d *Process* § 184 (2009). Also, states "ordinarily provide for the mode of service upon an infant defendant," requiring service upon designated persons. *Id.*

Follow-Up Questions

1. In the past, service was carried out by exclusively marshals in the federal system and sheriffs in the states. In recent years, however, servers may be anyone of a certain age (usually 18 or older) and not a party to the case. Thus, the person carrying out service for you may have little experience. What instructions should you give the person serving process? When advising a process server, you routinely should consider various situations that the server might

face, such as the defendant's absence but another person's presence at the residence. What questions should the process server ask to ensure she complies with the law of your jurisdiction? What should the process server tell the person receiving service about the contents of the process? In your jurisdiction, must the return of service be filed with the court and, if so, does the server that you employ understand that the return must be completed and filed?

2. Assume that you have met with your process server. She then goes to the defendant's residence and waits until the defendant arrives home from work. As the defendant walks to his front door, the process server asks him his name. Figuring out that he's about to be served, the defendant becomes belligerent and yells at the process server to "get off his property or he'll sue for trespass." When the process server tries to hand the process to the defendant, he refuses to accept anything. The process server then tosses the process at the defendant's feet and says: "You've been served with process in _____ case." As she's driving off, the process server hears the process packet hit the back of her car and sees it fall into the street. In the state in which you intend to practice, would a court consider this to be proper service on an individual defendant?

Practice Problems

Practice Problem 5-1

Jefferson's car collided with Hamilton's car. Hamilton filed suit to recover from Jefferson $20,000 for damage to Hamilton's car. A deputy sheriff attempted to serve process on Jefferson, who was not home to accept it. The deputy taped the summons and complaint to the front of Jefferson's curbside mailbox and told Jefferson's fourteen-year-old son, "Be sure your father sees this when he gets home." In your jurisdiction, has process been served properly?

[handwritten margin note: improper service, but if D gets it, if is, it is valid under cure statute]

[handwritten note: improper]

Practice Problem 5-2

Bruce Wayne was driving his automobile in the capital city of your state, when he struck and injured Christian Bale, a pedestrian. A week later, Wayne and his wife locked up their home, leaving no one in charge, and left for a vacation in the Bahamas. While they were gone, Bale brought an action against Wayne by filing a complaint to recover $500,000 for his injuries. A summons issued by the clerk was attached to a copy of Bale's complaint and delivered to a process server. The process server found no one present at the Wayne's home and, thus, posted the papers on the front door of the residence and made his return of proof of service to the court. Counsel for Bale then mailed the summons and complaint to Wayne's residence address via certified mail. When Mr. and Mrs. Wayne returned home, they were surprised to find that Bale had obtained judgment by default against Wayne for $500,000. In the state in which you plan to practice, was service proper and will the judgment stand?

Practice Problem 5-3

James Bowie spent half the year working as a businessman and living in a residence in a large city located in the same state where you plan to practice. He spent the rest of the year, during hunting and fishing season, living in his cabin on a lake in a rural area. Bowie entered into a business contract with Antonio

Santa Anna. Believing that Bowie had breached the contract, Santa Anna sued him for $100,000 and had a summons and complaint served at Bowie's cabin. Because no one was there, the process was posted on the front (and only) door. Santa Anna soon thereafter had a certified mail version of the summons and complaint mailed to the cabin's address. The service was mailed at a time when Bowie ordinarily would have been at his cabin, but in this instance he happened to be visiting an old friend, Sam Houston, in Texas. Research the law of the state in which you plan to practice and determine whether service on Bowie was proper.

Serving Corporate Entities

When serving a corporation, service of process must be made to a corporation's agents because corporations are, of course, made up of actual persons. 62B Am. Jur. 2d *Process* § 238 (2009). Generally, under Federal Rule of Civil Procedure 4 and similar state rules, "a summons and complaint are served upon a domestic or foreign corporation by delivering a copy of the summons and of the complaint to an officer, a managing or general agent, or to any other agent authorized by appointment or by law to receive service of process and, if the agent is one authorized by statute to receive service and the statute so requires, by also mailing a copy to the defendant." *Id.* Additionally, service may be made on corporate representatives "so integrated with the organization that he or she will know what to do with the papers." *Id.* As with the approach of the Federal Rules and those states that follow them, the options noted are not hierarchical. *See* Appendix 5-1 (showing most states follow non-hierarchical Federal Rules approaches). Thus, you need not try one method before using another permitted one.

Service by Delivering a Copy of the Summons and of the Complaint to an Officer

Service on a corporate officer is universally accepted as a means of serving process on a corporation. 62B Am. Jur. 2d *Process* § 241 (2009). When the corporate officer receives service of process, the corporation has actual notice of the action. *Id.* Corporate employees only temporarily within the state may also be served on behalf of the corporation provided that "reasonable assurance exists that the corporate defendant will receive actual notice." *Id.* § 243. However, service on such a temporary employee is effective only if the corporate defendant meets the "minimum contacts" personal jurisdiction test for the state in question. *Id.*

Service by Delivering a Copy of the Summons and of the Complaint to a Managing or General Agent

Another popular means of serving a corporation is by "delivering a copy of the summons and the complaint to a managing or general agent." 62B Am. Jur. 2d *Process* § 245 (2009). Neither managing nor general agents need be "specifically authorized by the corporation to accept service." *Id.* § 245. The employee's responsibilities, not her title, determine whether she qualifies as a managing or general agent. *Id.* § 247. For example, the title "manager" is not determinative. Instead, the key is whether the person has the type of responsibility such that she would be likely to get the process to the appropriate corporate official. *Id.*; *see also id.* § 248 (determining whether a sales representative or distributor exercises sufficient authority over the corporation to qualify as an agent).

Service by Delivering a Copy of the Summons and Complaint to Company Agent

Another typical option for corporate service is on a corporation's "registered agent." Such an agent is "authorized by appointment or by law to receive service of process and, if the agent is one authorized by statute to receive service and the statute so requires, by also mailing a copy to the defendant." 62B Am. Jur. 2d *Process* § 250 (2009). Many states have statutes constructively appointing a state officer as an agent (*e.g.*, official of the state corporation commission) for the corporation if it has failed to appoint a registered agent.

Follow-Up Question

Assume that you are retained to sue a corporation incorporated outside of your jurisdiction but which does regular business in the state in which you intend to practice. Most states require nonresident companies that do business regularly in a state to appoint a registered agent in the state for purposes of receiving service of process. Serving the registered agent, therefore, is likely to be the easiest and least expensive method of serving the corporation. What state agency is most likely to have records of the name and address of the registered agent for a company?

Professional Identity Question

Your client has a dispute with a corporation and asks you to handle the suit. The client wants to serve the president of the corporation in a manner best calculated to embarrass the president and to bring negative publicity to the corporation. According to your client, the corporation's president will be speaking at a local public event soon. There should be a large crowd and media coverage of the event. The client asks you whether you would be willing to have the president served in front of the crowd and media. How would you respond?

Practice Problems

Practice Problem 5-4

Carol sued Home State Corporation, a company organized and existing in the same state in which Carol lives and in which suit is filed. Her lawyer sends a process server to the defendant's corporate offices. When the process server asks the receptionist to see an officer, no officer responds. The only person who comes out to the lobby is the secretary to the corporation's public relations manager. The process server delivers the summons and complaint to this secretary. Is service valid? What criteria will determine whether the secretary is a person who qualifies as one on whom service may be effected for a corporate defendant?

Practice Problem 5-5

Gotcha Insurance Company has refused to pay a claim by your client, the insured, for no good reason. You search and cannot find a registered agent for Gotcha in your jurisdiction. Thus, you determine that you will likely have to sue Gotcha, using the statute accompanying the long arm statute for your state. (You have concluded that both the long arm statute and the due process principles would be satisfied by the exercise of personal jurisdiction.) In the law of the state where you plan to practice, what steps would you need to take so as to serve process on the nonresident? Is there a state representative on whom you can serve process who forwards the process on to the nonresident? If so, is the date that will govern the nonresident defendant's response (a) the date the nonresident receives the mailing, (b) the date the state representative's confirmation of compliance with state law and of mailing to the nonresident is received in the court clerk's office, or (c) some other date?

Service on Unincorporated Entities

Serving an Unincorporated Association

Similar to service of process on corporations, service of process on unincorporated associations — under Federal Rule of Civil Procedure 4 and similar state rules — may be effected when the association "is subject to suit under a common name; by delivering a copy of the summons and complaint to an officer, a managing or general agent, or to any other agent authorized by appointment or by law to receive service of process; and ... by also mailing a copy to the defendant [if the statute so requires]." 62B Am. Jur. 2d *Process* § 257 (2009).

Serving Partnerships

A partnership "or other unincorporated association which is subject to suit under a common name" may be served "by delivering a copy of the summons and complaint to an officer, a managing or general agent, or to any other agent authorized by appointment or by law to receive service of process, and ... by also mailing a copy to the defendant [if the statute so requires]." 62B Am. Jur. 2d *Process* § 258 (2009).

If you sue not only a partnership by serving its "general partner" or a "general manager of a partnership" but also seek relief from one or more partners "in their individual capacity," service upon the general partner or general manager must comply with the rules for service upon individuals. *Id.* Furthermore, even though partners may be liable for the torts of each other, "a vicariously liable partner" must be "individually named and served in the action." *Id.*

Follow-Up Question

If you are suing a partnership, how can you determine the partners in the partnership? Should you serve the partners that you identify at their places of business or at their homes? Does your answer depend on whether you are suing the partnership, an individual partner, or both?

Professional Identity Question

Suppose you have reason to believe that a partner you are about to sue for your client, if served individually and for the partnership as a whole, will hide the lawsuit from the other partners. Would you feel comfortable serving process only on that partner in those circumstances?

Practice Problem

Practice Problem 5-6

Pizza Partnership is a general partnership in your jurisdiction. Your client sues Pizza Partnership for negligence because she was seriously injured when she ate one of its pizzas that contained a piece of sharp metal under the cheese topping. You find out that there are three partners, Adam, Bob, and Carl, each of whom are businessmen in three different cities within the state where you intend to practice. After filing suit, how should you effect service of the suit seeking compensation for your client's injuries?

Serving a State or Municipal Corporation, and Other State Governmental Organizations

Plaintiffs usually accomplish service of process upon a state, a municipal corporation, or upon another governmental organization by serving a copy of the summons and complaint personally on the municipality's chief executive officer. 62B Am. Jur. 2d *Process* § 264 (2009). Typically, state laws also specify another "person or officer upon whom service of process is to be made" (*e.g.*, city or county attorney), and no other person may be substituted. *Id.* Service by mail upon a governmental entity is prohibited, absent a specific state or federal statute stating otherwise. *Id.*

The chief executive officer of a state is the Governor. *See* 62B Am. Jur. 2d *Process* § 264 (2009). Typically, however, statutes will authorize serving the Attorney General of a state in lieu of the Governor. *See id.*

Practice Problems

Practice Problem 5-7

Gladys had her son, Ray, committed to Southeastern State Mental Hospital ("Southeastern State") because of his lack of mental capacity. Southeastern State is owned and operated by the state in which you expect to practice. Ray is considered psychotic and, without supervision, represents a danger to himself. The hospital negligently failed to supervise Ray, and he left the grounds. He jumped off the overpass above a passing train and was killed. Gladys brought a wrongful death action against the State for negligence resulting in her son's death. What are her options in serving the State?

Practice Problem 5-8

Parade City holds a parade monthly. During one of its parades, a City-owned float veered off track and hit a young boy. The boy broke his leg and he had to wear a cast for six months. His parents retain you to sue the City for negligence. In the state in which you intend to practice, what are the options for serving the City?

[handwritten marginal note: notice will 6 months to city attorney + then serve city attorney]

Necessity for a Process Server's Return of Service

"A return of service completes the service of process, giving assurance that service really has been made and establishing that proceedings implementing the constitutional requirements of due process were followed." 62B AM. JUR. 2d *Process* § 278 (2009). Filing a return proving service affects the validity of service and also supports a default judgment entered against a defendant. *Id.* § 280. A sample of a return is included in the last half of the summons set forth earlier in this chapter. Usually, however, if the defendant does not raise the issue of failure to file a return of service, the issue is waived. The delay and added expense if failure to file is raised, however, provide the incentive to get it right the first time.

Follow-Up Question

Why should your process server make filing the return of service a routine practice?

Professional Identity Question

Suppose your process server typically does file a return of service. However, one time he does not and then leaves town. He left the incomplete return at your office because he was in a hurry. When he calls you from out of town, he asks whether you could complete the return and sign his signature for him. Would you do that?

Practice Problem

Practice Problem 5-9

Pat Plaintiff sues Nosy Neighbor for repeated trespasses. Pat's process server attaches a summons and complaint to the front door of the defendant's residence (no one was home). Within a week of such posting, Pat's lawyer sends a certified copy of the summons and complaint to the defendant. The process server fails to file a return of service. Defendant Neighbor moves to dismiss for insufficient service of process. Under the law of the state where you plan to practice, should the court grant the motion? If the court does grant the motion, would Pat be permitted to file again and have a second chance at serving Neighbor?

D. Methods to Reinforce and Integrate Topics Covered in This Chapter

A useful exercise is to compare the service requirements for each type of defendant. Make a chart with several columns. Label the headings as follows: Individual, In-State corporation, Out-of-State Corporation, Partnership, State Government, City Government (or in any other categories that makes sense to you). Under each column, list the service requirements for each type of defendant in the state where you intend to practice. Consider using the chart as a resource for training the process server(s) who you will hire to perform service of process.

E. Written Assignments

1. Assume the State of Illyria has the same service requirements as the state in which you plan to work. Further assume that the City of Arcadia is a city within that state. Identify the City personnel that are considered authorized representatives of the City for purposes of service. Then describe the steps you would take to serve the City on behalf of Sally in her suit against Arcadia.

2. As noted above, assume the State of Illyria is the State in which you will end up practicing law. Identify (1) the State personnel that are considered authorized representatives of the State for purposes of service; (2) who, under the State Tort Claims Act of the state in which you will practice, is identified as an authorized representative upon whom process may be served under the Tort Claims Act; (3) whether the persons identified in response to subparts (1) and (2) are different persons. Then describe what steps you would take to serve the State on behalf of Sally in her suit against Illyria.

3. Assume that the State of Illyria requires service on out-of-state defendants, such as HorsePower, Inc., in the same way as the state in which you intend to prac-

tice. Describe (1) how you can serve an out-of-state defendant such as HorsePower, Inc.; (2) what steps you would have to take in your State to send information, materials, fees, etc. to the appropriate state representative; and (3) what the State representative would then prepare, send to the nonresident, send to the trial court, etc. For purposes of this assignment, assume that the address of Horse-Power, Inc.'s corporate headquarters (where its president works), is 12345 Main Street, San Franco, Texafornia 54321.

Chapter 6

The Defendant Strikes Back: Responding on Behalf of a Client Who Has Been Sued

A. Sally's Case at This Stage of Litigation Process

You have been the associate representing Sally up to this point. As the next chapter on discovery process emphasizes, you could and probably should still be building your case. However, the ball is in the defendants' court now that the complaint has been served. Therefore, this chapter will ask you to shift roles. Now you will be alternately an assistant city attorney representing Arcadia, an assistant attorney general representing Illyria, and an associate in the law firm representing the manufacturer.

B. Tasks and Decision-Making at This Stage of a Case

The phase of litigation where the case now stands is highlighted in Diagram 6-1.

As defense counsel, you may start at a disadvantage. The plaintiff's lawyer has had the case for a longer period of time and, if she is worth her salt, has made valuable use of that time. In the pre-suit stage, plaintiff's counsel should have researched the law of each potential claim, the statute of limitations on each claim, and all possible defenses. Moreover, as suggested more fully in Chapter 4, plaintiff's counsel should have performed a thorough investigation, preserved evidence, and generally be in command of the case by the time of filing a complaint.

The reality is that most plaintiffs' lawyers do not take command of a case. Effective lawyers do, but they are in the minority. Even when facing an effective plaintiff's lawyer who has a strong command of the case, a defendant's lawyer can always catch up. She just has to be willing to work. The order of decisions and tasks will hinge on priorities. First and foremost, defense counsel must determine the best means to respond to the complaint in time to avoid default. That in turn requires her to determine the deadline for responding to the complaint. More strategically, defense counsel must help her client decide on the optimal pleading to file in response to a complaint.

Diagram 6-1

Cause of Action (events leading to suit)
Prefiling Matters to Consider; Choice of Forum [Chs. 2–3]
Π and Δ Decide on Offensive Pleadings & Joinder (of claims & parties); Filing Suit; Service [Chs. 4–5]
Motions, Responsive Pleadings; Default; Voluntary & Involuntary Dismissals [Chs. 6–7]
Discovery Phase (developing proof to establish claims & learning about the adversary's case) [Ch. 8]
Right to Jury Trial; Pretrial Motions & Practice [Ch. 9]
Final Pretrial Conference & Other Events within Last Month before Trial [Ch. 10]
Procedure at Trial [Ch. 11]
Post-Trial Motions & Calculating the Date of Final Judgment to Know Key Deadlines Such as for Notice of Appeal [Ch. 12]

For purposes of this chapter, we will assume that the defendant either has no basis for removing her case to federal court, or does not wish to do so.[1] Regardless, responsive pleadings may need to be filed in state court to avoid the possibility of being held in default if the case is remanded. *See, e.g.*, *Levine v. Lacy*, 204 Va. 297, 130 S.E.2d 297 (1963) (defendant removed case from state court to federal court without filing a responsive pleading in state court and, upon remand of the case to state court, defendant was held in default).

C. Overview of Applicable Law

Calculating the Response Deadline

The task of determining the date by which a response must be filed can be a surprisingly complicated one. If a defendant is served within the state in which the action is pending, the deadline typically is easy to calculate. The jurisdiction's law (and the sum-

---

1. Federal law provides that a defendant who wishes to remove his case to federal court must do so "[w]ithin 30 days after receipt by the defendant, through service or otherwise" of a pleading that indicates that the case is removable. 28 U.S.C. § 1446 (2008). In *Murphy Bros. v. Michetti Pipe Stringing*, 526 U.S. 344 (1999), the United States Supreme Court clarified the rather confusing language in the removal statute and held that the 30 day time period begins to run once proper service is effected on the defendant.

mons served with the complaint) will specify the amount of time a defendant has to respond (*e.g.*, 20 days, 21 days). Using the method of judicial counting described *supra* in Chapter 2 at pages 24–27, Day 1 of the prescribed period would be the day after a defendant has been served. Thus, if the deadline for a response is 21 days, the deadline will be 21 days after the day on which the defendant was served with process.

What if the defendant served is an out-of-state person or business entity? As noted in Chapter 5, almost every state allows a representative in the state where suit is pending (*e.g.*, secretary of the state) to be served as an "agent" of the nonresident if the long-arm statute of that jurisdiction is satisfied. Such statutes, moreover, typically set the date for when the defendant must file a response to the complaint. Unlike the general rule above, the deadline here is not based on the date that the defendant actually receives process (usually by mail in this situation). Instead, the deadline for responding (*e.g.*, 20 days, 21 days), typically runs from the date that the clerk of the court in which the action is pending receives and files the "certificate of compliance" that the state agency mails to the clerk simultaneously with its mailing of process to the nonresident defendant. Thus, defense counsel will misjudge the actual responsive pleadings deadline if she assumes that the period for responding runs from either (1) the date of service on a state agency, or (2) the date a nonresident receives the mailing from the state agency. Instead, in many if not most states, the deadline that will trigger the period for responsive pleadings is the date on which the clerk of court receives a certificate from the state agency confirming that process has been mailed to the nonresident.

Imagine this scenario. The jurisdiction in question requires a response within 21 days of service on a defendant or, when a nonresident is served through the secretary of the state, 21 days from filing of a "certificate of compliance" in the clerk's office. Plaintiff serves the nonresident defendant through a state agent (usually the secretary of state), who mails the process to the defendant and simultaneously mails a certificate of compliance to the court. The clerk receives the certificate and files it on March 1, and the nonresident receives the process on March 5. Defendant's counsel assumes that March 5 is the trigger date for the response deadline and further assumes she has until March 26 to respond. Proceeding on this assumption, defendant responds on March 25. However, because the trigger date for the response deadline in fact was March 1, defense counsel's failure to determine the correct response deadline has resulted in the default of her client. She may be able to get the client out of default through one of the ways discussed in the next chapter. However, counsel who has created a default scenario will face the embarrassment of explaining the problem to her client. How can defense counsel charge any fees for getting a client out of default when the lawyer's mistake caused the problem? In short, knowing when a response to a complaint must be filed is the "bread and butter" of defense counsel's job.

Deciding Whether, as a Nonresident, to Appear in Another State to Challenge Jurisdiction

Typically, the most difficult decision at the outset of litigation is not when to file, but what type of motion, pleading, or combination of these, presents the best strategic response. Sometimes a defendant, even after calculating her deadline, chooses not to file anything. This choice makes sense for an out-of-state defendant who has a strong basis for challenging personal jurisdiction. If a court entering a judgment lacks jurisdiction, the judgment will be void. A plaintiff who brings such a judgment from the state in which she received it and seeks to enforce it in the defendant's home state, may find that the defendant's home state is unwilling to enforce the judgment. However, the tactical decision here is important. Suppose the defendant's prediction is wrong and the defendant's home state court considers the out-of-state court to have had jurisdiction. If so, the home state court will have to enforce the other state's judgment, and there will be no trial on the merits. *See* U.S. CONST. art. IV (states required to give full faith and credit to judgments of other states). Thus, by deciding to wait and challenge personal jurisdiction, the defendant will lose her shot at being heard on the merits.

Defendants have been known to make half-hearted challenges when suit is brought in another state. An example would be to go to the other state, challenge personal jurisdiction solely, but then fail to appeal an adverse decision. The following case illustrates the danger of such an approach.

Baldwin v. Iowa State Traveling Men's Association
283 U.S. 522 (1931)

Mr. Justice ROBERTS delivered the opinion of the Court.

[The respondent (Iowa State Traveling Men's Association, defendant in the trial court), an Iowa corporation, asserted a lack of personal jurisdiction in a Missouri court proceeding. The Missouri court disagreed and maintained jurisdiction. The respondent then refused to participate further, and the Missouri court entered a default judgment against it. When the petitioner (Baldwin, plaintiff in the trial court) sought to enforce his judgment in Iowa, the respondent again raised the lack of personal jurisdiction argument and prevailed. The Supreme Court's reversal of that decision highlights the strategic blunder of the defendant's approach in choosing to appear in an out-of-state proceeding, but then failing to litigate the merits there or to appeal the adverse decision to the appellate court in that proceeding.]

The special appearance gives point to the fact that the respondent entered the Missouri court for the very purpose of litigating the question of jurisdiction over its person. It had the election not to appear at all. If, in the absence of appearance, the court had proceeded to judgment, and the present suit had been brought thereon, respondent could have raised and tried out the issue in the present action, because it would never have had its day in court with respect to jurisdiction.... It had also the right to appeal from the decision of the Missouri District Court.... It elected to follow neither of those courses, but, after having been defeated upon full hearing in its contention as to jurisdiction, it took no further steps, and the judgment in question resulted.

Public policy dictates that there be an end of litigation; that those who have contested an issue shall be bound by the result of the contest; and that matters once tried shall be considered forever settled as between the parties. We see no reason why this doctrine should not apply in every case where one voluntarily appears, presents his case and is fully heard, and why he should not, in the absence of fraud, be thereafter concluded by the judgment of the tribunal to which he has submitted his cause.

....

The judgment is reversed and the cause remanded for further proceedings in conformity with this opinion.

Reversed.

As already noted, *Baldwin* presents an odd twist—the defendant appeared in the litigation away from its home state, but after losing, stopped all litigation. Conversely, the safest approach—if a defendant wants to preserve her opportunity not only to defend on the merits, but also to raise personal jurisdiction—is to commit to litigate in the state where suit is filed. If the defendant chooses to challenge jurisdiction in the state away from her home, she should choose to defend to the end—through to trial and on to appeal. To do so, the defendant would (1) challenge jurisdiction; (2) if she loses, raise whatever defense on the merits she has; and then (3) if she loses on the merits, appeal to the appellate courts of that state not only the personal jurisdiction decision, but any error in trial on the merits. Conversely, if the defendant believes that lack of personal jurisdiction is so clear that it cannot reasonably be debated, she could choose to ignore the out-of-state proceedings, but she had better truly ignore them, as *Baldwin* teaches. Any appearance will trigger the opportunity for her "day in court." Even if the defendant makes a special appearance in a state that still allows one to do so without submitting to the court's jurisdiction, she will be stuck there if the court rejects the challenge. A defendant who has confidence in her personal jurisdiction defense should thus instead wait and, if the plaintiff seeks enforcement of the out-of-state judgment in the defendant's home state, then defend on the ground that the judgment is void due to lack of personal jurisdiction. An exception to the Constitution's Full Faith and Credit Clause, which otherwise requires a state to give effect to judgments of a sister state, is that void judgments get no such respect. *See, e.g., Milliken v. Meyer*, 311 U.S. 457, 462 (1940).

Follow-Up Questions

1. Baldwin sued the Iowa State Traveling Men's Association in Missouri. Baldwin entered a special appearance challenging personal jurisdiction over him in Missouri. (A "special appearance," discussed more fully *infra* at page 127), allows a defendant to appear in a case to contest personal jurisdiction without having the appearance waive her challenge to personal jurisdiction). The Missouri court rejected the challenge of the Iowa State Traveling Men's Association and upheld personal jurisdiction. Having lost on his personal jurisdiction challenge in the trial court, the defendant gave up. Why do you think the defendant gave up? Could the defendant have then litigated the merits of the case and, if she lost, appealed any errors in the trial and in the rejection of its personal jurisdiction defense?

2. Assume the facts set forth in the immediately preceding question. After a default judgment was entered in Missouri, plaintiff Baldwin filed suit in Iowa to enforce the judgment entered in Missouri, as a citizen is entitled to do under the Full Faith and Credit Clause of the U.S. Constitution. At that point, the defendant Iowa State Traveling Men's Association raised its personal jurisdiction defense again. However, the Court held that the defendant had had its day in court on the personal jurisdiction issue by choosing to raise it in Missouri. If, however, the defendant had chosen not to appear at all in Baldwin's Missouri suit, and Baldwin then sued on a default judgment in Iowa, would the Court in that scenario have held the defendant precluded from litigating the question of personal jurisdiction?

3. Assume the defendant Iowa State Traveling Men's Association chose to stay in Iowa after learning of the Missouri suit and, when plaintiff Baldwin came to Iowa with a Missouri default judgment, what could a defendant who waits at home like the Iowa State Traveling Men's Association litigate at the point when the plaintiff

is seeking to enforce the default judgment in Missouri? Is the defendant who takes this approach limited solely to challenging the question of whether the Missouri court had subject matter and personal jurisdiction? Can such a defendant also defend on the underlying merits of the plaintiff's claim—*i.e.*, whether the plaintiff was entitled to relief in the first state that entered the default judgment?

The following Practice Problem offers an illustration of the difficult decisions that defendants face in these situations.

Practice Problem

Practice Problem 6-1

Defendant, a small Texafornia[2] company called Pack-Tight, Inc. made a unique device—a scooter that could be folded up and carried like a large brief case, then unfolded and ridden. The device cost $15,000. Pack-Tight, Inc. maintained an Internet site with images of the scooter and business information (address, phone number, etc.). However, it was not interactive: customers could not place orders through the Internet site. Most of its sales were local, but it also sold scooters to customers who ordered the product by telephone and had it shipped to the customers' home states.

On a visit from his home in the state in which you plan to live, Aldo saw the scooter, bought one, and took it back to your state. After using it three times, the scooter fell apart. Aldo sued Pack-Tight in the court of general jurisdiction in your state. He served Pack-Tight, Inc. through the applicable long arm statute.

Assume that Pack-Tight does not respond, that Aldo gets a default judgment against it, and that Pack-Tight has no assets in your state. To enforce the judgment, Aldo must hire an attorney in Texafornia and rely on the Uniform Enforcement of Foreign Judgments Act.[3] This Act, which has been adopted with some variation in every state,[4] allows a person to "domesticate" a judgment from another state by filing suit, attaching the other state's judgment, and seeking to enforce the judgment in the new state. Why strategically may Pack-Tight have a sound basis for choosing not to respond in the suit in your state and to allow the case to go into default there? If it did so, would it have any defenses if Aldo came to Texafornia to enforce the judgment? Would those defenses be limited? If the scooter instructions stressed that certain maintenance must be completed each time the scooter was used, and Pack-Tight's inspection showed that the maintenance had not been done, would Pack-Tight be able to raise such a defense to the merits of Aldo's claim if Pack-Tight had chosen to sit and wait in Texifornia to defend any litigation? Conversely, if Pack-Tight goes to your state, challenges personal jurisdiction and loses, it will be unable to appeal the jurisdiction decision until after a trial and final judgment on the merits, and will also have to bear the expense of litigating. But could Pack-Tight in this scenario raise the defense of improper maintenance? After considering all of the above questions, assume that your research leads you to conclude that the odds

---

2. Texafornia should be considered the fictional fifty-second state in the Union, after Illyria, the fictional fifty-first state introduced in the Master Problem.

3. For a full discussion of this Act, see *Validity, Construction, and Application of Uniform Enforcement of Foreign Judgments Act*, 31 A.L.R. 4th 706 (1984).

4. *See id.* § 1.

are less than 50% that a court would rule that a court in your state has personal jurisdiction over Pack-Tight. In short, Aldo could obtain a default judgment in your state, have a copy of that judgment certified by the court in your state, and then file suit in Texafornia to enforce the judgment, but a Texafornia court more likely than not should hold the judgment void for lack of personal jurisdiction. Would you advise Pack-Tight that a decision to wait and fight in Texafornia is defensible because, even with a strong defense on the merits, Pack-Tight should win if it waits and attacks any judgment as void—not to mention it will spend less overall by this approach? What risk would you ensure Pack-Tight understands if it choses the wait-and-defend approach?

Ensuring a Responsive Pleading Is Filed and All Defenses Are Preserved

The preceding Practice Problem illustrates that the question of *whether* to respond is not an academic one. It also illustrates another important point—the first challenge a defendant should consider is personal jurisdiction. Historically, the easiest way to unintentionally waive the personal jurisdiction defense was to file a pleading that qualified under state law as a "general appearance" of the party in court, thereby submitting the action to the court's jurisdiction. By making a general appearance, the party would lose the ability to challenge personal jurisdiction. 4 Am. Jur. 2d *Appearance* § 2 (2009). Under the "General Appearance Doctrine," a defendant who wished to challenge personal jurisdiction had to make a special appearance in court for the sole purpose of raising that issue. Waiver by general appearance is now less prevalent because the majority of states (as under Federal Rule of Civil Procedure 12) permit the defendant to challenge personal jurisdiction simultaneously with other defenses, so long as it is raised in the initial filing. *See* Appendix 6-1 (showing majority of states follow Fed. R. Civ. P. 12). However, you should be aware that some states still follow the general appearance and special appearance doctrines. *See, e.g.*, Cal. Civ. Proc. Code § 410.50 (2009); Tex. R. Civ. P. 120(a) (2009); *see also* Appendix 6-1 (majority follows Fed. R. Civ. P. 12's approach).

Even if lack of personal jurisdiction is not a defense at issue, the attorney still must be on guard. For purposes of filing a response, not just any pleading will do. Some pleadings do not stop the clock on a defendant's deadline for filing responsive pleadings. If a defendant files such a pleading, she will go into default every bit as quickly as if she had filed nothing. Defense counsel must file a response that qualifies as a "responsive pleading"—*i.e.*, a pleading that stops the clock on the defendant's time to respond and, thus, precludes default. Furthermore, defense counsel must be careful not to inadvertently waive other defenses (discussed below) on behalf of her client. 72 C.J.S. *Pleading* § 161 (2009). Most often, a defendant will inadvertently waive a defense by failing to raise it along with her answer.

In most states a defendant can file an answer and a motion to dismiss (based on lack of personal jurisdiction, insufficient service, etc.) simultaneously. Marilyn J. Berger et al., Pretrial Advocacy 164 (2d ed. 2007). If the defendant chooses to file an answer as her only initial pleadings, she can avoid waiving possible defenses by listing them as affirmative defenses in her answer. *Id.* This strategy is useful when the defendant recognizes that she may have a better chance of successfully arguing a defense at a later time. At that point, she will have preserved all possible defenses and can raise them in a motion supported by facts gathered during the process of discovery process. Preserving defenses is important because, generally, defenses that are not asserted in the pleadings are waived. 71 C.J.S. *Pleading* § 161 (2009).

After (1) filing within the required deadline for responsive pleadings; and (2) preserving any defenses (by a motion and/or an Answer), the defendant can begin to choose between different litigation strategies. At this time, defense counsel's decision tree will separate along two branches. Diagram 6-2 illustrates the framework of such a decision tree upon which you may build in light of the particular law in your jurisdiction.

Diagram 6-2

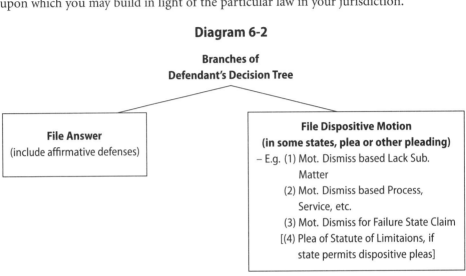

Branches of
Defendant's Decision Tree

File Answer
(include affirmative defenses)

File Dispositive Motion
(in some states, plea or other pleading)
– E.g. (1) Mot. Dismiss based Lack Sub.
    Matter
    (2) Mot. Dismiss based Process,
        Service, etc.
    (3) Mot. Dismiss for Failure State Claim
    [(4) Plea of Statute of Limitaions, if
        state permits dispositive pleas]

A defendant may choose to bring one or more challenges which, if successful, will end the lawsuit. (This choice is illustrated on the right branch of Diagram 6-2). Such challenges are typically by pre-answer motion raising a defense such as lack of personal jurisdiction. Some jurisdictions use other terms, often derived from common law pleading (*e.g.*, "pleas" or "pleas in bar") that raise an issue which, if decided in defendant's favor, brings the litigation to a close. (These jurisdictions that allow pleas are effectively permitting what are early summary judgment motions on a dispositive issue, such as the statute of limitations or res judicata). The defenses in this category may be referred to collectively as "dispositive challenges." Dispositive challenges may include the following:

1. Motion to dismiss for lack of subject matter jurisdiction;

2. Motion to dismiss for lack of personal jurisdiction;

3. Motion to dismiss for insufficient process (the summons is not proper, not filled out by the Clerk, etc., or the plaintiff fails to serve both a summons completed by the Clerk and a complaint, but rather serves only the complaint);

4. Motion to dismiss for insufficient service of process;

5. Motion to dismiss for failure to serve within the time period required by the jurisdiction in question;

6. Motion to dismiss for failure to state a claim upon which relief can be granted; and/or

7. Motion for summary judgment (or plea) seeking dismissal based on a single factual defense, unrelated to the merits that, if true, should result in dismissal (includes dismissal based on statute of limitations, res judicata, illegality of alleged contract, etc.).

If the defendant prevails on a dispositive challenge, the suit will be dismissed. A successful attack at the outset, on grounds separate from the merits of the case, saves considerable time and expense. If the court allows an amendment to cure the defect that led to dismissal, then the pre-answer motion simply delays matters. Later, this chapter will explore potential dispositive challenges in more detail.

The other branch of the decision tree is a simple response: answer the allegations in the complaint. An answer puts the parties at issue, and gets the litigation into the discovery phase. An answer can preserve defenses such as lack of personal jurisdiction, statute of limitations, res judicata, or the like, that might be brought as dispositive challenges. Thus, defense counsel has the option of pursuing dispositive challenges at the outset or preserving them in an answer by including them as affirmative defenses. Then she can prepare to bolster the challenge through discovery and research. After counsel believes that she has gathered sufficient evidence and discovery to prevail on the defense, she typically would file a summary judgment motion. (Summary judgment motions are discussed *infra* in Chapter 9.)

Deciding whether to bring a pre-answer motion or other dispositive challenge, or to file an answer and preserve defenses to be raised later, is precisely the kind of strategic decision-making in which effective lawyers must engage. Strategic decision-making at any stage of a lawsuit is more art than science. All too often, lawyers do their clients a disservice when they reflexively file pre-answer motions, especially when they might have a greater chance of prevailing on a particular issue if they wait. In other words, without thinking (or worse, to justify billing as much as possible), lawyers often file motions that either have little chance of success or can be easily fixed by an amended pleading. They may be able to charge an unsophisticated client for such motions. The effect often is a waste of time and resources. The effective defense counsel takes a different tack. Just as a plaintiff's lawyer should thoroughly research the elements of each claim that is pled, effective defense counsel research the elements of the plaintiff's claims, and all available defenses that could defeat the claims, so as to timely identify deficiencies and affirmative defenses. A lawyer can form an effective defense strategy and help her client make informed decisions only after doing appropriate legwork and research. Following this approach, the defense lawyer may realize that filing a motion will only alert the plaintiff to a deficiency that can be amended. If so, the defendant may wait until plaintiff puts on her evidence at trial and rests, and then move to have the case dismissed based on the deficiency of which plaintiff's counsel never became aware until too late. Such judgments by defense counsel are the essence of effective advocacy.

At this point, a skilled defense lawyer will also consider the "momentum" or "credibility" component to litigation. The policy favoring a case's going forward ("momentum") presents an obstacle to the a defendant seeking dismissal for failure to state a claim upon which relief can be granted. Influenced by the philosophy of the Federal Rules of Civil Procedure, which were adopted in 1938, most state court systems traditionally have stacked the cards in favor of a plaintiff's case at the early stages of the case—allowing it to proceed beyond the pleading stage in the interest of resolving cases on the merits rather than on a lawyer's ability to draft pleadings. *See supra* Chapter 4 at pages 75–77 (discussion of pleading standards); *see also* John B. Oakley & Arthur F. Coon, *The Federal Rules in State Courts: A Survey of State Court Systems of Civil Procedure*, 61 WASH. L. REV. 1367 (1986). Very few states allow a defendant to take issue with the facts pled in a plaintiff's complaint, and inferences from the facts that are pled are viewed in the light most favorable to the plaintiff. *See supra* Chapter 4 at page 75; *see also* 61A AM. JUR. 2d *Pleading* § 84 (2009). Especially in state courts, modern pleading practice ensures that the allegations in a pleading will be liberally construed in favor of the pleader. *Id.* §80. True, the recent U.S. Supreme Court's decisions adopting an apparently heightened pleading standard under Federal Rule 8 have influenced some state supreme courts[5] and could have a broader impact on other states over time. *Ashcroft v. Iqbal*, 129 S. Ct. 1937 (2009); *Bell Atlantic Corp. v. Twombly*, 550 U.S. 544 (2007). Although a defendant can rely on these decision to more aggressively challenge pleadings than in the past, she ought not be surprised if state courts are slow to accept the notion that plaintiff must plead with specificity matters other than fraud, mistake, or such matter traditionally considered to be the only ones requiring particularized pleading.

When reviewing the complaint, defense counsel should ask at least two questions: (1) has the plaintiff alleged enough facts on each element of a claim so that my client knows why she is being sued; and (2) are the claims actionable in my jurisdiction? If the answer to both questions is "yes," filing a motion to dismiss for failure to state a claim makes little sense. The most likely result is that you will waste your client's time and money. Even if the court grants the motion, the plaintiff will receive leave to amend and can correct a deficiency. Needless to say, if the answer to either question is a resounding "no," a motion to dismiss for failure to state a claim is appropriate. Knowing when to file, and when not to file, takes sound judgment.

As noted above, yet another strategic factor urges caution before launching a motion to dismiss. When defense counsel files a motion to dismiss, she will often highlight the weaknesses in the plaintiff's case. Plaintiff's counsel then will have ample opportunity to strengthen her case and amend the complaint if necessary. Consider the alternative: the defendant does not file a motion, plaintiff's counsel fails to recognize one or more vulnerabilities, and then the defendant challenges them at a time when the plaintiff can do little or nothing—such as at summary judgment or at trial. In other words, the defendant's motion to dismiss is often a road map for the plaintiff's counsel to prepare her case. Conversely, a plaintiff's lawyer is far less likely to pay attention to an affirmative defense subtly tucked away in an answer. There, the defense is still preserved, and defense counsel can raise the challenge at an appropriate time.

Although the preceding paragraphs urge caution in bringing dispositive challenges, two scenarios justify bringing these challenges at the outset, or at least reasonably early in the litigation. First, if the defendant believes that the challenge has a strong basis, and that the plaintiff cannot fix the problem, then the challenge should be brought at the outset. One example would be a personal jurisdiction defense that is rock solid. A second example would be a plaintiff's complaint that asserts a claim not recognized under applicable law. For that defect, the plaintiff cannot amend the complaint in order to correct the problem. The complaint will be defective no matter how many times it is amended.

In addition, defense counsel should recognize that certain defenses are more likely to be granted if pursued earlier in the litigation rather than later. Theoretically, the defendant can choose to forego a pre-answer motion and raise personal jurisdiction, insufficient process, or insufficient service of process at a later time by preserving these defenses in an answer. However, at some point a court will consider the defendant to have waived such a defense by actively litigating in the forum. Such a result is only common sense. If

---

5. *Compare Iannacchino v. Ford Motor Co.*, 888 N.E.2d 879, 889–90 (Mass. 2008) (noting a heightened standard for pleading based upon the language used by the Court in *Twombly* to "retire" the "no set of facts" pleading standard of *Conley*), *with Bock v. Gold*, 184 Vt. 575, 576, 959 A.2d 990, 992 (2008) (maintaining adherence to notice pleading stand and finding any reliance on *Twambly* "misplaced").

a court and parties have invested considerable resources in a case, the court will be reluctant to pull the rug out from under the plaintiff by dismissing a case based on a defense that could have been brought much earlier.

Deadline for, and Options in, Responding to Complaint

Once served, a defendant has a limited time within which to file responsive pleadings, or she will be in default. This time period varies by state, but it is generally about 20 days (absent waiver of process which extends the time period). *See* Appendix 6-1 (states adopting Federal Rule of Civil Procedure 12, though with some variation on the 21-day period in that Rule for responding). To keep a defendant out of default, defense counsel must file a pleading that properly qualifies as a "responsive pleading" in the jurisdiction where the case was filed. Various pre-answer motions qualify as responsive pleadings and will serve to keep the defendant out of default. Most state courts have adopted pleading rules that closely follow the federal system, providing the defendant with the option of filing either a pre-answer motion or an answer. *See* Appendix 6-1. Because complete uniformity does not exist, however, defense counsel should research the rules of procedure in the jurisdiction in which the case is pending to be sure that the pleading she files qualifies as a responsive pleading.[6]

Much, if not all of the previous discussion focused on the defendant's perspective. However, the rules concerning pre-answer motions, answers, and defenses to a complaint apply equally to a plaintiff who has had claims asserted against her in a counterclaim. Likewise, when a defendant asserts a cross-claim against a co-party, the co-party must consider these rules in responding to the claim. Finally, a third-party defendant brought into the suit by an original defendant would, of course, have to engage these questions as well.

Pre-Answer Motions

Many states now follow the model of Federal Rule of Civil Procedure 12. *See* Appendix 6-1 (reflecting states that follow the approach of Fed. R. Civ. P. 12). Rule 12 provides in pertinent part as follows:

Rule 12

(a) TIME TO SERVE A RESPONSIVE PLEADING.

(1) *In General.* Unless another time is specified by this rule or a federal statute, the time for serving a responsive pleading is as follows:

(A) A defendant must serve an answer:

(i) within 21 days after being served with the summons and complaint; or....

(b) **How to Present Defenses.** Every defense to a claim for relief in any pleading must be asserted in the responsive pleading if one is required. But a party may assert the following defenses by motion:

(1) lack of subject-matter jurisdiction;

---

6. For an interesting discussion of variances between procedural rules, see Stephen N. Subrin, *Federal Rules, Local Rules, and State Rules: Uniformity, Divergence, and Emerging Procedural Patterns,* 137 U. Pa. L. Rev. 1999 (1989).

(2) lack of personal jurisdiction;

(3) improper venue;

(4) insufficient process;

(5) insufficient service of process;

(6) failure to state a claim upon which relief can be granted; and

(7) failure to join a party under Rule 19.

Rule 12 [handwritten margin note]

Fed. R. Civ. P. 12 (emphasis added); *see* Appendix 6-1 (reflecting states that follow Fed. R. Civ. P. 12).

Waivable Defenses

The four defenses emphasized in bold above are sometimes called "disfavored" defenses. Joseph W. Glannon, Civil Procedure: Examples and Explanations 369 (6th ed. 2008). Others prefer to call them the easily "waivable" defenses. Federal Rule 12 and state counterparts provide that these defenses must be raised in a defendant's initial response—specifically, in a pre-answer motion, or as an affirmative defense in the answer within the time period allowed for responding to the complaint—or the defendant will waive the defense permanently. *Id.*; *see, e.g.*, Ohio R. Civ. P. 12(h).

response = pre-answer motion OR affirmative defense in answer [handwritten margin note]

Requiring the defendant to raise these defenses in her initial response promotes both judicial efficiency and fairness to the opposing party. Otherwise, a defendant could knowingly "save a defense" for later when the case is going poorly on the merits, and then pull out that defense as her "ace" by which to obtain dismissal, and thus waste substantial time and resources. Unlike other defenses that a defendant may not discover until later in the litigation process, waivable defenses are ones of which the defendant should be aware of at the onset of litigation. To illustrate, a defendant knows the manner in which she was served and can determine whether service was "proper." She also knows the degree of contacts she has with a particular state and can challenge personal jurisdiction at the outset of the case if the contacts are insufficient.

purpose ✕ of easily waived def's [handwritten margin note]

judicial efficiency & fairness [handwritten margin note]

Under the Federal Rule 12 model followed in most states, a defendant can waive defenses in two ways. The first way is by making a pretrial motion that does not include the defense. The second is, if the defendant foregoes a pre-answer motion, by failing to include the defense in the answer or an amendment to it. The importance of the waiver provisions deriving from subsections (g) and (h) of Federal Rule 12 bears emphasis. Many states have the same provisions. *See* Appendix 6-1. Following are the entirety of subsections (g) and (h) in Rule 12:

how to waive [handwritten margin note]

(g) **Joining Motions.**

(1) *Right to Join.* A motion under this rule may be joined with any other motion allowed by this rule.

(2) *Limitation on Further Motions.* Except as provided in Rule 12(h)(2) or (3), a party that makes a motion under this rule must not make another motion under this rule raising a defense or objection that was available to the party but omitted from its earlier motion.

(h) **Waiving and Preserving Certain Defenses.**

(1) *When Some Are Waived.* A party waives any defense listed in Rule 12(b)(2)-(5) by: *(the easily waived def's)*

> (A) omitting it from a motion in the circumstances described in Rule 12(g)(2); or

> (B) failing to either:

>> (i) make it by motion under this rule; or

>> (ii) include it in a responsive pleading or in an amendment allowed by Rule 15(a)(1) as a matter of course.

more flexible →

(2) *When to Raise Others.* Failure to state a claim upon which relief can be granted, to join a person required by Rule 19(b), or to state a legal defense to a claim may be raised:

> (A) in any pleading allowed or ordered under Rule 7(a);

> (B) by a motion under Rule 12(c); or

> (C) at trial.

most flexible

(3) *Lack of Subject-Matter Jurisdiction.* If the court determines at any time that it lacks subject-matter jurisdiction, the court must dismiss the action.

Even the best of lawyers find the interplay between Rules 12(g) and 12(h) somewhat perplexing. However, an experienced lawyer would work through the provisions in a step-by-step fashion. In so doing, she would understand that the possibilities of waiver (some would call them traps) are quite clear. Our lawyer would begin with the subdivision that refers to "waiving" defenses, subdivision (h). That section speaks to a party who has filed a motion under Rule 12. The lawyer would have to know whether the defendant answered first or had filed a pre-answer motion. We will assume here that the defendant filed a pre-answer motion and we will deal with the "answer scenario" next. Our seasoned lawyer would then read the first part of subdivision (h), which provides that the moving party waives a defense by failing to "make it by motion under this rule." Fed. R. Civ. P. 12(h)(1)(B)(1). However, the defendant did make a motion, so what is the problem? "Well," as our lawyer would say, "you must go back up to Rule 12(g) to see what kind of failure this is referring to." Specifically, Rule 12(g) precludes a party who has filed a Rule 12 motion from filing "another motion under this rule raising a defense or objection that was available to the party but omitted from its earlier motion." Rule 12(g)(2). This scenario, our experienced lawyer would say, requires that someone has filed a pre-answer motion but has left out one of the following specified defenses—12(b)(2) (personal jurisdiction), 12(b)(3) (venue), 12(b)(4) (improper process), 12(b)(5) (insufficient service of process)—that was available under Rule 12 and *could have been* included in the first motion. Concluding her analysis, our lawyer would then read, at the end of subdivision (g), the effect of omitting some basis for a motion under Rule 12 in the initial motion is that: a "party waives any of the defenses in Rule 12(b)(2)-(5)." Thus, the expert would announce: "Filing the Rule 12 motion here, but having left out one of the four defenses in 12(b) available at the time of the initial Rule 12 motion, resulted in waiver of the defense left out of the initial motion."

The second way to waive a defense is, if the defendant chose not to file a pre-answer motion, by failing to include it in the answer. Rule 12 and its state counterparts mandate this type of waiver as well. *See* Appendix 6-1. Here, again, we would benefit from observing the cognitive process of a seasoned lawyer as she reads through the rest of Rule 12. As she notes, Rule 12(h) specifically singles out—after it refers to waiver by a motion that omits one of these defenses—another way to waive the four defenses of lack of personal jurisdiction (Rule 12(b)(2)), improper venue (Rule 12(b)(3)), insufficient process (Rule 12(b)(4))

[handwritten margin notes: Scenario 1: motion • (h) — start here • b did Δ fail to make a motion? (g) did she have ability to make motion? • on (b)(3)(2)(4) er (5). If so, & if rule 12 not filed, & there was basis to file rule 12(b)(2)-(5) then no (2)-(5) are waived]

and insufficient service of process (Rule 12(b)(5)). Rule 12(h) provides, as she observes, that these four defenses will be waived "if … neither made by motion under this rule nor included in a responsive pleading or an amendment thereof permitted by Rule 15(a) to be made as a matter of course." The lawyer recognizes that the first part of the quoted language describes waiver by omission from a Rule 12 motion (the same waiver scenario she analyzed above). However, the second part also provides for waiver when one of the four defenses is not raised "in a responsive pleading or an amendment thereof permitted by Rule 15(a) to be made as a matter of course." Because the language allows for an exception (the amendment as a matter of course), she turns to Rule 15(a)(1)(B), which states that a party may amend its pleading (*i.e.*, answer) once as a matter of course "within 21 days after serving the pleading if a responsive pleading is not allowed and the action is not yet on the trial calendar." Thus, the second way in which a party can waive one of the four waivable defenses is by failing to include the defense in her answer or to amend that answer in the typically brief period permitted "of right" after a responsive pleading is filed.

Follow-Up Question

Do the rules regarding waiver seem "harsh" to you? Are you surprised by any of the "waivable" or "disfavored" defenses? Or do you consider the waiver rules necessary incentives for defendants who are prone to causing delays in the litigation process? These rules grounds for dismissal seems geared more towards getting Δ to sit in one place & not try to move around later on if their case starts to go against their favor

Professional Identity Question

If you had no basis for asserting personal jurisdiction over a defendant in the forum in which you want to sue, would you consider filing such a suit appropriate? Could you justify the filing based on the possibility that the defendant would waive the personal jurisdiction defense by failing to raise the defense in a timely fashion?

Practice Problems

Practice Problem 6-2

Peppy Plaintiff and Dierdre Defendant are citizens of different states. Peppy brings a personal injury claim seeking damages arising out of a car accident that occurred while he was visiting family in the state of which Dierdre is a citizen. Peppy files suit in the state where he lives so as to minimize litigation expenses. The only time that Dierdre has ever set foot in Peppy's home state was 10 years earlier when he temporarily worked on a job assignment there. Peppy serves Dierdre but, in the process of mailing by the appropriate state official, the summons is damaged by water—on receiving the summons and complaint, Dierdre can read the response deadline but cannot make out the clerks's signature.

Dierdre files a motion to dismiss based solely on insufficiency of process. The court denies the motion. Dierdre files a second motion to dismiss, including this time a challenge to personal jurisdiction. Plaintiff opposes the motion on the ground that the defendant has waived any challenge to personal jurisdiction. Research the law of the state in which you intend to practice and determine whether the personal jurisdiction defense has been waived.

Practice Problem 6-3

Plaintiff, Cardservice International, Inc. ("CSI") is incorporated in Texafornia and has its principal place of business there. CSI is the owner of certain trade secrets by which it has been able to provide credit and debit card processing services less expensively than competitors. WRM Associates, Inc. ("WRM") is a company with its principal place of business in a state other than CSI. WRM has set up an Internet website offering card processing services and calls itself "The Cardservice Company." A former officer of CSI set up WRM and used CSI's trade secrets to accomplish card processing in the less expensive manner only CSI had accomplished to date. CSI has had some business activity in the state in which you intend to practice, but its main connection with the state is the location of its preferred outside counsel. A couple of businesses in the state in which you intend to practice have seen the WRM website, but there is no evidence of a person or business in that state using WRM's card processing services.

CSI sues WRM in a court of general jurisdiction in your state. CSI's complaint alleges misappropriation of trade secrets, a claim actionable in your state. WRM files an answer denying the allegations in CSI's complaint. Two months after filing its answer, WRM moves for leave to file an amended answer raising lack of personal jurisdiction and improper venue as defenses. CSI opposes the motion on the grounds that WRM has waived these defenses. Research the law of your state and determine whether the defenses have been waived.

[handwritten margin notes: answer / motion for leave to file amend answ.]

Other State-Specific Waivable Defenses

Each state may have other defenses that will be waived if defense counsel does not raise them as required by state law. For example, most states' civil procedure rules will provide a deadline for serving the complaint, usually measured from the date the action is filed. The court can dismiss the plaintiff's claim if the plaintiff fails to properly serve the summons and complaint on the defendant within the jurisdiction's service deadline. 62B AM. JUR. 2d *Process* § 121 (2009). The majority of jurisdictions emulate Federal Rule 4(m), which provides that the trial court can dismiss the case *without prejudice* if the complaint is not served within 120 days. *Id.* § 123. Some states allow longer—for instance, a year from filing suit—and in return make the failure to serve within a year one in which dismissal can be *with prejudice*. *See, e.g.*, VA. SUP. CT. RULE 3:3 (2009) (requiring service within one year of filing); *Gilbreath v. Brewster*, 250 Va. 436, 463 S.E.2d 836 (1995) (failure to serve within one year requires dismissal with prejudice).

[handwritten margin note: turn in service or then or be dismissed w/ prej.]

Jurisdictions that have adopted Federal Rule 12(f) provide the defendant with the option of filing another type of responsive pleading—a "motion for a more definite statement." In some states, the motion is called a "motion for bill of particulars." *See, e.g.*, 735 ILL. COMP. STAT. ANN. § 5/2-607 (West 2009); N.Y. C.P.L.R. § 3041 (McKinney 2009). This type of motion may be filed when the allegations in the complaint are so vague, unintelligible, or ambiguous that the defendant cannot prepare a response. 61A AM. JUR. 2d *Pleading* § 464. Failure to bring this type of pre-answer motion should result in waiver of the defendant's right to

[handwritten margin note: motion for bill of particulars/ 12(f) must move for early]

challenge the complaint's definiteness at a later time. *Id.* § 467. In the notice pleading system, however, discovery provides a vehicle for fleshing out the facts of the case. *Id.* § 464.

Motions to Dismiss (Not all about 12(b)(6), but some)

Motions to Dismiss When Claim Asserts Grounds Other Than Fraud, Mistake, or Another Matter Typically Required to Be Pled with Particularity

The most common defense motion is a motion to dismiss for failure to state a claim upon which relief may be granted, often referred to in federal practice as a "Rule 12(b)(6) motion," or in some state jurisdictions as a "motion for failure to state a claim." 61A Am. Jur. 2d *Pleading* § 536 (2009). *See, e.g.,* Fla. R. Civ. P. 1.140(b) (motion to dismiss for failure to state a cause of action).

In common law pleading, the demurrer serves as the functional equivalent of the federal system's Rule 12(b)(6) motion to dismiss. 71 C.J.S. *Pleading* § 666 (2009). The Federal Rules abolished demurrers, and most states followed. *See, e.g.,* N.C. R. Civ. P. 7(c). However, some states still employ the demurrer or a similar device. *See, e.g.,* Va. Sup. Ct. R. 3:8 (recognizing "demurrers" as a responsive pleading); *cf.* Pa. R. Civ. P. 1028(a)(4) (illustrating a state's unique terminology for a device that serves the same function as a demurrer: "preliminary objection"). Regardless of a state's name for this kind of challenge, it serves the same function — challenging the legal sufficiency of the pleading as a matter of law. 61A Am. Jur. 2d *Pleading* §§ 536, 666 (2009). The rules for deciding whether to dismiss a case are also the same. The court must stay within the record, typically the complaint, and treat the well-pled facts as true. *Id.* § 537. In other words, the defendant cannot dispute the facts of the complaint and the court affords all reasonable inferences from the facts to the plaintiff.

In two scenarios, the defendant often prevails on a motion to dismiss for failure to state a claim upon which relief can be granted. The first occurs when the plaintiff has asserted a claim, such as social host liability, and the jurisdiction in question does not recognize such a claim. *See, e.g., Charles v. Siegfried,* 651 N.E.2d 154 (Ill. 1995) (court dismissed complaint for asserting a claim not recognized as actionable in Illinois). When the claim simply is not actionable, the court is unlikely to grant leave to amend. 71 C.J.S. *Pleading* § 358 (2009). In the second scenario, the claim is actionable, but the plaintiff has failed to allege facts supporting one or more elements of the claim. Here, the court is likely to grant leave to amend so that the plaintiff can allege these facts if she is able. *Id.* § 355. In keeping with modern notice pleading practice, an attack on a complaint for defect of form typically has been difficult. However, recent U.S. Supreme Court decisions appear to raise the bar in pleading facts under Federal Rule 8 and have influenced some state supreme courts in their interpretation of state rules based on the Federal Rule. *See Aschroft v. Iqbal,* 129 S. Ct. 1937 (2009); *Bell Atlantic Corporation v. Twombly,* 550 U.S. 544 (2007).[7] Although it remains to be seen, these decisions could have a broader effect over time and lead states to require more specificity in pleading claims. If that happens, the ability to challenge complaints based on insufficiently pled facts will be greater.

Often plaintiffs will allege claims based on instruments, such as contracts, leases or deeds that are not attached to the complaint. Unless these instruments are made a part

---

7. *See supra* this chapter note 5.

[handwritten margin notes: "1. Claim not recognized as actionable" / "2. failure to support main claim (failure to amend) (likely: leave to amend) (more likely to be raised) See Twiqbal" / "Statutory Attachment requirement"]

[handwritten: attachment cont.]

of the record, the court cannot consider them on a motion to dismiss but rather must wait until a summary judgment motion. Because in some instances the instrument will provide the basis for a dispositive challenge to the complaint, defense counsel should be aware of methods to get such instruments into the record immediately. Many states have a statute requiring that a document on which a suit is based be attached to the complaint as an exhibit. *See* Fla. R. Civ. P. 1.130 (West 2009) (complaint based on a written instrument does not state a cause of action until the instrument or an adequate portion thereof is attached to, or incorporated, in the pleadings); Ill. Comp. Stat. Ann. 735 § 5/2-606 (West 2009);[8] 71 C.J.S. *Pleading* § 526 (2009). If the instrument is not attached to the complaint, the pleading is considered defective, and the defendant may file a motion to dismiss. *See, e.g.,* Fla. R. Civ. P. 1.130.

[handwritten: craving oyer]

In the alternative (or in a jurisdiction that does not have a statute or case requiring attachment of the document), a defendant can move to require the plaintiff to file with the pleadings the written instrument that forms the basis of the suit. The plaintiff may be required to furnish a copy of the instrument to the defendant within a certain amount of time. 71 C.J.S. *Pleading* § 525 (2009). Traditionally called "craving oyer," this mechanism—a vestige of common law pleading—allows a defendant to move for production of a document that is referred to in, but not attached to, the complaint. *Id.* § 521. The court may order a copy of the document (*e.g.,* contract, deed, or lease) to be produced and placed in the record so that the defendant can properly prepare a defense. *Id.* §§ 520, 525.

For example, suppose the plaintiff is suing on a contract that the defendant suspects is invalid. The contract is not attached to the complaint. In ruling on a motion to dismiss at this stage of the litigation, the court is limited to the facts pled. Thus, the defendant cannot get the case dismissed without this crucial document on the record. Recognizing the ability to achieve early dismissal if the contract is included in the record, the defendant moves for the contract to be produced and included in the record. After the defendant has in common law parlance "craved oyer," the court may properly consider a document such as the contract as part of the facts pled. *See* 71 C.J.S. *Pleading* § 522 (2009). Once a document sued upon is made a part of the record, the defendant at times can rely on provisions in that document showing that the plaintiff's claim lacks merit. This procedure saves the time and expense of discovery when the instrument at issue provides a dispositive defense. A document required by statute or, through the common-law mechanism of "craving oyer," is considered part of the complaint. Thus, the court would not be going beyond the plaintiff's own complaint in ruling on a motion based on the instrument. If a defendant can rely on the instrument sued on (*e.g.,* contract, lease), it effectively can bring a more robust motion to dismiss for failure to state a claim. By relying on such a document, the defendant will not always win a dispositive motion, but she will win in some cases. In those cases, defense counsel's knowledge of and ability to use craving oyer, or the equivalent, will save her client a great deal of expense. Some states lack a statute requiring the instrument supporting a claim to be attached to the complaint, or the craving oyer mechanism. In these states, a defendant will have to seek summary judgment, as soon as possible, as the method of raising a defense based on an instrument on which a plaintiff bases her claim.

[handwritten: No attachment req. or craving oyer req.]

---

8. The Illinois statute reads as follows:

Exhibits. If a claim or defense is founded upon a written instrument, a copy thereof, or of so much of the same as is relevant, must be attached to the pleading as an exhibit or recited therein, unless the pleader attaches to his or her pleading an affidavit stating facts showing that the instrument is not accessible to him or her. In pleading any written instrument, a copy thereof may be attached to the pleading as an exhibit. In either case the exhibit constitutes a part of the pleading for all purposes.

Motions to Dismiss When Claim Is for Fraud, Mistake, or Other Matter Typically Required to Be Pled with Particularity

If the complaint alleges fraud, mistake, or some other matter that requires particularized pleading, the defendant may file a motion to dismiss (or demurrer) if the complaint is not sufficiently specific. *See* 37 Am. Jur. 2d *Fraud and Deceit* §450 (2009). For example, in a fraud claim, the plaintiff must plead each element of fraud and the specific facts relied upon to satisfy each element. *Id.* §452; *see, e.g.*, Mass. R. Civ. P. 9. Typically, the plaintiff must allege the specific communications, the parties to these, the dates of any such communications, the manner in which they are fraudulent, and why the plaintiff could reasonably rely on the statements. 37 Am. Jur. 2d *Fraud and Deceit* §464 (2009). One reason for requiring particularity in certain types of claims is that the claims involve matters that are more difficult to defend without specifics, so the defendant needs to be properly put on notice of the specifics of the claim in order to prepare a defense. *Id.* §453. Another reason for the requirement is that a fraud claim implicates a person's reputation—somthing that the law does not want plaintiffs to be able to do casually. *See id.* Also, if the plaintiff is asserting other claims in which the defendant's reputation could suffer from the complaint's allegations, a jurisdiction may require particularized pleadings, just as with fraud or mistake. *Id.*

Practice Problems

Practice Problem 6-4

In Chapter 4, Brad T. Rex sues Ena Hurry over a motor vehicle accident and the subsequent pushing, shoving, and yelling. (*See supra* pages 82–86). He also sues, however, Dr. Lovey Payne for malpractice related to the physician's treatment at the hospital after the accident. (*See supra* pages 85–86). Many jurisdictions would consider the events (accident, medical treatment, etc.) to be separate occurrences. In such jurisdictions, could either defendant file a motion to dismiss based on the inappropriate joinder of parties? What alternative remedy might a defendant pursue here?

Practice Problem 6-5

Patty Plaintiff files a complaint against Defendant Yard Works, Inc. for $50,000 in the state's court of general jurisdiction within the applicable statute of limitations. The complaint alleges the following: (1) that Patty was injured as she tripped over a shovel that Simple Simon had negligently left on the street in front of Plaintiff's home; (2) that Simple Simon was an employee of Yard Works, Inc.; and (3) that Patty suffered damages as the result of her injury in the amount of $50,000. Recalling tort and agency principles, you determine that Yard Works, Inc. can file a motion to dismiss for failure to state a claim. Why?

Practice Problem 6-6

Pam Plaintiff witnessed Doug Defendant swinging a chain around his head in increasingly large concentric circles. Doug did not see a ten-year-old girl approaching from behind, but Pam observed the whole series of events and could not yell because, as she put it, she was frozen with fear. The chain knocked the girl out and left a gash across her face. Pam was not related to the girl, but was deeply disturbed at witnessing the incident. She continued to dream of it and could not shake its effects. Plaintiff sues Defendant for negligent infliction of emotional distress. However, the state where the incident occurred has never recognized such a claim. Would a motion to dismiss for failure to state a claim be appropriate? Should the court, if it grants the motion, allow Pam to amend her complaint if it agrees that no such claim is actionable in your state?

Practice Problem 6-7

Tom Tenant sues Larry Landlord claiming that Landlord has failed to maintain the premises as required by the lease, allowing the tenant an automatic reduction in the rent. The lease is not attached to the complaint. A provision in the lease makes it the Tenant's responsibility to notify Landlord if the particular type of maintenance for which it is complaining, in Tenant's opinion, needs to be performed—and failing such notice, Tenant cannot complain, sue, seek any reduction in rent, etc. Landlord moves for the lease to be made a part of the record. The court grants the motion, and the lease is made part of the record. Landlord then files a motion to dismiss for failure to state a claim, citing the language in the lease and the failure of Tenant to allege any notice to Landlord as required by the lease. How should the court rule?

Practice Problem 6-8

What if Tenant in the scenario described in Problem 6-7 had given notice to Landlord, but had failed to allege in the complaint that it had given notice. If the defendant moves to dismiss and the court grants the motion, should the court grant Tenant leave to amend?

Answers

Most states have adopted Federal Rule of Civil Procedure 8(b) governing answers. *See* Appendix 6-2 (reflecting states that have adopted Fed. R. Civ. P. 8(b)). Following is the text of Rule 8(b):

(b) **Defenses; Admissions and Denials.**

(1) *In General.* In responding to a pleading, a party must:

(A) state in short and plain terms its defenses to each claim asserted against it; and

(B) admit or deny the allegations asserted against it by an opposing party.

(2) *Denials—Responding to the Substance.* A denial must fairly respond to the substance of the allegation.

(3) *General and Specific Denials.* A party that intends in good faith to deny all the allegations of a pleading—including the jurisdictional grounds—may do so by a general denial. A party that does not intend to deny all the allegations must either specifically deny designated allegations or generally deny all except those specifically admitted.

(4) *Denying Part of an Allegation.* A party that intends in good faith to deny only part of an allegation must admit the part that is true and deny the rest.

(5) *Lacking Knowledge or Information.* A party that lacks knowledge or information sufficient to form a belief about the truth of an allegation must so state, and the statement has the effect of a denial.

(6) *Effect of Failing to Deny.* An allegation — other than one relating to the amount of damages — is admitted if a responsive pleading is required and the allegation is not denied. If a responsive pleading is not required, an allegation is considered denied or avoided.

(c) **Affirmative Defenses.**

(1) *In General.* In responding to a pleading, a party must affirmatively state any avoidance or affirmative defense, including:

• accord and satisfaction;

• arbitration and award;

• assumption of risk;

• contributory negligence;

• discharge in bankruptcy;

• duress;

• estoppel;

• failure of consideration;

• fraud;

• illegality;

• injury by fellow servant;

• laches;

• license;

• payment;

• release;

• res judicata;

• statute of frauds;

• statute of limitations; and

• waiver.

If a defendant does not have a basis for filing a pre-answer motion, or strategically chooses to save certain defenses for later in the litigation, the defendant must file an answer. The answer is one of the most important pleadings in a case. Too often it is treated casually as a perfunctory step to get the case moving.

In the answer, the defendant must respond to each of the allegations in the complaint. The applicable rule in most jurisdictions is that the defendant must "fairly admit or deny the allegations in the complaint." *See, e.g.,* OHIO R. CIV. P. 8(b). Defense counsel must categorize a complaint's allegations. One important category to identify first includes the allegations for which the defendant's counsel, who typically, is new to the case, lacks a sufficient basis to determine the accuracy of allegations. More often than not, a defendant who has just been sued does not have sufficient facts to admit or deny a factual allegation. Recognizing this reality, almost every state allows a defendant to respond that it lacks information sufficient to form a belief as to the accuracy of the allegation. 61A AM. JUR. 2d *Pleading* § 406 (2009). As Rule 8 provides, such a statement has the effect of a denial. If the state in which you intend to practice does not make clear that such a response effectively serves as a denial, then the safer course is to state that "defendant lacks information sufficient to form a belief as to [XYZ allegation] and therefore denies the allegation." Why be careful? Because most state's rules, like Rule 8, provide that the failure to respond to an allegation operates as an *admission. Id.* § 249. In litigation, an "admission" is an allegation that is accepted as true for all purposes — meaning that no proof need be offered on the matter at trial. Following is a case that illustrates the effect of failing to respond to all of the allegations in a complaint.

Martin v. Lilly
505 A.2d 1156 (R.I. 1986)

[Weisberger, J., delivered the opinion of the Court]

This appeal raises three issues (two of which were raised by counsel): (1) whether [Defendant/Appellant] Dean's appeal of the action brought by [Plaintiff/Appellee] George for property damage is properly before this court; (2) whether the trial justice's denial of the motion to amend Dean's answers to add the defenses of lack of consent and ownership was proper; and (3) whether the trial justice's denial of the motion for directed verdict was proper. We answer the first issue in the negative and the second and third issues in the affirmative....

DENIAL OF THE MOTION TO AMEND

After plaintiffs had rested and after the defense had presented two witnesses, Dean filed a motion to amend its answer to assert the defenses of lack of ownership and lack of consent. The trial justice denied this motion, and Dean appealed. Before reaching the merits on this issue, we think it is necessary to discuss briefly the operation of R.I. GEN. LAWS §§ 31-33-6 and 31-33-7 so as to clarify the manner in which these statutes operate.

The actions against Dean were based on § 31-33-6 [a statute making the owner of a motor vehicle liable for injuries to others caused by persons who use the owner's motor vehicle with the owner's permission]. There was no allegation of the application of § 31-33-7 [entitled "Prima Facie Evidence of Consent of Owner"] in the complaint, and the judge did not instruct the jury concerning § 31-33-7. Having not alleged § 31-33-7 in their complaint, plaintiffs did not raise § 31-33-7 and were not entitled to its benefits.... Because the complaint did not assert the application of § 31-33-7, Dean was not required to plead affirmatively lack of consent. If the complaints had alleged the application of § 31-33-7, Dean would have been required to plead affirmatively lack of consent. However, even if § 31-33-7 had been invoked, Dean would not have been required to plead affirmatively lack of ownership or registration. An answer denying plaintiffs' allegations would have sufficed. To achieve the benefits of § 31-33-7, plaintiffs would have first to prove registration. *Gemma v. Rotondo*, 62 R.I. 293, 295–96, 5 A.2d 297, 299 (1939), and defendants could traverse the fact of registration without the necessity of an affirmative plea.

General Laws 1956 (1968 Reenactment) § 31-33-6 provides:

> Owner's liability for acts of others. Whenever any motor vehicle shall be used, operated, or caused to be operated upon any public highway of this state with the consent of the owner, or lessee, or bailee, thereof, expressed or implied, the driver thereof, if other than such owner, or lessee, or bailee, shall in case of accident be deemed to be the agent of the owner or lessee, or bailee, of such motor vehicle unless such driver shall have furnished proof of financial responsibility in the amount set forth in chapter 32 of this title, prior to such accident; and for the purposes of this section the term 'owner' shall include any person, firm, copartnership, association or corporation having the lawful possession or control of a motor vehicle under a written sale agreement.

As we have stated, the case against Dean was premised solely on § 31-33-6. Without question, plaintiffs must prove each essential element of their action to recover.... To recover under this statute, plaintiffs were required to prove four elements: (1) that the driver (Maria) was negligent; (2) that the car was being operated on a public highway; (3) that the car was owned by defendant; and (4) that the car was driven with the owner's (Dean's) consent....

To oppose any of these elements, all a defendant must do is file an answer disputing the essential facts asserted in the complaint... Therefore, we conclude that an answer denying plaintiffs' claim based on § 31-33-6 would entitle defendant to produce evidence challenging plaintiffs' allegations on any essential elements. However, if a plaintiff alleges that the defendant is the registered owner, then § 31-33-7 would be applicable and defendant would be required to plead affirmatively absence of consent. In the case at bar, an answer that denied ownership and consent would have sufficed to meet the allegations of this complaint.

.... Rule 8(b) of the Superior and District Court Rules of Civil Procedure requires a party to "admit or deny the averments upon which the adverse party relies." Under Rule 12(a) of the Superior and District Court Rules of Civil Procedure, the answer must be filed within twenty days of service of the complaint. Failure to deny an averment results in a judicial admission of the alleged fact. Super. R. Civ. P. 8(d); Dist. R. Civ. P. 8(d); 1 Kent, R.I. Civ. Prac. § 8.5 at 86 (1969); McCormick, Evidence § 262 at 776 (3d ed. Cleary 1984). A judicially admitted fact is conclusively established ... that is, removed from the area of controversy, obviating the need of the plaintiff to produce evidence on the fact and precluding the defendant from challenging the fact.... By not answering the allegations of ownership and consent, Dean admitted these facts and every other allegation relating to liability in the complaint. The trial justice therefore properly precluded Dean from introducing evidence to challenge the facts of ownership and consent.

....

For the reasons stated above, we affirm the trial justice's denial of the motion to "amend" the answer. Further, although Dean's motion with respect to No. 74-749 was not a Rule 15(b) motion because no answer existed to amend, the trial justice's denial of Dean's motion to amend a nonexistent answer and preclusion of evidence challenging lack of ownership and lack of consent was correct. The trial justice had determined that to allow Dean to challenge ownership and consent at that juncture would severely prejudice plaintiffs because of the impossibility of obtaining registry records to verify ownership.... As the trial justice pointed out, trial by ambush is no longer allowed under our modern view of pleadings. The purpose of modern pleadings is "to define with clearness and reasonable certainty the issue to be tried." ... Dean's attempt to challenge ownership, raised for the first time after plaintiffs had rested and at a time when plaintiffs could no longer obtain registry records, would constitute trial by ambush, and the motion to amend was properly denied....

DENIAL OF THE MOTION FOR DIRECTED VERDICT

The final issue under review is whether the trial justice properly denied Dean's motion for a directed verdict. Dean claims that he was entitled to a directed verdict because the only evidence produced by plaintiffs to show Dean's ownership of the car was inadmissible hearsay and, therefore, plaintiffs failed to make out a prima facie case.

In the ordinary case, as we stated in *Young v. Park*, 417 A.2d 889, 893 (R.I. 1980), in reviewing a trial justice's decision on a motion for directed verdict, "we have the same duty as the trial justice to view the evidence and the inferences to which it is reasonably susceptible in the light most favorable to [the plaintiff]. We do this without weighing the evidence or assessing the credibility of witnesses. Instead, we decide whether the evidence is sufficient in law to support a verdict for the plaintiff."... In the case at bar the trial justice could have reached only one conclusion.

In the instant case all allegations in respect to liability, ownership, and consent had been admitted by the failure of Dean to file an answer denying the essential averments of the complaint. Consequently, any evidence purportedly admitted in support of these allegations was mere surplusage. Therefore, we need not reach the issue of the admissibility of Maria's hearsay declaration. In light of Dean's judicial admissions, the only issue remaining to be resolved was damages. 1 Kent, §8.5 at 86 (averments of damages are not admitted if not denied). Since an entry of appearance had been made on Dean's behalf, it was entitled to an evidentiary hearing on the issue of damages just as it would have been in the case of the entry of a formal default. See Super. R. Civ. P. 55(b)(2). Since no default had been entered, the case was submitted to a jury. No error inhered in this procedure.

For the reasons stated, the purported appeal from civil action No. 76-747 is not properly before us and is dismissed pro forma; the appeal from civil action No. 76-749 is denied and dismissed. The judgment of the Superior Court is affirmed, and the papers in the case may be remanded to the Superior Court....

———————

To avoid results such as illustrated in the above case, the careful attorney will compare the complaint's allegations with the defendant's answer to ensure that the answer responds to each of the complaint's allegations. In addition, the defendant should add affirmative defenses to the answer. Rule 8(c) provides a non-exhaustive list of affirmative defenses. In the writ pleading days of old, the matters now listed as affirmative defenses would have been considered issues of "confession and avoidance." Affirmative defenses are not denials; they are a way for the defendant to "avoid" liability for the plaintiff's claim. 61A Am. Jur. 2d *Pleading* §288 (2009). An affirmative defense asserts a legal point, for which the defendant bears the burden of proof that if true will elude liability in whole or in part. *Id.* The defendant can raise an affirmative defense (such as statute of limitations) and provide additional facts in support of the defense. *Id.* In other words, even if the plaintiff's allegations are true, the affirmative defense allows the defendant to avoid liability by alleging additional facts to undermine a plaintiff's ability to recover on the claim. *Id.* §287. For example, if the statute of limitations has run on a plaintiff's claim, the defendant may avoid liability by raising the limitations defense. Even though the plaintiff may be able to prove every element of the claim, bringing the claim beyond the limitations period will "avoid" judgment against the defendant if she proves that the statute of limitations has run on the claim. (For a thorough discussion of the analysis for determining whether the limitations period has run on a claim, *see supra* Chapter 2). Counsel's failure to raise an affirmative defense typically results in waiver of the defense. 61A Am. Jur. 2d *Pleading* §291.

Following is a chart comparing the *Rex v. Hurry* complaint (*supra* Chapter 4, at pages 82–86) with a sample answer to that complaint. The complaint is in the left column, and responses typically seen in an answer appear in the right column. A comparison such as this will help to ensure that the answer responds to every allegation in the complaint. Note that most of the responses in the answer column below are of the "without information to respond and therefore denies the allegations" variety. Such responses are legitimate in most cases because, at the outset of a case, defense counsel usually has limited facts. Defense counsel, in good faith, can give such a response. Because it serves effectively as a denial, *see* Fed. R. Civ. P. 8(b)(5), it provides a safe way for a party to respond without making a costly admission.

Sample Complaint	Sample Answer
IN THE CIRCUIT COURT FOR THE CITY OF ARCADIA	IN THE CIRCUIT COURT FOR THE CITY OF ARCADIA

BRAD T. REX,
    Plaintiff,
v.   Case No. 2008cv10
ENA HURRY,
    Defendant,
and
LOVEY PAYNE, M.D.,
Defendant.
	BRAD T. REX,
	    Plaintiff,
	v. Case No. 2008cv10
	ENA HURRY,
	    Defendant,
	and
	LOVEY PAYNE, M.D.,
	Defendant.

COMPLAINT The Plaintiff, Brad T. Rex, by counsel, for his Complaint against defendants, Ena Hurry and Lovey Payne, states as follows:	ANSWER The Defendant, Ena Hurry, by counsel, for her Answer to Plaintiff's Complaint, states as follows:
Parties 1. The Plaintiff, Brad T. Rex, is a citizen of the State of Illyria, and the Defendants, Ena Hurry and Lovey Payne, are citizens of the same State.	Parties 1. Defendant admits only that she is a citizen of the State of Illyria. Defendant lacks information sufficient to form a belief as to the truth of the remaining allegations in paragraph 1 of the Complaint and therefore denies them.
Facts Common to All Counts 2. On January 18, 2008, the Plaintiff was driving a motorcycle owned by a friend, Harley Davidson, who had given the Plaintiff permission to ride the bike while the Plaintiff's motorcycle was in the shop for repairs.	Facts Common to All Counts 2. Defendant lacks information sufficient to form a belief as to the truth of the allegations in paragraph 2 of the Complaint and therefore denies them.
3. The Plaintiff was driving Davidson's motorcycle between the minimum speed limit of 15 miles per hour and the maximum speed limit of 35 miles per hour. He was driving the motorcycle during daylight at around 4:00 p.m. on a public, single-lane road called Easy Street in Arcadia, Illyria, which intersects with Dangerous Drive ("The Intersection"). The Intersection is controlled by a traffic light. The Plaintiff, who was traveling west on Easy Street, entered the Intersection immediately after other vehicles traveling in the same direction had done so.	3. Defendant admits only that Easy Street and Dangerous Drive intersect in the City of Arcadia. Defendant lacks information sufficient to form a belief as to the truth of the remaining allegations in paragraph 3 of the Complaint and therefore denies them.

4. On the same day and at the same time described in the preceding paragraph, the Defendant Hurry was operating her car on Dangerous Drive in the right hand lane of the two lanes heading north. Defendant Hurry proceeded through the intersection negligently despite the lack of a green light.

4. Defendant admits only that, on the day alleged, she was operating her car on Dangerous Drive at the intersection with Easy Street. Defendant denies the remaining allegations in paragraph 4 of the Complaint.

5. The Defendant Hurry, who was traveling at a high rate of speed that exceeded the speed limit, proceeded through the Intersection at an unsafe speed and/or despite traffic signals indicating she should have stopped.

5 Defendant admits only that, on the day alleged, she was operating her car on Dangerous Drive. Defendant denies the remaining allegations in paragraph 5 of the Complaint.

6. The Plaintiff and his motorcycle collided with the side of the Defendant Hurry's car. The Plaintiff was thrown over the car onto the asphalt and received numerous and serious injuries throughout his body, for which he has received—and will continue to receive—medical care. The Plaintiff has experienced pain, suffering, discomfort, and significant disruption to his life. The collision and aftermath damaged Davidson's motorcycle in an amount that will likely exceed $50,000 or more to repair.

6. Defendant admits only that her vehicle and Plaintiff's motorcycle collided. Defendant is without information sufficient to form a belief as to the truth of the remaining allegations in paragraph 6 of the Complaint and therefore denies them.

7. Rex was wearing a new state-of-the art motorcycle airbag jacket manufactured by Kagasaki, Inc. Kagasaki advertises the jacket as an essential safety device that will inflate immediately when a rider is thrown from a motorcycle and protect him from serious trauma. The air bag jacket that Rex was wearing did not inflate when Rex was thrown from the motorcycle.

7. Defendant is without information sufficient to form a belief as to the truth of the allegations in paragraph 7 of the Complaint and therefore denies them.

8. Stunned by these events, the Plaintiff stood up after great effort—only to have the Defendant Hurry approach him in a threatening manner and push him with both of her hands on his shoulders.

8. Defendant denies the allegations in paragraph 8 of the Complaint.

Negligence Claim

9. The preceding allegations are hereby restated and incorporated as if set forth here.

Negligence Claim

9. Defendant incorporates her responses to the allegations preceding paragraph 9 of the Complaint as if set forth here.

10. The Defendant Hurry had a duty at the time of the events to use ordinary care to avoid injury to others and to the property of others.

10. Defendant states that the allegations in paragraph 10 of the Complaint set forth conclusions of law to which she is not required to respond. To the extent any factual allegations are implicit in this paragraph, plaintiff denies them.

11. The Defendant Hurry breached her duty to use ordinary care in a variety of ways, including but not limited to, driving at an unsafe speed,

11. Defendant denies the allegations in paragraph 11 of the Complaint.

failing to observe the traffic signals controlling the Intersection, and/or observing a traffic signal indicating she should stop and proceeding through the intersection anyway.

12. The Defendant Hurry's breach is described in the preceding paragraph.

13. As a proximate result of the Defendant Hurry's breach of her duty, the Plaintiff suffered severe injuries to his cervical spine and neck among other severe injuries, was prevented from attending school and/or transacting business, suffered great pain of body and mind, and incurred expenses for medical attention and hospitalization.

Assault

14. The preceding allegations are hereby restated and incorporated as if set forth here.

15. When the Defendant Hurry intentionally approached the Plaintiff after the collision in a physically threatening manner, she created a reasonable apprehension of immediate, offensive bodily contact.

16. The Defendant Hurry had the apparent ability to carry out the threatened offensive bodily contact.

17. The Defendant Hurry's actions constituted an assault for which she is liable to Plaintiff for both compensatory and punitive damages.

Battery

18. The preceding allegations are hereby restated and incorporated as if set forth here.

19. The Defendant Hurry intentionally touched Plaintiff in a manner offensive to a reasonable person.

20. The Defendant Hurry's actions constitute a battery for which she is liable to Plaintiff for both compensatory and punitive damages.

12. Defendant denies the allegations in paragraph 12 of the Complaint.

13. Defendant denies the allegation that she breached any duty to Plaintiff and denies any factual allegations implicit in such allegation. As to the remaining allegations in paragraph 13 of the Complaint, Defendant is without information sufficient to form a belief as to the truth of the allegations and therefore denies them.

Assault

14. Defendant incorporates her responses to the allegations preceding paragraph 14 of the Complaint as if set forth here.

15. Defendant denies the allegations in paragraph 15 of the Complaint.

16. Defendant denies the allegations in paragraph 16 of the Complaint.

17. Defendant states that the allegations in paragraph 17 of the Complaint set forth conclusions of law to which she is not required to respond. To the extent any factual allegations are implicit in this paragraph, Defendant denies them.

Battery

18. Defendant incorporates her responses to the allegations preceding paragraph 18 of the Complaint as if set forth here.

19. Defendant denies the allegations in paragraph 19 of the Complaint.

20. Defendant states that the allegations in paragraph 20 of the Complaint set forth conclusions of law to which she is not required to respond. To the extent any factual allegations are implicit in this paragraph, Defendant denies them.

Malpractice

21. The preceding allegations are hereby restated and incorporated as if set forth here.

22. Defendant Payne had a duty to exercise reasonable care consistent with that of a reasonable physician in Arcadia so as to avoid injury to Plaintiff.

23. Defendant Payne breached his duty to exercise reasonable care consistent with the standard of care of a reasonable physician in Arcadia by failing to treat the Plaintiff's concussion at all, much less in a manner consistent with how a reasonable physician in Arcadia would treat a concussion.

24. Defendant Payne's breach of duty set forth above has proximately resulted in, and will continue to result in, injuries and symptoms that are likely to be long-lasting and possibly permanent.

25. Defendant Payne's actions constitute malpractice for which he is liable to Plaintiff for compensatory damages.

Malpractice

21. Defendant incorporates her responses to the allegations preceding paragraph 21 of the Plaintiff's complaint as if set forth here.

22. Defendant states that the allegations in paragraph 22 of the Complaint set forth conclusions of law to which she is not required to respond. To the extent the allegations in paragraph 22 state factual allegations, Defendant is without information sufficient to form a belief as to the truth of those allegations.

23. Defendant is without information sufficient to form a belief as to the truth of the allegations in paragraph 23 of the Complaint and therefore denies them.

24. Defendant is without information sufficient to form a belief as to the truth of the allegations in paragraph 24 of the Complaint and therefore denies them.

25. Defendant states that the allegations in paragraph 25 of the Complaint state conclusions of law to which she is not required to respond. To the extent the paragraph contains factual allegations, Defendant is without information sufficient to form a belief as to the truth of the allegations in paragraph 25 of the Complaint.

26. Any and all allegations in the Plaintiff's Complaint not explicitly admitted in this Answer are hereby denied.

AFFIRMATIVE DEFENSES

Defendant hereby alleges the following defenses:

1. Negligence of the Plaintiff proximately caused any or all of his injuries.

2. [Any other defense that under applicable law represents an affirmative defense—*i.e.*, a defense that, if proved, will avoid liability of the Defendant even if the Plaintiff's allegations are true, or at

This paragraph (para. #26) is not required but offers a safe method to ensure that, if one of a defendant's responses does not address an allegation in plaintiff's Complaint, defendant will correct the omission by this "back-up" denial

The first paragraph of Affirmative Defenses is included because contributory negligence states will bar recovery to a negligent plaintiff; in comparative negligence states, one would state that any recovery by a plaintiff must be reduced by the percentage of negligence attributable to plaintiff

least lessen liability such as where the duty to mitigate damages applies].

WHEREFORE, the Plaintiff demands the following relief judgment against the Defendant:
a) compensatory damages in a sum exceeding Seventy Five Thousand Dollars ($75,000) exclusive of interests and costs, the complete amount to be determined at trial;
b) compensatory damages in a sum to be determined at trial against Dr. Lovey Payne; and
c) punitive damages in an amount to be determined at trial against Defendant Ena Hurry.

WHEREFORE, having fully answered, the Defendant respectfully requests that the plaintiff's actions be dismissed with prejudice.

BRAD T. REX _____
Of Counsel

ENA HURRY _____
Of Counsel

The Law Offices of Jim Justice, Esq.
111 Liberty Street
Arcadia, Illyria 23464
757.222.3333
jim@justice.com

Counsel for Plaintiff

Dee Fender, Esq.
1000 Liberty Street
Arcadia, VA 23510
757.625.5000
deefender@yahoo.com

Counsel for Defendant

Pleas

In some states, a defendant can file a "plea" or similar challenge when a dispositive fact will end the litigation. 61A Am. Jur. 2d *Pleading* § 253 (2009). "Pleas" are traditionally a common law mechanism and have been abolished in some jurisdictions. However, in other jurisdictions they (or a device called something else but serving the same function) are still a proper mechanism for raising defenses that, if true, would end the litigation immediately. *Id.* § 262. If, for instance, the statute of limitations has run on the plaintiff's claims, filing a motion to dismiss or demurrer will not achieve dismissal because the trial court does not accept facts outside the record. However, jurisdictions that permit pleas will allow a party to file a pleading raising the pertinent facts upon which the defendant maintains that the litigation should be ended. *Id.* Classic examples would be pleas of statute of limitations, res judicata, incompetency, illegality of a contract, etc. Where pleas or a similar procedural mechanism are available, the trial court will hold an evidentiary hearing concentrating on the issue raised. If the state allows for a jury trial, the defense should consider whether to demand a jury on the factual question. Both parties should, if the court conducts a hearing on facts raised in a plea, consider whether they have a right to have a jury decide the facts.[9]

_____

9. As noted in Chapter 9, the Seventh Amendment to the U.S. Constitution has not been incorporated via the Fourteenth Amendment so as to be applicable to states. Thus, a party's right to a jury trial in state court depends on the applicable state's constitution, statutes, or procedural rules of the jurisdiction.

A Final Note on Answers

The key to filing effective answers is research. The list of affirmative defenses provided by Federal Rule 8 (and its state counterparts) is not exhaustive. Therefore, defense counsel must research the applicable jurisdiction's law to see what affirmative defenses apply. For a list of defenses that courts have recognized as affirmative defenses beyond the scope of Rule 8, see 61A Am. Jur. 2d § 370 (2009). Furthermore, a practitioner must discipline herself to continue the research process as a case proceeds. An affirmative defense may only become apparent after conducting discovery and learning more facts. (See Chapter 8 *infra* on the discovery process.) Only by continued research in light of facts as they become known in discovery can an attorney be sure that she has protected her client by raising affirmative defenses that may avoid liability, or at least lessen the damages a client may face.

Follow-Up Questions

1. How will you decide whether, in a given case, your client's interests are best served by (a) a dispositive motion (such as a motion to dismiss), or alternatively, (b) filing an answer preserving defenses and waiting until you have sufficient factual support to assert the defense?

2. Can you envision a scenario in which you would wait until trial and, only after the plaintiff has rested her case, press a challenge to the complaint or an affirmative defense?

Professional Identity Question

In answering, some lawyers deny every fact in a complaint, regardless of whether her client has affirmed the accuracy of the plaintiff's allegation. The rationale of such lawyers is that most courts expect the defendant to deny allegations in a complaint and are unlikely to sanction the lawyer for denying such facts. However, if your client makes clear that a fact alleged is accurate — or if the fact is undeniable in light of, for example, physical conditions (*e.g.*, a street runs north), would you deny such facts? If not, can you admit the facts that are true in a certain paragraph of the complaint, but make clear you do not admit other facts in that paragraph? Why would you be careful to separate factual allegations in a paragraph in this manner?

D. Methods to Reinforce and Integrate Topics Covered in This Chapter

The process of responding to a complaint is full of strategic decisions and traps. Thus, a chart or diagram highlighting them would be a helpful tool for a defendant's lawyer.

Diagram 6-3 provides an outline of strategic questions for defense counsel as she decides whether to respond to the complaint and how. The diagram is a general outline only, and the practitioner needs to research the law of the applicable jurisdiction to fill in the specifics. Consider how, in light of your jurisdiction's law, you would tailor a diagram like the one below, or develop a variation of your own choosing.

Diagram 6-3

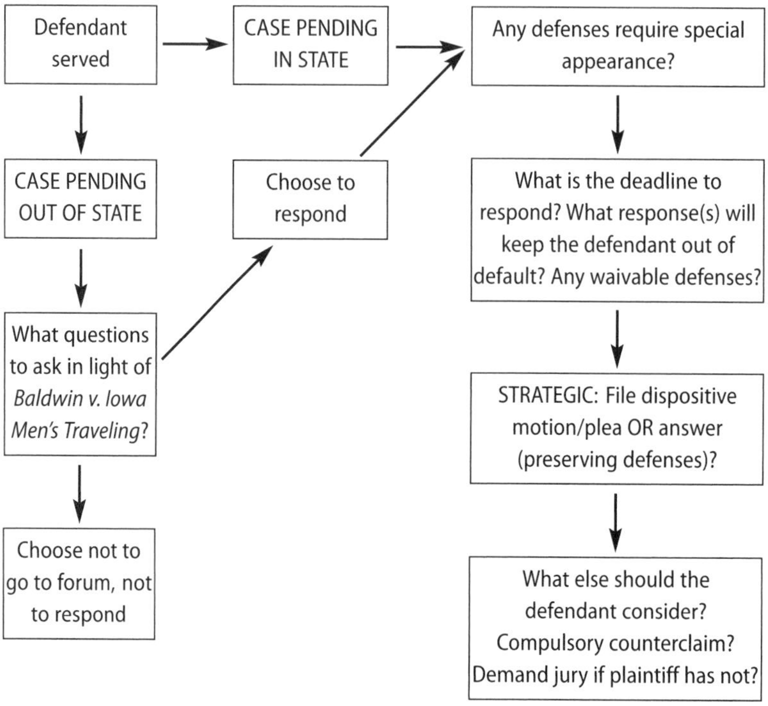

E. Written Assignments

1. Assume for this assignment only that Sally did not give notice to the State of the accident or allege negligence as required by the State Tort Claims Act of the state in which you intend to practice. You are an assistant attorney general, and the State has been served with Sally's complaint. Draft an appropriate pleading in response to her complaint.

2. Assume that you are an associate in the law firm hired by HorsePower, Inc., which has just been served in Sally's case. Identify affirmative defenses, in addition to those listed in Federal Rule of Civil Procedure 8(c), that should be considered for inclusion in the manufacturer's answer.

Chapter 7

Defaults, Limbo, and Pretrial Dismissal

A. Sally's Case at This Stage of Litigation Process

Lucky Sally. The defendant manufacturer was served through Illyria's secretary of state. As required by Illyria law, the secretary mailed the process to the manufacturer and simultaneously mailed a completed certificate of compliance (noting the mailing of process to the defendant) to the clerk of court in Arcadia. Counsel for the manufacturer made the mistake (noted in Chapter 6) of assuming that the 21-day responsive pleading deadline began when the manufacturer received the mailing. Assume that, in fact, under applicable law the time period began when the clerk received the certificate of compliance several days earlier. When defendant manufacturer submitted a response, it was beyond the 21-day period and "out of time." Thus, the clerk noted this defendant as in default. Being "in default" does not mean, however, that the defendant has had a default judgment entered against it. The manufacturer still may be able to get out of default status and defend the suit as if none of this had happened.

This chapter will discuss the effect of default and a defendant's options once in default. It also will discuss other ways in which a case, or part of a case, may come to an early resolution: voluntary dismissals and involuntary dismissals.

B. Tasks and Decision-Making at This Stage of a Case

The point at which you now find yourself in the timeline of a case is set forth in diagram 7-1.

The decision-making process and tasks at this stage vary depending on whether you are a plaintiff like Sally or a defendant like the manufacturer. Both this section on tasks and strategic decision-making, and the section entitled "Applicable Law," will first discuss defaults and then discuss voluntary and involuntary dismissals in that sequence.

Diagram 7-1

Cause of Action (events leading to suit)
Prefiling Matters to Consider; Choice of Forum [Chs. 2–3]
Π and Δ Decide on Offensive Pleadings & Joinder (of claims & parties); Filing Suit; Service [Chs. 4–5]
Motions, Responsive Pleadings; Default; Voluntary & Involuntary Dismissals [Chs. 6–7]
Discovery Phase (developing proof to establish claims & learning about the adversary's case) [Ch. 8]
Right to Jury Trial; Pretrial Motions & Practice [Ch. 9]
Final Pretrial Conference & Other Events within Last Month before Trial [Ch. 10]
Procedure at Trial [Ch. 11]
Post-Trial Motions & Calculating the Date of Final Judgment to Know Key Deadlines Such as for Notice of Appeal [Ch. 12]

Strategy Regarding Defaults

The decision-making process concerning defaults hinges on whether the litigant is a plaintiff or a defendant. A plaintiff loves defaults. A plaintiff cannot be held in default because, after all, she brought the suit. Moreover, if a defendant remains in default, the plaintiff gets to litigate against a defendant in a manner unlike that which takes place in the course of normal litigation. The defendant cannot contest liability, although typically a defendant can take part in a hearing or trial related to the amount of damages owed. In many places, the plaintiff need not even send notices to a defendant in default. The defendant has to figure out when to appear to contest damages.

Conversely, defense counsel must act quickly if her client is in default. The longer a party stays in default, the less likely a court will be to allow leave for the defendant to file responsive pleadings and become a full-fledged litigant. A defendant can move for leave to file responsive pleadings and ask to be relieved from default. States vary in the criteria for relief from default, but lawyers may discern some general principles from various states' rules. *See* Appendix 7-1. In the early phases, the actual criteria—and their application—are likely to favor the defendant. For instance, prejudice to the plaintiff in allowing a defendant to file responsive pleadings is almost always a factor. Prejudice to the plaintiff at the beginning of the case is minimal, and relief from default will thus be easier to achieve. However, prejudice to the plaintiff will be much greater at the later stages when the plaintiff is well into a case and prepared for trial. Having the trial date continued at that point will cost the plaintiff more money and delay resolution of her claim. Consequently, the defendant's chances of obtaining relief from default are slimmer.

Strategy on Voluntary and Involuntary Dismissals

Voluntary and involuntary dismissals involve a case being terminated prior to going to trial. The meaning of those terms should be clarified. A "voluntary dismissal" is one sought by the plaintiff and not opposed by a defendant. *See* Appendix 7-2 (identifying states' approaches to voluntary dismissals).

An "involuntary dismissal" is one sought by the defendant but which the plaintiff opposes.

Voluntary Dismissals

A plaintiff may use the tool of voluntary dismissal strategically. The tool can be used in several ways. A plaintiff initially files every claim available and can support each one with some factual basis. However, once the case has proceeded into discovery, she may be unable to muster the evidence necessary to present one of the claims persuasively. As to the other claims, however, the plaintiff believes she will be able to put on a compelling case. Wise lawyers realize that unimpressive claims will weaken persuasive claims if they are combined. Although theoretically a jury could keep separate the persuasive claims from the unpersuasive, a weak claim in reality can hurt a plaintiff's credibility in the jury's eyes. Voluntarily dismissing a weak claim or claims can prevent the watering down of a plaintiff's strong claims. Taking such a step is hard for lawyers who like to cover the waterfront and do not want to be second-guessed. A relatively new associate would probably struggle with dropping a claim. However, effective lawyers make these types of judgment calls, and most clients will understand the rationale for dismissing a weak claim.

A plaintiff also may voluntarily dismiss an entire case as a way to retreat and "fight again another day." Some states allow at least one voluntary dismissal, sometimes called "non-suit," and provide a period in which the plaintiff can re-file without the statute of limitations beginning to run again on the claims. Such an approach is admittedly a minority one among states. *See* Appendix 7-2. However, if your state is in the minority, this tool is a powerful one. If the litigation does not go well, or if plaintiff's counsel finds a new lead that she cannot pursue because of the court's deadlines, taking a voluntary dismissal offers a way out. Plaintiffs particularly like voluntary non-suits if they are "without prejudice," the term used for a dismissal that allows a plaintiff to re-file the suit again. Even then a plaintiff must be careful that the statute of limitations has not run on her claims during the pendency of the suit. Often state law will provide that, during the period in which an action has been pending (and often some period of time after voluntary dismissal), such time will not be counted against the statute of limitations. If she can avoid the bar of a statute of limitations, the plaintiff can start over, get an expert needed to prove her case, or otherwise better prepare for and bring suit again.

Voluntary dismissals are more complex than defaults for defendants. Some defendants are happy when a plaintiff wants to end a suit: it might be an end to their problems and litigation expenses. Maybe the plaintiff will disappear and never resurface. On the other hand, if the plaintiff is seeking dismissal because of a potential vulnerability in her case, defendants are often less willing to agree to a voluntary dismissal. Forcing the plaintiff to go forward despite the vulnerability increases the defendant's chances of (a) prevailing, or (b) gaining a settlement more favorable than if the plaintiff were not force to go forward. If the jurisdiction's law allows a dismissal as of right, the defendant has no opportunity to object. However, if the state follows the approach of the federal system, a defendant can object and urge the court to refuse the request.

One instance in which both plaintiffs and defendants would agree to a voluntary dismissal is when they settle the case. There, a voluntary dismissal order is a usual step in the process of settling.

Involuntary Dismissals

Concerning involuntary dismissals, plaintiffs need to be wary. Such dismissals can be "with prejudice," meaning the claims are barred if brought again. Alternatively, the dismissal could be "without prejudice" and permit a limited time in which the plaintiff can amend to overcome the basis for the involuntary dismissal. Thus, the wise plaintiff's lawyer anticipates potential grounds on which defendants will seek dismissal. Pleading the case with sufficient specificity that addresses each of the elements of a claim will avoid a motion to dismiss for failure to state a claim.

As explained in the last chapter on defensive strategy, a defendant has to make judgments about the best grounds on which to attack a suit. If a dispositive ground that would result in dismissal exists, such as lack of personal jurisdiction, the defendant has to decide whether to raise it as a motion at the outset or preserve the defense in the answer and pursue dismissal later. In other words, the defendant must ascertain the strength of her basis for seeking involuntary dismissal.

C. Overview of Applicable Law

Default Judgments, Voluntary Dismissals, and Involuntary Dismissals

This section has three parts. The first discusses the law of default judgments and is followed by questions and practice problems related to defaults. The second relates the law of voluntary dismissals, again followed by questions and practice problems. The last section addresses the law of involuntary dismissal and, as with the other two sections, includes questions and practice problems on the topic.

Default Judgments

A party who fails to respond to the complaint, or who responds after the deadline, is "in default." *See* Appendix 7-1 (identifying states' approaches to defaults); *see also* 46 Am. Jur. 2d *Judgments* § 255 (2009). In some states, the failure to respond within the appropriate time frame classifies the non-responding party as in default, *by operation of law*, without the court (or clerk) taking any action. *See* 46 Am. Jur. 2d *Judgments* § 255 (2009). In others, the court (typically the clerk) notes in the file that the party is in default. *Id.* § 257. The difference between being in default and having a default judgment entered is comparable to the difference between being arrested and actually being locked up. Even after default is entered, the defendant may avoid the effect of going forward to a default judgment hearing.

Anytime before entry of a default judgment, a party may be granted leave to file responsive pleadings. 61B AM. JUR. 2d *Pleadings* § 908 (2009). If a defendant has missed the filing deadline by a few days, a court will almost surely grant her leave to file responsive pleadings. 47 AM. JUR. 2d *Judgments* § 686 (2009). The defendant will then be "out of default." Some jurisdictions separate litigation into phases for purposes of specifying deadlines and applying the criteria for granting leave to file. *Id.* The longer a case is pending and the further it proceeds, the chances of relief from default lessen. Id. § 689. Unless the party in default can show good reason for the delay, the court more often will deny leave to file responsive pleadings. *See generally Kirtland v. Ft. Morgan Auth. Sewer Serv. Inc.*, 524 So. 2d 600 (Ala. 1988).

If a party remains in default, the effect of that status varies by jurisdiction. Some states provide that no notice is necessary to a party in default. *See* 46 AM. JUR. 2d *Judgments* § 278 (2009). In those states, the party in default will have to monitor the court's docket to determine when a hearing or trial will be held. Other jurisdictions provide that, if she makes an appearance, the party in default should receive notice of pleadings, court dates, etc. *See* Appendix 7-1 (reflecting states that follow FED. R. CIV. P. 55(b)(2)); *see also* 55 MOORE'S FEDERAL PRACTICE: CIVIL § 55.10(2) (3d ed. 1999). An "appearance" means simply that the party or, more usually, her attorney has taken some act (usually the filing of a pleading) by which she submits to the jurisdiction of the court. C.J.S. *Appearance* § 1 (2009).

Jurisdictions also vary on the effect of default status at the hearing or trial. Many states consider the issue of liability to be resolved. FED. R. CIV. P. 55(b)(2); *see* Appendix 7-1 (showing whether states are aligned with the Federal Rule, which does consider liability to be resolved). The only question then is the amount of damages, provided they are not liquidated. FED. R. CIV. P. 55(b)(2); *see* Appendix 7-1. A party in default who attends a hearing or trial, therefore, will be limited to contesting damages. *See* GENE R. SHREVE & PETER RAVEN-HANSEN, UNDERSTANDING CIVIL PROCEDURE § 11.02(2) (4th ed. 2009). Solely on the issue of damages, the defendant may cross-examine and offer her own witnesses, challenge and offer jury instructions, and the like. *See id.* In some jurisdictions, the effect of default is not quite so severe. The defaulting party is deemed to have admitted all facts pled by the plaintiff, but not questions of law. 10 MOORE'S FEDERAL PRACTICE § 55.12(1) (3d ed. 1999); *see also* 10A CHARLES ALAN WRIGHT ET AL., FEDERAL PRACTICE AND PROCEDURE § 2688 (3d ed. 1998) (stating that "[a] party in default does not admit mere conclusions of law."). Thus, the court has the discretion to rule in favor of the defaulting party if the claims are not legally viable. *Overcash v. United Abstract Group, Inc.*, 549 F. Supp. 2d 193, 195 (N.D.N.Y. 2008); *see also* GENE R. SHREVE & PETER RAVEN-HANSEN, UNDERSTANDING CIVIL PROCEDURE § 11.02(2) (4th ed. 2009).

When a party fails to respond by the responsive pleading deadline, a court does not simply enter a default judgment. The plaintiff must jump through certain procedural hoops before a default judgment is entered. For instance, the jurisdictions that follow the federal model require: (1) an application for default by the party seeking recovery; and (2) notice to the party in default of the application for a default judgment and the date and time of any hearing thereon. FED. R. CIV. P. 55(b)(2); *see* Appendix 7-1.

After a final default judgment (including a determination of damages) is entered, the bases for setting aside such a judgment are fairly narrow. *See* GENE R. SHREVE & PETER RAVEN-HANSEN, UNDERSTANDING CIVIL PROCEDURE § 11.02(2) (4th ed. 2009). In every jurisdiction, a default judgment will be set aside if there was fraud in obtaining the judgment, or the judgment is void (*e.g.*, entered by a court lacking subject matter jurisdiction). Other common reasons for allowing relief from default are mistake, inadvertence, surprise, or excusable neglect. An example of surprise or excusable neglect would be where a party shows that she never received notice of the action. Death of a party or her family member may also serve as grounds for setting aside default, and even confusion over representation (counsel withdrew and defendant thought new counsel would take over). *See, e.g.,* 10A CHARLES ALAN WRIGHT ET AL., FEDERAL PRACTICE & PROCEDURE § 2695 (3d ed. 1998).

Follow-Up Questions

1. As discussed, a defendant can be held in default for failing to respond in the time allotted (usually around three weeks). Absent relief from the default, the defendant loses her "day in court"—at least on liability. Does this strike you as harsh? Does that consequence place incentives on defendants? What policies, if any, support such incentives?

2. Imagine a civil judicial system that lacks a default process. How would the absence of default affect the system? What interests does the default process protect?

3. What procedures protect the defendant's interests and how do they do so? Does the default process, on balance, fairly account for the interests of both plaintiff and defendant, or is it skewed toward one party?

Professional Identity Question

You represent a client who is suing a large in-state company. Assume that your jurisdiction now allows service by certified mail to an entity's post office box or to a street address. You have two addresses for the company: (1) a post office box where it receives payments, but which it visits once a month; and (2) the street address of the company's headquarters. If you serve the company by certified mail to the post-office box immediately after it has picked up the monthly payments, the chances of a default are greater than if you mail to the headquarters address. Would you, in an effort to have the defendant go into default, serve the company at the post-office box address rather than its headquarters' address?

Practice Problems

Practice Problem 7-1

Here is a variation on Practice Problem 5-2 in Chapter 5 *supra* at page 113. While driving his automobile through a street intersection in the capital city of your state, Bruce Wayne struck and injured Christian Bale, a pedestrian who also resided in the city. While Wayne and his wife were on vacation in the Bahamas, Bale brought an action against Wayne seeking $500,000 for his injuries. Because no one was home, the sheriff attached process to the front door and filed a return of service. Counsel for Bale then mailed the summons and complaint to Wayne's residence via certified mail. When Wayne came home, he was surprised to find that he was in default. When Wayne called the court, he discovered that a hearing has been set for the following week on the amount of damages that the court should award to Bale. Wayne comes to you and asks what can be done about his situation. What would you advise him? If he retains you to represent him at the hearing, will you be able to participate and what, if any, form would that participation take?

Practice Problem 7-2

Assume the same facts as Practice Problem 7-1 except that, when Wayne returns from Florida, he learns not only that a default judgment had been entered but also that a hearing finding the plaintiff's damages to be $500,000 had occurred. The result of the hearing was memorialized in a final judgment order that, by the time they brought it to your attention, was more than 30 days old. Wayne asks you what can be done. What would you advise him?

[handwritten margin notes: "past 21 days", "can try to claim negligence, fraud", "explain to see if you could get good cause"]

Practice Problem 7-3

Big Corporation, Inc., has been sued in a $1 million lawsuit in your state. The General Counsel faxes you, the company's outside counsel, a summons and complaint to which an answer should have been filed two weeks ago. You ask why the summons and complaint had not been forwarded to you sooner. The General Counsel explains that process was served on the assistant to the president of Big Corporation. General Counsel agrees that the assistant is a person with responsibilities that should qualify her as a "managing agent" for purposes of service of process. The assistant placed the summons and complaint in the Chief Executive Officer's (CEO's) in-box and expected her to see it. Although the CEO usually reads any items placed in her in-box promptly, she had been out of the office on a trip and was behind on reading papers in her in-box. She discovered the summons and complaint right before the General Counsel faxed it to you. What could you do to seek relief from default status for Big Corporation? What would you emphasize in your argument to the court? In return for granting such relief, could the court require something of Big Corporation to offset any prejudice to the plaintiff, who may have taken any actions or incurred expenses in reliance on Big Corporation's being in default?

"General Counsel" is the head of a corporation's in-house legal department. "Outside Counsel" is an independent law firm that undertakes representation of the company

Voluntary and Involuntary Pretrial Dismissals

The Meaning of "With Prejudice" and "Without Prejudice" Dismissals

The following discussion of voluntary and involuntary dismissals will refer to the terms "with prejudice" and "without prejudice." Understanding the difference between them is crucial. Voluntary and involuntary dismissals may be "with prejudice" or "without prejudice." Dismissing a claim "with prejudice" means that it cannot be brought again. 4 Am. Jur. 2d *Appellate Review* § 155 (2009). If the claim is voluntarily dismissed with prejudice, the plaintiff cannot appeal. Conversely, if a plaintiff's claim is involuntarily dismissed with prejudice (*e.g.*, on a motion to dismiss), she can appeal. *Id.* In most cases, however, the appeal will have to await a final judgment. If some claims survive a motion to dismiss and others are dismissed with prejudice, the plaintiff typically can appeal the dismissal of the claims only after resolution and final judgment on the surviving claims. *Id.*

Dismissing a claim "without prejudice" means that the claim will not be precluded *by the terms of that dismissal order* from being filed again. *Umbenhauer v. Woog*, 969 F.2d 25, 39 n.6 (3d Cir. 1992). Even if a dismissal is without prejudice, however, other reasons may later prevent the plaintiff from proceeding with the claim dismissed without prejudice. For instance, if a tolling provision does not apply, the limitations could begin running again on a claim. *See id.* Or the claim could be lost another way. For example, a plaintiff may have several claims arising from the same set of facts. Suppose one claim is dismissed without prejudice. Assume the case then goes to trial on the other claims and results in a final judgment. Ordinarily, under principles of res judicata, the previously dismissed claim is merged into the final judgment and cannot be filed again. Thus, the "without prejudice" label can give a false sense of security. If the final judgment is adverse to the party who had a claim dismissed "without prejudice," she would need to appeal not only dismissal of that claim but the other claims. Whether serving as plaintiff's or defendant's counsel, an effective lawyer will consider these possibilities and decide whether to seek or fight dismissal without prejudice.

Voluntary Dismissals

Every system allows a plaintiff to voluntarily dismiss some or all of her claims. Jurisdictions that follow the common law approach represent the minority. These jurisdictions give a plaintiff the right to a voluntary dismissal (also called a nonsuit) throughout the litigation up until some defined point, such as when the jury retires. *See, e.g.,* Va. Code Ann. § 8.01-380 (2009).

Most jurisdictions allow voluntary dismissal as of right early in a case, typically before responsive pleadings have been filed, but require court approval afterward. Appendix 7-2; *see generally* D.W. O'Neill, Annotation, *Time When Voluntary Nonsuit of Dismissal May Be Taken as of Right Under Statute So Authorizing at Any Time Before "Trial," "Commencement of Trial," Trial of the Facts," or the Like,* 1 A.L.R. 3d 711 (1965). Later in the case, many states allow voluntary dismissal if all parties consent. *See, e.g.,* Fed. R. Civ. P. 41(a)(1)(A)(ii). Otherwise, voluntary dismissal in these jurisdictions requires court approval. *Id.* (a)(2). As with getting out of default, the longer a case is pending and the further it progresses, it becomes less likely that a court will allow voluntary dismissal — especially if the defendant opposes it. States that require court approval to dismiss will, if all parties consent, be more likely to grant the request even late in a case's progress. *See id.*

Reasons for voluntary dismissal are varied. As suggested above in this chapter's discussion of strategy, plaintiff's counsel may want to wipe the slate clean and start over. *See, e.g.,* Susan Clark Taylor, *Rule 41(a)(2) Dismissals: Forum Shopping for a Statute of Limitations,* 20 Mem. St. U. L. Rev. 629 (1990). Plaintiff's counsel will be especially inclined to seek voluntary dismissal if a weakness in the case has become apparent and court deadlines preclude fixing the weakness. *See id.* For instance, in the next chapter, we will see that the last stage of discovery is the deposition of experts. Suppose a defense expert offers persuasive testimony to which the plaintiff has no expert to respond. By that time, the deadline for identifying experts will probably have passed. Plaintiff can always move for a continuance, but the trend across the nation has been toward resolving cases in a shorter period of time and avoiding continuances. *See* National Center for State Courts, *Civil Action, Improving Management of Complex Cases* Vol. 3, No. 1 (2004). Thus, in this scenario, the plaintiff would do well to seek voluntary dismissal without prejudice, re-file the action, and find an expert to counter the defense's expert. Some states model their voluntary dismissal approach on Federal Rule 41. *See* Appendix 7-2. Those states allow dismissal without court approval early in a case but, short of settlement, any other efforts to dismiss after initial pleadings require court approval. Other states allow dismissal without prejudice much later in the proceedings, sometimes even at trial. Hence, the ability to exercise strategic maneuvers such as dropping a case and getting an expert will depend on a jurisdiction's flexibility in this regard.

As also suggested in this chapter's discussion of tasks and decision-making at this stage, a truly effective litigator will abandon claims that she pled originally but which, after discovery, are less persuasive than other claims. In this process, the voluntary dismissal would be only partial. Even late in the game, courts will allow a party to dismiss some claims because it streamlines a case. *See, e.g., Neitzke v. Williams*, 490 U.S. 319, 326 (1989). To avoid piecemeal litigation, a court may require that the dismissal be with prejudice. If the court allowed a dismissal of some claims without prejudice, the plaintiff could try the remaining claims, and then re-file a new case on the other claims. If the claims dismissed without prejudice are not time-barred when re-filed and are not barred by principles of res judicata, then piecemeal litigation would result.

Most often, cases are dismissed voluntarily after the parties settle. *See, e.g.*, Samuel P. Jordan, *Early Panel Announcement, Settlement, and Adjudication*, 2007 B.Y.U. L. Rev. 55 (2007). Typically, the parties reach a settlement agreement in which the plaintiff receives consideration in return for a release of claims. Afterward, the parties usually submit a consent order stating that the case has been settled and that the case is dismissed "with prejudice." *See, e.g.*, Robert Timothy Reagan, *The Hunt for Sealed Settlement Agreements*, 81 Chi.-Kent L. Rev. 439 (2006). Of course, the settlement could provide otherwise. The parties could, for instance, agree that the case would be dismissed "without prejudice" and include an agreement that statutes of limitation defenses will not be raised if the parties are unable to work out their settlement. Counsel should be particularly careful when the plaintiff and some, but not all, defendants reach a settlement. If fewer than all defendants pay for a settlement that secures a release of all defendants, and the defendants have joint liability (*e.g.*, joint tortfeasors, parties who implicate vicarious liability principles, etc.), then the settling defendant(s) usually will have a claim against the non-settling defendant(s). *See, e.g., Garrison v. Navajo Freight Lines*, 392 P.2d 580, 582 (N.M. 1964). If the settlement agreement does not release the other defendants, the settling defendant(s) will not have a claim, *see, e.g.*, 42 Pa. C. S. § 8324 (2009), but the plaintiff can proceed against the non-settling defendant(s). If the trial results in a verdict for the plaintiff, the non-settling defendant(s) in joint liability scenarios will be entitled to a credit against the judgment amount. *See id.* The jury is not informed of the credit, but after the verdict, the court applies the amount paid by the settling defendant(s), and the nonsettling defendant(s) are responsible for the remainder. *See* Susan Lyons Cockrell, *Joint Tortfeasors Beware: Double Recovery May Be Allowed*, 50 S.C. L. Rev. 1081 (1999).

Follow-Up Questions

1. Compare the common law system, which allows a plaintiff to dismiss the case without prejudice one time for any reason, with the Federal Rules model that requires, after responsive pleadings are filed, court approval for a voluntary dismissal. What values does each system favor? What is the approach of the state in which you intend to practice?

Professional Identity Question

Assume you are in a state that allows voluntary dismissals freely (either a common law system, or simply a state where the courts are encouraged by the Supreme Court to grant voluntary dismissals without prejudice). Would you file suit, even if you were not truly prepared to proceed to trial, simply to educate yourself on how the defendant will handle the action, the experts that may be necessary, etc.? In other words, would you consider filing suit with no intention of going to trial but with the intention of taking a voluntary dismissal and then doing the preparation you need to do to "really" file and seek relief?

Practice Problems

Practice Problem 7-4

You file suit against a manufacturer for negligent design of a forklift on which your client is injured while operating the machine. Your suit is filed days before the statute of limitations runs on the claim. The case then is pending less than a year when you realize that you need to retain several experts if you are going to succeed. At this point in the proceedings, courts in your state routinely grant voluntary dismissals without prejudice. What must you nevertheless check before seeking such dismissal with plans of refiling the suit?

Practice Problem 7-5

Suppose you file a breach of contract and business conspiracy suit on behalf of a company who had failed business relations with another company. The suit has been pending over two years, and the court entered a pretrial order with a discovery cutoff that has passed. You are a month from trial. You realize that you lack a damages expert essential to demonstrating the amount of money that the defendant's actions have cost your client. You move for a voluntary dismissal without prejudice. (Assume the governing law does not follow a one-dismissal-of-right approach, but rather requires court approval). The defendant opposes the motion. What is the likelihood that the court will grant the voluntary dismissal? How can you increase your chances of at least avoiding trial without the necessary expert by moving for something other than dismissal?

Practice Problem 7-6

You have been representing a plaintiff in a breach of contract case for over a year. Ultimately, the plaintiff and defendant compromise and reach an agreement on the amount the defendant will pay the plaintiff. The parties enter into a settlement agreement. You then move for a voluntary dismissal, and the defendant insists that it be with prejudice. Should your client agree to such a dismissal? Will the court likely grant the request? *[handwritten: could bring suit on the later settlement agreement]*

[handwritten: suit could be on settlement agreement]

Involuntary Pretrial Dismissals

Involuntary pretrial dismissals may involve a variety of grounds. For instance, granting a motion to dismiss for insufficient service of process is an involuntary dismissal. *See* GENE R. SHREVE & PETER RAVEN-HANSEN, UNDERSTANDING CIVIL PROCEDURE § 11.04(2) (4th ed. 2002). Other involuntary dismissals include dismissal for lack of subject matter jurisdiction, lack of personal jurisdiction, insufficient process, or failure to join an indispensable party. FED. R. CIV. P. 41(b). Indeed, any of the grounds listed in Federal Rule of Civil Procedure 12(b) would represent bases for involuntary pretrial dismissal. *Smith v. Sidney Moncrief Pontiac, Buick, GMC Co.*, 120 S.W.3d 525 (Ark. 2003). If the problem can be solved by an amended pleading, the court will almost always allow leave to amend. *See, e.g.*, FED. R. CIV. P. 15(a); MASS. R. CIV. P. 15(a). For example, an amended pleading would cure a dismissal for failure to state a claim upon which relief can be granted if the plaintiff simply neglected to allege an element of a claim for which the plaintiff had factual support. Allowing leave to amend, however, would do no good if the basis for dismissal is lack of subject matter jurisdiction, personal jurisdiction, or the like. *See, e.g.*, FED. R. CIV. P. 41(b).

Other reasons could lead a court to dismiss a case involuntarily. If a party fails to comply with court orders, the court can dismiss the case with prejudice. *See, e.g., Link v. Wabash R.R. Co.*, 370 U.S. 626, 635 (1962). Most often, failure to comply with discovery orders has been the basis for such an extreme sanction. *See, e.g., Smith v. Gold Dust Casino*, 526 F.3d 402, 405 (8th Cir. 2008). Because all American jurisdictions favor resolution of cases on the merits, courts will not dismiss a case lightly. *Id.* However, involuntary dismissals may be necessary to prevent a litigant from flaunting the litigation process and to preserve the dignity of the court. *See generally Link v. Wabash R.R. Co.*, 370 U.S. 626 (1962) (holding that dismissal was proper when counsel failed to appear at a pre-trial conference and the litigant consciously acquiesced to his attorney's actions).

Follow-Up Questions

1. In a system designed to give litigants their opportunity to have a day in court, what purposes do involuntary pretrial dismissals serve? If the plaintiff's complaint fails to state a claim upon which relief can be granted, why does it make sense to grant an involuntary dismissal? What happens if the plaintiff's amended pleading still fails to state a claim upon which relief can be granted?

2. Some litigants abuse the system. If a plaintiff repeatedly fails to abide by court orders regarding discovery, is it fair to dismiss the plaintiff's case before it gets to trial? Why or why not?

Practice Problems

Practice Problem 7-7

Pauline Plaintiff retains an auction company to sell items from her mother's estate. Pauline and auction company enter into a contract. The contract includes the following terms: the auction company will use its best efforts to sell estate items, the auction company cannot make representations about items without adequate documentation, and the auction company does not guarantee a certain sale price per item. In return for its sales, the auction company receives a commission. One of the estate items was a bed that Pauline called a "plantation bed," by which she meant a bed from an eighteenth-century plantation. She did not provide documentation of this claim, so the auction company advertised the bed as a "plantation style" bed. Disappointed with the sale price, Pauline sued. After the auction company moved to have the contract made part of the record, the court ordered the contract to be produced and considered as part of the complaint. The court then dismissed Pauline's complaint based on a failure to state a claim upon which relief can be granted, but allowed leave to amend. After Pauline amends and asserts again that the bed was from a plantation, but still fails to allege any documentation supporting the assertion, the court grants a second motion to dismiss for failure to state a claim upon which relief can be granted. This time the court denies leave to amend and enters an involuntary dismissal order with prejudice. Was the court's decision a proper exercise of an involuntary dismissal?

Practice Problem 7-8

Pierre files suit for negligence against a SuperSaver Supermarket in maintaining an aisle where he slipped and suffered "major injuries." Pierre failed to respond to interrogatories or requests for production of documents sent by Supermarket. Defendant obtained a court order compelling responses, and Pierre still failed to respond. Moreover, Pierre failed to appear for a deposition properly scheduled and for which a timely notice was sent to Pierre's counsel. Defendant moves for a dismissal with prejudice, and the court grants the motion. Is the court's action appropriate? *(Yes) Valid remedy*

D. Methods to Integrate and Reinforce Topics Covered in This Chapter

Prepare two timelines based on the law of your jurisdiction. The first timeline is for defaults. On your default timeline, include the following: the time for a party to be placed in default, the time at which a party in default will have a judgment entered, and the date on which that judgment will become final (and, thus, hard to undo). The second timeline is for voluntary dismissals. (If you are in a common law jurisdiction where voluntary dismissals can be taken as of right through trial, you can omit this timeline.) On your voluntary dismissal timeline, label the various stages of the case and the likelihood that a court will grant a voluntary dismissal without prejudice at each stage. Be sure to include any considerations unique to your jurisdiction and/or any significant case law from your jurisdiction. Diagram 7-2 illustrates the first timeline. Diagram 7-3 illustrates the second.

Diagram 7-2

Suit Filed	Response Due	Δ in "Default" Status	Judgment Entered	Judgment Becomes Final

Diagram 7-3

Suit Filed	Response — Typically able to Voluntarily Dismiss	Discovery Starts — Likelihood of Voluntary Dismissal Begins to Become Less Certain	Likelihood of Involuntary Dismissal Being Granted Diminishes	Close to or at Trial: Little Chance of Voluntary Dismissal (except states with one-dismissal-of-right approach)

E. Written Assignments

1. In Sally's suit, HorsePower, Inc., HorsePower mistakenly assumed that the date it received the summons and complaint at its offices in Texafornia was the starting point for calculating the deadline for a responsive pleading. In fact, the jurisdiction requires that when an out-of-state defendant is served through a state representative, the date that triggers the response deadline is the date that the clerk of court receives the "certificate of compliance" from the state agency who mailed the certificate simultaneously with mailing process to the nonresident defendant. As a result, HorsePower, Inc. failed to respond within the time prescribed and is "in default." In an effort to get HorsePower, Inc. out of default, prepare a motion for relief from default and for leave to file responsive pleadings.

2. Assume that instead of filing a few days late, HorsePower sits on the summons and complaint for months before sending them to you. By the time you have them, HorsePower is in default and a hearing on damages has been scheduled to take place. The court refuses to allow HorsePower out of default because it failed to show sufficient grounds warranting such relief. HorsePower asks you to do everything you can to keep the damages as low as possible. What steps should you take to prepare for the hearing, what do you expect to do at the hearing, and if you can call any witnesses, who would you call and what would you ask them?

Chapter 8

Discovery: The Battle for Information

A. Sally's Case at This Stage of Litigation Process

You review the defendants' answers to Sally's complaint. (You should assume that HorsePower, Inc., though technically in default as described at the outset of the preceding chapter, received leave to file a responsive pleading so that it no longer is in default.) In response to each of Sally's allegations, the defendants either denied the allegations or stated that they lacked information sufficient to respond. In your jurisdiction, like every other one, a party's lack of information sufficient to verify allegations in a complaint operates as a denial. Mr. Befayre says the issues are "joined" or, as some other lawyers phrase it, the parties are "at issue." When you ask what he means, he tells you that the case reaches the point he described when the plaintiff has alleged facts that the defendant denies. Reaching this phase is good news because you have at least passed the first round of challenges to the suit. He says that the parties will engage in discovery and that they need to remain mindful of gathering evidence on each element of Sally's case so as to overcome any summary judgment motion after discovery is done. Then, he concludes, you can get her case to trial where you want it—in front of a jury.

As the supervising partner, Mr. Befayre assures you he will meet with you once you have developed a discovery plan. However, he is occupied with a big case and is giving you a great deal of freedom. You have observed that your firm's lawyers keep their clients informed at each stage of the litigation via letters and reports. Thus, you realize that after meeting with Mr. Befayre, he will want Sally and her daughter to be notified of the plan, and a range of potential expenses, so that they are in tune with their lawyers' strategy. You have also heard lawyers from other firms speak with admiration of your firm's uncanny ability to keep clients happy. These lawyers often ask, "What is your firm's secret?" You were not sure at first. However, you are starting to see that this practice of keeping clients informed and part of the decision-making process is most likely one of the main reasons for the client satisfaction.

B. Tasks and Decision-Making at This Stage of a Case

The point in the litigation process to which Sally's case now has progressed is shown in Diagram 8-1.

Diagram 8-1

Cause of Action (events leading to suit)
Prefiling Matters to Consider; Choice of Forum [Chs. 2-3]
Π and Δ Decide on Offensive Pleadings & Joinder (of claims & parties); Filing Suit; Service [Chs. 4-5]
Motions, Responsive Pleadings; Default; Voluntary & Involuntary Dismissals [Chs. 6-7]
Discovery Phase (developing proof to establish claims & learning about the adversary's case) [Ch. 8]
Right to Jury Trial; Pretrial Motions & Practice [Ch. 9]
Final Pretrial Conference & Other Events within Last Month before Trial [Ch. 10]
Procedure at Trial [Ch. 11]
Post-Trial Motions & Calculating the Date of Final Judgment to Know Key Deadlines Such as for Notice of Appeal [Ch. 12]

"You cannot win cases in discovery but you sure can lose them there," said Mr. Befayre. You asked him what he meant by that, and he explained that an attorney has to gather information and facts with the ultimate goal of successfully winning over a judge or jury should a case go to trial. However, because a claim cannot prevail *until* trial, discovery is a necessary (but not sufficient) means to that end. He further explained that if a lawyer failed to develop sufficient evidence to support *each* element of the client's claims, an opponent's summary judgment motion will expose these failures. "A chain is only as strong as its weakest link" is another of Mr. Befayre's pet refrains. By this comment, he means that a client could have great evidence on three elements of a claim, but if the claim requires four elements to be proved, that fourth element could be the weak link that breaks the chain if the lawyer does not establish evidence on *each* part of a case.

You realize, therefore, your plan has to both evaluate Sally's case critically and determine how to build it. You would have to identify which evidence you could develop to prove each essential element of each of Sally's claims. The burden of proof in civil cases, as you well know, is proof by a preponderance of the evidence. Thus, Sally's evidence would have to convince the fact-finder that each of the elements of her claim is more likely than not, true. Or, simply put, if the plaintiff's and defendants' evidence sits on a scale, the scale would need to tip (if only slightly) in her favor. You also realize that any defenses raised by defendants need to be considered. Although the defendant would bear the burden of proof on any such defenses, Sally will need to have evidence showing that the defenses lacked merit.

Your plan now accounts for the exact nature of Sally's claims. You believe that her best claims are against the City, the State, and HorsePower, Inc. As for her negligence claim against each defendant, she will have to prove the classic four elements of the tort—duty, breach, causation, and damages. However, you also realize that for each claim the evidence will vary. Moreover, the evidence showing that the City and State were responsible for the large hole will overlap. How will you show that part of the hole was within the jurisdiction of the City and that it was the City's responsibility to maintain safe roads within its jurisdiction? How will you show that part of the hole was outside the jurisdiction of the City and therefore within the State's jurisdiction so that it had responsibility to maintain that part of the road? What public or private documents might help to establish these facts? Are there witnesses who would need to be called to prove what the documents represent? Alternatively, should you hire your own expert surveyor to establish both the location of the accident and the fact that part of the hole was on City land and part of the hole was on State land?

If you conclude that the City and State had to have been aware of the defective road conditions in order to be found negligent, how will you show that they were negligent and failed to do anything about it? Can you simply call witnesses who traveled the route regularly to verify that the hole was there for a long period of time, gradually worsened, and the City and State officials must have been aware of the condition? Or should you pinpoint the City and State representatives responsible for that portion of the road and take their depositions? Moreover, your research has shown that you will not be able to recover punitive damages against the State but that your jurisdiction has left open the possibility of recovering punitive damages against a municipality like Arcadia upon a showing of willful or grossly reckless conduct.[1] How will you be able to offer proof to justify punitive damages against the City?

Were there any witnesses to the accident? Can you rely on Sally to testify about what happened? Has she, after the coma, regained memory of events immediately preceding the accident? What are Sally's recoverable damages to date? What future damages, if any, does she expect to incur as a result of the accident? What documents will verify damages? What experts are necessary to verify past or future injuries and damages?

In the claim against the vehicle manufacturer, how will you prove that the failure of the vehicle's roll-bar was due to the manufacturer's negligence? Recognizing that against HorsePower, Inc., you have pled not only negligence but also breach of Uniform Commercial Code implied and express warranties, what will you need to prove the elements of those claims? What documents would you request from the manufacturer? Could a governmental agency have documents that might be helpful in building a case, and if so which ones would you request?

Effective lawyers not only know how to answer these kinds of questions, but also know *which* discovery tools to use, the order in which to use them, and when to get the court involved if someone is recalcitrant. The following section will outline the array of discovery methods available.

---

1. *See, e.g.*, Joel E. Smith, *Recovery of Exemplary or Punitive Damages from a Municipal Corporation*, 1 A.L.R. 4th 448 (1980).

C. Overview of Applicable Law

Discovery Methods and Sanctions

As the previous section illustrates, discovery is necessary to building a case. Discovery is a pretrial mechanism that provides parties to the litigation the tools with which to obtain evidence and facts from the opposing party. 23 Am. Jur. 2d *Depositions and Discovery* § 1 (2009). Discovery eliminates the element of "surprise" at trial by allowing the parties to access any facts that may be admitted as evidence at trial. 27 C.J.S. *Discovery* § 2 (2009). Additionally, discovery ideally allows parties to narrow the issues and distinguish claims that have supporting evidence from those that do not. *Id.*

Most jurisdictions allow discovery by any of the following methods: depositions, requests for production of documents or things (or for permission to enter upon land or property for inspection), written interrogatories, requests for admission, and physical and mental examinations. 23 Am. Jur. 2d *Depositions and Discovery* § 7 (2009). None of the discovery tools is exclusive; they may be used in conjunction with one another. *Id.* Unless the court orders otherwise, the rules do not dictate a particular sequence. *Id.* § 8.

An attorney who rushes into the discovery process without a plan does her client a disservice for at least two reasons. First, an attorney can inadvertently educate her opponent, allowing the opponent to script responses to discovery and to prepare her case for trial. Without the prompting of discovery requests, opposing counsel may neglect to prepare for a key element of her client's case. Although a lawyer always takes a risk in underestimating her opponent, a good lawyer recognizes that rote discovery requests that are not necessary for her client but which prompt the opponent to focus on an issue make little sense. Second, discovery conducted without a proper plan typically increases the client's costs.

Informal Discovery

Informal discovery should be the place where every lawyer starts building her case and developing a case strategy. Informal discovery is more efficient and less costly than using the methods provided by the procedural rules. Roger S. Haydock et al., Fundamentals of Pretrial Litigation 206 (7th ed. 2008). An attorney should attempt to locate all of the favorable and unfavorable information. She can then target focused formal discovery on obtaining necessary evidence and on supporting the strong points of her case and negating weak points. Marilyn J. Berger et al., Pretrial Advocacy 242 (2d ed. 2007).[2]

Conferring with the client is the most common type of informal discovery and is the most convenient way to glean information about a case. An attorney can request documents and materials directly from her client. The documents will educate her about the issues at hand, the damages incurred, and possible future damages. A client's documents may also lead to third-party witnesses who can testify to important facts. For injured clients, the documents will provide a record of health care professionals. These persons

---

2. *See also, e.g.,* Corey David Kintzer, *Informal Discovery: An Effective Strategy and Cost-saving Solution,* http://www.abanet.org/yld/tyl/june07/kintzer.html (visit the ABA Young Lawyers Division for other informative articles).

often serve as a cross between factual and expert witnesses because they provide factual background about treatment but also may offer expert opinions.

Informal discovery need not stop with your own client. For example, in a personal injury case, an attorney should visit the scene of the accident as soon as possible. A lawyer should visit the accident scene with a witness, ideally one not employed by her firm or otherwise interested in the case. The attorney and witness can make a record of the accident scene, gather facts, take photographs from different view-points, and measure pertinent distances, heights of objects, etc. Often the location of an accident undergoes physical changes by the time a case is tried. A proactive attorney will preserve evidence of the location of the accident as close to the time of the accident as possible. Having done so may prove to be invaluable information when the case goes to trial and may prevent the attorney from having to rely on a witness's recollection of the condition of the scene. The attorney can have the witness testify to the physical features she observed on the visit to the scene. The witness also can provide the foundation for photographs by testifying that they fairly depict the scene at the time, that measurements are consistent with her recollection, etc. Although the attorney can at times find witnesses who will verify these facts if she took the photographs and took the measurements herself, she risks becoming a witness (and potentially having to withdraw as counsel) if no one else can verify the facts documented in the informal investigation.   *Why 2d person broughtalong*

Each time an attorney gathers information informally, she advances her client's case. Bit by bit, she learns more about the case. The difference between hearing a description of an accident scene and actually visiting the scene is comparable to the difference between listening to someone describe the taste of an apple and actually eating one. At an accident scene, the lawyer can view it from every angle, measure relevant distances, and observe physical conditions that simply could not be appreciated without being on the scene. Throughout the remainder of the case, the lawyer who has visited the scene and gathered evidence will continue to benefit from that effort. When she drafts the written discovery requests, or questions witnesses under oath in the depositions (both described below), she will draft more intelligent document requests and ask better questions than an attorney who handles the case from her desk. Informal investigation may, and should, involve more than merely visiting an accident scene and recording facts there. If vehicles or other physical evidence have been towed away or placed in a location other than the accident site, the attorney should secure this evidence. Securing such evidence may require placing it in storage. Physical evidence owned by others must be dealt with differently. If owned by a nonparty, the attorney can ask for the evidence (possibly pay a nominal amount to obtain and preserve it), and preserve it exactly as found. If a non-party or a party has physical evidence and will not agree to preserve it, the attorney may have to seek an immediate court order requiring such preservation.   *× court order requiring preservation*

What if people live near the location where events giving rise to the suit occurred? The attorney or other agent for the client should interview these persons. Did they see the events? Do they know anyone who did? How long has a physical condition, such as a hole in the ground or a sharp pipe sticking out of the ground, existed? Do they know of anyone who has been hurt there? After speaking with witnesses, the attorney or other agent often asks these people if they are willing to sign a statement reciting the facts related.   *→ locals who can attest to facts*

What if a company is likely to be sued? Can the lawyer still engage in informal investigation? Well, if a company is being sued, a fair chance exists that the company has been sued before. Through computer-assisted research, such as internet searches, a lawyer will often find the other cases. Nothing prevents a lawyer from calling plaintiff's counsel in these other cases. If documents produced by the company in another case have either be-   *internet searches*

how do you know that?

come public records or are not under an order preventing their dissemination, the attorney can ask for and receive all documents produced by the company. The advantage to a lawyer who seeks and gathers such information cannot be exaggerated.

One other advantage of informal discovery is the possibility that an adversary, once formal discovery is underway, may not ask for facts, documents, or information gathered through informal discovery. If requested, counsel must, of course, identify any facts learned regardless of how she learned them. Moreover, documents that are not protected by a privilege will have to be produced, as discussed more fully below. However, counsel's opponent does not always ask for every fact an attorney has learned. And counsel's opponent does not always ask for every document she has gathered. In these instances, the opponent may not be ready at trial when such facts or documents come to light. Moreover, the opponent will have no one to blame except her lawyer, who failed to do her job.

The American system is an adversarial one. An attorney's job is to represent her client to the best of her ability and to handle herself professionally and ethically. If counsel for your opponent fails to ask for certain information or documents, the opponent may have a malpractice claim against her attorney but cannot blame you for her attorney's laziness. In short, hard work for your client may at times pay off with valuable information or documents that provide significant leverage for your client.

leverage.

Practice Problem

Practice Problem 8-1

This exercise illustrates the value of brainstorming on potential sources of informal discovery. The group members can use the questions raised above to get started, and ideally will then develop some of their own ideas about the kinds of inexpensive informal discovery that could be performed in different kinds of cases. After considering the kinds of informal discovery you could pursue in a case arising from a vehicular accident (such as *Brad T. Rex v. Ena Hurry* described in Chapter 4 *supra* at pages 82–96), discuss how you could take advantage of informal discovery in a variety of cases. For instance, take a dispute with an insurance company over its refusal to honor an insured's claim. What could the lawyer for the insured do, prior to formal discovery, to ensure she is knowledgeable about insurance practices? Or, assume you were retained to sue a car dealership under a state "Lemon Law Statute" allowing car buyers who have excessive trouble with cars bought from dealers to seek relief if the dealer will not take the car back and refund the purchase price. How would you prepare yourself to discuss issues related to continuing engine malfunctions or the like?

Formal Discovery

The Scope of Discovery

Today, most jurisdictions embrace the scope of discovery that was outlined in Federal Rule of Civil Procedure 26 prior to the recent amendments to that Rule. *See* Appendix 8-1 (showing that many of Fed. R. Civ. P. 26's provisions are included in state rules or statutes, though often in a number of different rules and statutes). Under the pre-amend-ment standard, "parties [could] obtain discovery for any matter relevant to the subject mat-ter involved in the action." FED. R. CIV. P. 26(b)(1).

In an effort to limit the scope of discovery, Rule 26 was amended in 2000 so that the scope of discovery provision states that "parties may obtain discovery regarding any non-privileged matter that is relevant to any party's claim or defense...." FED. R. CIV. P. 26(b)(1). (Previously the provision allowed discovery "of any matter relevant to the subject matter of the pending action.") Even in federal courts, this change has had little impact on nar-rowing the scope of discovery. *See, e.g., Equal Employment Opportunity Comm'n v. Caesar's Entm't, Inc.,* 237 F.R.D. 428 (D. Nev. 2006) ("There seems to be a general consensus that the [2000] Amendments to Rule 26(b) 'do not dramatically alter the scope of discovery'.... Most courts which have addressed the issue find that the amendments to Rule 26 still con-template liberal discovery, and that relevancy under Rule 26 is extremely broad."); *see also* CHARLES ALAN WRIGHT ET AL., FEDERAL PRACTICE & PROCEDURE § 2008 n.13.1 (2009) (collecting cases reaching the same conclusion as *Caesar's Entertainment* decision).

States have largely retained the broad definition based on the pre-2000 version of Fed-eral Rule of Civil Procedure 26(b). *See* Appendix 8-1. Thus, most modern jurisdictions have a broad "relevance" standard, and consequently, the scope of discovery is broad as well. Appendix 8-1; 23 AM. JUR. 2d *Depositions and Discovery* § 2 (2009). Under the fed-eral rules and comparable state rules, "relevance" includes any matter that pertains to, or could reasonably lead to a matter that pertains to, any issue presented in the case. 23 AM. JUR. 2d *Depositions and Discovery* § 24 (2009).

Discovery is not restricted to the search for evidence that will be admissible at trial. Even if the information or documents sought would not be admissible under the rules of ev-idence, a discovering party can obtain such information or documents. She need only show that the information or documents *could reasonably lead* to admissible evidence. *Id.* Also, because a primary purpose of discovery is to narrow the issues in the case, the parties can pursue discovery on matters beyond the pleadings. *Id.* § 23.

Nevertheless, discovery does have its limits. Matters that are clearly outside the scope of a reasonable search are not discoverable. *Id.* For example, asking a party about her sex life in a breach-of-contract action would be out of bounds.

Specific Tools of Discovery

Automatic Disclosures

Initial Automatic Disclosures

The automatic discovery disclosures introduced within the past decade into federal practice have not, except in few states (*see, e.g.,* COL. R. CIV. P. 26(a)(1)), caught on in state practice. *See, e.g.,* John B. Oakley, *A Fresh Look at the Federal Rules in State Courts,* 3 NEV. L. J. 354, 361-84, 386-87 (2003). Because more states may adopt the practice, how-ever, the approach is outlined here. Federal Rule of Civil Procedure 26(a)(1) reads as fol-lows:

(a) Required Disclosures.

(1) *Initial Disclosure.*

(A) *In General.* Except as ... otherwise stipulated or ordered by the court, a party must, without awaiting a discovery request, provide to the other parties:

Automatic

(**i**) the name and, if known, the address and telephone number of each individual likely to have discoverable information—along with the subjects of that information—that the disclosing party may use to support its claims or defenses, unless the use would be solely for impeachment;

(**ii**) a copy—or a description by category and location—of all documents, electronically stored information, and tangible things that the disclosing party has in its possession, custody, or control and may use to support its claims or defenses, unless the use would be solely for impeachment;

(**iii**) a computation of each category of damages claimed by the disclosing party—who must also make available for inspection and copying as under Rule 34 the documents or other evidentiary material, unless privileged or protected from disclosure, on which each computation is based, including materials bearing on the nature and extent of injuries suffered; and

(**iv**) for inspection and copying as under Rule 34, any insurance agreement under which an insurance business may be liable to satisfy all or part of a possible judgment in the action or to indemnify or reimburse for payments made to satisfy the judgment.

Adopted in 2000, the automatic disclosure provisions are designed to get the process of exchanging information underway without delay. *See* Federal Rule of Civil Procedure 26 advisory committee's note to the 2000 amendment. Requiring a party to provide a computation of damages, and documents upon which the computation is based, is a valuable requirement. Although parties are supposed to produce the best damages calculations of which they are capable at the outset of litigation, the Rule does not require a party asserting a claim to have detailed damage calculations, and parties are permitted to amend. *See* 6-26 P. HIGGINBOTHAM, MOORE'S FEDERAL PRACTICE & PROCEDURE § 26.22 (2009). Moreover, the requirement of early production of any insurance agreements that may be liable to satisfy a judgment likely helps to promote settlement. If a party has limited insurance coverage, the claimant will perhaps be less inclined to seek damages to the same degree as otherwise.

The two other automatic disclosures, of witnesses and of documents, allow counsel to see what a party considers significant to her case. Note, however, that both Rule 26(a)(1)(A) and 26(a)(1)(B) qualify the witnesses and documents that must be produced if the party "may use them *to support* its claims or defenses." (emphasis added). In other words, a disclosing party can know of eyewitnesses or documents crucial to the case but which it deems to be unhelpful to its claims or defenses. If so, the party has no obligation to disclose them under the automatic disclosure provisions. That major hole in these automatic disclosure provisions requires a litigant to count on the traditional discovery tools discussed below—interrogatories, requests for production of documents, requests for admission, and depositions. If worded correctly by the party sending the discovery or asking the question at a deposition, the opponent must respond even if the witnesses identified or the documents produced *hurts* the opponent's case. In other words, formal discovery should identify the witnesses and the documents that the opponent both will and *will not* rely upon. An attorney wants all of the witnesses identified and all potentially relevant documents produced, especially those that do not support your opponent's case. The reason is obvious: these are the witnesses and documents that have the most potential to support your client's case. In traditional discovery, an attorney can uncover a "smoking gun"—a litigator's phrase for a piece of evidence of great value to her client (and damaging to your opponent). Automatic disclosures, due to the phrase limiting them to witnesses or documents that "may support" a litigant's case, assure that smoking guns will not be produced through that form of discovery. Hence, formal discovery must seek *all* facts, witnesses, and documents related to the case.

Automatic Disclosures Regarding Experts

The amendments to Federal Rule of Civil Procedure 26(a) also include automatic disclosure of certain expert testimony. Following is the Rule's language:

(2) *Disclosure of Expert Testimony.*

(A) *In General.* In addition to the disclosures required by Rule 26(a)(1), a party must disclose to the other parties the identity of any witness it may use at trial to present evidence under Federal Rule of Evidence 702, 703, or 705.

(B) *Written Report.* Unless otherwise stipulated or ordered by the court, this disclosure must be accompanied by a written report—prepared and signed by the witness—if the witness is one retained or specially employed to provide expert testimony in the case or one whose duties as the party's employee regularly involve giving expert testimony. The report must contain:

(i) a complete statement of all opinions the witness will express and the basis and reasons for them;

(ii) the data or other information considered by the witness in forming them;

(iii) any exhibits that will be used to summarize or support them;

(iv) the witness's qualifications, including a list of all publications authored in the previous 10 years;

(v) a list of all other cases in which, during the previous four years, the witness testified as an expert at trial or by deposition; and

(vi) a statement of the compensation to be paid for the study and testimony in the case.

(C) *Time to Disclose Expert Testimony.* A party must make these disclosures at the times and in the sequence that the court orders. Absent a stipulation or a court order, the disclosures must be made:

(i) at least 90 days before the date set for trial or for the case to be ready for trial; or

(ii) if the evidence is intended solely to contradict or rebut evidence on the same subject matter identified by another party under Rule 26(a)(2)(B), within 30 days after the other party's disclosure.

(D) *Supplementing the Disclosure.* The parties must supplement these disclosures when required under Rule 26(e).

Notice that this automatic disclosure rule, even if it has been adopted in a state, has significant "holes." In particular, the Rule requires disclosure "if the witness is one retained or specially employed to provide expert testimony in the case or one whose duties as the party's employee regularly involve giving expert testimony." FED. R. CIV. P. 26(a)(2). What if a health care professional was involved in treating a person? Or, consider the employee of a party who is an expert but does not regularly give expert opinions. Are such persons required to provide expert disclosures? As written, these categories of experts were not covered by the automatic disclosure rules. *See* C. WRIGHT, A. MILLER & C. MARCUS, FEDERAL PRACTICE & PROCEDURE § 2031.1 (2009). Thus, a party would need to issue an interrogatory to her opponent to learn of such experts or risk surprise late in the trial process. However, a proposed amendment that would take effect on December 1, 2010, would close these gaps and requires some automatic disclosure even of treating health care professionals and employee experts.[3]

 Final Pretrial Disclosures

Finally, Federal Rule of Civil Procedure 26(a)(3) provides for so-called final automatic pretrial disclosures. This part of the Rule reads as follows:

(3) *Pretrial Disclosures.*

(A) *In General.* In addition to the disclosures required by Rule 26(a)(1) and (2), a party must provide to the other parties and promptly file the following information about the evidence that it may present at trial other than solely for impeachment:

(i) the name and, if not previously provided, the address and telephone number of each witness — separately identifying those the party expects to present and those it may call if the need arises;

(ii) the designation of those witnesses whose testimony the party expects to present by deposition and, if not taken stenographically, a transcript of the pertinent parts of the deposition; and

(iii) an identification of each document or other exhibit, including summaries of other evidence — separately identifying those items the party expects to offer and those it may offer if the need arises.

(B) *Time for Pretrial Disclosures; Objections.* Unless the court orders otherwise, these disclosures must be made at least 30 days before trial. Within 14 days after they are made, unless the court sets a different time, a party may serve and promptly file a list of the following objections: any objections to the use under Rule 32(a) of a deposition designated by another party under Rule 26(a)(3)(A)(ii); and any objection, together with the grounds for it, that may be made to the admissibility of materials identified under Rule 26(a)(3)(A)(iii). An objection not so made — except for one under Federal Rule of Evidence 402 or 403 — is waived unless excused by the court for good cause.

FED. R. CIV. P. 26(a)(3).

As with the weakness of initial pretrial disclosures, a lawyer would do her client a disservice to rely on this automatic disclosure, even if her state has adopted a version of it into its rules. The rule requires identification of witnesses and exhibits that a party "will" call (or offer), or which the party "may" call (or offer) at trial. What does this leave out? As noted in the discussion of initial pretrial disclosures, it leaves out those witnesses, documents, or other evidence supporting *your* case — and which the opponent (disclosing party) would just as soon that your client not see. Thus, the traditional rules of discovery discussed more fully below are as important as ever. Only by employing them will a party have a degree of certainty that she has learned *all* the facts, seen *all* the documents, and found out about *all* the witnesses that are significant to her client's case. Although as the next section points out, an effective attorney will push for a final pretrial conference

---

3. For a schedule regarding Rule amendments including the one to Rule 26(a)(2), see the Federal Judiciary Website at http://www.uscourts.gov/rules/Civil_Docket.pdf (last visited Dec. 11, 2009).

deadline at which, typically, the court will require identification of witnesses, exhibits, and the like. Thus, even if a person's state lacks the automatic disclosure provisions above, she can ensure identification of the same items by moving the court to impose the same disclosure obligations and deadlines. The place to do this is at the initial pretrial conference, usually heard early in a case (*e.g.*, after a defendant has answered), so that a schedule is in place and everyone knows the requirements and deadlines well ahead of time.

Initial Discovery Conference

Many ignore initial pretrial conferences in jurisdictions that do not require them, but intelligent attorneys know better. In many jurisdictions, discovery may not be sought by either party until an initial discovery conference has taken place. *See* Am. Jur. 2d *Depositions and Discovery* § 8 (2009). In those that follow the Federal Rules, the timing of the automatic disclosures that were just discussed is triggered by the initial pretrial conference. *See, e.g.*, Col. R. Civ. P. 26(a)(1)(C) (automatic disclosures due 14 days after the conference of parties required by Col. R. Civ. P. 26(f)). Although even the Federal Rules do not require an initial pretrial conference because Federal Rule of Civil Procedure 16 provides that the court "may" order one, almost every federal court—and states that follow the Federal Rules—have an initial pretrial conference to set a trial date, discovery cutoffs, and similar deadlines. It is within the trial court's discretion to order the parties to appear before it for a pretrial conference. *See* Appendix 10-1 (reflecting the states that have adopted rules or statutes similar to Fed. R. Civ. P. 16). Even if your jurisdiction's rules do not require a pretrial conference, a party can always move for a pretrial conference. For the reasons discussed below, attorneys should seriously consider seeking a conference if the court does not require one.

A pretrial conference promotes settlement of the case and narrowing of the issues, as well as the ability of counsel to set out a timeline and discovery plan. 23 Am. Jur. 2d *Depositions and Discovery* § 10 (2009). A pretrial conference often aids in the resolution of cases with less expense to the parties. *See, e.g.*, Tex. R. Civ. P. 166. Jurisdictions that require a pre-trial conference usually mandate a written report outlining that the discovery plan be filed with the court within a specified period of time following the conference. 23 Am. Jur. 2d *Depositions and Discovery* § 10 (2009). Plaintiff's counsel should beware that, by prematurely certifying that a case is ready for trial, she can inadvertently cut off her ability to seek discovery. Conversely, defendant's counsel may waive the ability to seek further discovery by not requesting it early enough. *Id.* § 8. In short, be aware of the rules in your jurisdiction concerning limitations on discovery once a trial date is set. [handwritten margin note: *don't be too eager to set trial date w/o checking time limits on discov.*]

Effective lawyers recognize that a pretrial conference and the order resulting from such a conference typically serve their clients' best interests. The conference and order impose discipline and limitations on the parties, resulting in reduced litigation expenses. The pretrial conference and order allow the court to exercise judicial control over the scope of discovery and to order the discovery process to be limited in some way(s). *Id.* § 10. Unbounded discovery, coupled with the growth in electronic discovery, are two main factors in the explosion in litigation costs.

By employing the procedural tools available to her, a lawyer can effectively limit discovery costs. For example, assume you represent a defendant. At the pretrial conference, defense counsel can seek a stay of discovery until a particular matter is resolved by the court. (A "stay" would mean that the court suspended any discovery until further notice.) If a defendant files a pretrial motion or pleading that has the ability to end the litigation (*e.g.*, personal jurisdiction challenge), the court may take months to resolve the issue.

Without a discovery stay, time and resources could be wasted by all of the parties to the litigation. Conversely, plaintiff's counsel in virtually any case does her client a favor by imposing a time-line on discovery. Given time, lawyers tend to use that time to seek increasing amounts of information, regardless of whether they really need it. Much, if not most of the time such discovery derives from a fear of not having every last document or piece of information. If a lawyer has sought everything, so the thinking goes, she cannot be second-guessed. If plaintiff's counsel is humble enough to recognize her own need for discipline and deadlines, she will ask the court at a pretrial conference for a discovery cut-off date and a trial date. Without time constraints, attorneys usually do not exercise the self control necessary to handle cases in a manner that best serves the client. Even if the items about which opposing counsel fight are within the realm of reason, nothing forces a lawyer to prioritize the matters most important to her case like a deadline. Lacking a deadline, parties spend literally tens of thousands of dollars in some cases in the endless back-and-forth disputes of discovery. In large cases, costs escalate even more.

During the past decade, many states have adopted judicial case management plans that require cases to be disposed of within a specified period of time, often a year. Other states have rules allowing trial court judges to create local rules that are designed to expedite a court's business. *E.g.*, CAL. CIV. PROC. CODE § 575.1 (West 2009). The days of cases sitting around for years are coming to a close. However, some jurisdictions may not actively implement such a plan. Other courts may leave to litigants the option of whether to place a case on the fast track. For the reasons set forth above, a lawyer in most instances will serve her client's best interests by choosing that option.

The United States District Court for the Eastern District of Virginia learned this lesson in the second half of the Twentieth Century. For many years, Judge Walter E. Hoffman was the only United States District Judge in the Norfolk and Newport News Divisions of that court. Facing a large docket and believing that part of justice involved resolving cases in a reasonable period of time, Judge Hoffman developed a plan in which cases had to be tried within six months of an answer being filed. *See* Heather Russell Koenig, *The Eastern District of Virginia: A Working Solution for Civil Justice Reform*, 32 U. RICH. L. REV. 799 (1998); *see also generally* 23 AM. JUR. 2d *Depositions and Discovery* § 8 (2009) (explaining that federal judges have the right to enforce a strenuous discovery schedule). Continuances were unheard of. *See* Koenig, 32 U. RICH. L. REV. at 802-19. Lawyers complained. *Id.* But the cases began to be heard. No matter how complex, every case had to adhere to the deadlines. Parties adapted to the deadlines and completed the necessary discovery, even in this shorter-than-usual time frame. Gradually, this court became known as the fastest at disposing of cases within the federal system and accordingly, earned the name, the "Rocket Docket." *Id.*

The example of the Rocket Docket has led many other jurisdictions to implement case management plans.[4] Implementing an accelerated case management plan is fairly simple. The first step is, early in the case, to set a firm trial date.[5] After doing so, the court typically will work back chronologically—setting a final pretrial conference three weeks to a month before trial. Continuing to work backwards chronologically, the key deadlines would be two in particular—(1) the deadline for summary judgment motions after the close of discovery, and (2) the cut-off date by which all discovery will be completed. Courts have taken such

---

4. The impact has led to reforms in state court practice. *See Discovery Guidelines for State Courts*, http://www.abanet.org/jd/ncstj/pdf/GuidelinesWithCommentary.pdf. (2001) (Developed by the National Conference of State Trial Judges of the A.B.A.).

5. Carrie E. Johnson, *Rocket Dockets: Reducing Delay in Federal Civil Litigation*, 85 CAL. L. REV. 225, 233 (1997).

case-management steps because they realized that the delays in resolution of cases were increasing expenses to both the parties and taxpayers. The other lesson of the Rocket Docket was to debunk the myth that some cases are too complex to be tried on a fast track.

Unless a compelling reason justifies delay, plaintiff's counsel should seek as early a trial date as possible and for an appropriate discovery schedule that takes the trial date into account. Counsel may want to cite the example of the Rocket Docket and the emerging trend across the nation in support of obtaining a speedy resolution of a particular dispute. If plaintiff's counsel has pursued informal discovery, the plaintiff ought to be farther along in preparing the case than the defendant. Strategic pressure for an earlier trial date can give the plaintiff the advantage of maintaining any leverage gained by previous trial preparation.

The initial pretrial order need not be complex. Below is a sample based on an actual case in the State of Washington. Ultimately, the plaintiff's failure to abide by the order in part supported a judgment against the plaintiff based on the trial court's ability to impose sanctions for noncompliance.[6] (The question of sanctions to enforce discovery will be addressed more fully below.)

Sample Pretrial Scheduling Order

IN THE SUPERIOR COURT OF KING COUNTY,
STATE OF WASHINGTON

ALI SHEKARCHI,	)
	)
Plaintiff,	)
v.	) No. 121602
	)
ALLSTATE INSURANCE COMPANY,	)
	)
Defendant.	)
	)

Initial Scheduling Order

The trial in this case shall occur on May 17, 2004.

Each party shall file a list of the witnesses that the party will or may call at trial no later than December 15, 2003.

Both parties shall complete discovery by March 29, 2004. By "complete," the court means that the party shall have served the requested discovery (if a written request) so that the time for responding under the rule shall occur before March 29, 2004. Moreover, any depositions must be arranged, noticed, and subpoenas issued in sufficient time before March 29, 2004, so that the deposition may occur on or before that deadline.

The deadline for hearing final dispositive motions such as pretrial motions for summary judgment shall be May 3, 2004. All briefs must be filed in a sufficient time before that deadline so that the court will have the opportunity to read them and be prepared for oral arguments on May 3, 2004.

---

6. *See Shekarchi v. Allstate Insurance Co.*, 127 Wash. App. 1028, 2005 WL 1178053 (Wash. App. Div. 1 2005).

A settlement conference shall occur on May 10, 2004.

IT IS SO ORDERED

ENTERED:

Superior Court Judge

Jan. 5, 2004

King County, Washington

Follow-Up Questions

1. Consult the rule or statute in the state in which you intend to practice concerning pretrial conferences. Will you be required to set a trial date with pretrial deadlines leading up to it? If the rule or statute does not require a trial date and deadlines, how can you go about moving for a conference and order setting deadlines?

2. How can you convey to your client, in terms that the client will likely take seriously, the necessity to respond promptly to discovery requests of the opponent, so that you can keep pressure on that opponent to do the same?

Professional Identity Question

A lawyer who is looking out for her client's best interests ought to, as noted above, seek the earliest trial date possible. A lawyer with a billable-hour arrangement has a competing interest—the more time the lawyer spends on a case, the more she makes. Lawyers may not consciously think out loud: "I want to extend this case for a sustained period so as to maximize fees." However, do you believe that unconsciously someone can be influenced by pressures either to satisfy a firm's billable hour requirements, or simply to make as much money as one can? How can you implement safeguards so as to avoid your allowing such pressures to cloud your judgment about a client's best interests?

The Importance of Considering Electronic Data Early

Another crucial issue militates in favor of an early pretrial conference and order. The escalation of the use of electronic data management and storage of records has created additional issues that must be considered. "Electronic media discovery" is becoming more and more prominent in practically every type of lawsuit.[7] "North American businesses create [i]n excess of 3.25 trillion e-mails per year and create more than 90 percent of their information in digital form." Bradford S. Babbitt & Kori E. Termine, *in The New Reasonable Accessibility Standard: What's So Reasonable About It*, E-Discovery: A Special Publication of the Section of Litigation of the American Bar Association 42 (2007). Paper is on the way out, as "bytes" of data, stored in electronic form, take its

---

7. For an interesting discussion regarding discovery of deleted electronic records, see Marjorie A. Shields, *Discovery of Deleted E-mail and Other Deleted Electronic Records* 27 A.L.R. 6th 565 (2007).

place. All of this may make environmental enthusiasts happy, but those who are accustomed to discovery of paper documents must change the way they consider the discovery process. Realizing the significance of electronic data at the outset of a case is crucial. The convenience and efficiency that is attached to electronic storage of data also makes it easy to delete. With the click of a button, crucial evidence can be destroyed.

An attorney should write opposing counsel at the very beginning of a case, especially if the defendant is a corporate, governmental, or similar entity that deletes e-mail on a regular basis. For instance, most e-mail systems are programmed to automatically delete certain types of data after a certain amount of time. Information Technology ("IT") personnel often encourage employees to delete certain types of electronic data because it is necessary for an organization's computer system to run efficiently. These representatives may not know about impending litigation (or the need for preservation of certain data) *unless you ensure that they become aware of it.* An attorney can request the court to issue an order preventing the destruction of electronic data or ask opposing counsel to agree to a cessation of data destruction — something typically called a "litigation hold order." Counsel should memorialize the consent in an order and, if opposing counsel will not consent, she should file a motion to require a litigation hold order.[8]

"A duty to preserve evidence exists when a party has notice that the evidence is relevant to litigation or when a party should know that the evidence may be relevant to future litigation." Maria Perez Crist, *Preserving the Duty to Preserve: The Increasing Vulnerability of Electronic Information* 58 S.C. L. Rev. 7, 9 (2006). The intentional destruction of evidence is termed "spoliation," and in some jurisdictions is recognized as a separate cause of action.[9] Most jurisdictions follow the federal rules, which allow for the court to impose sanctions, including but not limited to dismissal of the case, default judgment, or monetary sanctions. *Id.* at 10–11. In *United States v. Phillip Morris Inc.*, 327 F. Supp. 2d 21, 26 (D.D.C. 2004), the court ordered Phillip Morris to pay $2,750,000.00 in sanctions for the "reckless disregard and gross indifference displayed" toward the company's duty to preserve documents for discovery. *Id.*

The modern lawyer must also be familiar with "metadata"—embedded data automatically created by software that, unless the user is knowledgeable, will often go unnoticed. "Most metadata is not visible on the computer screen, does not appear on the electronic file when a copy is printed, and is often completely unknown to the person who generates the file." 7-37A John K. Rabiej, Moore's Federal Practice §37A.03 (2009). The information stored within a document usually includes not only the identity of authors, but also dates of creation and revision, the parts that a particular author worked on, and the like. *See id.* Such embedded information could be privileged, such as communications between an attorney and client on documents such as a contract, lease, or similar document. A recent ethics opinion interpreting the American Bar Association Code of Professional Responsibility concluded that a party who received documents containing metadata can, unless she is aware that it was produced unintentionally, use such data freely. *See* ABA Comm. on Ethics and Prof'l Responsibility, Formal

---

8. *See* Martha J. Dawson, et al., *Electronic Discovery Today*, 716 P.L.I. 7, 32–44 (2004); Stanley M. Gibson, *Litigation Holds: Turning on—and off—the Switch to Avoid Sanctions and Costly E-Discovery Blunders*, 766 P.L.I. 151 (2007).

9. *See, e.g., RSC Quality Measurement Co. v. IPSOS-ASI, Inc.*, 196 F. Supp. 2d 609, 615 (S.D. Ohio 2002) (explaining that Indiana and Ohio recognize spoliation of evidence as an intentional tort and a separate cause of action). Louisiana, Florida, Montana, New Jersey, and West Virginia also recognize spoliation as an intentional tort.

Op. 06-442 (2006). The opinion notes that a party producing electronic data can "scrub" the data from the document or produce the document in a form that does not contain the metadata. *See id.* The "scrubbing" of metadata represents using a program, such as Adobe Acrobat®, to remove metadata from an electronic file.

Follow-Up Questions

1. Does the state in which you intend to practice have a rule or statute concerning electronically stored information (perhaps added as part of a previously existing rule)? What does the rule or statute require?

2. How can you convey to your client, in terms that the client will likely take seriously, the need to preserve electronic data?

Professional Identity Questions

1. Suppose you represent a large company with countless forms of electronic data. You have received a request for production of documents from opposing counsel. You have consulted with your client and reviewed the printed documents and electronic documents that it has. You realize that the client has so much documentation and electronic data that you can likely overwhelm your opponent by flooding them with papers and electronic data that are at best marginally relevant and mixing in documents (hard copy and electronic) within the large quantity of marginally relevant data. If you produced these documents all together as a large response, you realize that it will take some digging and effort for the opponent to find documents that could help the opponent's case. Would you engage in production of documents in this manner? Why or why not?

2. Suppose you are a plaintiff suing a large company with countless forms of electronic data. Your suit is on a claim that, in your judgment, barely passes the Rule 11 test such that you have a good faith basis in fact and law or for the extension of existing law. Recognizing that your case is not strong, you consider that, by requesting a "freeze" (or more often called a "hold") on discarding of electronic data, you may be able to gain leverage over the defendant. In other words, solely to seek an early settlement before the defendant company realizes that it will likely prevail in the suit, you use the company's large electronic data as one of the ways to be a "nuisance." (The phrase "nuisance settlement" derives from scenarios such as this where a defendant will pay simply to avoid the cost and hassle of dealing with litigation burdens.) Would you seek leverage in this way in an attempt to get a nuisance settlement? Why or why not?

3. What if you have an electronic document prepared by a corporate client in which several authors worked on revising a document that will be important in the case. Knowing who worked on which part would aid your opponent greatly — something she could learn by viewing the metadata in the electronic version. If your opponent asks for electronic documents but does not include in the definitions or requests a specific request for "metadata," would you feel com-

fortable removing (by the "scrubbing" process (mentioned *supra* at page 180) metadata from the document? What if the document request specifically requested "metadata"?

Practice Problem

Practice Problem 8-2

Break into groups and discuss how you can become sufficiently proficient on the following topics: (1) electronic data, the hardware and software involved in storage, methods used to "back-up" such data, metadata and how, if appropriate, to "scrub" it from an electronic document; and (2) how best to pursue discovery of electronic data, especially cost-effective methods.

Most classrooms have students with varying levels of expertise concerning computer hardware and software. In the groups, those with reservations about their level of knowledge ought to be encouraged to be frank about that. Those with more knowledge should consider how to explain technical concepts related to computer technology in laypersons' language.

Technology continues to change at a rapid pace. Do you believe that a lawyer today can represent her clients effectively without some proficiency in computers, electronic data, etc? If you realize that you do not have such proficiency, how can you obtain it? Even if you have it at the moment, how will you continue to stay abreast of changes in technology so that your level of proficiency continues to match clients' needs? Also, how would such knowledge help you advise your client about handling of its electronic data so as to (1) help the client defend herself in litigation, and (2) avoid claims of destruction (spoliation) of documents that could prejudice her position or even lead to liability?

The Primary Written Forms of Discovery: Requests for Production of Documents, Interrogatories, and Requests for Admission

After ensuring that you have a pretrial schedule that benefits your client, and that you have preserved data as far as possible, an intelligent discovery plan will begin with written discovery requests.

Requests for Production of Documents or Other Tangible Things to Parties and Subpoenas Duces Tecum to Nonparties
Requests for Production of Documents to Parties

Modeled on Federal Rule of Civil Procedure 34, every jurisdiction has "requests for production of documents and tangible things." Appendix 8-2; 27 C.J.S. *Discovery* § 104 (2009).[10] A party may request production of "documents or other tangible things," as

---

10. Some states refer to this discovery mechanism as a "subpoena duces tecum." *See, e.g.*, N.Y. C.P.L.R. § 3120 (McKinney 2009). However, most states reserve that phrase solely to describe the mechanism for requiring production of documents and tangible items from *nonparties*.

long as the requested matter is within the scope of discovery. 23 Am. Jur. 2d *Depositions and Discovery* § 146 (2009). The request should specify the items requested, along with the time, location, and manner in which the items should be produced for inspection. *See id.*; *see also* Kan. Stat. Ann. § 60-234 (2008). The material must be within the custody or control of the party from whom it is requested. *E.g., id.* The rules of the applicable jurisdiction provide a response and objection deadline. *See, e.g.*, Mass. R. Civ. P. 34(b). Typically, state rules do not place a presumptive limit on the number of requests for production (unlike interrogatories). Theoretically, you can include as many requests as you wish. If you ask so many requests that it is obvious you are on a fishing expedition, or if you duplicate requests repeatedly, the party receiving the requests can object.

A crucial thing to know is this: even if you cannot respond to each request by whatever deadline your jurisdiction sets, you *must* serve all objections to those requests by the applicable deadline. Some jurisdictions have local rules. Local rules often set deadlines to object to discovery requests. 27 C.J.S. *Discovery* § 113 (2009). Typically, the deadline for objecting imposed by local rules is *before* the deadline for producing documents, answering interrogatories, etc. Thus, the wise attorney will always check for applicable local rules. 23 Am. Jur. 2d *Depositions and Discovery* § 15 (2009). If the attorney fails to object by the applicable deadline, a party's objections will be deemed waived. That party can then be subjected to enormous burden and expense due to the simple failure to object. *Id.* § 165.

> Local rules are rules that govern a court, or group of courts within a judicial district, and place requirements on parties that, though not inconsistent with the State's rules, often are more demanding, such as by imposing an earlier deadline for objecting to discovery

In general, a party has 30 days from receipt of service in which to provide written responses or objections. *Id.* As already noted, however, courts within a particular jurisdiction may have rules that provide for an *earlier* deadline in which to object or rules that are specific to the jurisdiction. For example, in New York, a party must serve a written response stating any objections within 20 days of receipt of service of the requests. N.Y. C.P.L.R. § 3122(a) (McKinney 2009). Another typical provision in any jurisdiction's request for production of documents provision is the requirement, such as in Federal Rule of Civil Procedure 34, that the documents be produced "as they are kept in the usual course of business or must organize and label them to correspond to the categories in the request." *E.g.*, W. Va. R. Civ. P. 34(b); Wyo. R. Civ. P. 34(b)(i). If a responding party provides responses by a "document dump" of boxes of unorganized documents, that party has not complied with the above requirement to produce documents so as to respond fairly to each request. Rather than attempt to sort out what documents relate to which request, the attorney should insist that the responding party do so.

Below is the beginning of a sample request for production of documents based on the *Brad T. Rex v. Ena Hurry* case introduced in Chapter 4, *supra* at pages 82–96.

In the Circuit Court for the City of Arcadia

[PARTY'S NAME],	)	
Plaintiff,	)	
	)	
v.	)	Case No. 123456
	)	
[PARTY'S NAME],	)	
Defendant.	)	

REQUEST FOR PRODUCTION OF DOCUMENTS

Pursuant to Rule __ [insert applicable rule for jurisdiction], Plaintiff [or Defendant if Defendant is making the requests] requests production of the following documents at the office of Plaintiff [or Defendant, if Defendant is issuing] within __ days [the time allotted by the jurisdiction's rule]:

Definitions

[Here, the drafting party should define "documents" or "tangible things" so that, when the term is used in specific requests, it will include everything included in the definition. Many believe definitional sections of discovery requests have gotten out of hand. Some definitional sections go on for pages. The point of the definitions is to ensure that the key terms used in the Request for Production, most often the term "document," comprise every kind of document that might exist — originals, copies, handwritten documents, typed documents, electronic documents of all varieties, etc. The Definitions and Requests should emphasize that you are requesting every version of a document, regardless of whether multiple versions exists. Doing so can be crucial if, for instance, there are handwritten comments on a printed version. Moreover, a printed version will not show metadata that, if a document is produced in electronic form, will be available — if counsel knows how to look for the metadata. For a discussion of metadata in electronic documents see *supra* pages 178–80. So long as the definitional section in your jurisdiction is broad enough to ensure a responding party cannot fail to respond because the Request does not define the requested materials broadly enough, you should be safe. A sample definition of documents found online for a Continuing Legal Education program in Utah offers a reasonable compromise between extreme tedium and appropriate breadth:

"Document(s)" means all materials within the full scope of FED. R. CIV. P. 34 including but not limited to: all writings and recordings, including the originals and all non-identical copies, whether different from the original by reason of any notation made on such copies or otherwise (including but without limitation to, emails and attachments, correspondence, memoranda, notes, diaries, minutes, statistics, letters, telegrams, minutes, contracts, reports, studies, checks, statements, tags, labels, invoices, brochures, periodicals, telegrams, receipts, returns, summaries, pamphlets, books, interoffice and intraoffice communications, offers, notations of any sort of conversations, working papers, applications, permits, file papers, indices, telephone calls, meetings or printouts, teletypes, telefax, invoices, worksheets, and all drafts, alterations, modifications, changes and amendments of any of the foregoing), graphic or aural representations of any kind (including without limitation, photographs, charts, microfiche, microfilm, videotape, recordings, motion pictures, plans, drawings, surveys), and electronic, mechanical, magnetic, optical or electric records or representations of any kind (including without limitation, computer files and programs, tapes, cassettes, discs, recordings), including metadata.[11]

The Definitions should also define terms such as "you" or "your" to include the opposing party, any agent of the opposing party, or anyone acting on behalf of the opposing party. Likewise, the facts of the case will dictate terms that would be used repetitively in the Requests if counsel did not define them. For instance, in a personal injury case over a vehicular accident, counsel would do well to define "accident" to mean the accident on (insert date) at (insert location) involving plaintiff and defendant.]

1. All documents identified in response to the accompanying Interrogatories.

2. All documents showing persons with knowledge of any fact related to the accident.

3. All documents related to any drugs, medications, alcohol, or other chemical substances that the defendant ingested within a 48-hour period prior to the accident.

4. All documents related to the defendant's vision, including but not limited to a copy of the defendant's license, any vision tests, and any prescriptions.

5. ....

[PARTY'S NAME]

By _____
                    Counsel

[Name of Party's Counsel]
[Address of Party's Counsel],
[Tele. No., E-Mail (and in some
States, State Bar No.)]

CERTIFICATE OF SERVICE

I certify that on this __ day of _____, 20__, a true copy of the foregoing REQUEST FOR PRODUCTION OF DOCUMENTS was served by first-class mail on the following:

[insert name and address of counsel for all other counsel in the case]

By _____
            Counsel

Subpoenas Duces Tecum to Nonparties

Modeled on Federal Rule of Civil Procedure 45, virtually every jurisdiction allows a party to issue a subpoena to a person or entity that is not a party to the suit (usually called a "subpoena duces tecum"). *See* Appendix 8-3. This subpoena to nonparties mirrors the request for production on issue to a party. If a nonparty will provide such documents without a subpoena, a subpoena is not necessary. Following is a blank subpoena duces tecum form available from the Federal Judiciary website:

Anyone can access this document, fill in information, and print it at the following link on the Federal Judiciary's website: http://www.uscourts.gov/forms/forms_Civil.cfm#Others. State supreme court websites, or websites for courts of general jurisdiction in a state, typically have forms including one for a subpoena duces tecum. The key difference to re-

---

11. Found at http://www.utahbar.org/cle/fallforum/materials/sample_request_production.pdf (last visited June 25, 2009).

AO 88B (Rev. 06/09) Subpoena to Produce Documents, Information, or Objects or to Permit Inspection of Premises in a Civil Action

UNITED STATES DISTRICT COURT

for the

_____ District of _____

_____)	
Plaintiff)	
v.)	Civil Action No.
)	
_____)	(If the action is pending in another district, state where:
Defendant)	_____ District of _____)

SUBPOENA TO PRODUCE DOCUMENTS, INFORMATION, OR OBJECTS
OR TO PERMIT INSPECTION OF PREMISES IN A CIVIL ACTION

To:

✕ *Production:* YOU ARE COMMANDED to produce at the time, date, and place set forth below the following documents, electronically stored information, or objects, and permit their inspection, copying, testing, or sampling of the material:

Place:	Date and Time:

✕ *Inspection of Premises:* YOU ARE COMMANDED to permit entry onto the designated premises, land, or other property possessed or controlled by you at the time, date, and location set forth below, so that the requesting party may inspect, measure, survey, photograph, test, or sample the property or any designated object or operation on it.

Place:	Date and Time:

The provision of Fed. R. Civ. P. 45(c), relating to your protection as a person subject to subpoena, and Rule 45 (d) and (e), relating to your duty to respond to this subpoena and the potential consequences of not doing so, are attached.

Date: _____

    CLERK OF COURT

           OR

  _____   _____
   Signature of Clerk or Deputy Clerk   *Attorney's signature*

The name, address, e-mail, and telephone number of the attorney representing (*name of party*) _____, who issues or requests this subpoena, are:

member between Requests for Production of Documents and Subpoenas Duces Tecum is how they must be served. Because they go to an opposing party, Requests for Production need only be mailed to opposing counsel. However, a subpoena duces tecum is being served on a person or entity who is *not a party*. By serving such a person, counsel is invoking the subpoena power of the court to aid in gathering information for purposes of litigating the case. However, because that person or entity is not a party, the person or entity must be served with the subpoena duces tecum as if that person or entity were being sued. In other words, you must serve the subpoena duces tecum through a process server. If the party fails to respond, you can bring that party before the court to answer why she should not be held in contempt. More often, if the request is a broad one, the person or party served may move to quash the subpoena duces tecum and schedule a hearing. Out of that would come some resolution of what the nonparty has to produce, but it may not be everything requested. Often, when such a motion to quash is filed, counsel for the nonparty and counsel issuing the subpoena can reach an agreement limiting the scope to the documents that the requesting party really needs.

Professional Identity Question

Requests for production of documents and other discovery tools are subject to abuse. Although this chapter will discuss below methods in which to protect a client from abusive discovery, this question focuses on you as the attorney sending out discovery to opposing parties. Some clients will ask you, either explicitly or implicitly, to "load up" your discovery requests to opponents as a means of discouraging the opponents from litigating the merits, by making litigation as difficult as possible, and by draining their financial resources. Will you agree to send such discovery — i.e., the type that has little value in advancing your client's case, duplicates requests already made, etc. — where your primary purpose is discouraging the opposing party and draining that opponent's financial resources? If you find yourself rationalizing how the 125th request for production of documents in a set you have prepared might lead to discoverable evidence on some theory, can you do a reality check to say "enough is enough"?

If you decide that you will not engage in discovery designed not primarily to further your client's case but rather for an ulterior motive such as to discourage the opponent, precisely because you do not want to be the kind of lawyer who engages in tactics such as those described above, how will you explain your position to a client who asks you to take the pile-them-on approach? Consider how, if the matter comes before the court on a motion to compel (as is likely to be the case if you send this many requests for production), you and the client will be viewed by the court. If you were the judge, how would you perceive a lawyer who sends such requests? Ultimately, is it your decision or the client's whether you would follow the client's direction to employ discovery for leverage and to require the adverse party to spend significant money in responding? In an adversarial system, cannot a lawyer always say that, if opposing counsel finds the discovery requests to be objectionable, then it is up to that opponent to object? What, if any, problem is there with this way of thinking?

Practice Problem

Practice Problem 8-3

Students should assume the role of counsel for plaintiff and for defendant in the case of *Brad T. Rex v. Ena Hurry* the facts of which are set forth *supra* in Chapter 4 on pages 82–96. Assume for this exercise that Dr. Lovey Payne has been dismissed from the case. What documents would you request if you represented the plaintiff. Draft five requests for production of documents that you would serve on the defendant, Ms. Hurry. Ponder how to phrase each request so that it is not only clear, but phrased in a way that the responding party will have to produce all documents that you seek. For instance, would you ask for all documents "*supporting* Defendant Hurry's contention that _____" (phrasing similar to the wording of automatic disclosures under Federal Rule 26(a)(1))? If you can as easily ask for "all documents supporting or otherwise related to Defendant Hurry's contention that _____," what would be the advantages of such phrasing? Also discuss in what circumstances, under a request for production or *other tangible things*, a litigant would list actual objects, not just documents, to be produced. Finally, discuss what documents from nonparties you could obtain through a subpoena.

Students should then switch sides and represent the Defendant Hurry. Draft five requests for production of documents for the defendant to serve on Plaintiff Rex. Observe how your requests for production can differ because you are representing the defendant. How would you phrase them to ensure that they were not interpreted narrowly to avoid disclosure of documents in Rex's posession? What tangible items other than documents might you request of plaintiff Rex so that you can inspect these items? To which nonparties would you issue a subpoena so as to gather further evidence?

Interrogatories

Modeled on Federal Rule of Civil Procedure 33, interrogatories are available in every jurisdiction. Appendix 8-4; 27 C.J.S. *Discovery* § 74 (2009). A party serves the opposing party with a document containing specific written inquiries. 23 Am. Jur. 2d *Depositions and Discovery* § 155 (2009). The party answering them then must do so under oath. *See id.* Answering under oath simply means that the client appears before a notary public and swears that the answers are accurate.

> A notary public is an official, typically appointed by courts in a jurisdiction for specified terms, who are authorized to administer oaths and verify on a document that a person has sworn to the accuracy of the contents of the document

Generally, a party has 30 days from the date of service of the interrogatory to serve a written response. *E.g.*, Tex. R. Civ. P. 197.2(a) (providing 30 days from the date of service of interrogatories to respond, except when a defendant is served with interrogatories before his answer is due, in which case she has 50 days to respond). Some jurisdictions provide a shorter time for response or objections. Appendix 8-4; *see, e.g.*, La. Code Civ. Proc. Ann. art. 1458 (2008) (providing that a party must serve answers and objections to interrogatories within 15 days of being served). As with requests for production, a particular court often has local rules that set the deadline for objections earlier than a Rule's deadline for responding. Moreover, unlike requests for production, written interrogatories typically are limited in number, often to 25 interrogatories. 23 Am. Jur. 2d *Depositions and Discovery* § 122 (2009). The limit also typically provides that the maximum number shall include "parts and subparts" so that lawyers do not circumvent the limit by cramming a number of interrogatories together and designating them with one number. *See, e.g.*, Wyo. R. Civ. P. 33(a) (allowing 30 written interrogatories including discrete subparts).

Interrogatories are unique because the client must answer every interrogatory question and verify under oath the accuracy of the answers. "Signing under oath" means that the client will repeat an oath and swear to the accuracy of the answers before an official authorized to give oaths, usually by a notary public. When pressed for time, attorneys sometimes sign answers to interrogatories for their client. Such a shortcut presents the opportunity for embarrassment, not to mention potential sanctions from the court. If the lawyer for a client attests to the accuracy of facts, opposing counsel may be able to depose that lawyer. Indeed, if it turns out that facts provided by a client but sworn by her lawyer are not true, the lawyer could be prosecuted. Needless to say, therefore, the better practice is to insist that the client always be the person to swear to the accuracy of answers.

In a document that combines interrogatory answers with objections to certain interrogatories, an attorney must sign as to the objections. 23 Am. Jur. 2d *Depositions and Discovery* § 125 (2009). However, she can sign the interrogatories "As to Objections Only," to protect herself by limiting the scope of her signature to objections, leaving to the client the job of signing so as to verify answers. Just as with responses to request for production of documents or tangible things, you *must* serve objections to interrogatories by the deadline imposed by the applicable jurisdiction. Failure to observe a deadline to serve an objection typically results in waiver. 27 C.J.S. *Discovery* § 84 (2009). As with objections to document requests, many jurisdictions allow courts to set local rules for a particular court or courts within a judicial district that provide for an *earlier* deadline in which to object to interrogatories. Counsel has to check for such local rules rather than assume that the state-wide rules provide all applicable deadlines. Again, if a lawyer misses one of these earlier deadlines for objecting, her client will end up having to respond to requests that the client would otherwise not have to respond to.

Below is the beginning of a sample set of interrogatories:

In the Circuit Court for the City of Arcadia

[PARTY'S NAME],	)	
Plaintiff,	)	
	)	
v.	)	Case No. 123456
	)	
[PARTY'S NAME],	)	
Defendant.	)	

INTERROGATORIES

Pursuant to Rule ___ [insert applicable rule for jurisdiction], Plaintiff [or Defendant] requests the Defendant [or Plaintiff, if Defendant is issuing] to answer the following interrogatories under oath on or before _____ [insert time allotted by the jurisdiction's rule]:

Definitions

[Here, as with a Request for Production of Documents or Other Tangible Things, the drafting party should define "documents" or "tangible things" so that, when the term is used in specific interrogatories, it will incorporate everything included in the definition. Many believe definitional sections of discovery requests have gotten out of hand. Some definitional sections go on for pages. The point of the definitions is to ensure that the key terms used in the interrogatories, most often the term "document," comprise every kind of document that might exist—originals, copies, handwritten documents, typed documents, electronic documents of all varieties, etc. So long as the definitional section of your jurisdiction is broad enough to ensure a responding party cannot avoid responding because the interrogatory does not define the requested materials broadly enough, you should be safe. Following is a typical definition of documents:

"Document(s)" means all materials within the full scope of FED. R. CIV. P. 34 including but not limited to: all writings and recordings, including the originals and all non-identical copies, whether different from the original by reason of any notation made on such copies or otherwise (including but without limitation to, emails and attachments, correspondence, memoranda, notes, diaries, minutes, statistics, letters, telegrams, minutes, contracts, reports, studies, checks, statements, tags, labels, invoices, brochures, periodicals, telegrams, receipts, returns, summaries, pamphlets, books, interoffice and intraoffice communications, offers, notations of any sort of conversations, working papers, applications, permits, file papers, indices, telephone calls, meetings or printouts, teletypes, telefax, invoices, worksheets, and all drafts, alterations, modifications, changes and amendments of any of the foregoing), graphic or aural representations of any kind (including without limitation, photographs, charts, microfiche, microfilm, videotape, recordings, motion pictures, plans, drawings, surveys), and electronic, mechanical, magnetic, optical or electric records or representations of any kind (including without limitation, computer files and programs, tapes, cassettes, discs, recordings), including metadata.[12]

The Definitions should also define terms such as "you" or "your" to refer to include the opposing party, any agent of the opposing party, or anyone acting on behalf of the opposing party. Likewise, the facts of the case will dictate terms that would be used repetitively in the interrogatories if you did not define them. For instance, in a personal injury case over a vehicular accident, counsel would do well to define "accident" to mean the accident on [insert date] at [insert location] involving plaintiff and defendant.]

1. Identify any drugs, medications, alcohol, or other chemical substances that the defendant ingested within a 48-hour period prior to the accident, all persons with knowledge of your ingestion of any of these, and all documents relating to ingestion of these.

2. Identify all facts supporting your denial of allegations contained in paragraphs 2 through 14 of the complaint. Also identify all persons with knowledge of such facts and all documents related to such facts.

3. Please list all insurance agreements you have made regarding the vehicle you were operating at the time of the occurrence, including the name of the owner, the name of the insurance carrier, the policy number, the type of coverage, the amount of coverage (specifying its upper and lower limits) and the effective dates of the policy for the past five years.

4. Identify your vision (*e.g.*, 20-20, 20-30, 20-40, etc.) within six months prior to the accident and at the time of the accident (or if your vision is unknown, describe the vision test results closest in time to the accident), whether you wear corrective lenses, and whether you were wearing corrective lenses at the time of the accident.

5. Identify any and all expert witnesses you may call at the trial of this case, regardless of whether such witnesses are persons retained by you to testify and describe the information to which each such expert has been exposed (oral communications, documents, etc.), any opinions such expert has formed, the basis or bases for any such opinions, and any reports produced by such experts.

6. ....

---

12. *See supra* this chapter, note 11, for the source of the definition quoted. The definition of "documents" used in a Request for Production of Documents and in accompanying Interrogatories are usually identical. Other terms, however, may need to be added and defined depending on wording of one's interrogatories.

[PARTY'S NAME]

By _____
                    Counsel

Name of Counsel for Party[13]
Address of Counsel
Tele. No., E-Mail
(and in some States, State Bar No.)

CERTIFICATE OF SERVICE

I certify that on this __ day of _____, 20__, a true copy of the foregoing INTER-ROGATORIES were served by first-class mail on the following:

[Insert names and addresses of all other counsel in the case]

By _____
             Counsel

Practice Problem

Practice Problem 8-4

In addition to the four interrogatories set forth above designed to get the discussion going, what others would you ask? Do any of the above interrogatories contain subparts that could increase the actual number of interrogatory subparts counted against the 25-interrogatory limit — the typical limit in light of the rule that each subpart will be counted as if it is a separate interrogatory? Why would the limit on numbers of interrogatories be something to keep in mind in drafting interrogatories early in a case?

Interrogatory No. 2 in the above sample is called a "contention interrogatory." It is so dubbed because it asks an opponent to reveal facts, persons with knowledge (witnesses), and documents concerning a contention that the party has made. When a defendant denies contentions or a claim set forth in a series of paragraphs in a complaint, such denials represent the defendant's contention or contentions. Why would identifying all facts, witnesses, and documents related to such contentions be important? In the same way that a plaintiff can ask contention interrogatories, a defendant can ask interrogatories of the plaintiff seeking facts, documents, and witnesses supporting the allegations in the complaint. For instance, here, Ena Hurry (see *supra* Chapter 4, pages 82–96 for facts and pleadings in the case of *Brad T. Rex v. Ena Hurry*) could ask: "state all facts, persons with knowledge of, and documents related to your contention in paragraphs ___ of the complaint that defendant was negligent." Then the plaintiff, Brad, would have to identify all facts upon which he predicated the claim that encompass the contentions, all persons with knowledge of such facts, and all documents related to such facts. (If the defendant simultaneously serves request for production of documents that seek all documents identified in response to interrogatory answers, the plaintiff will have to produce all documents related to

---

13. Note that counsel for a party sends Interrogatories and signs them. It is only the response to Interrogatories that a party, not counsel, herself must sign and swear to the answers before an official authorized to administer oaths.

the contentions supporting his claim.) Can you see the value of contention interrogatories? Will they assist in determining persons to depose, what documents
to focus on, etc.? Moreover, at a final pretrial conference or a trial, if you have
asked contention interrogatories on every one of your opponent's contentions,
and the opposing party lists in the pretrial disclosure of witnesses a person that
has not been listed in answers to your contention interrogatories, what objection
can you make? Can you also object if your opponent seeks to offer documents
not identified in response to a contention interrogatory that should have prompted
their identification?

Now, as your practice exercise, draft five interrogatories for the plaintiff, Rex,
to serve on Defendant Hurry to answer. Then, switch sides and draft five interrogatories for defendant, Ena Hurry, to be answered by Plaintiff Rex. Do both
your interrogatories served on the plaintiff and on the defendant include contention interrogatories? Do your interrogatories include an expert interrogatory? Why should you always include an expert interrogatory among your limited
number of interrogatories? Why, even in states that adopt Federal Rule of Civil
Procedure's 26(a)(2)'s requirement of pretrial expert disclosures (discussed *supra*
pages 173–74), would you still be wise to issue an interrogatory asking about
your opponent's experts and any opinions they may offer?

Requests for Admission

Modeled on Federal Rule of Civil Procedure 36, requests for admission in every jurisdiction are quite simply requests seeking to achieve agreement on certain facts. *See* Appendix 8-5 (reflecting Fed. R. Civ. P. 36 as essentially followed in the majority of states);
27 C.J.S. *Discovery* § 164 (2009). Requests for admission remove uncontested factual issues before trial—promoting efficiency of the trial process. 23 AM. JUR. 2d *Depositions
and Discovery* § 181 (2009). A party may serve on its opponent a document that refers
to the applicable rule in the jurisdiction and request that the opponent categorically
admit or deny each item in the request. *Id.* § 183. In general, the party must admit, deny,
or object to a request for admission. *Id.* § 185. An objection must specify the reason why
the party cannot admit or deny the request. *Id.* When an item is deemed admitted, it is
taken as "true," and a party is bound by the admission at trial. *Id.* § 197. A factual issue
is deemed admitted for purposes of trial in two ways: (1) the party affirmatively admits
its truth and serves it on the requesting party; or (2) the party fails to respond to the request by the response deadline. 27 C.J.S. *Discovery* § 174 (2009). Statutes and local rules
will provide the manner and time period within which a party must answer a request for
admission as well as the permissible scope[14] of the requests. *Id.* § 163. Typically, the rule
will not place a presumptive limit on the number of requests for admissions. A response
to request for admissions will be signed by counsel for the party on whom they are
served.

Some call requests for admission the "hot potato" of litigation. Why? Put aside the
prospect of waiving an objection, as can happen with any discovery requests. The rule
on requests for admission provides that, if a response is not provided within the applicable

---

14. For an interesting discussion of the permissible scope of requests for admission in different states,
see Russell G. Donaldson, *Permissible Scope, Respecting Nature of Inquiry, of Demand for Admissions
under Modern State Civil Rules of Procedure*, 42 A.L.R. 4th 489 (1985).

deadline, the matter sought in the request is *deemed admitted*. FED. R. CIV. P. 36; Appendix 8-5. If an attorney wants to object to a request, she should file it within the required deadline — sometimes earlier than the date for responding to the requests for admissions. Regardless of whether the responding party has an objection, she should file *some* response. An adversary will often write a request in a manner most favorable to her client. Counsel should not only respond in time, as is reiterated below, but she must also be careful how she responds. Responses to requests for admissions can be offered as evidence at trial and are often read to the jury. When presented with a request for admission that contains implicit facts that are not disputed but which also contain characterizations with which the lawyer disagrees, she ought to consider how the response would be read at trial. She can deny the request as written, isolate the facts that are not disputed, and characterize them in a way most favorable to her client. If you follow this practice, lawyers will likely stop sending you "loaded" requests for admissions and more likely stick to the facts not in dispute. That is, after all, the point of seeking admissions.

In any event, a lawyer must object or respond to a request for admissions within the time that will ensure the matter requested is not deemed admitted. To fail to do so would fall below the standard of care in virtually every jurisdiction and, thus, provide the basis for a malpractice action. A lawyer bears the responsibility for failing to respond within the proper time frame so as to avoid crucial facts from being "deemed" admitted when they ought not to be. That is not to say that counsel for the responding party ought to ignore the Rule's requirement that the responding party admit as much of the request as possible and to be fair in her responses. However, failure to respond within the required time frame — and having an opponent's characterization of factual matters "deemed" admitted purely because of the failure — is inexcusable.

Also, the rule typically provides that, if a party denies a requested matter, and the proponent has to bear expenses to prove the matter at trial, that party can request those expenses after trial if the court determines the matters should have been admitted. FED. R. CIV. P. 36; Appendix 8-5. The threat of paying such expenses often motivates parties to at least admit the genuineness of documents so that witnesses need not be subpoenaed, for example, to testify solely to lay the foundation for the genuineness of a document. In other words, the party refusing to admit the genuineness of a document ought to have a good reason or risk paying for her refusal. Counsel of course does not waive other objections, such as hearsay or other grounds for exclusion, simply by admitting the genuineness (also referred to as authenticity) of a document.

Below is the beginning of a sample request for admission:

In the Circuit Court for the City of Arcadia

[PARTY'S NAME],	)	
Plaintiff,	)	
	)	
v.	)	Case No. 123456
	)	
[PARTY'S NAME],	)	
Defendant.	)	

REQUEST FOR ADMISSIONS

Pursuant to Rule __ [insert applicable rule for jurisdiction], Plaintiff [or Defendant if issuing] requests production of the following documents at the office of Plaintiff [or Defendant if issuing] within __ days [the time allotted by the jurisdiction's rule]:

Definitions

[Here, the drafting party should define "documents" or "tangible things" so that, when the term is used in specific requests, it will include everything included in the definition. Many believe definitional sections of discovery requests have gotten out of hand as some definitional sections go on for pages. The point of the definitions is to ensure that the key terms used in the Request for Admissions, most often the term "document," comprise every kind of document that might exist including originals, copies, handwritten documents, typed documents, electronic documents of all varieties, etc. An attorney will be safe as long as her definitional section is broad enough to cover the different forms in which documents exist. Doing so will ensure that the responding party cannot avoid responding fairly because the Request does not define the requested materials broadly enough. Following is a sample definition[15] of documents:

> "Document(s)" means all materials within the full scope of Fed. R. Civ. P. 34 including but not limited to: all writings and recordings, including the originals and all non-identical copies, whether different from the original by reason of any notation made on such copies or otherwise (including but without limitation to, email and attachments, correspondence, memoranda, notes, diaries, minutes, statistics, letters, telegrams, minutes, contracts, reports, studies, checks, statements, tags, labels, invoices, brochures, periodicals, telegrams, receipts, returns, summaries, pamphlets, books, interoffice and intraoffice communications, offers, notations of any sort of conversations, working papers, applications, permits, file papers, indices, telephone calls, meetings or printouts, teletypes, telefax, invoices, worksheets, and all drafts, alterations, modifications, changes and amendments of any of the foregoing), graphic or aural representations of any kind (including without limitation, photographs, charts, microfiche, microfilm, videotape, recordings, motion pictures, plans, drawings, surveys), and electronic, mechanical, magnetic, optical or electric records or representations of any kind (including without limitation, computer files and programs, tapes, cassettes, discs, recordings), including metadata.[16]

The Definitions should also define terms such as "you" or "your" to include the opposing party, any agent of the opposing party, or anyone acting on behalf of the opposing party. Likewise, the facts of the case will dictate terms that would be used repetitively in the Requests if they were not defined. For instance, in a personal injury case over a vehicular accident, counsel would do well to define "accident" to mean the accident on [insert date] at [insert location] involving plaintiff and defendant.]

1. Admit that the accident report dated [date of accident] is a genuine copy of the report filled out and signed by Officer ___ after the accident.

2. Admit that you ingested six beers within ___ hours before the accident.

3. Admit that you have 20-40 vision and a restricted driver's license requiring corrective lenses.

4. Admit that you were not wearing the corrective lenses at the time of the accident.

5. ....

---

15. *See supra* this chapter, note 11, for the source of the definition quoted. The definition of "documents or tangible things" used in a Request for Production of Documents and in Requests for Admissions are usually identical. Other terms, however, may need to be added and defined depending on the wording of one's Request for Admissions.

16. Found at http://www.utahbar.org/cle/fallforum/materials/sample_request_production.pdf (last visited June 25, 2009).

PAM PLAINTIFF

By _____
              Counsel

[Name of Counsel for Party (here, Plaintiff)]
[Address of Counsel]
[Tele. No., E-Mail]
[(and in some States, State Bar No.)]

CERTIFICATE OF SERVICE

I certify that on this __ day of _____, 20__, a true copy of the foregoing REQUEST FOR ADMISSIONS was served by first-class mail on the following:

[insert names and addresses of counsel for all other counsel in the case]

_____
      Counsel

Practice Problem

Practice Problem 8-5

The above discussion highlights the value of Requests for Admissions in avoiding having to prove the genuineness of a document. In practical terms, how does an admitted request on the genuineness of a document make your trial presentation more efficient, and avoid unnecessary witnesses? If the opposing party admits the requests, can you avoid calling witnesses to authenticate the documents? Are there other less controversial facts for which requests for admissions would serve as a useful tool?

How Best to Employ the Above Discovery Tools before Taking Depositions—The Optimal Sequence of Discovery

Having reviewed the ground rules for the three primary written forms of discovery requests, the attorney can now consider the optimal sequence in which to pursue discovery. As this section will note, an attorney should also consider how to obtain discovery from non-parties because parties are not the only ones with documents and information about a case.

Lawyers who think strategically recognize the logical sequence in which discovery should be pursued. They will issue the written discovery requests outlined above so that they have sufficient time to follow up with depositions of the "persons with knowledge" identified in the discovery. They realize that interrogatories are not the best means of asking some questions because of the ability of the lawyer to script answers with a client. However, interrogatories are highly useful for identifying preliminary facts, documents related to the case, and persons with knowledge of the facts. Hence, interrogatories should be used for this kind of information.

Many jurisdictions, like Federal Rule of Civil Procedure 30, place a presumptive limit of 10 depositions on a party. *See* Appendix 8-6. Moreover, in most cases, a party's litigation budget will limit counsel in the number of persons deposed. (Depositions cost thousands of dollars in light of the court reporter's fee, transcription costs, attorneys' fees, etc.) Again, contention interrogatories—ones that force an opponent to identify persons who support key contentions—help to prioritize the persons to be deposed. Such interrogatories reveal the persons who know the facts on which the opponent is basing her claims or defenses. If counsel's opponent lists dozens of witnesses in response to a contention interrogatory, counsel may have to move to compel answers that separate the persons who know more facts from those who may have superficial or limited factual knowledge and are thrown into the mix in order to make counsel's job harder. Yes, some counsel will respond to contention interrogatories with dozens of persons, in the same way that some counsel will produce thousands of pages of marginally relevant documents, in an effort to make it harder to identify the key witnesses and documents within a mound of information. Your job is to rely on the rules and motions (discussed more below), to offset such tactics. Another way to undercut such evasive tactics is to call a witness, if you can identify one, who you know has significant knowledge. You can then depose that person as a means of narrowing down the significant from marginal witnesses.

In the optimal sequence of discovery, requests for production of documents and subpoena duces tecum are usually the first tools on which an attorney relies. Responses to Requests for Production of documents allow the attorney to gather and review documents *prior to* the depositions. Hence, an attorney can determine the appropriate witness to be questioned for each document. Often counsel will need to file a motion to compel to overcome objections. (*See infra* pages 210–12 this chapter for a discussion of discovery motions.) For instance, a motion to compel will seek to obtain complete responses in order to force parties who have failed to produce the documents in a manner in which they can be categorized with the particular topic in a request. In other words, counsel need not let a party shower her with documents that are not identified as responsive to particular requests. If an opponent attempts to do this, your job is to force them to play by the rules.

Requests for admission are less useful at early stages of litigation unless counsel wishes to determine whether her opponent will challenge the authenticity of certain documents. Thus, counsel will typically take depositions before sending out requests for admissions.

Depositions — The Most Powerful Discovery Tool

Depositions are by far the most powerful tool in a lawyer's discovery arsenal. They offer the opportunity to ask spontaneous questions of an opposing party or witness, to follow up on answers, and to get unscripted responses to the questions. Depositions are also an area in which more seasoned lawyers can take advantage of less experienced ones. Thus, it is imperative to know not only how to prepare for a deposition, but also the rules by which they operate. If well prepared, any associate, even in her first deposition, can effectively represent her client.

Preparation is the key to success in depositions. An attorney should have studied interrogatory answers and all potential documents prior to the deposition. Having the court reporter mark the documents with exhibit stickers before the deposition begins makes the deposition proceed more crisply. If an attorney moves from one pre-marked exhibit to the next, the witness will be more likely to follow along at her pace. If the attorney is searching around for documents during the deposition, handing them back and forth to the witness and court reporter, the deposition will not only take longer, but she will find that the witness begins to offer spontaneous clarifications to her testimony during pauses. Often these spontaneous responses are ones that dilute the deponent's testimony. Again, if the attorney is setting the pace, and not taking long pauses, she cuts out these opportunities for the opponent to volunteer information and editorialize answers.

Next, an attorney will want to know who will be attending the deposition. The court reporter, who is trained in stenographic transcription (so that he or she can take down everything that is said and reproduce it), will be present. The reporter is the closest to a court representative at the deposition. He or she will administer the oath to the person answering questions (the "deponent"), who may be a party or a nonparty witness. In addition, the counsel for the parties, the deponent, the parties, and, at times, expert witnesses will also be there. Different jurisdictions vary on limits regarding who can appear at depositions. 23 AM. JUR. 2d *Depositions and Discovery* § 80 (2009). Most will allow a party, or if a party is an entity, a party representative, to be present. *Id.* § 92. Moreover, experts are often allowed because they can base their opinions on witnesses' testimony. 27 C.J.S. *Discovery* § 68 (2009). If a deposition is being videotaped as well as transcribed, then a videographer will also be present. 23 AM. JUR. 2d *Depositions and Discovery* § 98 (2009).

A party must send a notice of deposition to the party's opponent and all other counsel for parties in the case. This notice must allow reasonable notice of the date and time of the deposition, the location of the deposition, and the manner in which it is to be recorded. *Id.* § 91. The majority rule among states requires "reasonable notice" before a deposition. *See* Appendix 8-6. A significant minority of states allow notice of a deposition to range from 7 to 30 days. *See id.* Professional courtesy urges that the notifying counsel check opposing counsel's available dates before sending a notice. If a party to the action is to be deposed, the notice itself is sufficient to require the party's appearance. If a nonparty witness will be deposed, however, the party initiating the deposition is responsible for subpoenaing that nonparty witness. *Id.* § 94. If the notifying party fails to do so, counsel or her client can be liable for the attorney's fees of opposing counsel appearing at a deposition where the witness fails to show up. *Id.* § 82. If counsel wants the deponent to bring any documents or tangible things to the deposition, the notice and, in the case of a nonparty, the subpoena, must include a subpoena for production of documents (called a subpoena duces tecum). *Id.* § 91. As noted earlier in this chapter, the lawyer taking a deposition should already have seen all documents and prepared to ask questions about them. It is irresponsible for counsel, on the day she is taking a deposition, to view the documents for the first time. She may however, want originals of the witnesses' files brought to the deposition, in which case the subpoena duces tecum offers the mechanism for having these produced. The notice of deposition should reflect any such subpoena for documents or tangible things to be produced at the deposition.

Proper Questions and Objections at Deposition

As with discovery in general, the scope of questions permitted at a deposition is relatively broad, so long as counsel is asking questions that are relevant to the cause of action or a defense at hand. 27 C.J.S. *Discovery* § 72 (2009). If questions can arguably lead to admissible evidence regarding the case in controversy, they are usually permitted. *Id.* § 68.

Objections allowed at depositions are limited. The only objections that truly need to be made, other than objections protecting a privilege, are ones "as to the form of the question." 23 AM. JUR. 2d *Depositions and Discovery* § 113 (2009). An objection to the form of the question presumes that the question, as stated, cannot be answered. Some attorneys will ask long, compound questions that cannot be answered effectively because they pack too much into the question. For example: "Didn't you get in the car, turn on the ignition, put the car in gear, back up, start to drive, stop at the stop sign, travel some distance up to Stingray Street, and then slam into the rear of my client's convertible?" The question asks so many separate questions that a witness cannot possibly answer it with one response.

Opposing counsel properly may state: "Objection. Compound question." Such an objection does not prevent the witness from answering the questions. If the witness has any common sense, however, she will realize that the question is too confusing and, in some parts, vague (*e.g.*, the phrase in the question "traveled some distance"). A witness who has been properly prepared before a deposition should be sensitive to the difference between everyday communication and the precision required of answers to questions in depositions. Such a witness will be cautious of questions that cannot be answered precisely and accurately and will let the questioning lawyer know that she has difficulty with the question. The lawyer will then have to break the question into parts, as the lawyer should have done to begin with. The value of objecting to form is that, if the questioning lawyer does not rephrase the question, and then attempts to use the deposition testimony at trial, the objecting lawyer can rely on her objection to form. Then the court can rule at trial that the question was inappropriate and, thus, the deposition testimony cannot be used. *Id.* §97.

Objections to relevance, hearsay, and other grounds of admissibility at trial of testimony or exhibits are preserved in every jurisdiction until trial, even if the attorney never objects at the deposition. *Id.* §113. Thus, a new lawyer should realize that most questions will be answered at a deposition. Even if she asks the question in a manner that violates the proper form, opposing counsel can register her objection, but the question should still be answered if the witness is able. *Id.* §97. The area in which young counsel ought to be most on guard is the practice of "speaking objections." Some counsel will object and include in their objection signals to the witness of whether to answer a question and what problems might lie in doing so. For example, interrogating counsel asks, "please identify all facts surrounding the accident leading to this case." What if opposing counsel objects: "Objection, overly broad and vague. The witness cannot possibly identify *all* facts surrounding any instance." A witness, hearing this objection, may then say "I cannot recall all of the facts." Such a response suggests that the lawyer's responses are influencing the witness's response. Some lawyers are more strategic and save their speaking objections for questions that are pivotal to the case. The best way to spot speaking objections is that they generally involve some clues to the witness on how the witness should answer the question. Federal Rule of Civil Procedure 30(d) provides a strong statement against the practice of speaking objections:

> An objection must be stated concisely in a nonargumentative and nonsuggestive manner. A person may instruct a deponent not to answer only when necessary to preserve a privilege, to enforce a limitation ordered by the court, or to present a motion under Rule 30(d)(3) [concerning motions to limit or suspend a deposition when confronted with bad faith or oppressive conduct in the taking of a deposition].

Quite simply, an attorney should not direct her client how to answer a question.

A representative state court opinion reflecting the views of most judges on speaking objections follows:

Paramount Communications v. QVC Network
637 A.2d 34 (Del. 1994)

VEASEY, Chief Justice.

In this appeal we review an order of the Court of Chancery dated November 24, 1993 (the "November 24 Order"), preliminarily enjoining certain defensive measures designed to facilitate a so-called strategic alliance between Viacom Inc. ("Viacom") and Paramount Communications Inc. ("Paramount") approved by the board of directors of Paramount (the "Paramount Board" or the "Paramount directors") and to thwart an unsolicited, more valuable, tender offer by QVC Network Inc. ("QVC"). In affirming, we hold that the sale of control in this case, which is at the heart of the proposed strategic alliance, implicates enhanced judicial scrutiny of the conduct of the Paramount Board.... We further hold that the conduct of the Paramount Board was not reasonable as to process or result.

QVC and certain stockholders of Paramount commenced separate actions (later consolidated) in the Court of Chancery seeking preliminary and permanent injunctive relief against Paramount, certain members of the Paramount Board, and Viacom. This action arises out of a proposed acquisition of Paramount by Viacom through a tender offer followed by a second-step merger (the "Paramount-Viacom transaction"), and a competing unsolicited tender offer by QVC. The Court of Chancery granted a preliminary injunction....

The Court of Chancery found that the Paramount directors violated their fiduciary duties by favoring the Paramount-Viacom transaction over the more valuable unsolicited offer of QVC. The Court of Chancery preliminarily enjoined Paramount and the individual defendants (the "Paramount defendants") from amending or modifying Paramount's stockholder rights agreement (the "Rights Agreement"), including the redemption of the Rights, or taking other action to facilitate the consummation of the pending tender offer by Viacom or any proposed second-step merger, including the Merger Agreement between Paramount and Viacom dated September 12, 1993 (the "Original Merger Agreement"), as amended on October 24, 1993 (the "Amended Merger Agreement"). Viacom and the Paramount defendants were enjoined from taking any action to exercise any provision of the Stock Option Agreement between Paramount and Viacom dated September 12, 1993 (the "Stock Option Agreement"), as amended on October 24, 1993. The Court of Chancery did not grant preliminary injunctive relief as to the termination fee provided for the benefit of Viacom in Section 8.05 of the Original Merger Agreement and the Amended Merger Agreement (the "Termination Fee").

Under the circumstances of this case, the pending sale of control implicated in the Paramount-Viacom transaction required the Paramount Board to act on an informed basis to secure the best value reasonably available to the stockholders. Since we agree with the Court of Chancery that the Paramount directors violated their fiduciary duties, we have AFFIRMED the entry of the order of the Vice Chancellor granting the preliminary injunction and have REMANDED these proceedings to the Court of Chancery for proceedings consistent herewith.

We also ... [address] serious deposition misconduct by counsel who appeared on behalf of a Paramount director at the time that director's deposition was taken by a lawyer representing QVC.

....

The issue of discovery abuse, including lack of civility and professional misconduct during depositions, is a matter of considerable concern to Delaware courts and courts around the nation. One particular instance of misconduct during a deposition in this case demonstrates such an astonishing lack of professionalism and civility that it is worthy of special note here as a lesson for the future—a lesson of conduct not to be tolerated or repeated.

On November 10, 1993, an expedited deposition of Paramount, through one of its directors, J. Hugh Liedtke, was taken in the state of Texas. The deposition was taken by Delaware counsel for QVC. Mr. Liedtke was individually represented at this deposition by Joseph D. Jamail, Esquire, of the Texas Bar. Peter C. Thomas, Esquire, of the New York Bar appeared and defended on behalf of the Paramount defendants. It does not appear that any member of the Delaware bar was present at the deposition representing any of the defendants or the stockholder plaintiffs.

Mr. Jamail did not otherwise appear in this Delaware proceeding representing any party, and he was not admitted pro hac vice. Under the rules of the Court of Chancery and this Court, lawyers who are admitted pro hac vice to represent a party in Delaware proceedings are subject to Delaware Disciplinary Rules, and are required to review the Delaware State Bar Association Statement of Principles of Lawyer Conduct (the "Statement of Principles"). During the Liedtke deposition, Mr. Jamail abused the privilege of representing a witness in a Delaware proceeding, in that he: (a) improperly directed the witness not to answer certain questions; (b) was extraordinarily rude, uncivil, and vulgar; and (c) obstructed the ability of the questioner to elicit testimony to assist the Court in this matter.

The phrase "pro hac vice" means "for this case only"; virtually every state has a rule by which a lawyer admitted to practice in a state other than the forum may be admitted for a particular case although such an attorney may be required to have as co-counsel someone admitted to practice in the forum

To illustrate, a few excerpts from the latter stages of the Liedtke deposition follow:

Q. (By Mr. Johnston [Delaware counsel for QVC], hereafter MR. JOHNSTON) Okay. Do you have any idea why Mr. Oresman was calling that material to your attention?

MR. JAMAIL: Don't answer that.

How would he know what was going on in Mr. Oresman's mind?

Don't answer it.

Go on to your next question.

MR. JOHNSTON: No, Joe —

MR. JAMAIL: He's not going to answer that. Certify it. I'm going to shut it down if you don't go to your next question.

MR. JOHNSTON: No. Joe, Joe —

MR. JAMAIL: Don't "Joe" me, [ass___].[17] You can ask some questions, but get off of that. I'm tired of you. You could gag a maggot off a meat wagon. Now, we've helped you every way we can.

MR. JOHNSTON: Let's just take it easy.

MR. JAMAIL: No, we're not going to take it easy. Get done with this.

MR. JOHNSTON: We will go on to the next question.

MR. JAMAIL: Do it now.

MR. JOHNSTON: We will go on to the next question. We're not trying to excite anyone.

MR. JAMAIL: Come on. Quit talking. Ask the question. Nobody wants to socialize with you.

MR. JOHNSTON: I'm not trying to socialize. We'll go on to another question. We're continuing the deposition.

MR. JAMAIL: Well, go on and shut up.

---

17. Mr. Jamail actually used the full eight-letter word in the deposition.

MR. JOHNSTON: Are you finished?

MR. JAMAIL: Yeah, you—

MR. JOHNSTON: Are you finished?

MR. JAMAIL: I may be and you may be. Now, you want to sit here and talk to me, fine. This deposition is going to be over with. You don't know what you're doing. Obviously someone wrote out a long outline of stuff for you to ask. You have no concept of what you're doing.

Now, I've tolerated you for three hours. If you've got another question, get on with it. This is going to stop one hour from now, period. Go.

MR. JOHNSTON: Are you finished?

MR. THOMAS: Come on, Mr. Johnston, move it.

MR. JOHNSTON: I don't need this kind of abuse.

MR. THOMAS: Then just ask the next question.

Q. (By Mr. Johnston) All right. To try to move forward, Mr. Liedtke, … I'll show you what's been marked as Liedtke 14 and it is a covering letter dated October 29 from Steven Cohen of Wachtell, Lipton, Rosen & Katz including QVC's Amendment Number 1 to its Schedule 14D-1, and my question—

A. No.

Q.—to you, sir, is whether you've seen that?

A. No. Look, I don't know what your intent in asking all these questions is, but, my God, I am not going to play boy lawyer.

Q. Mr. Liedtke—

A. Okay. Go ahead and ask your question.

Q.—I'm trying to move forward in this deposition that we are entitled to take. I'm trying to streamline it.

MR. JAMAIL: Come on with your next question. Don't even talk with this witness.

MR. JOHNSTON: I'm trying to move forward with it.

MR. JAMAIL: You understand me? Don't talk to this witness except by question. Did you hear me?

MR. JOHNSTON: I heard you fine.

MR. JAMAIL: You fee makers think you can come here and sit in somebody's office, get your meter running, get your full day's fee by asking stupid questions. Let's go with it.

    . . . .

Staunch advocacy on behalf of a client is proper and fully consistent with the finest effectuation of skill and professionalism. Indeed, it is a mark of professionalism, not weakness, for a lawyer zealously and firmly to protect and pursue a client's legitimate interests by a professional, courteous, and civil attitude toward all persons involved in the litigation process. A lawyer who engages in the type of behavior exemplified by Mr. Jamail on the record of the Liedtke deposition is not properly representing his client, and the client's cause is not advanced by a lawyer who engages in unprofessional conduct of this nature. It happens that in this case there was no application to the court, and the parties and the witness do not appear to have been prejudiced by this misconduct.

Nevertheless, the Court finds this unprofessional behavior to be outrageous and unacceptable. If a Delaware lawyer had engaged in the kind of misconduct committed by Mr. Jamail on this record, that lawyer would have been subject to censure or more serious sanctions. While the specter of disciplinary proceedings should not be used by the parties as a litigation tactic, conduct such as that involved here goes to the heart of the trial court proceedings themselves. As such, it cries out for relief under the trial court's rules.... Under some circumstances, the use of the trial court's inherent summary contempt powers may be appropriate....

Although busy and overburdened, Delaware trial courts are "but a phone call away" and would be responsive to the plight of a party and its counsel bearing the brunt of such misconduct. It is not appropriate for this Court to prescribe in the abstract any particular remedy or to provide an exclusive list of remedies under such circumstances. We assume that the trial courts of this State would consider protective orders and the sanctions permitted by the discovery rules. Sanctions could include exclusion of obstreperous counsel from attending the deposition (whether or not he or she has been admitted pro hac vice), ordering the deposition recessed and reconvened promptly in Delaware, or the appointment of a master to preside at the deposition. Costs and counsel fees should follow.

Depositions are the factual battleground where the vast majority of litigation actually takes place.... Thus, it is particularly important that this discovery device not be abused. Counsel should never forget that even though the deposition may be taking place far from a real courtroom, with no black-robed overseer peering down upon them, as long as the deposition is conducted under the caption of this court and proceeding under the authority of the rules of this court, counsel are operating as officers of this court. They should comport themselves accordingly; should they be tempted to stray, they should remember that this judge is but a phone call away.

....

Counsel attending the Liedtke deposition on behalf of the Paramount defendants had an obligation to ensure the integrity of that proceeding. The record of the deposition as a whole ... demonstrates that, not only Mr. Jamail, but also Mr. Thomas (representing the Paramount defendants), continually interrupted the questioning, engaged in colloquies and objections which sometimes suggested answers to questions, and constantly pressed the questioner for time throughout the deposition.... As to Mr. Jamail's tactics quoted above, Mr. Thomas passively let matters proceed as they did, and at times even added his own voice to support the behavior of Mr. Jamail. A Delaware lawyer or a lawyer admitted pro hac vice would have been expected to put an end to the misconduct in the Liedtke deposition.

Rule 30(d)(1) of the revised Federal Rules of Civil Procedure, which became effective on December 1, 1993, requires objections during depositions to be "stated concisely and in a non-argumentative and non-suggestive manner." ... The Delaware trial courts and this Court are evaluating the desirability of adopting certain of the new Federal Rules, or modifications thereof, and other possible rule changes.

[W]e share [the trial court's] view not only of the impropriety of coaching witnesses on and off the record of the deposition ... but also the impropriety of objections and colloquy which "tend to disrupt the question-and-answer rhythm of a deposition and obstruct the witness's testimony." ... To be sure, there are also occasions when the questioner is abusive or otherwise acts improperly and should be sanctioned.... Although the questioning in the Liedtke deposition could have proceeded more crisply, this was not a case where it was the questioner who abused the process.

This kind of misconduct is not to be tolerated in any Delaware court proceeding, including depositions taken in other states in which witnesses appear represented by their own counsel other than counsel for a party in the proceeding. Yet, there is no clear mechanism for this Court to deal with this matter in terms of sanctions or disciplinary remedies at this time in the context of this case. Nevertheless, consideration will be given to the following issues for the future: (a) whether or not it is appropriate and fair to take into account the behavior of Mr. Jamail in this case in the event application is made by him in the future to appear pro hac vice in any Delaware proceeding; and (b) what rules or standards should be adopted to deal effectively with misconduct by out-of-state lawyers in depositions in proceedings pending in Delaware courts.

As to (a), this Court will welcome a voluntary appearance by Mr. Jamail if a request is received from him by the Clerk of this Court within thirty days of the date of this Opinion and Addendum. The purpose of such voluntary appearance will be to explain the questioned conduct and to show cause why such conduct should not be considered as a bar to any future appearance by Mr. Jamail in a Delaware proceeding. As to (b), this Court and the trial courts of this State will undertake to strengthen the existing mechanisms for dealing with the type of misconduct referred to in this Addendum and the practices relating to admissions pro hac vice. [Conclusion of opinion]

Again, the most important thing an inexperienced lawyer can do before a deposition is to prepare. You should always make sure you have thorough knowledge of the rules of what can, and cannot, be objected to in a deposition. Be sure that you bring the court's telephone number to the deposition. As the above opinion suggests, counsel should call the trial court to deal with inappropriate deposition conduct. If you are questioning a witness and opposing counsel begins to make inappropriate speaking objections, you should ask the court reporter to mark in the record the questions and objections. Then, the interrogating attorney should state for the record that the objection is inappropriate and why. If opposing counsel continues to make speaking objections, call the court and ask for a judge to resolve the deposition dispute. You can have the court reporter at that point read back questions, objections, whatever the witness says, etc. If the attorney cannot reach a judge at that time, suspend the deposition and move for a protective order directing counsel to cease speaking objections. You can also seek fees and expenses associated with the motion. 23 AM. JUR. 2d *Depositions and Discovery* § 93 (2009). Before suspending a deposition and filing a motion, the attorney would be wise to have several questions on the record to which opposing counsel makes speaking objections. In that way, the chances increase of a judge's ruling in favor of the protective order, granting a request for fees and expenses, and probably censuring opposing counsel.

The interrogating counsel must keep her poise throughout this process and avoid getting into arguments with opposing counsel. Again, knowing the rules, showing opposing counsel that you know them, and seeking the court's intervention if opposing counsel interferes in the deposition — all go a long way to keeping you in charge of your deposition and opposing counsel in her proper place. In addition, another technique some lawyers use — particularly for lawyers with a reputation for being obstreperous — is to notice the deposition to be taken down stenographically by the court reporter and videotaped. Lawyers are far less likely to misbehave when they know that a court (or bar disciplinary committee) could end up seeing their behavior in living color.

Objections to questions that invade privilege are exceptions to the above rules. Counsel "defending" a deposition — *i.e.*, not interrogating, but rather representing her client while that client or another witness is being deposed—must remain alert for questions that invade the attorney-client privilege or work product doctrine. MARILYN J. BERGER ET AL., PRETRIAL ADVOCACY 339 (2d ed. 2007). *See generally* 27 C.J.S. *Discovery* § 42 (2009). These types of questions, and others that invade other privileges recognized by law, are the kind of deposition questions that an attorney can instruct a witness not to answer, in addition to objecting for the record. *Id.*

The attorney-client privilege applies to any oral or written communications between an attorney and a client concerning legal advice. 23 AM. JUR. 2d *Depositions and Discovery* § 29 (2009). The manner in which the privilege can be compromised is often subtle. Suppose the president of a pharmaceutical company had received a letter from an independent chemist who had tested a drug produced by the company. The chemist's letter alleges that one of the company's drugs contains chemicals that are known to be harmful to humans. The letter gives the impression that the chemist is planning to inform people whom he knows have used the drug. The president speaks with outside legal counsel (or with her in-house counsel). The president and counsel decide that it is in the best interest of the pharmaceutical company to conduct some tests on the drug in question in anticipation of impending litigation.

Assume that a plaintiff then sues the pharmaceutical company and that the president of the company is being deposed. What if plaintiff's counsel asks: "Identify all persons with whom you have had any conversations about the drug referred to in the letter from the chemist, and also identify the exact nature of those conversations." Although the question does not specifically ask the president anything regarding his conversations that he had with a lawyer, it does ask the president to identify "all persons" with whom he has discussed the drug, and the nature of those conversations. Counsel for the defendant should, at that point, state: "Objection based on privilege to the extent that the question asks about any conversations with lawyers and the witness is instructed not to answer as to any such conversations." Such an objection can, and indeed must, be made. If it is not, and the deponent testifies about the conversation with the lawyer, the privilege is deemed waived. *Id.* § 29.

Now, suppose the plaintiff's counsel in the same deposition asks whether the company has performed any tests on the drug. Here, the defendant's counsel should object along these lines: "Object based on *Hickman v. Taylor*[18] and the work product doctrine as to any tests performed in anticipation of litigation." (The work product doctrine will be discussed further, as it relates to discovery in general, below.) Federal Rule 26(c) actually protects only written work product, but most recognize that the *Hickman* case contemplated work product in a broader sense. *See* 23 AM. JUR. 2d *Depositions and Discovery* § 45 (2009). If opposing counsel could ask questions about the tests performed in anticipation of litigation, the holding in *Hickman* would be gutted. Indeed, the Court in *Hickman* specifically rejected interrogatories that invaded work product.

Professional Identity Question

Sometimes counsel will, in preparing a witness to be deposed, advise the witness that if she hears the attorney object at all, to pay close attention to the question. The attorney may even urge the witness that, if an objection is made, to ask

---

18. *Hickman v. Taylor*, 329 U.S. 495 (1947).

for the previous question to be repeated. Thus, the attorney might object to a question, "Objection to form. Vague." If a witness followed the attorney's instructions and remembered to ask for the question again, and sought out what in it might be vague, has the attorney engaged in coaching the witness? Would the attorney's objection, in these circumstances, be a "speaking objection"?

Corporate or Entity Depositions

Federal Rule 30(b)(6) and the procedural rules of virtually every state allow a litigant to send a notice to a corporate or other entity requesting for a deposition the persons most knowledgeable on matters listed in the deposition notice. 23 Am. Jur. 2d *Depositions and Discovery* § 92 (2009). The notion here is that a litigant cannot be expected to know who in a company or entity is most knowledgeable on every subject. Thus, when a notice is properly served on such a corporation or entity, that corporation or entity has the responsibility to determine the one or more persons on each item specified most knowledgeable and to produce the person(s) at the deposition to answer questions. *Id.* Again, the deposition should properly be noticed. The notice would salute the applicable rule or statute requiring that the person who is most knowledgeable from an entity be produced. The notice would then list all subjects on which the party wishes to ask questions of a person with knowledge of a designated topic. *Id.* §§ 91, 92. The person answering on behalf of the company or entity does so as if she were the company's spokesperson on the subject for which she was produced. *Id.* § 108. Thus, if the company is a party, the answers of the person or persons designated to answer at a Rule 30(b)(6) deposition will bind the company. *Id.* They may be offered at trial as binding testimony. *Id.* Hence, this mechanism is a powerful one for a party suing an entity, and a party defending a company or entity should recognize the significance of such depositions.

Professional Identity Question

Suppose your opponent serves a deposition notice directed to your corporate client that lists over twenty subjects on which it requests production at a deposition of a person most knowledgeable on each subject. You interview several witnesses and conclude that it would be necessary to produce more than one person if you were to truly produce the persons most knowledgeable on the different categories of the topics. However, you have one representative who knows something about all of the items listed, and it would be more convenient to produce that person. You tell yourself the person knows enough to answer on each question and thus should not be criticized for choosing one rather than having to deal with several persons being deposed. Should you go with the one witness or the several?

Whether a Deponent Should Read a Deposition or Waive Doing So

An area of great confusion surrounds what a deponent may do when a deposition has concluded. Deposition rules usually allow a party to waive the reading and signing of a deposition. *See generally* 27 C.J.S. *Discovery* § 71 (2009). Too often lawyers recommend such a practice. The problem with this practice is that, if the court reporter transcribes anything in the deposition inaccurately, and a witness has waived reading and signing, the inaccuracies cannot be corrected. *Id.* Conversely, if a witness requests the opportunity to review the deposition before signing a confirmation as to its accuracy, she will have the opportunity to correct errors in the transcript. 23 Am. Jur. 2d *Depositions and Discovery* § 100 (2009). Some lawyers mistakenly tell deponents that they may only correct "typographical errors" upon reviewing the transcript. In fact, the witness may correct any errors she sees, including substantive errors in testimony. *Id.* A deponent who makes substantive changes to her deposition testimony may, of course, have to face questions from counsel that implicate the deponent's credibility. But the myth that a deponent can only make typographical corrections is just that—a myth unsupported by the rule.

Strategy in Deposition-Taking

Described above are the steps a lawyer would take in preparing for a deposition. You might assume that a lawyer deposing a witness should ask every question she may have — just to be sure she has done so before trial. Without weighing the pros and cons of doing so, the choice to ask every question and leave no stone unturned is almost always a mistake. After thoroughly preparing for a deposition, a lawyer should decide *whether* to ask about everything. Sometimes the best strategy is not to ask a question at the deposition and to save the question for trial. Again, strategy comes into play. If counsel asks the party or witness at the deposition about a subject you anticipate as an Achilles heel in the opposing party's case, opposing counsel will surely be alerted and prepare at trial to deal with the question more effectively there. Whether counsel asks about an area of vulnerability depends on factors such as whether she believes it will provide the foundation for summary judgment. If so, she may want to ask the question on the expectation that there will not be a trial at which opposing counsel can arrange for a response that puts the best face on a set of facts. If, however, the attorney anticipates the case going to trial, then she can choose to save her ammunition for trial. Although it is dangerous to underestimate opposing counsel, the chance exists that if you do not ask about it, opposing counsel will either not become aware of the vulnerability or will think you are not aware of it. Either way, opposing counsel is less likely to be equipped to deal with an attack on the vulnerable point at trial.

Suppose, for instance, that a witness had been at a local bar before the events leading to the suit. Assume further that your opponent relies heavily on the witness to corroborate her version of events. Say that you have learned by means of thorough informal investigation that the witness was at the bar. If he denies being there, you actually have a receipt with his credit card and the date showing that he paid for several drinks. Do you confront the witness with this fact at the deposition? If you do, your opponent will surely deal with the unfavorable fact. Perhaps the opponent will even find another witness. A legitimate strategic choice would be to not ask about being at the bar prior to the events in question. Then, at trial, you would certainly ask about the key witness having been at a bar. You really do not care so much how the witness responds. He may be surprised, which will almost certainly show. If he admits being at the bar but claims to have had only one beer, jurors are not likely to believe that. These are the kinds of questions in which you really cannot lose. By waiting until trial to confront the witness with unfavorable facts affecting the weight of his testimony, you likely will undercut his testimony. The general approach to taking depositions is to seek a thorough understanding of a witness's knowledge of the facts and the documents. However, as suggested, thoughtful attorneys will decide whether certain questions are better left unasked until trial. Such decisions require judgment. But they are the essence of effective lawyering.

Group Exercise in Exploring Deposition Techniques

The problem with "Ugh Ugh" answers in depositions is that, on reading the transcript, the phrase will be ambiguous. "Ugh ugh" could mean "yes" or "no" and without the non-verbal language, such as a witness shaking her head up and down for "yes" or side to side for "no" — something that court reporters typically do not record — the reader cannot tell which answer the witness meant

Form groups in which each student takes turns playing the role of the interrogating attorney, the attorney "defending" the person being deposed, the witness (called "deponent"), and court reporter. Practice having the witness sworn in and ensuring the witness understands the process of a deposition requires audible answers other than "ugh ugh" or body language, which will not reflect the deponent's response in the transcript taken by the reporter. Pretend that the deposing attorney is plaintiff Brad Rex's counsel who is deposing Ena Hurry about the accident and the ensuing events that led to Rex's complaint and her counterclaim. (*See supra* pages 82–92 for a summary of Rex's complaint and Hurry's counterclaim.) At some point, counsel for Rex can ask about any discussions Hurry has had "with anyone" concerning the accident. At that point, why should counsel for Hurry object? Can counsel for Rex rephrase the question to avoid the objection? How?

Work Product Doctrine and Attorney-Client Privilege

Work Product

Work product refers to the information and materials an attorney (or other agent of a party) gathers for a party in anticipation of litigation. Work product can be categorized as both "non-documentary" work product and "documentary" work product. Many do not think of work product protection in non-documentary terms. However, the *Hickman* case dealt with precisely that issue — interrogatory questions to a lawyer who had gathered information in anticipation of litigation and was asked to provide information (some from his memory and some from materials he had gathered). *See Hickman v. Taylor*, 329 U.S. 495, 498-99 (1947). If asked about anything related to information that was gleaned by a representative of a party (the doctrine is not restricted to attorneys, but includes investigatory agents, etc.) in anticipation of litigation, an attorney should remember to object based on the work product doctrine.

Hickman recognizes that the discovering party may be able to overcome work product protection by showing substantial need. *Hickman*, 329 U.S. at 511–12. However, if the discovering party fails to make such a showing, answers in depositions or to interrogatories should be just as off-limits under the work product doctrine as requests for documents.

Document requests, however, more typically set the stage for a work product battle. In their rules of court, most states have provisions similar to Federal Rule of Civil Procedure 26(b). Appendix 8-1 (showing majority of states' general discovery provision equivalent to Fed. R. Civ. P. 26(b)). The provisions on work product in such rules state that documents or other materials prepared in anticipation of litigation are protected from disclosure. *See, e.g.*, Ala. R. Civ. P. 26(b)(3). The same rules contain other provisions similar to the Federal Rule. For instance, a party withholding documents under the work product doctrine should identify the documents with sufficient specificity so that the discovering party can determine whether to seek to overcome the privilege. *See, e.g.*, Fed. R. Civ. P. 26(b)(5). In addition, state rules typically allow a party to overcome a work product objection if the discovering party can show: (1) a substantial need for the materials; and (2) that the party cannot without undue hardship obtain the substantial equivalent of the materials by other means. *Id.* 26(b)(3). Even if a party overcomes the work product objection by such showings, however, opinion work product (*e.g.*, the lawyer or other representative's mental impressions, conclusions, opinions, or legal theories) will be "redacted" (*i.e.*, blacked out or otherwise deleted) in the materials produced. *Id.*

You may wonder who will police the party from whom work product is obtained to ensure that relevant materials are not redacted. An attorney should ask the judge to review the documents "in camera" (*i.e.*, in chambers, without them becoming public). Thus, if a party has any doubt about whether the opponent is fairly redacting only those parts of work product that represent opinion work product, then she can seek in camera review so that the judge can regulate this process. *See, e.g., Kerr v. United States*, 426 U.S. 394, 404-05 (1976) (approving the use of in camera review by judge of documents sought that non-disclosing party claims to be privileged).

Attorney-Client Privilege

An illustration above portrays a pharmaceutical company's president being asked in a deposition about oral communications that he had with his lawyer concerning legal advice. (*See supra* this chapter at page 203.) This example shows the attorney-client privilege as clearly applying to oral communications. *See* 23 Am. Jur. 2d *Depositions and Discovery* § 29 (2009). The privilege also applies to written communications to or from the attorney and client regarding legal advice. *Id.* A party seeking discovery can overcome the attorney-client privilege only in very narrow circumstances. If a party shows the "crime fraud exception" (where the attorney is participating in a crime or fraudulent activity that can only be revealed by piercing the attorney-client privilege), then that party may pierce the attorney-client privilege and force disclosure of attorney-client communications. *Id.* Note, however, that even though you ordinarily will be able to withhold materials that fall within the attorney-client privilege, states, like the federal system, require a listing of the documents that are withheld under the privilege. *E.g.*, Mass. R. Civ. P. 26(b)(5). An attorney should always specify the documents that are being withheld based on the attorney-client privilege or the work product doctrine in the log that she provides to opposing counsel. The privilege log should be produced at the time counsel serves her response to request for production of documents. (If local rules or the applicable request for production rule require objecting, and virtually every request for production rule requires responding "or objecting" within the specified time, counsel had better object on attorney-client and/or work product grounds or risk waiving these privileges.) More often than not, counsel will seek production of documents withheld under the work product doctrine rather than attempt to overcome the attorney client privilege. If the opposing counsel can show substantial need and inability to obtain the substantial equivalent to the withheld documents, she can force production of the documents withheld under the work product doctrine. *See* Fed. R. Civ. P. 26(b)(5).

[handwritten margin note: list of AC privilege docs & wp too]

Avoiding Waiver of Attorney-Client Privilege and/or Work Product Doctrine

Counsel should recognize that, if she produces a document to opposing counsel that qualifies under the attorney-client privilege or work product doctrine, she will have waived the protection that would otherwise be provided. 23 Am. Jur. 2d *Depositions and Dis-*

covery §§ 29, 30 (2009). In certain (limited) circumstances,[19] if the production is inadvertent, counsel can have the document returned to them and still be deemed protected. *See, e.g.*, Wyo. R. Civ. P. 26(b)(5)(B). Indeed, with the advent of electronic discovery, most rules contain a specific provision providing a mechanism by which electronic documents that are inadvertently disclosed may be recovered. *Id.*

What if you have withheld a document under the attorney-client privilege or work product doctrine, but the court has nevertheless ordered its production? Can you produce the document without waiving the protection of attorney-client privilege or work product doctrine? The answer is "no." Because rulings during the course of a case are typically not immediately appealable, you must take the approach that the defense attorney took in *Hickman*. The lawyer resisting discovery should let the court know that she is refusing to produce the materials because she plans to appeal and needs to be held in contempt of court. *Hickman*, 329 U.S. 495, 500. Usually, counsel's asking a trial court to hold her in contempt would be called leading with one's chin. However, trial courts understand that such a holding is the only means of obtaining appellate review and avoiding waiver. Thus, courts typically release an attorney on her own recognizance even after holding her in contempt. *See, e.g.*, Richard L. Marcus, *The Story of Hickman: Preserving Adversarial Incentives While Embracing Broad Discovery, in* Civil Procedure Stories 307, 320 (Kevin M. Clermont ed., 2004).

Discovery of Experts

Experts are persons who have knowledge beyond that of the ordinary person on a topic pertinent to the case. *See* Fed. R. Evid. 701. Discovery of testifying expert witnesses is an area with particular rules, but fortunately these rules generally are uniform among states. One major difference between federal and (most) state jurisdictions' approaches to experts now is that the Federal Rules rely on expert reports as the main vehicle for disclosing expert testimony. *See* Appendix 8-1; Fed. R. Civ. P. 26(a)(2). (The requirements for expert reports are discussed *supra* pages 173–74.) By contrast, most state jurisdictions approach discovery of testifying experts in the way the Federal Rules did before adopting the expert report approach. *See* Richard D. Freer, Introduction to Civil Procedure § 8.2.1 (2006). A party may ask an interrogatory seeking the identification of any experts who may testify, an explanation of such experts' opinions, the information reviewed in forming such opinions, and an explanation of the grounds for the experts' opinions. *See, e.g.*, Colo. R. Civ. P. 26(b)(4)(B). Indeed, the sample interrogatories included *supra* at pages 188–90 illustrate just such an interrogatory. Furthermore, a party may take depositions of an opponent's testifying experts. *See, e.g., id.* 26(b)(4)(A).

Although an attorney is wise to include an expert interrogatory in her first round of interrogatories, counsel ordinarily would not want to depose the other side's experts until after depositions of fact witnesses. The reason is simple: experts may rely on the testimony of fact witnesses, and counsel would want to know—at the time the expert is deposed—everything on which he or she relies. Typically, the party taking an expert's deposition is responsible for paying that expert's fee for the time during which the ex-

---

19. Beware that codes of professional responsibility and state bar ethics opinions are far from uniform on this issue. Some allow an opponent to keep privileged documents even where inadvertently produced.

pert is being deposed. *See* 23 Am. Jur. 2d *Depositions and Discovery* § 52 (2009). For some experts the fee can be quite large. Thus, counsel should ensure that she takes the expert's deposition once and once only, so as to avoid unnecessary trouble and expense.

A party may retain non-testifying experts, usually referred to as "consulting" experts. Generally, counsel cannot ask discovery questions of such an expert because the rules state that discovery may only be had from an expert who may testify at trial. *See id.* § 50; *see, e.g.,* Colo. R. Civ. P. 26(b)(4). They are treated as part of the trial team and, thus, communications with them are comparable to "work product" and should not ordinarily be discoverable. In cases where the subject matter is technical or complicated and the attorney needs assistance in order to understand the subject matter, a consulting expert can be invaluable in the attorney's preparation. However, counsel should be sure that her consulting expert and testifying expert do not exchange information. If so, that could expose the consulting expert to being deposed. The testifying expert often will have to disclose any such communications because generally any information a testifying expert is exposed to will be fair game in discovery.

A final category of experts are those persons with specialized knowledge but who happen to be involved in the facts of the case. For instance, a physician who treated the plaintiff in a personal injury case may be one of the most effective experts in a case. Others, such as a mechanic who worked on a car that malfunctioned, an equipment operator, or the like, would fall into this category. These experts should be identified in response to interrogatory answers, and counsel would do well to at least interview them. Because the expert is not allied with any party, sometimes the expert will actually offer helpful information for your side of the case. In any event, an attorney ought not to overlook the experts who happen to be part of the history of a case.

Objections to Discovery and Protective Orders

Courts know that counsel tend to be overly zealous in discovery. Some lawyers practice a "scorched earth" method of discovery designed to require so much work and resources of an opponent, that the litigant gives up. The system allows for objections to discovery and protective orders to prevent abusive practices such as this. Indeed, as will be shown below, the objections can even take into account the different level or resources of opposing litigants. Because too few counsel are aware of their ability to shield a client from abusive discovery, some clients with legitimate claims do in fact give up pursuing a more "well-heeled litigant." Realistically, some litigants will find litigating against an opponent with considerable resources to require them to either settle or end the litigation. However, a client with lesser resources should never have to do so because her lawyer failed to seek protection under the rules. In other words, inequitable resources will likely always play a part in denying justice to some, but that happens far more than it needs to happen simply because lawyers fail to know how to protect their clients.

Objections

Some objections derive directly from a discovery rule. For instance, most interrogatory rules limit the number of interrogatories to 30 including parts and subparts. 23 Am. Jur. 2d *Depositions and Discovery* § 122 (2009). If a party exceeds that number, the person on whom they are served can object based on the rule. Virtually every state recognizes the following general objections to discovery that are found in Federal Rule 26(b)(2)(C):[20]

- The discovery sought is unreasonably cumulative or duplicative, or can be obtained from some other source that is more convenient, less burdensome, or less expensive;

- The party seeking discovery has had ample opportunity to obtain the information by discovery in the action; and

- The burden or expense of the proposed discovery outweighs its likely benefit, considering the needs of the case, the amount in controversy, *the parties' resources*, the importance of the issues at stake in the action, and the importance of the discovery in resolving the issues.

See Appendix 8-1 (reflecting states with such rules). Note the italicized language—a common provision in state rules on objections, as also stated in Federal Rule 26(b), explicitly permits the court to weigh parties' differing resources in ruling on discovery objections.

Protective Orders

In addition to objecting to discovery, a party may also move for a protective order. Protective orders are a flexible, powerful tool by which the court can hold parties in check and prevent abuse. Most jurisdictions have a rule modeled on Federal Rule of Civil Procedure 26(c), which is reprinted below. The rule permits courts, upon motion and for good cause, to issue an order to protect a party or person from annoyance, embarrassment, oppression, or undue burden and expense, including one or more of the following:[21]

(A) forbidding the ... discovery;

(B) specifying terms, including time and place, for the ... discovery;

(C) prescribing a discovery method other than the one selected by the party seeking discovery;

(D) forbidding inquiry into certain matters, or limiting the scope of ... discovery to certain matters;

(E) designating the persons who may be present while the discovery is conducted;

(F) requiring that a deposition be sealed and opened only on court order;

(G) requiring that a trade secret or other confidential research, development, or commercial information not be revealed or be revealed only in a specified way; and

(H) requiring that the parties simultaneously file specified documents or information in sealed envelopes, to be opened as the court directs.

See Appendix 8-1 (states whose rules or statutes incorporate such protections).

Discovery Motions and Sanctions

Few attorneys will get through a case without filing a motion to compel discovery. This unfortunate fact likely results from the mindset that is fostered by an adversarial sys-

---

20. Appendix 8-1; *see also, e.g.,* Wyo. R. Civ. P. 26(b)(2)(C).
21. Appendix 8-1; *see also, e.g.,* Wyo. R. Civ. P. 26(c).

tem of justice. Lawyers who receive discovery requests commonly look for a way to interpret them so as to justify providing less information (or materials) than an objective reading of the request would call for.

The introduction of broad discovery into American civil litigation was supposed to foster cooperative exchange of information, avoid surprises, and foster settlements. 23 Am. Jur. 2d *Depositions and Discovery* § 1 (2009). To some extent, broad discovery probably has achieved those goals. A high percentage of cases settle before trial, and a major contributing factor is the exchange of information that allows parties to see how their case is likely to turn out. *Id.* Unfortunately, the reality in our modern adversarial system is that a litigant will have to fight for much of the information to which she is fairly entitled. Rarely will an attorney receive responses to interrogatories or requests for production without some objections upon which her opponent may very well be withholding valuable information. Even attorneys who seek to maintain a level of professionalism will justify withholding discoverable information that *could* be produced upon a fair reading of a discovery request. They rationalize that the adversarial system dictates that if they have any arguable objection to responding (especially with a document that is harmful to their party's case), that they should raise the objection and withhold the requested information with the knowledge that opposing counsel can move to compel, and the court will rule on whether the information must be submitted. Although the goals of avoiding surprises and fostering settlements seem to have been somewhat furthered, the goal of cooperation has not been advanced to the same extent.

Thus, an attorney should enter discovery with her eyes wide open. She must expect to relentlessly pursue her discovery requests until they are fully answered. Then and only then can an attorney be confident that she has *all* of the information (or documents) to which her client is entitled. Additionally, through thorough discovery the attorney can gain whatever leverage is appropriate to the strength of her client's claims or defenses. Counsel will need to be persistent in discovery to ensure she gains that leverage appropriate to her client's position so that, if there is a settlement, it is based on full disclosure of the facts—providing an accurate picture of the likely outcome of the trial—rather than a settlement based on an incomplete view of the facts and likely outcome.

Every jurisdiction recognizes that the discovery process presents unique issues, and therefore motions to compel and discovery sanctions are treated separately from sanctions regarding other aspects of litigation, such as the pleading of claims. *See* Appendix 8-7 (states' approaches to motions to compel and discovery sanctions). Thus, Chapter 4 dealt with various jurisdictions' approaches to "Rule 11" violations—sanctions related to pleadings, motions, or arguments *other than* those involved in the discovery process. (*See supra* Chapter 4 at pages 78–79.) However, you must look to another part of your state's rules or statutes for the methods to deal with motions to compel discovery and sanctions for violations of the discovery rules. Usually, you will find such a rule at the end of the discovery section of your state's discovery rules. For instance, the federal sanctions rule (Rule 37) follows the rest of the discovery rules.

A healthy trend in discovery has been to require the moving party to certify that she has attempted to resolve the discovery dispute with opposing counsel prior to filing a motion to compel. When attorneys take the time to discuss the objections that have been made (by either side) they can often reach an agreement concerning the discovery that is being sought. That will at least narrow the controversy that the court has to resolve. If a jurisdiction requires such a certification, and the moving party does not make a good faith attempt to resolve the conflict and certify as much in her motion, the court will not hear the motion. *See* 23 Am. Jur. 2d *Depositions and Discovery* § 206 (2009); *see, e.g.,* Wyo. R. Civ. P. 37(a)(2)(A).

Assuming that counsel has attempted to resolve the motion and cannot, a motion to compel would follow. Unlike pleadings (*e.g.*, a complaint) and motions, discovery requests and responses are not filed with the court. Instead, it is served by counsel on each other. Thus, the only way the court will know what was requested, what objections were made, and what was provided is when the moving party files a motion explaining these facts—and attaching pertinent discovery requests, objections, and the responses deemed inadequate. After securing the dates that the opposing counsel is available for a hearing, an attorney would schedule a hearing with the court.

Promptly moving to compel is essential. If the case has a discovery cut-off, the attorney may not have all information needed to conduct depositions if she does not push for such disclosure early. Often it takes more than one motion to compel to get everything one needs. Unfortunately, even after being compelled, opposing counsel will often still not provide all information or documents called for. You may wonder how counsel responding to discovery can get away with doing so. In part the answer is that, unfortunately, some courts are not as willing as others to impose the sanctions for discovery abuse. Opposing counsel can often make some colorable claim for continuing to object to a discovery request, perhaps on a variation of the first objection that introduces new issues to argue. Rather than sanction an attorney for taking such a tack, courts are far more inclined simply to grant a second motion to compel and, if they do anything, chastise opposing counsel. Most states' rules allow for imposition of attorneys' fees and costs that result from a party having to make a motion to compel, but courts do not always impose these sanctions. 23 Am. Jur. 2d *Depositions and Discovery* § 208 (2009). Thus, the party responding to discovery has less incentive to respond fully on the first response to discovery. Again, the party seeking discovery should recognize that reality and expect to be required to move to compel more than once. The good news is that, if an attorney shows an opponent that she is unwilling to permit withholding of information or documents and that she will pursue them until they are produced, this often sends a powerful signal to the opponent. If that opponent faces potential liability, an aggressive approach to discovery can lead to forcing the hand of the opponent—*i.e.*, to settlement discussions, earlier rather than later.

Sanctions in discovery generally come in two forms. First, a recalcitrant party can face sanctions for failure to comply with an order compelling discovery. If the court has granted an order compelling discovery or otherwise ordered a party to produce information or make a witness available, the failure of such a party to comply with the order justifies sanctions. *See* 23 Am. Jur. 2d *Depositions and Discovery* § 210 (2009). The possible sanctions a court can order in this situation typically include: (a) having the matter sought to be discovered taken as established for purposes of trial; (b) prohibiting the party who failed to comply with the court's order from supporting claims or defenses or from introducing certain evidence; (c) striking pleadings, in whole or in part; (d) staying the case until the order is obeyed; (e) dismissing the suit in whole or in part; (f) entering a default judgment against the party who failed to comply, and/or holding the party who failed to comply in contempt of court. *E.g.*, Wyo. R. Civ. P. 37(b); see Appendix 8-7.

Second, a party may be sanctioned for certain failures even without a prior court order. The specific situations that would lead to a sanction without a court order include a party's failure to appear for a deposition properly noticed by her opponent, or a party who fails to provide *any* answers to interrogatories, *any* responses to request for production of documents, or who otherwise fails to respond at all to discovery requests. *See, e.g.*, Wyo. R. Civ. P. 37(c)(d).

D. Methods to Reinforce and Integrate Topics Covered in This Chapter

Students will likely benefit from grouping discovery tools into different phases. Below is one possible grouping. Students can take the tools in each category and identify the strengths and weaknesses of each.

INITIAL TOOLS: Obtaining a "Litigation Hold Order" to ensure no electronic or other documents are disposed of while case pending; Interrogatories; Request for production of documents or things; Rule 45 subpoena duces tecum for production of documents by nonparty;
Others?

_____
_____
_____

MID-PHASE TOOLS: Motions to Compel; Depositions (party deposition, corporate/entity deposition, nonparty deposition via subpoena under Rule 45); Second round of more focused Interrogatories and Request for production of documents or things; Determining how much electronic information is at issue and discussing with client plan for dealing with that.
Others?

_____
_____
_____

LATTER PHASE TOOLS: Depositions of experts; Request for Admissions.
Others?

_____
_____
_____

E. Written Assignments

The following are suggested written assignments that should help reinforce further the topics and analysis covered in this chapter.

1. Develop a written "trial preparation and discovery plan" for Sally in her case against HorsePower, Inc. The plan should refer to the elements of her claims and proof needed on these. Include your objectives, the discovery tools you plan to

use, etc. (In an actual case, you would have a trial preparation and discovery plan for proving your case against each defendant.) The plan should also include trial preparation, along with discovery, because you must consider what you can prove — through factual witnesses, documents, and experts — without exclusively relying on discovery from defendants. Although you will certainly have to request documents and take depositions of HorsePower, Inc., how will you prove that the vehicle's roll-bar was defective? If you need an expert to do so, what kind of expert? How will you find an expert? What information will that expert need? Will you have a consulting and a testifying expert? Your planning on the use of experts would be included in the trial preparation plan and the discovery plan. Your expert will need certain information from the manufacturer to help her or him to develop opinions. Identify that information in the plan. In addition, you will want to seek identification of the manufacturer's employees and outside experts and any information on which they rely before you take their deposition.

If you will not seek certain information in discovery for strategic reasons, identify that in your plan as well and how you would ensure Sally agrees with you and understands the potential risks.

2. Assume that the three defendants have each served extensive written discovery requests on Sally. Combined, she has received three sets of interrogatories and several hundred requests for production of documents. Many of these duplicate one another. What steps should you take to protect Sally's interests? Do the Rules have specific provisions supporting any steps you take to prevent Sally from excessive cost in responding to the discovery?

3. You asked HorsePower, Inc. ("HorsePower") for a "Litigation Hold" order preventing the discarding of electronic information while the suit is pending. HorsePower responds that doing so would bring its information systems to a halt and that the company must dispose of electronic files regularly or risks a "system crash." How do you deal with this problem? If you end up taking the matter to court by filing a motion for a "hold" order, what position will you take — that HorsePower must keep everything, or is there a compromise you might be willing to reach? If you answer that you will argue that HorsePower must keep everything, would it change your position if the judge said to do that she will require Sally to pay the costs of storing such data (say, $25,000 a month)?

Chapter 9

The Right to a Jury Trial and Summary Judgment

A. Sally's Case at This Stage of Litigation Process

At the beginning of the case, Sally preserved her right to a jury trial by demanding a jury within the required time. Moreover, her claims are the same kinds of claims that juries in the Anglo-American tradition have heard. She claims negligence against the City and the State, as well as negligence against the manufacturer. (Although some refer to a claim against a product manufacturer as a "products liability" claim, the claim usually includes both elements of negligence and, at times, strict liability depending on the jurisdiction.) Sally's remedies are also suitable for a jury: Sally does not seek equitable relief, but rather seeks money damages. Thus, her claims are precisely the kinds of claims that a jury hears routinely.

At this point, both sides have completed discovery. If the State, City, or HorsePower is going to try to avoid a trial, it will become clear at this stage of the litigation. The defendant will file a summary judgment motion. Sally has anticipated the possibility of a summary judgment motion from the outset of the case. Consequently, she will have sufficient evidence to bring before the court in the "paper preview" of the trial known as summary judgment practice.

B. Tasks and Decision-Making at This Stage of a Case

Diagram 9-1 illustrates where, in the stages of a case timeline, Sally now finds herself.

By demanding a jury early in the case, Sally did all that was necessary to ensure she will receive trial by jury on her claims. However, to actually get to trial, she must successfully fend off any summary judgment motions from a defendant. Her response must show the court that she has sufficient evidence supporting the required elements of each claim. Needless to say, she ought to put in front of the court (through the affidavits, depositions, or discovery responses attached to her brief) enough evidence that it convinces the court that reasonable jurors at least can disagree on each claim. Fortunately, the strategy and decision-making outlined in the preceding chapters have put Sally in an ideal position to respond to any summary judgment motions.

Diagram 9-1

Cause of Action (events leading to suit)
Prefiling Matters to Consider; Choice of Forum [Chs. 2-3]
Π and Δ Decide on Offensive Pleadings & Joinder (of claims & parties); Filing Suit; Service [Chs. 4-5]
Motions, Responsive Pleadings; Default; Voluntary & Involuntary Dismissals [Chs. 6-7]
Discovery Phase (developing proof to establish claims & learning about the adversary's case) [Ch. 8]
Right to Jury Trial; Pretrial Motions & Practice [Ch. 9]
Final Pretrial Conference & Other Events within Last Month before Trial [Ch. 10]
Procedure at Trial [Ch. 11]
Post-Trial Motions & Calculating the Date of Final Judgment to Know Key Deadlines Such as for Notice of Appeal [Ch. 12]

A case may involve pretrial motions other than motions for summary judgment. As suggested in Chapter 4 on pleading, one can file a motion for sanctions if the opponent asserts facts or legal grounds without a sound basis. As suggested in Chapter 8 on discovery, motions for a protective order, to compel discovery, and for discovery sanctions probably represent the greatest percentage of pretrial motions. Later, motions in limine challenging the admissibility of evidence will be discussed in Chapter 10 (Final Pretrial Conferences).

Nevertheless, no master list of motions exists. Any kind of relief a party needs in the process of handling a case provides the potential basis for a motion. One simply needs to title the motion "Motion for _____" (filling in whatever relief you are seeking). Of course, a litigant must have a basis for filing the motion. Rules, statutes, and cases represent obvious bases. Yet, as long as the relief requested is implicit in the necessary handling of the case, one can file a motion and title it appropriately.

This chapter focuses on the "800 pound gorilla" of pretrial motions: motions for summary judgment. These are by far the most significant of pretrial motions for a simple reason. They decide whether claims go forward to trial.

C. Overview of Applicable Law

The Right to Jury Trial and Motions for Summary Judgment

The right to a jury trial and motions for summary judgment are highly related. When a party demands a jury trial, she seeks a group of laypersons from the community to decide the disputed facts and apply the law to the facts. Usually, a major disputed fact will be the amount of damages necessary to compensate the plaintiff if the defendant is found liable. A summary judgment motion seeks to take the decision from the jury and place it in the hands of a judge. The rationale of a motion for summary judgment is that the party who bears the burden of proving her claim must show that her case is worthy of a jury trial. Essentially, summary judgment is a preview of the trial. The judge views the submissions of the moving party, and those of the party opposing summary judgment, and determines whether they reflect a genuine issue of material fact. A judge is not to decide in this process how persuasive the evidence is for the party with the burden of proof. Indeed, the judge cannot consider the credibility of witnesses. Instead, the judge considers solely whether the party who bears the burden of proof can produce sufficient evidence such that reasonable jurors can disagree on each of the essential elements of the claims.

[handwritten margin note: Not a question of credibility of evidence]

[handwritten margin note: B for Summary Judgment]

Why, then, are the right to jury trial and summary judgment motions related? The standard for granting summary judgment has been crafted so as to preserve a party's right to a jury trial. The reasonable-persons-can-differ standard is a generous one and reflects the preference under American law of allowing cases to be resolved by juries when possible. The judge intervenes in two general categories of cases. The first category includes cases in which the plaintiff asserts a claim that the jurisdiction does not recognize as actionable (*e.g.*, a claim against a social host when a guest gets drunk and, after a party, injures or kills another). The second category of cases in which the judge intervenes is when, the claimant—usually the plaintiff, but sometimes another party (*e.g.*, a counterclaimant)—fails to show that she has sufficient evidence such that reasonable jurors can disagree about the evidence supporting the claim. In the second category of cases, a judge will short-circuit the litigation process because the claimant can do no better at trial than at summary judgment. The judge here rules, in essence, that the case is not worthy of the time and effort involved in a jury trial. The judge can see from the summary judgment materials that judgment will have to be granted as a matter of law at trial due to the lack of sufficient evidence. American jurisprudence favors giving parties an opportunity to have their day in court. However, it does not guarantee the right to have every case heard in a court of law regardless of whether a party can show that there is a dispute to be tried.

The Right to a Jury Trial

In American law, few rights are held as precious as the right to a trial by jury. The right for an American citizen to have her claims decided by a group of her equals is fundamental to the American judicial system. Parties can point to support for this right not only in the U.S. Constitution, but also in the constitutions of the states, the statutes of the states, and/or state procedural rules. 47 Am. Jur. 2d *Jury* § 3 (2009). The foundation of the right to trial by jury can be traced back to the *Magna Carta*, the famous charter resulting from the revolt of English barons against their tyrannical king. Led by Archbishop Stephen Langton, the barons forced King John to sign the *Magna Carta* on June 15, 1215. Among the rights that the King recognized were the following:

> No free man shall be seized or imprisoned, or stripped of his rights or possessions, or outlawed or exiled, or deprived of his standing in any other way, nor will we proceed with force against him, or send others to do so, except by the lawful judgment of his equals....[1]

The *Magna Carta* decreased the centralized power of the king of England and is generally considered one of the foundations for English and American constitutional government.[2] Originally, the right to trial by jury afforded protection only to certain members of English society. Eventually, English common law and later American common law recognized this right as one owed to every member of society. RUSSELL KIRK, THE ROOTS OF AMERICAN ORDER, 185–86 (2004).

Unlike most of the Bill of Rights, the Seventh Amendment to the U.S. Constitution has not been held to apply to the states through the Due Process Clause of the U.S. Constitution's Fourteenth Amendment.[3] Thus, an attorney who represents her client in a civil case in state court, and who claimed that her client's right to a jury trial existed under the U.S. Constitution, would be wrong. In civil actions that are governed by state law, the law of the forum state controls whether the parties are entitled to a jury trial. 50A C.J.S. *Juries* § 12 (2009). A state court does not violate the constitutional right of due process "per se" by denying a party a trial by jury. 47 AM. JUR. 2d *Jury* § 7 (2009).

Many states extend the right to a jury trial by their constitution; others do so through statutes or procedural rules. If the right is not provided by the forum state's constitution, then the right to a jury trial can only be exercised if it is conferred by a statute or by a rule of court. *Id.* § 11. For example, Colorado's constitution states that, "a jury in civil cases ... may consist of less than twelve persons," but does not provide any other conditions regarding civil jury trials. COLO. CONST. Art. II § 23. Instead, both the substantive foundation and the procedural means to exercise the right to a jury trial are provided by Colorado Rule of Civil Procedure 38. The right to a jury trial exists insofar as the courts interpret Colorado Rule of Civil Procedure 38 to bestow it. SHEILA K. HYATT & STEPHEN A. HESS, 4 COLO. PRAC., CIVIL RULES ANNOTATED, R. 38 (4th ed., West 2008). In comparison, the Constitution of California declares the right to trial by jury in any cause of action to be inviolate, and available to all. WEST'S ANN. CAL. CONST. Art. 1 § 16 (1998). In any event, parties typically have—in state court as in federal court—the right to a jury trial in civil cases. 47 AM. JUR. 2d *Jury* § 4 (2009).

As with federal civil trials, however, the right does not apply to all classes of cases. However, the court must err on the side of granting a jury if a reasonable basis exists in state-law sources for a jury trial. *Id.* § 6. Moreover, the entitlement to a jury trial turns on the same two factors that federal courts consider under the Seventh Amendment. First, is the claim or issue in the case the type of claim that would ordinarily be heard by a jury rather than by a judge? 50A C.J.S. *Juries* § 25 (2009). Second, is the relief sought legal (*e.g.*, money damages) or equitable (*e.g.*, injunctive relief, rescission of contract)? *Id.* § 24.

---

1. MAGNA CARTA § 39 (1215).
2. *See, e.g.*, The Constitution of Maryland: Declaration of Rights, Art. 24 (2008) (quoting the *Magna Carta*).
3. *Pearson v. Yewdall*, 95 U.S. 294, 296 (1877) (holding that the court has stated "over and over" that the Seventh Amendment right to a jury trial applies only to courts of the United States).

[handwritten in top margin: another factor for determining jury]

If the particular case seeks ~~money damages~~, it will almost surely be heard by a jury; if it seeks ~~equitable relief only~~, the case will be heard by a judge. *Id* §§ 4, 24; *see, e.g.*, K.S.A. Const. Bill of Rights, §§ 5, 7.

If a case alleges claims that request legal and equitable relief on the same issue, the court must be careful not to infringe on a party's right to have the legal claim(s) tried by a jury. The court will have the jury resolve legal issues first so as to preserve the right to a jury trial on such issues. 50A C.J.S. *Juries* § 31 (2009). In this scenario, the jury would hear the evidence, receive instructions, and render its verdict on the legal issue(s) and relief. The judge would then render judgment on the equitable issue(s). If a fact found by the jury overlaps with a fact relevant to the equitable claim, the judge cannot reconsider and decide the fact differently. 47 Am. Jur. 2d *Jury* § 36 (2009). The opposite approach would not work. Having the judge resolve facts before the jury hears the entire case and renders its verdict would put the jury in a subservient role. *Id.* Because the judge is bound by the jury's findings of fact that are common to both the legal and equitable issues being tried, a judge cannot deny equitable relief based *solely* on a rejection of the jury's fact-finding. *Id.* However, because equity claims always require judicial discretion as a necessary part of the process, a judge can deny equitable relief even if legal remedies are awarded by a jury. *Id.*

[handwritten in right margin: Whether there are issues that have legal and equitable forms of relief]

The ability to have a jury determine a client's claims is a powerful and valuable right. However, a party can easily lose that right by failing to follow the deadline of the applicable jurisdiction, as well as other procedures for demanding a jury trial. Usually state rules (like Federal Rule of Civil Procedure 38) require the demand early in the pleading stage. At some point before trial, a party must demand a jury. Otherwise the court would not be able to know whether to schedule the case for a jury trial or a bench (judge) trial. If a party does not demand trial by jury, the right is deemed waived. *Id.* § 64.

Follow-Up Questions

1. Why do you believe so many litigants prefer a jury trial to a bench trial? →
2. In what circumstances as a plaintiff would you consider *not* having a jury trial, but would prefer a bench trial?
3. As a defendant in a civil case, are there circumstances where you would prefer a jury trial over a judge trial?

[handwritten in right margin: sympathetic jury / comparative negligence case · high tech technical contracts/business/FCRA case]

[handwritten in right margin: Where it was negligent · complicated/technical cases]

Professional Identity Question

Assume that you have been practicing for less than a year and are dying to get your first jury trial. You represent a defendant in a civil case concerning a car accident in which your client and the plaintiff dispute who changed lanes first and forced the other into a guardrail. Both cars ended up on the shoulder and were badly wrecked. Plus, the plaintiff suffered injuries, including whiplash to her neck that has required her to go to a chiropractor. The plaintiff is a well-spoken lady, and your client is a large, rough-mannered man with long hair, a Fu Manchu mustache, and tattoos all over his body, including his neck and fingers. It is the last day for demanding a jury trial. Plaintiff's counsel has not demanded a jury. You know her lawyer, who has a reputation for missing deadlines and, from what you have heard, is on vacation. If anyone claims a jury in this case, it will have to be you. Although you recognize that the plaintiff may be more sympathetic to a jury than your client, you really want to get your first jury trial. You tell yourself that you can overcome any sympathy factor for the plaintiff, and bias against your rough-looking client, by extra work in preparation for trial. Moreover, you believe most people think chiropractors are "quacks" and, thus, the plaintiff will not recover significant damages even if the jury decides in her favor. Would you make a jury demand?

Practice Problems

Practice Problem 9-1

A restaurant and museum business, the Restaurant and Museum, Inc., ("RMI") operates near a coal terminal operated by Carbon Coal Co. RMI claims that coal from the terminal is interfering with its business, causing it expenses such as repeated cleaning of facilities, lost restaurant and museum business, and the like. RMI sues Carbon Coal and seeks injunctive relief to prevent the alleged repeated trespasses (coal particles represent the alleged invasion of RMI's property) and nuisance. In addition, RMI seeks damages based on the same legal theories, trespass and nuisance, for damages up to the date of the suit, including lost business, cleaning expenses, etc. RMI timely demands trial by jury. Should it receive a jury trial in light of its claims? Will the jury consider the equitable claims? If not, when will the judge consider them? Even if the jury considers the claims for damages first, factual findings on those claims will overlap with factual findings affecting the equitable claims. How should the court treat such factual findings?

Practice Problem 9-2

PetroCo, a large gas company, not only sold petroleum products but owned certain gas stations that it allowed to be leased and used under a franchise agreement. PetroCo entered into a franchise agreement allowing the Smiths not only to lease one of its gas stations, but also to use the PetroCo name in selling gas. The Smiths fell on financial hard times and could not continue. The Torcomians heard of the situation from the Smiths, and approached PetroCo about the lease and franchise agreement. The Torcomians arranged with PetroCo to assume the franchise agreement, but the parties never entered into a final agreement. The parties engaged in several months of negotiations, and the Torcomians operated the station during this time despite the lack of a signed agreement. PetroCo made it clear that the Torcomians' operation of the station during this time was not a waiver of its standard requirement that any party operating its station do so under a signed franchise agreement. Finally, it became clear that the parties could not agree on terms, and that the Torcomians would not sign the franchise agreement that would substitute them for the Smiths. PetroCo instructed the Torcomians orally and then in writing to vacate the gas station, but the Torcomians refused. PetroCo sued the Torcomians seeking an injunction under a state unfair trade practices statute that authorizes injunctive relief when someone has used the trade name of another without written permission. The Torcomians counterclaimed against PetroCo seeking damages for the time when the Torcomians operated the station without a franchise agreement and, according to them, did not get paid sufficiently. The Torcomians demand a jury trial. Assume that PetroCo opposes the demand for a jury trial, and the court has to rule on whether the Torcomians have a right to a jury trial. How should the court rule? If the court finds that there is a right to jury trial on at least some issues, what issues will be resolved by the jury? What issues, if any, will be resolved by the judge? In what order should the issues be resolved?

[handwritten: T: argument for damages under quantum meruit k]

[handwritten margin: 2 pts. test p. 218 → Jury: money damages; Judge: equitable relief; order: jury → judge]

Motions for Summary Judgment

Summary judgment motions are the primary means by which cases are dismissed when they are not trial worthy—when there are no genuine issues of material fact. 73 Am. Jur. 2d *Summary Judgment* § 1 (2009). Most states follow the wording of Federal Rule 56(c) closely, if not exactly. *See* Appendix 9-1; *see also* Gene R. Shreve & Peter Raven-Hansen, Understanding Civil Procedure 369–70 (3d ed. 2002). Rule 56(c) states that judgment must be entered as a matter of law if the movant meets the burden of proof to "show that there is no genuine issue as to any material fact and that the movant is entitled to judgment as a matter of law." *See, e.g.*, Mass. R. Civ. P. 56(c); Or. R. Civ. P. 47(c).

The adoption of pleading Codes, such as the Field Code, and later in 1938 the Federal Rules of Civil Procedure, represented a major shift in the philosophy of the stage at which cases should be weeded out as not worthy of trial. Whereas previously the pleading stage had been significant and often a thicket the plaintiff could not penetrate, the Field Code and even more so the Federal Rules removed this barrier. However, they did contemplate that after a party had pled enough of a case to get to discovery, and had her opportunity to develop evidence, that summary judgment would serve as the threshing floor where cases lacking sufficient evidence would be weeded out.

Some believe that recent Supreme Court decisions are moving the threshing floor back to pleading. Even if these cases require more facts to be pled in federal court complaints than has been permitted within the last three decades,[4] the difficulty of pleading sufficient facts in most cases is not insurmountable. Thus, a party usually can get to the discovery phase of a case and have the opportunity to develop the evidence that she needs to prove each element of her claim.

The primary purpose of summary judgment motions continues to be what it always has been—to test whether genuine issues of material fact need to be tried. 73 Am. Jur. 2d *Summary Judgment* § 1 (2009). If a claimant cannot show disputed issues of material fact, then the issues at hand are a "matter of law" and, thus, for the judge to decide. 49 C.J.S. *Judgments* § 304 (2009). Summary judgment promotes judicial economy. *Id.* § 294. The mechanism allows courts to dispose of meritless claims and claims that exclusively involve questions of law. *Id.* As a result, the court saves substantial time and expense by discarding cases that do not require a full trial.

Generally a party may file a motion for summary judgment with or without supporting affidavits. 73 Am. Jur. 2d *Summary Judgment* § 22 (2009). In seeking summary judgment, the moving party has the burden of proving that the opposing party is not entitled

---

4. *See supra* Chapter 4 at pages 75–77 (discussing recent U.S. Supreme Court decisions suggesting a somewhat more rigorous pleading standard than has governed over the past several decades but which is not binding on state courts).

to have her claims heard by a jury because there is no legitimate (or triable) factual dispute. *Id.* § 17; *see, e.g.*, OR. R. CIV. P. 47. Effectively, the moving party claims that her opponent does not have enough evidence with which to support her claim, such that reasonable jurors might disagree about the evidence. 73 AM. JUR. 2d *Summary Judgment* § 17 (2009). All reasonable inferences as to whether there is a genuine factual dispute will be resolved in favor of the non-moving party. *Id.* The standard favoring a non-moving party is in keeping with the overarching policy of the American justice system that a party should be afforded the opportunity to have their case tried on the merits. Although summary judgment promotes judicial efficiency, the mechanism ought not prevent a party from having a fair trial where one is warranted. 49 C.J.S. *Judgments* § 294 (2009).

The movant must follow the applicable statute or rule governing proper procedure for filing a motion for summary judgment; otherwise, the motion will be denied. 49 C.J.S. *Judgments* § 314 (2009). *See, e.g., Discover Bank v. Stanley,* 757 N.W.2d 756 (2008) (holding that failure to follow the requirements of the applicable rule results in denial of motion for summary judgment). If a summary judgment motion is brought prematurely, before a party has had a sufficient opportunity to develop evidence in discovery to support her claim, the non-moving party can object to the motion for summary judgment on that basis or move for postponement until completion of discovery. *See, e.g.*, N.C. GEN. STAT. ANN. § 1A-1, Rule 56(f) (West 2009).

The following diagram is a helpful way to understand the process at work in a summary judgment decision.

Diagram 9-2

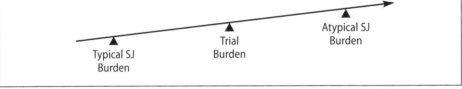

Typical SJ Burden

Trial Burden

Atypical SJ Burden

The first triangle depicts the typical threshold for a party opposing summary judgment and seeking trial. To survive summary judgment, the opposing party has to produce sufficient evidence to show that her case is beyond that benchmark. If the evidence on any one required element of her claim is insufficient, reasonable jurors could not decide for her at trial. The court should then grant summary judgment because the plaintiff cannot win. *See, e.g.*, OR. R. CIV. P. 47(c) ("No genuine issue as to a material fact exists if, based upon the record before the court viewed in a manner most favorable to the adverse party, no objectively reasonable juror could return a verdict for the adverse party on the matter that is the subject of the motion for summary judgment.").

On the far right, the triangle labeled "Atypical SJ Motion" is representative of the scenario in which — if the claimant produces sufficient evidence to go beyond that benchmark — reasonable jurors would *have* to find for the plaintiff. Occasionally a plaintiff's case is so compelling (and the defendant's position is so weak) that there is no other reasonable result to reach than for the plaintiff. Between the typical summary judgment and atypical summary judgment benchmarks, however, is the broad area in which reasonable jurors can disagree about the evidence. The majority of cases fall within this area.

The middle of Diagram 9-2, labeled "Trial Burden," represents a threshold that is the key to the burden of proof *at trial*, not at the summary judgment stage. In deciding summary judgment, a judge should not consider whether a party has met her trial burden on evidence. The trial burden for a claim or defense can vary. It may be proving the claim or defense is more likely than not — the preponderance-of-the-evidence trial burden. Or the trial burden may require proof beyond showing that the claim or defense is more likely than not, as when the trial burden requires clear and convincing proof. The judge adjusts the summary judgment burden to determine whether the party with the clear-and-convincing-evidence burden has produced sufficient evidence such that reasonable jurors could find for that party. The judge does *not* decide whether the party with that burden has proved her case by clear and convincing evidence. That decision is for the jury to decide after trial whether that party has proved her claim by clear and convincing evidence.

In other words, a judge — in considering a summary judgment motion — must assess whether the non-moving party has met her summary judgment burden in light of the trial burden. In a small percentage of cases, the judge will have to decide whether the evidence produced by the non-moving party is such that reasonable jurors could disagree about whether the trial burden of clear and convincing evidence has been met. Fraud is a good example of a claim that requires such a trial burden. Whether actual malice existed to support a public figure's libel claim was the issue in *Anderson v. Liberty Lobby*, 477 U.S. 242 (1986), and that claim required clear and convincing evidence. The Court in *Anderson* had to resolve whether the degree of evidence required of a non-moving party, to meet her summary judgment burden, should be greater in light of the greater trial burden. In answering "yes," the Court was careful to clarify that it was not changing the overall method by which judges must put aside their judgments concerning evidence and stick to the reasonable-jury standard. In other words, even in the small percentage of civil cases in which the clear and convincing trial burden applies, the judge is still not *deciding* whether the claimant has met the ultimate trial burden.

> Our holding that the clear-and-convincing standard of proof should be taken into account in ruling on summary judgment motions does not denigrate the role of the jury. It by no means authorizes trial on affidavits. Credibility determinations, the weighing of the evidence, and the drawing of legitimate inferences from the facts are jury functions, not those of a judge, whether he is ruling on a motion for summary judgment or for a directed verdict. The evidence of the non-movant is to be believed, and all justifiable inferences are to be drawn in his favor.... Neither do we suggest that the trial courts should act other than with caution in granting summary judgment or that the trial court may not deny summary judgment in a case where there is reason to believe that the better course would be to proceed to a full trial....
>
> In sum, we conclude that the determination of whether a given factual dispute requires submission to a jury must be guided by the substantive evidentiary standards that apply to the case. This is true at both the directed verdict and summary judgment stages. Consequently, where the ... "clear and convincing" evidence requirement applies, the trial judge's summary judgment inquiry as to whether a genuine issue exists will be whether the evidence presented is such that a jury applying that evidentiary standard could reasonably find for either the plaintiff or the defendant.... Thus, where the factual dispute concerns actual malice ... the appropriate summary judgment question will be whether

the evidence in the record could support a reasonable jury finding either that the plaintiff has shown actual malice by clear and convincing evidence or that the plaintiff has not.

Id. at 255–56.

In terms of Diagram 9-2, the judge should recognize that meeting of the "Typical Summary Judgment Burden" for a claim governed by the clear-and-convincing-evidence trial burden is greater than the amount of proof necessary to prove claims governed by the preponderance-of-the-evidence standard. Likewise, the trial burden will be correspondingly greater in matters of clear and convincing evidence than in proving something by a preponderance of the evidence. One could visualize the higher burdens by visualizing the arrow in Diagram 9-2 slanting further upward—representing the greater difficulty of each of the three burdens where the trial burden is clear and convincing evidence.) As with preponderance-of-the-evidence cases, the judge on summary judgment should not attempt to decide whether the claimant can carry that greater burden at trial. That job is for the jury. Regardless of the evidentiary standard, if sufficient evidence shows that reasonable jurors *could* find at trial that the trial burden has been met, then the judge should deny the summary judgment motion.[5]

And just what is it that a judge "sees" that enables her to make a decision when ruling on a summary judgment motion? She sees paper, and paper only, because a motion for summary judgment tests the legal sufficiency of a claim based on documents. 49 C.J.S. *Judgments* § 305 (2009). The judge does not hear live witnesses at summary judgment; she decides the motion based on what is presented to her. 73 Am. Jur. 2d *Summary Judgment* § 37 (2009). A summary judgment motion typically will rest only on depositions, affidavits, interrogatory answers, admissions on file, and pleadings. *Id.*; *see, e.g.,* Tex. R. Civ. P. 166(a). If upon reviewing the submitted material (depositions, pleadings, etc.) it is clear that there is no genuine issue of material fact to be tried, the court may grant judgment as a matter of law for the moving party. *See* 49 C.J.S. *Judgments* § 300 (2009); *see, e.g.,* Colo. R. Civ. P. 56(c).

Summary judgment is not about judges' determining the credibility of witnesses. Indeed, the law considers juries better at addressing witnesses' credibility than a judge. 47 Am. Jur. 2d *Jury* § 2 (2009). Moreover, the focus—even if not on credibility issues—has to be on whether there is no genuine issue of *material* facts. *See* G. Shreve & P. Raven-Hansen, Understanding Civil Procedure § 11.03[c][3][a] (4th ed. 2009). According to the Supreme Court in *Anderson*, a "material fact" is one "that might affect the outcome of the suit under the governing law." 477 U.S. at 248. If there is any doubt at all, the case should go to trial. 73 Am. Jur. 2d *Summary Judgment* § 38 (2009).

Most states closely follow Federal Rule 56. *See, e.g.,* Fla. R. Civ. P. 1.150(a). However, states differ regarding the deadline for filing a summary judgment motion. *Compare* Colo. R. Civ. P. 56(c) (deadline no later than 85 days before trial) *with* Or. R. Civ. P. 47(c) (deadline no later than 60 days before trial).

It is necessary that a party, by service of the motion, receive proper and timely notice that summary judgment is being sought against her. The rules on this issue vary somewhat

---

5. For an alternative description of the different burdens at play in summary judgment, see Richard D. Freer & Wendy Collins Perdue, Civil Procedure: Cases, Materials, and Questions 494 (5th ed. 2008).

among states. *Compare, e.g.,* Fla. R. Civ. P. 1.510(c) (requiring that the motion be served on the opposition at least 20 days prior to the hearing) *with, e.g.,* Mass. R. Civ. P. 56(c) (requiring that the motion be served on the opposing party no less than 10 days prior to the hearing). Nevertheless, the legitimacy of a summary judgment motion depends on proper notice to opposing counsel so that she may respond. 49 C.J.S. *Judgments* § 316 (2009).

In response to a summary judgment motion, a party cannot simply rest on denials contained in her pleadings, or on conclusory allegations. 73 Am. Jur. 2d *Summary Judgment* § 31 (2009). Instead, she must provide a response that is supported by whatever materials are permitted to be considered, such as deposition testimony, affidavits, discovery responses, and the like to show the court that there is a genuine issue of material fact to be tried. *Id*; *see, e.g.,* Ark. R. Civ. P. 56(e).

The goal of the party opposing summary judgment is simple — to show a genuine issue of material fact, that reasonable jurors could disagree over the evidence. Thus, the opposing party needs to know the elements of the claim to determine what issues are material to the case. A case will often have myriad facts. However, those facts that relate to the elements of a claim or defense that have the capability to change the outcome of a lawsuit are the ones that are "material." 73 Am. Jur. 2d *Summary Judgment* § 48 (2009). Moreover, the dispute over these facts needs to be a genuine, real, or triable issue that is supported by evidence and not merely non-essential details that parties are quibbling over. *Id.* § 47. Needless to say, if counsel has been following the advice of the earlier chapters, strategically considering the elements of the case from the outset, and developing evidence through a variety of means, then she should be able to overcome a motion for summary judgment.

[margin note: opposing party needs to know elements of claim, definition of material]

A defendant may bring a summary judgment motion in at least two scenarios. *See* 73 Am. Jur. 2d *Summary Judgment* § 17 (2009). First, she can gather evidence on one or more of the elements of a plaintiff's claim that tends to prove that the plaintiff is unable to carry her burden of proof. In this scenario, the defendant files her motion, attaches the proof she has gathered in discovery disproving the plaintiff's case, after which the plaintiff must respond or suffer summary judgment. 49 C.J.S. *Judgments* § 308 (2009). At this point, the plaintiff will typically answer with a brief in opposition to the summary judgment motion and attach discovery and affidavits attempting to show she can prove the matter at issue. *Id.*

[margin note: bringing SJ using proof the movant has gathered]

The other kind of summary judgment motion occurs when a party asks the opposing party for the evidence that the opposing party has on the various elements of a claim. For instance, a defendant may propound an interrogatory to the plaintiff seeking persons with knowledge of, or documents supporting, a key element of a claim. The defendant then takes the deposition of all persons identified and review the documents identified as supporting the key element. If these do not establish the required element, a movant may file a motion for summary judgment arguing (a) that her opponent bears the burden of proof at trial on material facts, (b) that discovery has revealed the plaintiff has insufficient evidence to prove the facts, and (c) thus no genuine issue of material facts exists. *See Celotex Corp. v. Catrett*, 477 U.S. 317–27 (1986).

[margin note: bringing SJ using proof the nonmoving party has gathered]

The party that has the burden of persuasion on a claim or an issue at trial may also move for summary judgment. Such motions are less typical because they require significant evidence. By moving for summary judgment, a party is claiming that her proof is so strong that it exceeds the third triangle in Diagram 9-2. In other words, the party with the burden of persuasion is putting evidence before the court that demonstrates reasonable jurors can only find that the party must recover on her claim. In other words, such

[margin note: i have so MUCH EVIDENCE that no any reasonable jury would rule in my favor]

a motion thus maintains that reasonable jurors could only reach one verdict, that verdict being for the party with the burden of proof. Although such motions are successful at times, the task of pushing a claim outside the broad middle area in which reasonable jurors can disagree is a formidable one.

In addition, a party may move for partial summary judgment. By doing so, the movant does not agree that the entirety of the case is subject to summary judgment, but rather that some claim or claims, or some aspect of the relief requested, cannot survive summary judgment. 73 AM. JUR. 2d *Summary Judgment* § 63 (2009). Here, as with a full summary judgment motion, the same process of filing a motion accompanied by the same type of papers, and the opposing party's response with similar papers, will allow the court to see whether sufficient evidence exists on the attacked claim or relief. *Id.* In some cases where the plaintiff's evidence is overwhelming on liability of the defendant, but the amount of damages is in dispute, partial summary judgment on liability will streamline the trial. *Id.* § 66.

partial summary judgment

Follow-Up Questions

1. Do the summary judgment procedures in the state in which you plan to practice mirror Federal Rule of Civil Procedure 56? If not, what are the differences between Rule 56 and your jurisdiction's procedures? Do these differences make it harder to obtain summary judgment, or easier to do so?

2. Because summary judgment is decided on a "paper record," are there some papers that a judge can review which would be more persuasive than others? For instance, would a well-developed deposition testimony be more effective in showing that your client has sufficient evidence to support a claim than answers to interrogatories?

Professional Identity Question

Some lawyers, even if they do not believe their client is entitled to summary judgment, will file a motion for summary judgment to force an opponent to respond. The thinking of such lawyers is that they will force the other side to explain how that party plans to prove her case at trial. In other words, the moving party gets a preview of the trial and can prepare accordingly. Would you file such a motion? If not, what would it take for you to feel that you could file a summary judgment motion and maintain the professional identity that you wish to have? In other words, where would you draw the line between motions that you could not justify and those you could?

Practice Problems

Practice Problem 9-3

Marge, the beneficiary of a life insurance policy owned by Mal, sues Insurance Company to collect the policy's proceeds. Insurance Company denies liability and asserts that Mal committed suicide. If true, Insurance Company would not have to pay under the policy. Insurance Company moves for summary judgment, attaching an affidavit that Mal had left a note saying he "did not see any reason to keep going on," and offering evidence of the person who found Mal on the ground next to the side of his house with the roof directly above him. Marge files a brief in opposition to the summary judgment motion, and attaches an affidavit in which she states under oath that "Mal would never commit suicide and did not do so here." How should the trial court rule on the summary judgment motion? What if Marge offered, instead, an affidavit affirming that a ladder was against the roof on a part that allowed access to the roof gutters, and that on the roof was a bucket with debris, mud, and other materials exactly like that in the gutter?

Practice Problem 9-4

Roddy Runner has a Ferrari of which he is very fond. One day, he takes the Ferrari out of the garage and, as he is about to drive away, remembers he has forgotten his wallet. He parks the car along the street and runs inside. When he comes back out, he is shocked to see the side of his car that is still parked on the side of the street, scraped to the metal in circular shaped scrapes. He looks in the distance and sees a truck with wheels so large that they are at about the same height as the side of his Ferrari, and the wheels have long spokes coming out of them. He sees "Dan the Man's Painting" on the back of the truck before it turns. He later finds out that a neighbor down the street had Dan the Man's Painting do a paint job on the day in question. Roddy sues Dan the Man's Painting. Dan denies scraping the Ferrari. On defendant's summary judgment motion, Roddy offers with his brief in opposition to the motion an affidavit testifying that he parked the car on the street, observed the circular scrape marks upon coming back out of his house, and saw the truck farther down the street. He also offers an affidavit verifying measurements that place the extended spokes on the truck at the exact same height as the scrapes on his car. Roddy also offers the neighbor's affidavit that Dan the Man's Painting was painting at his house before the incident. Defendant offers an affidavit of a metallurgist expert stating that the spokes on the truck have no more tensile strength than the metal on Roddy's Ferrari. How should the court rule on the motion?

Practice Problem 9-5

Plaintiff, WJAZ, is a radio station that has a covenant not to compete (also known as a non-competition clause) with a disc jockey, Jazzie Jeff, precluding the disc jockey from leaving WJAZ to work for any other radio station within a twenty-five mile radius of WJAZ's headquarters for one year. Jazzie Jeff leaves WJAZ and goes to WPOD during the term of his contract. Instead of suing Jazzie Jeff, WJAZ sues WPOD for the tort of intentional interference with contractual relations. The tort's requirements, in virtually every state, require a third party to know of a contract between two parties, to intentionally engage in conduct to induce a party to breach that contract, and to cause damages thereby. WPOD serves interrogatories on WJAZ seeking the identity of all persons with knowledge of WJAZ's contentions that WPOD knew of the contract or engaged in intentional interference with the contract to induce a breach. WPOD also served a request for production of documents seeking documents supporting these contentions. WPOD deposed the persons that WJAZ identified. The best testimony these witnesses could offer was that WPOD "must have known" that Jazzie Jeff had a contract with WJAZ containing a noncompetition agreement in it. Nor did the documents support WJAZ's contentions. Accordingly, WPOD filed a summary judgment motion attaching the relevant deposition testimony and its document requests with the documents produced. WJAZ responded with an opposition contending that, because WPOD failed to offer any proof that WPOD did not know of the contract and any affirmative proof that it had not engaged in conduct inducing the breach, it could not receive summary judgment. How should the court rule on WPOD's motion?

[handwritten margin notes:] grant WPOD's motion; WPOD takes strategy on p. 225; (1) WJAZ bears burden of prof @ trial; (a) discovery reveals that it has insufficient evidence to prove facts

D. Methods to Reinforce and Integrate Topics Covered in This Chapter

A useful way to appreciate how summary judgment works is to consider each element of a claim against the graphic depiction of the markers for sufficient and insufficient evidence shown before. Here is the graphic again:

Diagram 9-2

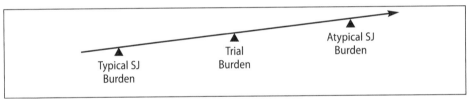

For instance, a negligence claim would require the plaintiff, if challenged by a summary judgment motion, to demonstrate in response that she had evidence upon which reasonable jurors could disagree: (1) the defendant was someone who owed a duty to plaintiff to use reasonable care to avoid injury; (2) defendant breached that duty; (3) the breach proximately caused; (4) damages to the plaintiff.

Because these elements are conjunctive (*i.e.*, they each must be met), the failure to have evidence upon which reasonable persons can disagree on any one element will result in summary judgment. In other words, the plaintiff must demonstrate in response to a summary judgment motion that she can arguably satisfy her trial burden as to each element of a claim. As the saying goes, a chain is only as strong as its weakest link. Plaintiff may have great evidence of breach of a duty, but failed to produce sufficient evidence upon which persons can disagree over whether the breach proximately caused plaintiff's damages.

An exercise that will help students understand summary judgment more completely would be to take various claims, identify the elements of each claim, and think about the kinds of evidence a client will need to satisfy the trial burden. Conversely, students can also consider how they can use the chain-is-only-as-strong-as-its-weakest-link truth to obtain summary judgment. Effective lawyering is pinpointing where a case is weak and preparing to show the inability to establish a particular element.

The exercise of thinking in terms of evidence that you will develop to avoid summary judgment (as plaintiff's counsel), or to demonstrate the weak link in a plaintiff's case (as defense counsel), allows students to connect the rule in question to practical application.

E. Written Assignments

The following are suggested written assignments that should help further reinforce the topics and analysis covered in this chapter.

1. Consider the elements of each claim Sally Wilreiz is asserting against Horse-Power, Inc. Refer to the Trial Preparation and Discovery Plan that you prepared in response to Written Assignment 1 to Chapter 8 at *supra* at pages 213–14. Recall the elements of each claim for which Sally will sue HorsePower, Inc., and demonstrate how your plan should produce sufficient evidence on each element of each claim to survive a summary judgment motion.

2. Assume that HorsePower, Inc.'s counsel develops evidence, through depositions of Sally and others who witnessed the incident, that she was thrown from the car, and regardless of whether the roll bar had stayed intact or not, it would not have prevented her injuries. Prepare a summary judgment motion identifying how this evidence supports a grant of summary judgment, and on which element of the negligence claim the manufacturer would argue Sally could not satisfy her burden of production in light of this testimony.

Chapter 10

Pretrial Considerations

A. Sally's Case at This Stage of Litigation Process

You have Sally's case in great shape. You have gathered the evidence necessary for her claims. You know what witnesses you will need to testify, what documents you will offer as exhibits, and the jury instructions you will propose. From discovery, you have also learned a good bit about the defendants' defenses and their strategy. You have considered how to address those as well. Having overcome their summary judgment motions, you feel confident in Sally's case. Yet, Mr. Befayre warns against overconfidence. The last 30 to 60 day period before trial, he explains, is when one's hard work earlier in the case bears fruit. You will have a pretrial conference and certain other essential preparation that will enable you to put on Sally's case successfully.

B. Tasks and Decision-Making at This Stage of a Case

The case at this stage is shown in Diagram 10-1.

The primary task you must accomplish now is to present a final pretrial order to the court after sharing your sections of the order with opposing counsel. This order will include the claims, contentions, and issues that each party expects to be tried. Ideally, the parties will have certain facts they agree upon. The order will also list all witnesses a party may call at trial. It will also typically list those exhibits a party may offer at trial.

The final pretrial conference is usually held about a month before trial. In addition to providing an opportunity for the court and parties to have a plan for the trial set forth in the pretrial order, this conference offers other opportunities. You can discuss the manner in which the judge will handle voir dire, whether you will be permitted to ask your own questions or whether the court wants your written submissions, etc. In addition, courts tend to prefer hearing motions in limine at the final pretrial conference rather than the first day of trial. Moreover, your trial preparation will benefit from rulings on such motions a month before trial. Motions in limine typically challenge the admissibility of certain evidence or even of witnesses' ability to testify. If a lawyer knows what evidence will come in at trial, then she can intelligently prepare her case (*e.g.*, opening statement, selection of witnesses and exhibits, closing argument). If

Motions in limine, from the Latin "on the brink," are motions traditionally heard just before the trial starts

Diagram 10-1

Cause of Action (events leading to suit)
Prefiling Matters to Consider; Choice of Forum [Chs. 2-3]
Π and Δ Decide on Offensive Pleadings & Joinder (of claims & parties); Filing Suit; Service [Chs. 4-5]
Motions, Responsive Pleadings; Default; Voluntary & Involuntary Dismissals [Chs. 6-7]
Discovery Phase (developing proof to establish claims & learning about the adversary's case) [Ch. 8]
Right to Jury Trial; Pretrial Motions & Practice [Ch. 9]
Final Pretrial Conference & Other Events within Last Month before Trial [Ch. 10]
Procedure at Trial [Ch. 11]
Post-Trial Motions & Calculating the Date of Final Judgment to Know Key Deadlines Such as for Notice of Appeal [Ch. 12]

you wait until the first day of trial to learn the court's rulings, you will be forced to make judgments "on the fly" and generally present your client's case less effectively. Hence, an attorney should welcome final pretrial conferences and the opportunity to bring such motions in limine at an earlier time. On some motions in limine, the court will defer ruling until the court can rule on the evidence in light of the other evidence presented. Nevertheless, you often will get a sense for how a court may rule on a motion even in these situations. In short, motions in limine are a powerful tool in trial preparation.

A motion in limine is also strategically wise because the court, if it denies your motion, will preserve your objection to that evidence. At trial you do not have to object, though you may remind the court of your motion. Thus, the motion in limine at a pretrial conference can also take some of the pressure off at trial by preserving for appeal issues that you ultimately may have to appeal to get a ruling on the trial court's evidentiary ruling. Again, you will not have to object in front of the jury nearly as much as you would have to if you chose not to file such a motion.

A lawyer must also make final decisions on the most effective evidence for proving her client's case and combating any defenses. That will require choosing among a number of witnesses. Putting on every conceivable witness is generally considered to be bad lawyering. Choosing among various possible witnesses the ones who not only have necessary testimony, but are credible, represents the kinds of judgment calls for which a client relies on her lawyer. Likewise, overloading a case with exhibits just "to be safe" is another bad habit of undisciplined lawyers. Even in complex cases, a relatively small number of documents (*e.g.*, under twenty-five documents easily) need to be offered as exhibits. Having the fortitude to offer less evidence rather than more can make a huge difference in the persuasiveness of a case. Your presentation will be focused, crisp, and to the point. You must ensure that, either through testimony, documentary, or other means (*e.g.*, judicial notice), the elements of each claim are proven. However, just because duplicative evidence (testimony or exhibits) exists does not mean you have to offer it. Indeed, you can virtually guarantee weakening your presentation by doing so. Seeking to prove the case effectively, but doing so efficiently, should be your goal.

Strategically, you have to decide whether to challenge certain evidence you believe is inadmissible but which the opponent is expected to offer at trial. In a jury trial, the motion in limine has value beyond that already discussed above. The court may well grant your motion and exclude the evidence. Alternatively, the court will often defer ruling until trial. However, by filing the motion, when the evidence first arises at trial, you are able to stand and say, "Your Honor, this testimony [or exhibit] deals with the matter Your Honor asked counsel to bring to your attention at trial." The court should then know to excuse the jury and to deal with the motion. In short, the motion in limine offers a more graceful way to object to anticipated testimony or evidence than to be a "jumping bean" objecting constantly in front of the jury—something no jury lawyer should do. If one objects repeatedly, jurors start to think a lawyer must be hiding something. You must exercise balance in your presentation and convince jurors you want to show them what happened and let them decide the consequences.

At this stage of the litigation, a lawyer should have prepared to subpoena witnesses far enough ahead of trial so that if a witness does not show up, the lawyer can argue for a continuance. The lawyer should also have prepared the jury instructions she will propose. In addition, the lawyer should have considered the value of her case. If the parties do not broach the subject of settlement, you can bet that the judge will do so. Methods for evaluating a case are thus included below. Having discussed with your client your evaluation of the case, you will be in a position to respond confidently if the judge presses for mediation prior to trial.[1] Even better, you will be able to negotiate from a standpoint of strength. Having prepared for negotiations, your preparation will show in the manner in which you handle such negotiations.

C. Overview of Applicable Law

Final Pretrial Conferences and Orders

Early in the case, the parties should have attended an initial pretrial conference that resulted in a pretrial order. The initial pretrial order includes matters such as the trial date, the final pretrial conference date, and the discovery cutoff, among other items. Many jurisdictions have statutes and rules in place providing for both an initial and final pretrial conference. 62A Am. Jur. 2d *Pretrial Conference* § 7 (2009) ("[S]tate trial courts have inherent power to require pretrial conferences in order to uncover the issues of a lawsuit.");

---

1. Mediation is different from settlement negotiations. In settlement negotiations, the parties and counsel participate. In mediations, an objective third party facilitates the negotiations. Mediations may be binding if, for instance, a contract requires mediation rather than trial. (Such an agreement would have to specify a person or persons who would decide the appropriate resolution if the parties cannot agree. Effectively. then, the parties would be engaging in a form of arbitration.) More often, the mediation is voluntary, but courts are increasingly forcing parties to engage in it before proceeding to trial.

see also, *e.g.*, Mary Elizabeth Carmody, Massachusetts Continuing Legal Education, Inc., *Litigating Under the Federal Tort Claims Act*, *in* 2 FEDERAL CIVIL LITIGATION IN THE FIRST CIRCUIT, ch. 15 (2008) (Massachusetts Superior Court, under § 15.4.4, requires a final pretrial conference). Indeed, those states that model their procedures on the Federal Rules tend to follow Federal Rule of Civil Procedure 16, which provides that at least one attorney from each side be present at any final pretrial conference. *Id.* § 16. As already suggested, however, regardless of whether a state's rules specifically require a final pretrial conference, a party may always move for any relief it deems appropriate, including scheduling a final pretrial conference. Moving for a final pretrial conference almost always serves the client's interests by imposing discipline on everyone, reducing costs by limiting the time a case is pending, etc. 62A AM. JUR. 2d *Pretrial Conference* § 9 (2009) ("[R]eason and common sense dictate that a [final] pretrial conference should be held even though one is not required.").

Both Rule 16 and similar state rules on pretrial conferences provide that the conference serves several purposes—to simplify and narrow the issues within a case, reduce expenses, and provide for a speedier process of resolving the case. *Id.* §§ 2, 8. Each attorney has a duty to disclose fully his or her views regarding the real issues for trial. *Id.* § 25. Another purpose of the conference is to get any admission of fact out of the way; parties are then bound to factual admissions made at the conference. *Id.* § 26. Discussed in more depth later in this chapter, settlement may also be considered at the pretrial conference. *Id.* § 34. Pretrial conferences also offer a convenient opportunity to control and schedule any matters involving last-minute disputes about (a) a matter not disclosed in discovery; (b) amendments to pleadings sought by the plaintiff or defendant; and (c) pending motions, questions of law, or other matters that "may aid in the disposition of the action." *Id.* § 36–45.

A final pretrial order supersedes any pleadings once it is entered following the pretrial conference. *Id.* §§ 46, 60, 63. This order states the issues as they have been limited for trial and controls the course of action. *Id.* §§ 15, 46. By superseding the pleadings, a matter pled by a party but not included in the final pretrial order may often be excluded at trial. *Id.* § 64 ("[A]n issue raised by the complaint but not included in the pretrial order is waived or abandoned"; similarly, "a defense pleaded in the answer but not stated in the order is … eliminated from consideration at trial.").

Under Rule 16 and similar state rules, the pretrial order should include a disclosure of all prospective trial witnesses, except those who will be used only for rebuttal. *Id.* § 32. Similarly, the final pretrial order should list potential trial exhibits; any objections to an opponent's exhibits should be addressed at the final pretrial conference. The court has discretion to exclude both witnesses and evidence not listed in the pretrial order. *Id.* § 74. The order will also typically address discovery to be offered at trial, such as deposition testimony of witnesses who are outside the subpoena power of the trial court. Parties may have, for instance, traveled to another state and subpoenaed a witness through a court in that location to appear to testify. In other words, although a witness cannot be forced to travel long distances to a trial, the lawyers can go to the witness, take a deposition (often by videotape, if the jury needs to observe the witness' demeanor, etc.), and then that deposition is admissible in evidence at trial. *See* AM. JUR. *Depositions and Discovery* § 109 (2009).

You may read at trial (or show videotape if taken by video) depositions taken where the witness is located to be read or shown later at the actual trial, sometimes called "de bene esse" depositions

Following is a model order, in the form specified by the Montana Rules of Civil Procedure, but which is typical of such orders nationwide, which the parties would discuss prior
to the final pretrial conference and then present to the judge after filling in the sections noted:

[CAPTION, INCLUDE IN NAME OF COURT AND CASE]

Pursuant to Rule 16 of the Montana Rules of Civil Procedure, a pre-trial conference
was held in the above-entitled cause on the _____ day of _____, 20__, at _____
o'clock __m.

_____ represented the plaintiff(s).

_____ represented the defendant(s).

_____ (other appearances) were also present.

AGREED FACTS

The following facts are admitted, agreed to be true, and require no proof:

(Here enumerate all agreed facts, including facts admitted in the pleadings.)

PLAINTIFF'S CONTENTIONS

Plaintiff's contentions are as follows:

1.
2.

DEFENDANT'S CONTENTIONS

1.
2.

EXHIBITS

Attached to the pre-trial order are exhibit lists identifying by number and
brief description each exhibit and stating any objections to the exhibits. Any exhibit offered at the trial to which no objection was made in the pre-trial order
will be admitted into evidence.

WITNESSES

The following witnesses and no others will (may) be called to testify except on
rebuttal:

Plaintiff

1.
2.

Defendant

1.
2.

ISSUES OF FACT

The following issues of fact, and no others, remain to be litigated upon the
trial: (Here specify each issue.)

1.
2.

ISSUES OF LAW

The following issues of law, and no others, remain to be litigated upon the trial:
(Here set forth a concise statement of each.)

1.
2.

DISCOVERY

The final pre-trial order shall refer to all those portions of depositions upon oral examination and interrogatories, requests for admissions, and answers and responses that the parties intend to introduce into evidence. Any objections to the use of the above documents shall be stated, and if not stated, shall be deemed waived....

ADDITIONAL PRE-TRIAL DISCOVERY

(Here specify any additional discovery contemplated by either party and the time within which such discovery will be completed.)

STIPULATIONS

(Here include any stipulations in addition to the agreed facts set forth above.)

DETERMINATION OF LEGAL QUESTIONS IN ADVANCE OF TRIAL

It was agreed that the following legal issues should be determined by the court in advance of the trial.

(Here specify issues and make provision for filing briefs with respect to such issues.)

ADDITIONAL ISSUES

Additional issues to be determined and/or addressed include: order of proof where there is a counterclaim; attorney's fees testimony and/or proof; time of filing and service of trial briefs and other issues.

JURY SELECTION AND PROCESS

Order and method of selection, stipulation that jury will be selected or drawn, numbering of panel, number of challenges, time to file instructions, length of time on voir dire.

TRIAL

It is estimated that the case will require _____ hours/days for trial.

The case will be tried before the court with (without) a jury.

IT IS HEREBY ORDERED that this pre-trial order shall supersede the pleadings and govern the course of the trial of this cause, unless modified to prevent manifest injustice.

IT IS HEREBY ORDERED that all pleadings herein shall be amended to conform to this pre-trial order.

DATED this _____ day of _____, 20__

_____District Judge

Approved as to form and content:

_____
Attorney for Plaintiff

_____
Attorney for Defendant

Mont. Unif. Dist. Ct. R. 5.

This order is typical of final pretrial orders although not all state's versions contain certain provisions (*e.g.*, "Additional Pre-Trial Discovery"). Moreover, the requirement that counsel collaborate in preparing the order prior to the conference has become a trend among jurisdictions. *See generally* David Steelman Nat'l Center for State Courts Study, Caseflow Management: The Heart of Court Management in the New

MILLENIUM (2004). The reason is easy to appreciate: the order becomes the master out-line for the trial, simplifies and streamlines the proceedings, and avoids waste of time. If counsel knows the court will require them to fill in the categories of material in the order, then they often will make great progress before the conference. In that way, they can avoid wasting a judge's valuable time.

Follow-Up Questions

1. You can plead a variety of claims or defenses and answer discovery responses by identifying the facts supporting such claims or defenses, but still fail to in-clude in the final pretrial order these claims or defenses as issues to be tried and contentions your client will make at trial. Generally, the order will super-sede all pleadings, discovery, etc. What effect would that have on your ability to offer evidence at trial on the claims or defenses omitted from the order?

2. If the court requires a pretrial order that supersedes pleadings and discovery responses and one runs the risk of having claims and evidence excluded if not set forth in the order, will you allow your opponent to prepare the order? Or will you insist that those sections related to your case are ones where you prepare the inserts and allow opposing counsel to prepare inserts for her part of the case? In other words, should the preparation of the final pretrial order prior to the final pretrial conference be a collaborative one? At what point prior to the final pretrial conference should you and opposing counsel begin to collaborate on the order?

Professional Identity Question

Suppose you have an opposing counsel known to be inattentive. After the close of discovery but before the final pretrial conference, you learn of evidence that would allow your client to seek not only a breach of contract claim (which you have pled) but also a tort claim for civil conspiracy (which you have not pled). You are tempted to add the conspiracy claim in the final pretrial order as issues to be tried and contentions your client will make. You are concerned that if you move for leave to amend instead, that may be denied. Would you put the tort claim into the final pretrial order with the expectation that opposing counsel will not catch it, and even if opposing counsel later realizes his error, you could argue that the order supersedes all pleadings and counsel waived any objections? In other words, how would you feel about playing a form of "gotcha" with opposing counsel?

Practice Problems

Practice Problem 10-1

Refer to the *Rex v. Hurry* case *supra* at pages 82–95. Research any require-ments in the jurisdiction where you will practice concerning whether you will have to submit anything to opposing counsel or the court, including whether you have obligations to participate in a pretrial conference, preparation of a pretrial order, submitting jury instructions, etc. If so, what would these requirements dictate that you prepare in the *Rex v. Hurry* case?

Practice Problem 10-2

In a personal injury action arising from a car accident, suppose the defendant has disclosed in discovery a number of prior accidents in which the defendant has been held at fault or been convicted of violating traffic laws. How can the defendant, at the pretrial conference, use the conference as an opportunity to move in limine to exclude any such evidence? What would the defendant argue at the final pretrial conference? What preparation would defense counsel have to do before the conference to be prepared to persuade the court?

Subpoenaing Witnesses for Trial

A lawyer's pretrial work is not complete upon entry of a final pretrial order. Just because witnesses are listed in a final pretrial order does not mean they will show up for trial. Indeed, you take a great risk to count on witnesses to show up for trial without having them subpoenaed. Each jurisdiction typically has a rule establishing the amount of time prior to trial by which a witness must be served with a subpoena if a lawyer wants the protection of a continuance if a subpoenaed witness fails to show up. *See generally* 17 Am. Jur. 2d § 17 (2009).

Lawyers in many jurisdictions are empowered by statute or rule to issue subpoenas themselves, without having to have the clerk issue them. Following is a sample subpoena provided for civil suits in Utah (typical of subpoenas in other states), where under Utah Rule of Civil Procedure 45 an attorney may sign the subpoena "as an officer of the court":

My Name   _____
Address   _____
Phone   _____
Email   _____

I am the   ❑ Plaintiff/Petitioner
              ❑ Defendant/Respondent
              ❑ Attorney for the ❑ Plaintiff/Petitioner ❑ Defendant/Respondent and my Utah
              Bar number is _____

In the ❑ District ❑ Justice ❑ Juvenile Court of Utah
_____ Judicial District _____ County
Court Address _____

_____	**Subpoena**
Plaintiff/Petitioner	Case Number _____
v.	Judge _____
_____	Commissioner _____
Defendant/Respondent	

. . . .

To: _____ (name of witness or other person served)
(1) ❑ You must appear at:
Date   _____ Time __:_____ ❑ a.m. ❑ p.m.
Address   _____
City   _____ Room _____

          ❑ to testify at a trial or hearing
          ❑ to testify at a deposition
          ❑ to permit inspection of the premises
          ❑ to produce the following documents or tangible things:

_____
_____
_____

(2) ❑ You must copy the following documents and to mail or deliver the copies to the person at the
address at the top of this Subpoena. You must comply no later than _____. (date)

_____
_____
_____

(3) Notice to Persons Served with a Subpoena* must be served with this Subpoena. The Notice explains your rights and obligations. If you are commanded to appear at a trial, hearing or deposition,
a one-day witness fee must be served with this Subpoena. A one-day witness fee is $18.50 plus $1.00
for each 4 miles you have to travel over 50 miles (one direction).
(4) You may object to this Subpoena for any of the reasons listed in paragraph 6 of the Notice by
serving a written objection upon the attorney listed at the top of this Subpoena. You must comply with
any part of the Subpoena to which you do not object.
. . . .
Date _____ Sign here ➤ _____
Typed or printed name
* Court Clerk ❑
* Attorney for the Plaintiff/Petitioner ❑
* Attorney for the Defendant/Respondent ❑

_____

    * The Notice attached to this Subpoena has been omitted.

As is true in most states, forms for subpoenas allow attorneys to serve witnesses for a variety of reasons, including depositions, production of documents at a deposition or at trial, or, most importantly, to appear at trial. Many lawyers are not aware of the fact that if a witness is subpoenaed, the witness is only released from the subpoena by the court's permission. Perhaps lawyers have the misimpression that they are unilaterally permitted to release witnesses because lawyers may issue the subpoena. Nevertheless, the lawyer in issuing the subpoena is relying on the court's power to compel attendance. *See* 81 AM. JUR. 2d *Witnesses* § 2 (2009). Generally, all subpoenaed witnesses must show up for the trial date at the time specified. *See id.* If the trial is likely to last numerous days, some courts will allow subpoenaed witnesses to remain on call to return. They are not released, however, until the court says that they are. *See, e.g., Anderson v. Commonwealth*, 63 S.W.3d 135, 142 (Ky. 2001) ("[O]nce subpoenaed, the witness is answerable to the court and can only be excused by the court."). Indeed, even if one party is the one who served a subpoena on a witness, the other party is thereafter permitted to rely on that subpoena until the witness is released. *See, e.g., id.* ("Any other view taken would require the issuance of multiple subpoenas to a witness whose testimony is deemed material by more than one party."). The safer practice, however, would be for counsel to subpoena any witness she considers significant even if her opponent has also done so. A witness is entitled to be paid for her expenses in attending the trial or hearing for which she has been subpoenaed. *See id.* § 70. You may end up splitting expenses for witnesses that both you and your opponent subpoena. However, the value of ensuring witnesses' presence is worth such expense. In other words, cutting corners at this stage of litigation is foolish.

Follow-Up Question

You represent the plaintiff, a party who certainly plans to be at trial. The plaintiff's sister witnessed the accident in which the plaintiff was injured. The sister is a key witness for your client. She assures you she will be at the trial, and you forego subpoenaing her. However, she is hospitalized with an illness and is unable to be in court when the trial begins. You ask the court for a continuance, arguing the absence of a key witness. The judge asks whether you subpoenaed this witness in the time frame recognized in the jurisdiction as potentially qualifying a party for a continuance if a subpoenaed witness fails to show up. You answer "no," and that because she was related to your client you did not think it necessary. The judge says that if you had subpoenaed the sister, a continuance likely would have been granted. However, because you did not, and because the opposing party objects to a continuance, the trial will go forward. Would you have second thoughts about failing to subpoena witnesses in future proceedings, no matter how much they assured you they would show up? Are you liable for malpractice for failing to subpoena the witness in this circumstance?

Professional Identity Question

You are counsel in a case in which many witnesses could be subpoenaed, but most of the witnesses would testify to matters that are tangential or duplicative. You believe, however, that by having as many witnesses as possible, you will intimidate your opponent into worrying about what these witnesses will say and how she will be able to cross-examine them. In other words, you are considering subpoenaing these witnesses not because you believe they would actually be necessary to prove the elements of your client's claims, but purely for the effect of having so many witnesses show up. Do you consider such a tactic appropriate? Would you do it?

Practice Problem

Practice Problem 10-3

Find a form used in your jurisdiction for subpoenas. Assume you represent Brad Rex in his case against Ena Hurry and want to subpoena Ed Eyewitness, who lives at 123 Easy Street in Arcadia, for a deposition a month from now. Then prepare the subpoena to require this witness's appearance.

Proposed Jury Instructions

Most courts require presenting proposed jury instructions either at or after the final pretrial conference. 6 AM. JUR. *Trials* § 923 (2009). Some judges will wait until trial to have a conference on instructions. The lawyer can then object to instructions she deems erroneous, and argue in favor of instructions she deems appropriate. The theory of judges who employ this practice is that until she hears the evidence, she cannot really decide on the instructions to be given. However, many judges require a party before trial to object by a specific deadline to instructions proposed by an opponent. *See id.* Most states also have model jury instructions (often called "pattern jury instructions"). These "pattern" or model instructions are generally the safest to follow and the easiest to convince a court to accept. The court recognizes that such instructions are prepared by an objective advisory committee who thoroughly research the law and seek to prepare instructions that not only reflect accurately the law, but present it in an even-handed way. Moreover, the trial court realizes the chances of reversal in using model instructions — as opposed to one created by counsel — are far lower.

Reviewing a model instruction is helpful to an attorney for determining which kind to propose for her case. The general categories of instructions include introductory instructions such as those instructing the jury of their role as jurors (*e.g.*, jurors should listen to the evidence and weigh credibility of witnesses; the jurors are the ones who will decide facts while the judge will instruct them on the law; jurors must not engage in bias or sympathy, etc.). Then the lawyer should tailor the instructions to her particular claims or defenses, instructing on the law relating to each claim or defense. For instance, in a negligence case, such instructions would define "reasonable care" as "the care a reasonable person in the circumstances would exercise to avoid injury to others or their property." Finally, the lawyer should include "finding" instructions. Such instructions are found in every model set of instructions, but usually require some editing by counsel to fill in blanks with the parties' names, events in the case, etc.

"Finding" instructions, included in all pattern or model sets of instructions, explain the elements of the case and who bears the burden of proof on which elements so that the jury can understand what it must decide in order to "find" for a party. *See* 6 AM. JUR. *Trials* 923 § 25 (2009)

For example, following is a sample finding instruction (typical of one that would be used in any state) from the Delaware Pattern Jury Instructions:[2]

> In this particular case, [*plaintiff's name*] must prove all the elements of [*his/her*] claim of [__state the nature of the claim__] by a preponderance of the evidence. Those elements are as follows: (1).... [__state element__] ... [etc.]
>
> {*If applicable*}: [*Party's name*] has alleged a [__counterclaim/cross-claim/third-party claim, etc.__] of [__state claim(s)__]. [*Party's name*] has the burden of proof and must establish all elements of that claim by a preponderance of the evidence. Those elements are as follows: (1).... [__state element__] ... [etc.]
>
> {*For an affirmative defense claiming comparative negligence*}:
>
> [*Defendant's name*] has pleaded comparative negligence and therefore has the burden of proving each of the following elements of [*his/her/its*] this defense:
>
> First, that [*plaintiff's name*] was negligent in at least one of the ways claimed by
>
> [*defendant's name*]; and Second, that [*plaintiff's name*]'s negligence was a cause of [*his/her/its*] own injury and therefore was contributorily negligent.

Most judges believe in giving each side's version of finding instructions so as to balance each side's position and avoid an argument of partiality. Thus, the following is one the court might give to balance the instruction quoted above:

> If the evidence tends equally to suggest two inconsistent views, neither has been established. That is, where the evidence shows that one or two things may have caused the [__accident/breach/loss__]: one for which [*defendant's name*] was responsible and one for which [*he/she/it*] was not. You cannot find for [*plaintiff's name*] if it is just as likely that the [__accident/breach/loss__] was caused by one thing as by the other. In other words, if you find that the evidence suggests, on the one hand, that [*defendant's name*] is liable, but on the other hand, that [*he/she/it*] is not liable, then you must not speculate about the suggested causes of the [__accident/breach/loss__]; in that circumstance you must find for [*defendant's name*].

Id.

You should observe an opponent's proposed instructions carefully. If they are not supported by the law of your jurisdiction, object to them. Failure to object to an opponent's jury instructions, even if they state the law of the jurisdiction inaccurately, often results in the law stated in the instruction becoming "the law of the case." 75 Am. Jur. 2d *Trial* § 1230. In other words, the "law" in the instruction will not serve as precedent in future cases, but the failure to object makes it permissible law that the trial court (on post-trial motions) or the appellate court (on appeal) can rely upon. *Id.*

If you object to a party's instruction, ensure that your objection is in the presence of a court reporter — or at least in writing in the record — and clearly identifies the instruction to which you are objecting. Otherwise, your objection can be waived. Moreover, if you offer an instruction that you believe is sound and necessary, but the court refuses to give it, ensure that you have it identified as an excluded instruction and placed in the record. *See* 75A Am. Jur. 2d *Trial* § 1230 (2009). Otherwise, any appeal based on the failure to give the instruction will likely be fruitless.

---

2. Del. P.J.I. Civ. (2000), *available at* http://courts.delaware.gov/Jury%20Services/pdf/?pattern jury_rev.pdf (last visited August 27, 2009).

Follow-Up Questions

1. Some instructions are ones not worth fighting over, and others are. Which instructions do you anticipate being worth your greatest attention?

2. If the court grants an instruction for an opposing party and you consider the phrasing to be such that it favors the opponent, should you seek to offer an instruction offsetting the impact of the other side's instruction? If you consider these instructions to be the kind of instructions worth arguing about, how can you persuade the court to grant your instruction?

Professional Identity Question

If you propose an instruction that is supported by the law of another jurisdiction, but which has not been addressed in your jurisdiction (because your case is one of first impression, for instance), would you feel obliged to bring that to the attention of the court?

Practice Problem

Practice Problem 10-4

Recall that the case of *Rex v. Hurry* described in Chapter 4 at page 82–95 *supra*. Assume counsel for both parties have to submit a set of proposed jury instructions before trial. Find a pattern or model set of instructions for your jurisdiction and consider ones that you would include in your proposed instructions. As if you were Brad's counsel, draft a finding instruction that instructs the jury on the findings it must make to rule for Brad on his negligence claim. Then, as if you were now Ena's counsel, draft an instruction that balances the instruction just drafted on Brad's behalf.

Valuing a Client's Case and Exploring Settlement

As already suggested above, an effective lawyer will have valued her client's case before the final pretrial conference. She may even have explored settlement with her opponent. Because the issue will certainly arise, the attorneys need to be confident when a judge asks whether the parties have discussed settlement. If they have not, judges are legitimately disappointed. They expect counsel to advise clients of the range of value of a case and see whether it can be resolved short of trial. The cost and vagaries of trials, not to mention the time a matter may linger in light of post-trial motions, appeals, etc., are realities that need to be communicated to the client. The client should then realize why pretrial settlement often presents the best resolution. Effective lawyers are able to value a client's case and explore the possibility of settlement. If an attorney's opponent fails to come within a range that is reasonable in light of counsel's evaluation, it will become apparent — either explicitly or implicitly by the manner in which one responds to a judge's inevitable query on the subject — that the opponent is failing to engage in good faith negotiations. In short, your credibility as a lawyer will in part be affected by whether you have done this work.

Though few agree on a single way to value a case, a lawyer must provide her client with an idea of the value of the case. Ideally, the client will then authorize the lawyer to settle within certain parameters. Many courts now assign a judge other than the trial judge to mediate a case. Alternatively, counsel may share the expense of a private mediator. Either way, you must have worked on the value of your case to have a solid basis for negotiating.

Methods of valuation range from the simple and crude to the sophisticated and complex. Likewise, attorneys' approaches to valuation range from an inexperienced lawyer's reliance on common sense intuition to sophisticated mathematical analysis. *See* Peter Toll Hoffman, *Valuation of Cases for Settlement: Theory and Practice*, 1999 J. Disp. Resol. 1, 6–7 (1991). Nevertheless, by considering certain criteria, even an inexperienced attorney should be able to come to a reasonably accurate value for a case.

Goals and Timing for Valuation

The goal to keep in mind when valuing any case is to identify a range of "monetary and nonmonetary elements of relief" and to then "monitor the various factors affecting the value of the case and to adjust the range accordingly." 53 Am. Jur. *Trials* § 44 (2009); Anthony F. Tagliamable, Practicing Law Institute, *Evaluating and Settling a Personal Injury Case: Plaintiffs' and Defendants' Perspectives*, in New York Practice Skills Course Handbook Series 71 (2000). Identifying a range for the client generally proves to be a more accurate portrayal of the case than attempting to arrive at a pinpointed valuation figure. Ideally, a lawyer has been considering valuation throughout the case. Lawyers should, for instance, ask themselves whether the defendant will be able to pay significant damages (insurance considerations play a part here) and whether the plaintiff will be able to prosecute the case effectively. *Id.* If not, the plaintiff likely should settle early for as much as she can convince the defendant to pay.

Valuation Schema

To assist lawyers with the inexact science of valuing claims, one scholar developed the following four-step approach: "(1) [D]etermin[e] the distribution of verdicts in similar claims; (2) adjust the distribution of verdicts in similar claims to reflect the unique facts of the particular claim; (3) adjust the revised distribution to reflect transaction costs; and (4) select a settlement value reflecting the client's preferences and values." Peter Toll Hoffman, *Valuation of Cases for Settlement: Theory and Practice*, 1999 J. Disp. Resol. 7 (1991). Reviewing verdicts in cases similar to your own case is particularly helpful when predicting abstract damages like those for pain and suffering. More concrete damages (*e.g.*, lost wages or the amount lost in a breach of contract) are easier to predict. *Id.* at 8–9. Other factors to consider when comparing past verdicts include factual similarity with the present case, verdicts from the same jurisdiction, how recent such judgments were rendered, and the quantity of similar cases. Venue tends to affect verdicts. Some courts have a reputation for awarding larger damage awards than others. Anthony F. Tagliamable, Practicing Law Institute, *Evaluating and Settling a Personal Injury Case:*

Plaintiffs' and Defendants' Perspectives, in NEW YORK PRACTICE SKILLS COURSE HANDBOOK SERIES 69 (2000). Considering each of these factors helps the attorney form a better prediction regarding her client's potential verdict. Hoffman, *Valuation of Cases for Settlement,* 1999 J. DISP. RESOL. at 12.

Step Two of this valuation method recognizes that the unique facts of each case must be a factor in predicting a verdict. Each claim or defense requires you to judge the "quality of proof" and which party bears the persuasion and production burdens for each issue. *Id.* at 16. You can, in other words, have an idea of whether your evidence should meet the evidentiary burden to prove certain elements — or at least whether you have sufficient evidence to get the matter to a jury.

Given unique legal and factual nuances in every case, you must approach this second "valuation adjustment" step differently. Some begin with the hypothetical perfect case and adjust it according to its unique factors. Others create a point system, assigning value to the factors affecting damage awards and apply the resulting "multiplier" to an expected verdict. *Id.* The *Personal Injury Valuation Handbook* systematically "adjusts [the value prediction] for jurisdictional differences, degrees of liability, quality of opposing counsel, and a number of other factors." *Id.*

Step Three of the method involves transaction costs: "(1) litigation expenses, (2) the time value of money; and (3) any tax consequences of the litigation to the plaintiff or defendant." *Id.* at 21. The "collectability of any judgment" and "any subrogation agreements" should also be considered at this point. *Id.* Examples of litigation expenses that should be considered when predicting a verdict include attorney and witness fees, discovery and court costs, and the monetary value of time expended in the litigation process. *Id.* at 21–23. In addition, the time value of money is a factor to consider. The "time value of money" simply means that money in hand now is worth more to someone now than the same amount is worth later. Tagliamable, *Evaluating and Settling a Personal Injury Case Plaintiffs' and Defendants' Perspectives, in* NEW YORK PRACTICE SKILLS COURSE HANDBOOK SERIES at 72. As a result, a "discount rate" should be applied to the future potential amount of the verdict. For a plaintiff, this rate usually represents "the interest rate at which the plaintiff can borrow the sum" and, for the defendant, "the rate of return the defendant can obtain through alternative uses of the money." Hoffman, *Valuation of Cases for Settlement,* 1999 J. DISP. RESOL. at 25. The transaction cost of taxes — when the plaintiff is taxed on his expected recovery, while the defendant considers the deductibility of his judgment — is the third factor. *Id.* at 26. Also, any potential recovery may be limited by both a defendant's lack of assets ("collectability") and any subrogation agreement between the plaintiff and any medical provider or insurance company. *Id.* at 26–27.

> Subrogation agreements involve someone (subrogee) who typically, in return for paying the debt of another (subrogor), assumes the rights of the subrogor against a third party

Fourth, the last step in the valuation schema emphasizes the importance of considering your client's preferences and values when predicting the value of a case. Though this factor is more pronounced when it comes to discussing an actual settlement, a litigant's attitude toward risk, fear of trial, aversion to settlement, changing opinions, emotions, and psychological makeup all come into play in the final outcome of any case. *Id.* at 28–41. In short, litigants and their attorneys are not one-dimensional. Any potential verdict will be influenced by several factors collectively.

Resources and Experts for Valuation

Nearly every legal scholar and attorney would agree on the importance of an objective opinion when it comes to valuing a case. Suggestions for sources to which one can refer when predicting a case's value include the following: newsletters and other jury verdict publications (*e.g.*, the New York Jury Reporter), other (especially experienced) attorneys, state and local bar associations, jury consulting firms, American Bar Association sections, Personal Injury Valuation Handbooks, and the Association of Trial Lawyers of America Law Reporter.[3] The more technically savvy attorney may even find software programs designed to calculate personal injury and wrongful death damages. 53 AM. JUR. *Trials* § 88 (2009).

Experts in valuation provide an especially valuable resource. For example, economists are the "essential" experts when it comes to valuing cases with future losses. Other helpful experts include rehabilitationists, treating physicians, and others who can predict the degree of expenses a client will likely incur in the future. *Id.* §§ 82–86; Tagliamable, *Evaluating and Settling a Personal Injury Case*, at 67.

Special Valuation Considerations for Personal Injury and Wrongful Death Cases

Valuing damages in personal injury cases is usually straightforward when it comes to damages already incurred such as medical expenses, often referred to as "special damages." Future medical expenses, however, are "hotly contested," often coming to a "battle of experts" in litigation. *Id.* at 60, 63. Lost earnings are also a broad enough category of damages to include past and future wage losses, loss of future career choices and economic opportunity, and "out of pocket expenses." *Id.* at 61.

Noneconomic damages add another wrinkle to estimating the value of a case because they are the "most speculative aspect of evaluating damages." *Id.* at 64. As previously noted, these damages require the attorney to consider verdicts from cases dealing with similar injuries. Noneconomic damages may include, among others, pain and suffering, loss of enjoyment of life, and loss of consortium. *Id.* at 64–65.

Additionally, beneficiaries' "pecuniary loss[es]" in wrongful death actions also require special attention in valuation. These pecuniary losses may include, among others, loss of financial support, services, "parental training and guidance," and funeral expenses. *Id.* at 65. In other words, estimating the value of a case with wrongful death and/or personal injury damages is no small task and usually requires the work of an expert such as an economist.

A solid case evaluation is vital if a lawyer wants to avoid settling a case for less than the actual value of the case. Conversely, the unequipped lawyer may refuse to recommend that her client accept an offer that one's client should accept. As already noted, you will likely be asked at a pretrial conference or some other occasion whether you have explored

---

3. 53 AM. JUR. *Trials* § 64 (2009); G. Nicholas Herman, *How to Value a Case for Negotiation and Settlement*, 31 MONT. LAW. 5, 6 (2005); Anthony F. Tagliamable, Practicing Law Institute, *Evaluating and Settling a Personal Injury Case: Plaintiffs' and Defendants' Perspectives, in* NEW YORK PRACTICE SKILLS COURSE HANDBOOK SERIES 68 (2000). Other intangible factors beyond the litigant's personal preferences and values also come into play, including potential sympathy toward a litigant (*e.g.*, a child as a plaintiff), or antagonism toward a litigant (*e.g.*, a corporate defendant). Tagliagame, at 70. These must be kept in mind during valuation as well.

settlement, regardless of whether mediation is required in the jurisdiction. If plaintiff's counsel responds that she has made no attempt to settle and has not developed a final value of the case, she loses credibility with the court. Some jurisdictions authorize courts to require mandatory settlement conferences, thus requiring litigants to engage in settlement negotiations. 62A AM. JUR. 2d *Pretrial Conference* § 35 (2009). Hence, the topic of settlement negotiations is well worth discussing.

Settlement of Cases

One of the areas in which young associates often are least prepared is engaging in settlement negotiations. The most important step a lawyer can take in settlement negotiations is to go through the process outlined above for valuing the case. The key to a successful settlement is to understand the strengths and weaknesses of both sides of the case. You cannot recommend agreeing to a settlement, or pushing forward to trial, unless you have (1) valued the case and (2) compared the final value to the likelihood of achieving that value or better via trial verdict or through settlement. *See, e.g.*, G. Nicholas Herman, *How to Value a Case for Negotiation and Settlement*, 31 MONT. LAW. 5, 5 (2005).

Settlement or Trial?

A settlement analysis should take into account what may be called the parties' "target" and "resistance" points. *Id.* at 5–6. From the plaintiff's perspective, the target point is the highest amount of money plaintiff receives in the best-case scenario. From the defendant's perspective, the target point is the lowest amount defendant would have to pay in the best-case scenario. *Id.* at 5. The parties' resistance points are the lowest amount that plaintiff will be willing to accept and the highest amount that defendant will be willing to pay. *Id.* at 6. Settlement occurs when the parties' resistance points overlap.

The Nature of Settlements and Its Various Forms

Settlement agreements are contracts and thus require offer and acceptance, consideration, and the capacity and authority to enter into the agreement. 62A AM. JUR. 2d *Pretrial Conference* §§ 38, 42 (2009). You should also know the variety of settlements to which your client could agree. The simplest and most common is called the "lump-sum" settlement. A lump-sum settlement refers to one in which legal claims (plaintiff's claims against the defendant) are exchanged for cash payments. 53 AM. JUR. *Trials* § 262 (2009). A variation of this settlement, called a "structured lump-sum settlement," occurs when the defendant pays the plaintiff in installments over a period of time. *Id.* § 263.

A different form of settlement is the "partial settlement." A partial settlement can refer to any of the following scenarios: one plaintiff settles with one or more defendants; one or more plaintiffs settle with one defendant; or one defendant settles with the plaintiff but continues the suit to receive indemnity from the other defendants. *Id.* § 278. A variation of the partial settlement is the "sliding scale," which "conditions the amount settling tort defendants pay on the amount ultimately recovered by the non-settling defendants." *Id.* You should know the rules in your jurisdiction because sliding scale settlements are void against public policy in some jurisdictions. *Id.* § 28 (*e.g.*, Florida). Whatever the form of settlement, the parties must "memorialize" it by stating the terms of the settlement either on the record or in writing. *Id.* § 298.

Suits against joint tortfeasors in which the plaintiff settles with some, but not all, tortfeasors have created problems for many lawyers unaware of the rules in their jurisdiction. Under the common law, if the plaintiff released one tortfeasor—something a settling defendant will certainly want—the release operated as a release of all tortfeasors, even if the other tortfeasor(s) did not contribute anything. *See* 66 Am. Jur. 2d § 36 (2009). Following the lead of the Uniform Contribution Among Joint Tortfeasors Act, many if not most states no longer leave this matter to common law. *See* 18 Am. Jur. 2d § 62. Anyone settling a case involving joint tortfeasors should determine the rules for the jurisdiction in question. In general, a settlement by one tortfeasor among multiple ones will release that tortfeasor from any claims (by the plaintiff or other tortfeasors) thereafter related to the incident. *See id.* The settling tortfeasor, however, has a contribution claim against the non-settling tortfeasors for any amount paid to the plaintiff if, as in most states, a Contribution Act has been adopted. Note that a Contribution Act will require the settling defendant to name a codefendant in a release if the settling defendant wishes to have a claim for contribution. Absent such a release, the non-settling defendant typically can be pursued only by the plaintiff. (The plaintiff's judgment against a second tortfeasor would typically be reduced, or offset, by the amount received in a prior settlement.)

Mediation

Many courts are requiring parties to engage in mediation at or around the time of the final pretrial conference. At that point both sides have finished discovery and should have a sense of the strengths and weaknesses of the clients' positions. For example, the District of Columbia requires parties to engage in alternative dispute resolution prior to a trial. 57 Am. Jur. *Trials* § 555 (2009). Often, the trial judge assigned to a case will refer the case to another judge in the court who will serve as the mediator. The trial judge should have no involvement in the mediation. The trial judge cannot communicate with the mediating judge. Otherwise, the trial judge's views of a case can be shaped by hearing the parties' respective settlement negotiations. If a trial judge attempts to take part in mediation, counsel should (politely) remind the judge of Rule 3.9 of the ABA Model Code of Judicial Conduct: "A judge shall not act as an arbitrator or a mediator or perform other judicial functions apart from the judge's official duties unless expressly authorized by law." Model Code of Judicial Conduct R. 3.9 (2007).

The mediator has to learn details of the parties' positions, the degree to which each party should account for the opponent's claims and defenses, and apply her own experience. A judge serving as mediator has particular credibility with parties. Parties tend to take note when a judge mediator tells the parties that, in similar trials where she presided, she saw results such as the plaintiff losing outright, or of a major jury verdict against a defendant. In a case where both sides have risks if the case goes to trial, the mediator's job is to ensure each side understands the risks. She can thereby move parties' valuations of a case into a range where settlement is possible. Hence, mediation often moves parties that have been too far apart into a range where their views of a case overlap sufficiently to get it settled.

Follow-Up Questions

1. Will the type of case you are handling affect how difficult it is to value the case for the client? Which types of cases should be easier, and which should be harder? In those cases where the damages are not easily quantified, what can you do to better develop a range of value?

2. Assume you have a personal injury case in which the plaintiff has sustained injuries that have manifested symptoms that have not fully matured. How can you begin to develop a value range to use in adjusting the value as the case proceeds? What are quantifiable criteria that you can value as the case proceeds? If there are expected future expenses resulting from injuries, what types of expert witnesses could help you to place a dollar value on these? On unquantifiable factors such as pain and suffering, what criteria could help you to assess what amounts a jury is likely to award in the jurisdiction in question?

3. Any personal injury lawyer will tell you that a case brought by a seriously injured person will likely produce a higher verdict than a wrongful death case by survivors of a person who died from personal injuries. Why should not a case in which someone was killed result in a higher verdict? What may account for the disparate results?

4. If you are representing a business seeking damages primarily for lost profits as a result of conduct you consider actionable by the defendant, what evidence would allow you to determine lost profits? What documents would need to be reviewed? What types of experts would be significant to prepare for and testify at trial regarding the damages?

Professional Identity Question

You represent the defendant in a suit in which the plaintiff alleges that your client, a competitor of plaintiff, had engaged in a conspiracy with others to drive your client out of business. You are able to establish sufficient facts to withstand summary judgment, and the case is going to trial. Business conspiracy statutes often permit treble damages, *i.e.*, three times the damages proved. The trial court orders the case into mediation with a judge other than the trial judge. Your client does not want to go to trial, recognizes the exposure as several million dollars, and wants you to settle if feasible (but of course for as little as possible). You are given authority of $1 million to settle, but the client says "he really would rather pay less if you can make it happen." After over a day of deliberations with each side separately and together, the mediator has the case in a position where it will settle if the defendant will pay $1 million. During the mediation, you are asked squarely whether you have authority of up to $1 million to settle. Can you answer that "your client is not comfortable settling for $1 million"? Would you answer in that way?

D. Methods to Reinforce and Integrate Topics Covered in This Chapter

One of the most difficult of the topics addressed in this chapter for many students is the last one—valuing a client's case. Assume you represent Brad Rex in his suit against both Ena Hurry and against Dr. Lovey Payne (Chapter 4, *supra*, at 82–96).

How would you go about categorizing the injuries he received at the accident itself? For instance, review verdicts in a city within your jurisdiction for persons with injuries similar to Brad's. Determine what publications in your state will allow you to see jury verdicts and list the kinds of injuries so that you can perform such an exercise.

How would you assess the damages against Dr. Payne for malpractice? Is there a cap on damages for malpractice claims within your jurisdiction?

E. Written Assignments

1. Write a memorandum to Mr. Befayre assessing the value of Sally's case. Employ the method for valuing a case suggested by Peter Hoffman described under the "Valuation Schema" above. In assessing the quality-of-proof element of the analysis, consider the description of the evidence Sally offers at trial, described in Chapter 12 on pages 263–65.

2. Search for model or "pattern" jury instructions in the state in which you intend to practice. Draft three "finding" jury instructions for Sally's claims against Horse-Power based on a set of pattern instructions from your jurisdiction. The first should be for Sally's claim against HorsePower for negligence (or strict liability if your jurisdiction approaches design defects in products from that approach). The second should be for her claim of breach of implied warranty of merchantability. The third should be for her claim of breach of express warranty.

Chapter 11

Procedures at Trial

A. Sally's Case at This Stage of Litigation Process

You have represented Sally throughout the pretrial process—pleadings, discovery, pretrial motions, and more. You evaluated her case and were prepared when the judge asked whether you had explored settlement. The defendants refused to respond at all and are taking an approach that they perceive as hard-nosed. They told the judge that their client simply cannot settle because the precedent of doing so here would be too damaging. That makes your job easier because you can focus on the trial. You must now represent Sally while she has her day in court.

This chapter will discuss the typical stages of a civil jury trial. It will not attempt to teach trial advocacy or address each aspect of handling the trial. Instead, it will focus on the procedural aspects of a trial, such as jury selection, motions during trial, and conduct that could result in a mistrial. Although this chapter does not discuss bench trials—*i.e.*, trials in which the judge serves as the fact-finder—such non-jury trials, albeit less complicated, entail many of the same procedural hurdles.

B. Tasks and Decision-Making at This Stage of the Case

The point at which you now find yourself in the timeline of a case is set forth in Diagram 11-1.

At this point (because she timely demanded a jury trial), Sally has opted to put her fate into the hands of the jury. Many reasons support that choice. She may trust in the collective judgment of a group over the judgment of one judge. Perhaps, recognizing she may not win or get everything she seeks, she is more willing to accept an anonymous collective verdict rather than that of one person.

The procedure during a civil trial is fairly consistent throughout most jurisdictions. *See generally* James A. Tanford, *An Introduction to Trial Law*, 51 Mo. L. Rev. 623 (1986). This reflects the influence of common historical origins and customs. However, much like the Federal Rules of Civil Procedure, most states' procedures deal primarily with pretrial and post-trial matters. They pay less attention to the trial process itself.

Diagram 11-1

Cause of Action (events leading to suit)
Prefiling Matters to Consider; Choice of Forum [Chs. 2-3]
Π and Δ Decide on Offensive Pleadings & Joinder (of claims & parties); Filing Suit; Service [Chs. 4-5]
Motions, Responsive Pleadings; Default; Voluntary & Involuntary Dismissals [Chs. 6-7]
Discovery Phase (developing proof to establish claims & learning about the adversary's case) [Ch. 8]
Right to Jury Trial; Pretrial Motions & Practice [Ch. 9]
Final Pretrial Conference & Other Events within Last Month before Trial [Ch. 10]
Procedure at Trial [Ch. 11]
Post-Trial Motions & Calculating the Date of Final Judgment to Know Key Deadlines Such as for Notice of Appeal [Ch. 12]

The best way to tackle the civil jury trial as a practitioner is to move through the process chronologically. Accordingly, the discussion below discusses procedural issues at trial in the order they typically would arise in trial.

C. Overview of Applicable Law

Jury Selection

After completing the pretrial process, usually on the first day of trial, counsel select a jury from the pool of potential jurors called to court. Selecting a jury is a two-step process: assembling the list (venire) of prospective jurors (venire members) and questioning the potential jurors (voir dire).

Venire

Generally, a "master roll" of the venire reflects a representative sample of the population and serves as the starting point from which to choose the jurors who will be summoned for trial. *See Taylor v. Louisiana*, 419 U.S. 522, 528–32 (1975) (holding that jury lists may not exclude certain groups, such as women or minorities, but instead must reflect a fair cross-section of the population). Courts rely on myriad statutory and procedural sources to compile the venire, such as voter registration lists or lists of licensed drivers. *See, e.g.,* GA. CODE ANN. § 15-12-40 (2009); VA. CODE ANN. § 8.01-345 (2009). Although the criteria for compiling the venire may differ from state to state, all venire share two components—they must be selected in a manner that is both comprehensive and random. *See* J. GOBERT & W. JORDAN, JURY SELECTION § 6.07 (2d ed. 1990).

Voir Dire

The purpose of the voir dire is to gather information from the venire members that would reveal potential biases, knowledge, opinions, or interests in the case that would disqualify them for cause. *See id.* § 9.04. For instance, a judge may strike a juror for cause if she has a close connection with any party or witness to the case, or if a juror's too-firmly entrenched and immutable opinions would render an impartial judgment impossible. *Patton v. Yount,* 467 U.S. 1025, 1035 (1984). Usually, the parties may exercise an unlimited number of for-cause challenges, but a limited number of peremptory challenges—challenges which allow the lawyer to strike a juror without the need to state a reason (subject to some limitations, discussed below). *See* J. GOBERT & W. JORDAN, JURY SELECTION § 7.01.

Courts in the different states have varied approaches to conducting voir dire. Venire members may be questioned as a group and, if the court permits it, individually. Moreover, voir dire may be conducted by the lawyers only, the judge only, and/or by the lawyers and the judge in succession. *See, e.g.,* KY. R. CIV. P. 47.01 (2009); *see generally* J. GOBERT & W. JORDAN, JURY SELECTION §§ 9.01–9.35. The types of questions allowed on voir dire also differ from state to state. For instance, the applicable statute may provide a list of acceptable questions, ranging from name, age, and marital status to knowledge of pre-trial publicity, or even involvement in another civil lawsuit or criminal prosecution. *See, e.g.,* PA. R. CIV. P. 220.1 (2009); *see also* J. GOBERT & W. JORDAN, JURY SELECTION §§ 9.13–9.14.

Peremptory Challenges

Lawyers may use a limited number of peremptory challenges to strike jurors without cause. *Compare* CAL. CIV. PROC. CODE § 231(c) (West 2009) (in a civil case, each side gets six peremptory challenges); 735 ILL. COMP. STAT. ANN. 5/2-1106 (LexisNexis 2009) (in Illinois, each side generally gets five peremptory challenges) *with* J. GOBERT & W. JORDAN, JURY SELECTION § 8.02 (noting that the federal number in civil cases is three peremptory challenges and that there is no constitutionally mandated minimum number). Traditionally, lawyers could exercise these challenges without offering any reason or explanation. However, the Supreme Court has ruled that litigants may not use their peremptory challenges to exclude jurors on the basis of race or gender. *See, e.g., Batson v. Kentucky,* 476 U.S. 79 (1986) (holding that the Equal Protection Clause of the Fourteenth Amendment governs the exercise of peremptory challenges by a prosecutor in a criminal trial); *Edmonson v. Leesville Concrete Co.,* 500 U.S. 614 (1991) (no exclusion on the basis of race); *J.E.B. v. Alabama,* 511 U.S. 127 (1994) (no exclusion on the basis of gender); *see also* J. GOBERT & W. JORDAN, JURY SELECTION §§ 8.05–8.11. *But cf. State v. Davis* 504 N.W.2d 767 (Minn. 1993) (although religious belief or activity is an allowable basis for exclusion, religious affiliation is not).

Follow-Up Questions

1. What is the purpose of thorough but random selection of the pool of potential jurors? *reflection of representative sample of population*

2. Which do you believe produces the most impartial and unbiased jury: (a) voir dire by counsel alone; (b) voir dire by the judge with questions proposed and selected by the judge to ask along with others from counsel if the judge deems them appropriate; or (c) voir dire solely by the judge? Why?

Professional Identity Questions

1. The *Batson* line of cases requires counsel, challenged with using peremptory strikes based on illegitimate reasons, to articulate a neutral, legitimate reason. How easily do you believe it is for counsel to articulate a seemingly neutral, legitimate reason when in reality she struck the juror due to race, gender, or other such illegitimate reason? Will you engage in striking jurors based on race? Will you engage in striking jurors based on gender?

2. Say you are representing an African American in a case against a Caucasian. Your voir dire questioning of an African American juror leads you to believe that this juror will factor race into her decision-making—thus offending the spirit of *Batson*. However, if you exercise a peremptory strike against this juror, an African American herself, you would be violating *Batson*. As a creative attorney, you could offer a good response to a *Batson* challenge during voir dire, explaining a peremptory strike in a way that does not implicate race or gender (*e.g.*, the juror is elderly while your client is young, and you want younger jurors). In weighing all of the above, what option would best achieve the ends of justice: striking the juror because you believe she will allow race to interfere in impartial decision-making, or allowing her to remain on the jury, and hope that you are wrong about the intuition that she will factor race into the case?

3. Implicit in Question 2 is the notion that, as an advocate in an adversarial system, you must employ methods that best position your client to prevail. However, can you choose to place limits on the extent to which you will engage in advocacy, such as refusing to consider race in jury selection even if your client wants you to strike jurors based on their race?

Practice Problems

Practice Problem 11-1

Fisherman's Financial Services is a small, suburban corporation that primarily serves fishermen and other small business owners in the rural town off a large body of water.

The company is operated by a board of directors, namely: Wally Whitefish, the president and CEO; Sally Swimmer, the sister of Wally Whitefish; and Chris Catchalot, a retired fisherman. All of the directors are licensed financial advisors and have been friends for many years.

Some time ago, the board of directors received a report from the State's Commerce Division expressing concern over various activities that appeared to be actionable under state business conspiracy statutes. The letter warned the company of the potential civil liability of the directors.

The Board hired Good-as-Gold, from the law firm of Gold, Fish & Fin to represent Fisherman's in any action taken by the State. Ultimately, the Division of Commerce assessed considerable fines against Fisherman's and its directors, jointly and severally. Fisherman's sued Good-as-Gold and his law firm, alleging legal malpractice. Fisherman's alleged that it hired Mr. Gold to shield the directors from individual liability. In defense, Mr. Gold claims that he was hired to shield the corporation only, and not the individual directors. The case is ready for trial.

Research the law of the state in which you plan to practice regarding the grounds on which jurors may be dismissed for cause. Assess whether these prospective jurors should be excused for cause. If the juror cannot be dismissed for cause, you can use one of your peremptory strikes so long as you do not base it on race or gender. For those that do not fit within the "for cause" categories in your jurisdiction, which would you consider as candidates for your peremptory strikes?

(1) **Wally Saylor** retired from the United States Navy as a Master Chief. He is a local fisherman and a fixture at the local watering hole. He is acquainted with Mr. Gold because Gold's law firm has chartered his boat for deep sea fishing expeditions. He knows Mr. Gold by name, but is not a personal friend.   *Peremptory*

(2) **Govial George** is a former dentist in a nearby town. He is seventy-one, and familiar with counsel on both sides of the case. He did not ask to be excused from jury duty because of his age. After losing some money in the stock market, he willingly admits that he distrusts companies and anything to do with investments in companies.   *For cause*

(3) **Ambitious Amber** works at a local restaurant that is famous for its fresh seafood. She moved to the area five years ago. She is considering procuring a financial advisor so that she can put together an investment portfolio and, someday, open her own restaurant. She had talked to Wally Whitefish at a cocktail party. In that conversation, Wally shared some advice, as he said, just because he liked Amber's ambition and did not see the need to have her come to his office and sign a client contract   *Peremptory*

(4) **Danny Do-Little** is twenty-five years old, and a high school graduate, but he has never been able to "hold down a job." He has never been fired from a position, but he always quits a month or two into being hired. He tells his family that he just gets "bored" and has not "found his niche," but his mother tells her friends that he is "lazy."   *Defense councel: don't want young people*

(5) **Frankie Felon** was convicted fifteen years ago of a felony. He says that he has reformed his ways and "can't wait to be a good citizen by sitting on a jury."

(6) **Had-a-Little Lamb** is fast becoming the most popular seafood chef in the area. He cannot read, write, or speak any English.

Practice Problem 11-2

Alan is a Caucasian male who ran a red light at a major intersection. Brandon, an African American male, was passing through the intersection when Alan struck his car. The point of impact was the rear passenger door of Brandon's vehicle, injuring Brandon's son who was riding in the back seat of the car. Brandon was so enraged by Alan's "lack of caution," and upset over his son's injuries, that he immediately got out of his car and punched Alan in the face, knocking out one of Alan's teeth. Brandon sued Alan for negligence, and the damages resulting from the car accident. Alan counterclaimed for battery.

After voir dire questioning of prospective jurors, each side made peremptory strikes. Before the jury was sworn, both Alan and the Brandon raised *Batson* challenges. Alan challenged Brandon's peremptory strike of a Caucasian prospective juror. Brandon in turn challenged Alan's peremptory strike of two African-American prospective jurors.

Alan's counsel explained that he struck each of the African-American prospective jurors because they did not make eye contact with him at all. Additionally, Alan's counsel pointed out that one of them rolled her eyes when the judge said that voir dire questioning would continue into the following day.

Brandon's counsel explained that the striking of the Caucasian prospective juror was at his client's request. Brandon's counsel also explained to the court that, from his observations during questioning, he felt that the prospective juror might actually be offended by some of the basic subject matter of the case and that it would affect her ability to be impartial.

Are the peremptory challenges legitimate? In other words, should the judge find that the reasons offered for one or more of the strikes are inadequate and, therefore, the jurors must remain so as not to infringe the United States Constitution's Equal Protection Clause? If you were the trial judge, how would you rule on each challenge?

Professional Identity Question

Assume the same facts as Practice Problem 11-2 except that Alan directed his lawyer to strike the African American jurors because, in the client's words, "I don't want Blacks on my jury." How should Alan's counsel respond to the client? How would you respond?

Motions at Trial

Directed Verdict Motions

After plaintiff completes her case-in-chief, the defendant often brings a mid-trial motion for a directed verdict. Gene R. Shreve & Peter Raven-Hansen, Understanding Civil Procedure § 12.01(6) (4th ed. 2009). In federal court, the motion under Federal Rule of Civil Procedure 50 is called a motion for judgment as a matter of law (JMOL). In other jurisdictions, the motion is called by different names, such as a "motion for an instructed verdict" or a "motion to strike the plaintiff's evidence." *See, e.g.*, Tex. R. Civ. P. 268 (calling it "motion for instructed verdict"); Va. Code Ann. § 8.01-378 (2009) (calling it "motion to strike the plaintiff's evidence"). For convenience's sake, the motion will be called a "directed verdict motion." Regardless of the title they use, a majority of states follow the same approach in dealing with these motions as shown in Appendix 11-1 and explained more fully below.

The directed verdict motion questions whether the plaintiff has met her burden of producing sufficient evidence such that a reasonable jury could find for her. If the plaintiff has met the burden of production—or if the question is a close one—the defendant's motion should be denied. *See, e.g., Saunders v. Lloyd's of London*, 779 P.2d 249, 252 (Wa. 1989).[1] As with the summary judgment standard discussed in Chapter 9 *supra* at pages 221–24, a judge should not seek to determine whether the party with the trial burden on a claim or defense has actually proved her case by a preponderance of the evidence, by clear and convincing evidence, etc. Instead, the judge keeps the trial burden in mind in determining whether the party has produced enough evidence to make out a case on whether jurors could disagree about whether a party may succeed. If the plaintiff has clearly and sufficiently failed to meet this burden, then it would be pointless and inefficient to submit the case to the jury because the judge would most likely set aside a verdict for the plaintiff on defendant's motion for judgment notwithstanding the verdict ("JNOV").[2] The standard for JNOV is the same as the standard for summary judgment; that is, the judge asks "whether a fair-minded jury could return a verdict for the plaintiff on the evidence presented." *Anderson v. Liberty Lobby, Inc.*, 477 U.S. 242, 252 (1986).

At the close of all the evidence, either party can move (or renew a prior motion made at the close of plaintiff's case) for a directed verdict. The motion is identical in the standard applied on directed verdicts at the close of the plaintiff's case; the motion differs solely in timing. Thus, a motion for directed verdict at the conclusion of trial contends that the party with the burden of proof has failed to produce sufficient evidence upon which reasonable jurors can disagree.

At the end of the day, if the judge submits the case to the jury, the judge may still set aside that verdict and direct entry of judgment for the other party (JNOV). The timing of post-trial motions is tricky. Thus, the next chapter (Chapter 12) deals with these and their cousins, new trial motions, separately.

Motion for Mistrial

The trial judge may order a mistrial when a party is either unfairly prejudiced in a way that would prevent her from receiving fair and impartial consideration of her claims or defenses, or when the jury is unable to reach a verdict. If a civil case results in a mistrial, the judge will order a new trial, or the plaintiff must drop the suit. Parties may move for a mistrial based on several circumstances. Generally, a judge may declare a mistrial due to a jury deadlock on the verdict; death of lawyer, judge, or juror; misconduct on behalf of jurors, parties, or counsel; or gross misconduct by the court that would unfairly bias a jury one way or another. A mistrial usually occurs because something has prejudiced the jury in such a way that its deliberations cannot proceed impartially. *Cf. Riley v. Davison Constr. Co.*, 409 N.E.2d 1279, 1286 (Mass. 1980) (denying numerous motions for mistrial and holding that the jury was not "hopelessly confused" by the jury instructions, nor did they violate instructions regarding the special verdict slip).

The most common bases for mistrials generally fall into four categories: (1) misconduct involving the jury; (2) misconduct involving counsel for a party; (3) misconduct of a witness; and (4) misconduct of the judge. Misconduct involving the jury can take a number of forms. Generally speaking, conduct affecting the jury can result in a mistrial if it results in information from outside the jury room being introduced into deliberations. The

---

1. In a bench trial, this motion testing the sufficiency of the plaintiff's case is called a motion for involuntary dismissal. The trial judge in that case is the fact finder; as such, she must decide both the sufficiency *and* weight of the evidence.

2. "NOV," in the phrase "JNOV," stands for the Latin phrase *non obstante veredicto*, which translates to "notwithstanding the verdict."

classic example is in a case involving an accident scene: a juror goes to the scene and reports what she saw to her fellow jurors. *See* Am. Jur. 2d *Trial* § 1484 (2009). Similarly, bringing sources into the jury room that were not introduced into evidence (*e.g.,* an almanac) would be grounds for a mistrial. *See* 58 Am. Jur. 2d *New Trial* § 206 (2009). Another frequent potential ground for mistrial involves communications between jurors and parties, or counsel for parties, that could influence the trial result. *See* C.R. McCorkle, *Contact or Communication Between Juror and Party or Counsel During Civil Trial as Ground for Mistrial, New Trial, or Reversal,* 62 A.L.R.2d 298 (1958). However, in most cases the jurors' deliberative processes are sacrosanct and cannot be impeached by juror affidavits or testimony. *See* 75B Am. Jur. 2d *Trial* § 1626 (2009). Some states will even prevent jurors from impeaching the jury's process when juror misconduct has been claimed. *See id.* However, many states do allow affidavits or juror testimony when the jurors themselves are alleged to have engaged in conduct such as considering facts obtained improperly (*e.g.,* by unauthorized jury view), facts brought into the jury room improperly (*e.g.,* bringing sources into the room not in evidence), or jurors communicating facts or information from parties, counsel, or witnesses. *See id.* 58 Am. Jur. 2d *New Trial* § 214 (2009).

Lawyer misconduct can easily result in a mistrial. *See, e.g., Davis v. Sams,* 542 P.2d 943, 944 (Ok. 1975) ("Where an attorney attacks opposing counsel in the presence of the jury, it constitutes grounds for a new trial if it appears that prejudice may have resulted."). In one case, defense counsel in a civil case asked on voir dire whether jurors realized that a verdict for plaintiff would result in their paying for the verdict as taxpayers; the court held that such conduct should have resulted in a mistrial. *See Bd. of County Road Comm'ns of Wayne County v. GLS Leasco, Inc.,* 394 Mich. 126, 229 N.W.2d 727 (1975). More generally, comparing the relative wealth or poverty of parties can lead to a mistrial, depending on the court's assessment of the existence of prejudice. *See* W. E. Shipley, *Counsel's Appeal in Civil Cases to Wealth or Poverty of Litigants as Grounds for Mistrial, New Trial, or Reversal,* 32 A.L.R.2d 9 § 7 (1953). Remarks about a party's nationality or race are particularly apt to be designed solely to arouse prejudice and will support a mistrial. *See, e.g., Solomon v. Stewart,* 151 N.W. 716 (Mich. 1915). Although many believe that a "golden rule" argument—*i.e.,* that jurors should treat a litigant as they would want to be treated—is per se error, courts generally find such an argument to be improper when the golden-rule argument addresses an issue of compensating the plaintiff as the jurors would want to be compensated. 75A Am. Jur. 2d § 547 (2009). Simply using that type of argument to ask jurors to consider whether a litigant has acted reasonably, however, is not considered improper. *See id.*

Witness misconduct is often inadvertent. Not knowing the rules of trials and of evidence, a witness may introduce evidence prejudicial to the jury's fair consideration. For instance, a witness may inadvertently mention inadmissible evidence such as the fact that a defendant that is being sued in a personal injury case has insurance. *See* 75 Am. Jur. 2d *Trial* § 519 (2009). An inadvertent mention of inadmissible evidence does not automatically result in a mistrial. *See id.* However, if the testimony creates prejudice, a mistrial is warranted. *See id.*

A judge's own misconduct may require a mistrial. Because judges in the American adversarial system are supposed to be fair and more like umpires than inquisitors, any disparaging comments by a judge about a party's case, about a witness, or other matters that could influence the jury can result in error. *See* Cristopher Vaeth, *Prejudicial Effects of Trial Judge's Remarks, During Civil Jury Trial, Disparaging Litigants, Witnesses, or Subject Matter of Litigation—Modern Cases,* 35 A.L.R. 5th 1 (2009). If the error is sufficiently prejudicial, it can justify a mistrial. *See* 75B Am. Jur. 2d *Trial* § 1492 (2009).

The trial court has the discretion either to grant or deny a motion for a mistrial. *Id.* § 1287. In some states, any misconduct which *might* influence the jury is sufficient for the judge to grant a motion for a mistrial and thus grant a motion for a new trial. *Davis v. Sams,* 542 P.2d 943, 944 (Okla. 1975) ("Jurors must be kept free from all possible influences. When exposed thereto it will not do to inquire into the probability as to the extent of these influences and their effect upon the verdict. There is no safety except in setting aside the verdict in a case where acts and conversations are shown which could have influenced the jury."). However, in other states, actual prejudice must have occurred—not just the possibility of prejudice. *Sturzenegger v. Father Flanagan's Boys' Home,* 754 N.W.2d 406, 429 (Neb. 2008) (holding that "a motion for mistrial must be premised upon actual prejudice, not the mere possibility of prejudice.").

If something justifying a mistrial occurs, the lawyer at trial must be careful to object in a timely way. Grounds for mistrial are easily waived. If the comment or event forming the basis for a motion is something of which counsel is aware, then she must object and move for a mistrial promptly. ROGER C. PARK, TRIAL OBJECTIONS HANDBOOK § 1.13 (1991). Otherwise, the matter will be deemed waived. *Id.* If the basis for mistrial is something that counsel learns after trial, such as from a juror about juror misconduct, then she must bring the matter to the trial court's attention as soon as possible. Again, each state's rules are different, so you should know the rules of the state in which you intend to practice. The following statement is typical of ones from state supreme court opinions nationwide:

> In order to preserve, as a ground of appeal, an opponent's misconduct during closing argument, the aggrieved party must have objected to the improper remarks no later than at the conclusion of the argument. And an aggrieved party wishing a mistrial because of an opponent's misconduct during argument is required to move for such before the cause is submitted.

Id.

In some states, either party may renew a motion for a directed verdict if a jury is unable to reach a verdict and no mistrial has been declared, *see, e.g., Nelson v. Data Terminal Sys., Inc.,* 762 S.W.2d 744, 748–49 (Tex. Ct. App. 1988), regardless of whether the party for whom judgment is granted requested a directed verdict at the close of the other party's case-in-chief. *See, e.g., Collora v. Navarro,* 574 S.W.2d 65, 67 (Tex. 1978).

The key question for the judge in deciding whether to grant a motion for a mistrial (and the key question you should remember) is whether the trial can proceed fairly with a cautionary or curative instruction. Whenever a comment or event occurs that could lead to a mistrial, the party who wishes the trial to proceed can suggest a "curative instruction." Cautionary or curative instructions arise when, after something occurs that the jury should not consider, the court cautions the jurors to disregard the event or comment and to ignore it. You may fairly ask how jurors can possibly wipe their minds of significant events or comments. However, courts regularly assume that cautionary or curative instructions *are* observed by jurors. Many a mistrial, new trial, or reversal has been avoided through such an instruction.

Follow-Up Questions

1. In each of the grounds for mistrial discussed above, what is the common denominator that could lead a trial court to grant a mistrial? By identifying this common denominator, are you more likely to recognize new situations that may arise at trial implicating grounds for a mistrial? *prejudice*

2. If something occurs at trial out of your and your client's control, such as a witness stating something that is inadmissible, and you want the trial to continue rather than having to go through the time and expense of a new trial, what action should you argue the court could take that would alleviate the effect of the comment/event? curative instruction

Professional Identity Questions

1. Suppose you are representing a person of Arabic descent. If in closing argument opposing counsel says, "Of course after 9-11 we know persons of Arabic descent cannot be trusted," could you move for a mistrial? Could you wait until closing arguments were over, and the jury took a recess, to make your objection to counsel's argument raising ethnicity as an issue? How would you argue that a cautionary or curative instruction in this instance would not be sufficient to overcome the effect of the statement? In your state, would delaying your objection until the end of the argument waive the objection? Do you believe a party's ethnicity would ever be relevant? Would you make this kind of argument? Would you even make an allusion—more subtle than the counsel's statement above—to a person's ethnicity?

2. Savvy counsel knows that courts do not like to grant mistrials. Courts will give cautionary instructions if possible, in lieu of a mistrial, to avoid the inefficiency of a new trial. In light of this, some counsel provide hints to a client that, even though a fact is inadmissible, if the fact somehow came to the jury's attention, it would help the client. For instance, suppose the client is suing a manufacturer for negligently designing a product that injured the plaintiff and, after the plaintiff's accident, the manufacturer changed its product. Generally, unless a manufacturer opened the door to testimony on the subject by contending that it was not feasible to change the product, such testimony is clearly inadmissible. However, you as plaintiff's counsel and the plaintiff are aware of the change. You tell the plaintiff that the court could grant a mistrial if the fact of the change in product design "happened to come up in the plaintiff's testimony," but that you are pretty confident that the judge would give a cautionary instruction. Your client makes the statement and your prediction of a curative instruction is accurate. Do you believe making this statement to the plaintiff was appropriate?

Practice Problems

Practice Problem 11-3

You are in a civil trial representing a plaintiff bringing a slander suit against the local newspaper. Your client is not a public figure, just an average citizen. The newspaper ran a story stating that your client had improperly claimed reimbursement as business expenses for trips that the story suggested were actually pleasure trips. You are satisfied that the stories are false. You know that the trial judge assigned to your case is a close friend of the newspaper's owner. You wisely had demanded a jury and were glad now that you had done so. Throughout the trial, however, the trial judge—whenever your client or one of your witnesses testifies—turns his chair 180 degrees and faces the back wall. The appearance is of one who could care less about the plaintiff's case. Conversely, whenever the newspaper calls a witness, the judge listens intently. Would such conduct of the trial judge constitute grounds for a mistrial? How would the appellate court, if the trial court denied the motion, have a record of what the trial judge had been doing and on which you based the mistrial motion?

Practice Problem 11-4

You represent the plaintiff in a car accident case. Prior to retaining you, the plaintiff had been interviewed by an insurance adjuster for the defendant. Needless to say, the parties had not been able to reach a settlement. In examining your client about what happened, you first have her describe the events leading up to the accident. You then ask, "What happened afterward?" You expect your client to talk about, as you had rehearsed, her series of medical problems and health care providers. Instead, she unexpectedly states that someone from the insurance company for the defendant contacted her the day after the accident. Defendant objects and moves for a mistrial. How would you best deal with this situation? Should the court grant a mistrial?

D. Methods to Reinforce and Integrate Topics Covered in This Chapter

You were asked in Practice Problem 11-1 to research the law of your state on challenging jurors for cause so that you could work out that problem. Now research the rules in your jurisdiction related to (a) size of a civil jury; (b) the number of peremptory strikes you will have; (c) what happens if there are multiple defendants (*e.g.*, must you share strikes); and (d) any other matter pertaining to selection of jurors in a civil case that, as you review your jurisdiction's rules, appears noteworthy.

Also research the grounds for mistrials in your jurisdiction. See if you can determine the most common basis on which courts have granted mistrials in civil cases. In discussing these grounds, has the court refused a mistrial because the trial court gave a cautionary instruction? Check the model (pattern) jury instructions for your state and see whether you can find a sample cautionary instruction. Of course, the instruction would have to be adapted in trial to refer to whatever happened that prompted the potential mistrial and/or a cautionary instruction.

E. Written Assignments

1. Sally has made it to the first day of trial. When you, Mr. Befayre, and she show up for the first day of trial, Mr. Befayre tells Sally that he has such confidence in you that with her permission he would like you to select the jury. He of course will give you his views and assist you. Sally has come to respect your abilities and heartily seconds that suggestion. Thus, you will be doing your first voir dire and are excited by that chance. The trial judge handling the trial al-

lows counsel to participate in voir dire. Write out a list of questions you will ask prospective jurors. Do you have any particular composition of a jury that you would like to end up with (*e.g.*, older versus younger jurors, jurors with certain experience, etc.)? If after voir dire you identify certain jurors that you believe present a potential basis for challenging them for cause, but do not want to offend either them or the rest of the jury panel, is there any reason you cannot ask the judge to have private questioning in chambers of such jurors with the judge, opposing counsel and defendants present — along with you and your client? Why might that be a valuable approach to moving to strike for cause? If the judge denies your request, what will you do in pursuing the challenges for cause?

2. You receive a list of 75 potential jurors 3 days before Sally's trial is set to begin. The list includes the prospective juror, her/his residence address, occupation, and her/his spouse's occupation — if the juror is married. You would like even more information on the group. Are there restrictions in your state affecting your ability to gather information on the prospective jurors, such as by visiting the jurors' homes (from street view only), noting information about jurors' homes, their vehicles, bumper stickers, etc.?

Chapter 12

Post-Trial Motions and Knowing the Deadline for Appeal

A. Sally's Case at This Stage of Litigation Process

Each of Sally's claims went to a jury. Before discussing the jury's factual findings and verdict, a review of the evidence Sally and the defendants offered is in order. This evidence will be the crux of the post-trial motions discussed in this chapter.

Sally called a number of witnesses to verify that the hole in the road on the border of Arcadia and Illyria had existed for several months and had become increasingly large as time passed, and that no one had done anything about it. Both she and other witnesses verified that it was difficult to see the magnitude of the hole until one was actually upon it, primarily because there was a slight grade uphill before a driver reached the spot. For someone like Sally who had not traveled on the road before, she would have had no way of knowing it was there. Sally testified that she was going below the speed limit and, all of a sudden, she found herself flipped over in the road. Another driver witnessed the accident and corroborated the above facts.

Sally also presented a surveyor who confirmed the hole was indeed partly on the City's property and partly outside, within Illyria's jurisdiction. She offered documents, sent to both the City and State transportation departments, from persons who complained about the dangerous condition of the hole well before her accident. One of the internal City transportation documents suggested that the reason the road was not being repaired was finances. Sally offered other documents showing that, at the same time as finances were offered as an excuse for failing to fix the road, the City had decided to upgrade the offices of its highest officials.

Sally provided expert testimony that the Stallion convertible's rollbar was defective not only in the manufacturing of the particular one on her car, but in the overall design of the rollbar. The experts in car design testified that although HorsePower had used a form of titanium in earlier models of the Stallion, it had switched to a composition employing both steel and aluminum for the year in which Sally's car was made. An internal company document produced in discovery (after Sally's counsel brought a third motion to compel) showed that the reason for the change in metals was to reduce costs of production. The experts testified, however, that roll bars of commercial titanium are far stronger and more likely to protect a vehicle's driver or passenger in a rollover accident than aluminum and steel composites. They testified that a design that included strong stainless steel might be defensible, but that using the composite of aluminum and steel represented a failure to exercise the kind of care that car manufacturers were able to exercise without undue expense. Moreover, the experts testified that there was a specific manufacturing defect in Sally's roll bar, because it showed air bubbles in the metal at the point at which it collapsed and failed to protect Sally. The experts testified as to how the air bubbles made the area in which they occurred even weaker than the bar would otherwise be, and that it was standard in the industry to check for air bubbles in roll bars and to replace the bars if bubbles existed. Finally, the experts testified that roll bars and protections against collapse of the cab of vehicles were a common feature not only in convertibles, but in all vehicles, because the prospect of vehicles turning over in accidents was well-known.

Sally also offered testimony about the express warranties HorsePower had made about the convertible being among the safest on the market, especially because of its representations about the roll bar. She testified that she relied on these claims and, indeed, they were what convinced her to buy a convertible—something she had never driven before. Her lawyer offered the documentation she had received from the dealer. The documents included disclaimers from the dealer, but anything about manufacturer disclaimers was in such small print that no one would ever notice them.

Sally's medical testimony established the severity of her injuries, including the concussion, broken bones, hospitalization, and grueling rehabilitation.

The defendants' testimony maintained that Sally was negligent herself for driving into a pothole. The manufacturer argued that its disclaimers prevented any claim of breach of implied or express warranties. Moreover, the defendants argued that Sally's advanced age accounted for much of her medical problems, rather than anything resulting from the accident.

Upon the completion of the evidence and post-trial motions, which the court denied, the judge gave the jury their instructions. Following that, counsel presented oral arguments. The jury members took a written version of the instructions to the jury room (a practice permitted in most jurisdictions) where they retired to deliberate.

After less than a day of deliberations, the jury returned a verdict for Sally. The jury found that the dangerous road condition existed for such a period of time that its lack of attention constituted not only negligent but also at least reckless conduct on the part of the City. The jury also found that this conduct proximately caused Sally's injuries. In its verdict form, it found for Sally and against the City of Arcadia, awarded compensatory damages of $5 million, and also awarded punitive damages of $10 million.

The jury also found that the State was liable for negligence under the State Tort Claims Act. It awarded compensatory damages of $5 million. As instructed by the judge, although the jury could award punitive damages against the municipality of Arcadia, it could not do so against the State because the State Tort Claims Act precluded such an award against the State. Thus, the jury was instructed that they were only to assess, if they found the State liable, compensatory damages.

Finally, the jury found HorsePower liable for more than one claim. First, it found HorsePower failed to use proper care in the manufacturing of the roll bars on Sally's Stallion convertible and that such negligence proximately caused her injuries. Second, the jury found that HorsePower breached the implied duty of merchantability, under the State's Uniform Commercial Code, requiring that goods covered by the Act be fit for the ordinary uses to which they would be put. It found that a rollover is something that a vehicle manufacturer could and should anticipate as an ordinary hazard of driving the vehicle. Finally, the jury found that HorsePower, under the State's Uniform Commercial Code, breached its express warranty that the Stallion's roll bars would not collapse in an accident. It found that the disclaimers in the sales documentation were so inconspicuous they were rendered ineffective. The jury found HorsePower liable for $5 million on each of the three claims.

The defendants asked the jury to be polled to ensure that these findings and verdict amounts were unanimous. Each juror confirmed the verdict. The judge then thanked the jurors for their service and excused them. On the same day as the verdict, the judge entered a "Judgment Order on Jury Verdict." This order recited the date the trial began, the impaneling of the jury, any incidents of the trial that she deemed significant (*e.g.*, denial of a motion for a directed verdict at the close of the plaintiff's evidence), the findings of the jury as noted above, and the verdict amounts. The judge then signed the order and directed the clerk to send the order to counsel immediately.

Less than 10 days from entry of the order, the City of Arcadia moved for a judgment notwithstanding the verdict or, alternatively, for a new trial. In its motion the City argued that the evidence was insufficient to support a claim of negligence or the finding of recklessness necessary to support the punitive damages award and, alternatively, that the court should order a new trial because the verdict and damages awards were against the great weight of the evidence and excessive. Also, less than 10 days after the judgment order, HorsePower moved for a judgment notwithstanding the verdict or, alternatively, for a new trial. HorsePower argued first, in support of the motion notwithstanding the verdict, that Sally's evidence was not sufficient to support the verdict on any of the claims. Alternatively, HorsePower argued that to the extent the court did not rule that the evidence was insufficient, the court should nevertheless rule that the verdict was against the great weight of the evidence and a new trial should be ordered. Finally, HorsePower argued that the damages as to each claim were excessive. The State timely filed a motion to reduce the compensatory damages award against it to the cap permitted under the State's Tort Claims Act.

Needless to say, Sally is pleased with the verdict. You and Mr. Befayre had explained to her, even before the jury returned with its verdict, that defendants often file post-trial motions after verdicts, seeking to have the judge set aside the verdict and enter judgment for them, or at least grant a new trial based on the contention that the verdict was contrary to the great weight of the evidence. In one of the funnier moments in the case, Sally responded: "What's all that legal gobbledygook mean? It sounds like the court just lets sore losers complain when they don't get what they want!" You explain to her that the first motion a defendant typically files after an adverse verdict—the motion for judgment notwithstanding the verdict—is essentially the same as the directed verdict motion at the close of the plaintiff's case. As you also explain, the court should not grant the motion if the court finds that the evidence was such that reasonable jurors could disagree, and that the court is not supposed to inject its own view of credibility or of the overall weight of the evidence. If the judge decides that she might have decided differently, but that the jury's findings are supported by evidence upon which reasonable persons could disagree, the judge should deny the motion. You do note that appellate court opinions urge district judges to avoid granting directed verdict motions at the close of the plaintiff's evidence or at the end of trial, even if the judge considers the motion to be one worth considering. In other words, appellate courts urge district judges to let the case go to the jury. If the jury decides against the plaintiff, the defendant's directed verdict motions become academic. Moreover, appellate courts want to be able to decide the case on appeal once and for all. If the district judge granted a directed verdict motion during trial, but the appellate court then rules that doing so was error, the entire case has to be put back on the jury trial calendar and tried before a new jury. By contrast, if the district judge allows the case to go to the jury in the first trial, and waits until after trial to grant a motion notwithstanding the verdict and enter judgment for the defendants, the plaintiff can appeal that decision. On appeal, the appellate court can reverse the trial court and reinstate the jury verdict. Such an approach, appellate courts have said, is much more efficient. You tell Sally this, and she seems to follow you but becomes a bit concerned that the judge might grant the defendants' motions if she wins a verdict. You tell her that you have explained the process so that she is fully informed. However, you also reassure Sally that you believe that the evidence Sally has presented should support the sufficiency of all of her claims. You note that Sally always has the ability to appeal, and that appellate courts give great deference to jury verdicts. Thus, if for some reason the trial court granted judgment to the defendants despite the jury verdicts in Sally's favor, she would have a strong basis for appeal.

Now that the jury has awarded verdicts to Sally, Mr. Befayre adds only the following sage comments. Even though Sally had as strong a case as he had seen in awhile, and she was a splendid witness, trial judges are prone to reduce damage awards through certain tools. One of these tools is "remittitur"—which he refers to as "a fancy word for reducing the amount of damages." In other words, as Mr. Befayre explained, if the verdict is higher than the judge thinks is appropriate, she can reduce the verdict to a lower amount. The plaintiff can take the reduced verdict amount or, if she refuses, she will have to go through a new trial, most likely limited to damages. The defendant may agree to pay the lower amount. Alternatively, the defendant may refuse to accept the remitted judgment, upon which the trial court can order a new trial solely on the issue of damages. Mr. Befayre tells Sally that he mentions this only so that she is not surprised. He assures her that, if they do not agree that the amount of any remittitur is appropriate, he believes she will ultimately receive a just result.

B. Tasks and Decision-Making at This Stage of the Case

The phase of litigation where the case now stands is shown below in Diagram 12-1.

If plaintiff's counsel performed the tasks and engaged in the strategic decisions with the client at each of the stages leading to the verdict, as suggested in the previous chapters, then the tasks and decision-making at this stage are simple. Once a jury has entered its verdict, seek a judgment on that verdict as soon as possible. Indeed, counsel can type a proposed order prior to the return of the verdict with blanks for the judge to fill in. Diagram 12-2 shows a sample draft order.

Diagram 12-1

Cause of Action (events leading to suit)
Prefiling Matters to Consider; Choice of Forum [Chs. 2-3]
Π and Δ Decide on Offensive Pleadings & Joinder (of claims & parties); Filing Suit; Service [Chs. 4-5]
Motions, Responsive Pleadings; Default; Voluntary & Involuntary Dismissals [Chs. 6-7]
Discovery Phase (developing proof to establish claims & learning about the adversary's case) [Ch. 8]
Right to Jury Trial; Pretrial Motions & Practice [Ch.9]
Final Pretrial Conference & Other Events within Last Month before Trial [Ch. 10]
Procedure at Trial [Ch. 11]
Post-Trial Motions & Calculating the Date of Final Judgment to Know Key Deadlines Such as for Notice of Appeal [Ch. 12]

Diagram 12-2

Sample Draft Order

STATE OF ILLYRIA:
IN THE CIRCUIT COURT OF THE CITY OF ARCADIA

SALLY WILREIZ,	)	
	)	
Plaintiff,	)	
	)	
v.	)	Civil Action No. 12345
	)	
	)	
CITY OF ARCADIA,	)	
	)	
STATE OF ILLYRIA,	)	
	)	
and	)	
	)	
HORSEPOWER, INC.,	)	
	)	
Defendants.	)	

FINAL JUDGMENT ORDER

[Continued on next page.]

This matter came before the Court on _____ for a jury trial on plaintiff's claims against the defendants. After voir dire, a jury was selected and counsel presented their opening statements. Plaintiff thereafter presented her case in chief, at which point she rested and defendants moved for a directed verdict, which this Court denied.

On _____ the defendants began putting on their evidence. The City presented its case and rested. Then the State presented its case and rested. Horsepower, Inc. began presenting its case in chief, but the case carried over to another day.

On _____, HorsePower, Inc. presented the remainder of its case in chief. At the close of all of the evidence, the defendants again moved for a directed verdict, which this Court denied. Thereafter the Court instructed the jury, and counsel presented closing arguments. The jury retired for deliberations and had not completed these before being excused.

On _____, the jury resumed its deliberations and at _____ announced it had reached a verdict. The Court then had the foreperson of the jury hand the verdict to the Clerk, who read the verdict. Defense counsel requested a poll of the jurors, and each juror confirmed the accuracy of the verdict as read. The Court then excused the jurors.

The Court, being of the opinion that the verdict is consistent with the law and is supported by sufficient evidence, hereby

ORDERS, ADJUDGES, AND DECREES that judgment is hereby entered for $_____ in compensatory damages against the City of Arcadia (1) $_____ in compensatory damages against the State of Illyria (representing the maximum permitted under the Torts Claims Act); (2) and Horsepower, Inc., jointly and severally; and (3) $_____ in punitive damages against the City of Arcadia.

The Clerk is directed to send a copy of this Order, once entered, to counsel for all parties.

ENTERED: _____

_____
Judge

I ASK FOR THIS:

_____
Benjamin Befayre
Artful Associate
BEFAYRE, DOGOOD & PROSPER

Unless the plaintiff loses or otherwise wants to challenge some part of the verdict, plaintiffs are almost always best served by having a final judgment entered on the verdict as soon as possible.

From the beginning of the case, the plaintiff should have been pressing for the earliest trial date possible. Having a verdict in her favor, the plaintiff ought not let up. The reason a judgment order needs to be entered is because post-trial motion and appeal deadlines will not apply until a final judgment is entered. As explained more fully below in the discussion of applicable law, the manner of pinpointing the date of a final judgment is fairly uniform. Knowing the exact date of a final judgment is crucial to calculating important post-trial deadlines. One is a deadline for motions for judgment notwithstanding the verdict and for new trials. The other is the deadline for a notice of appeal from the judgment.

As is explained more fully below, in most states, a motion for judgment notwithstanding the verdict or for a new trial will suspend the notice-of-appeal deadline until a ruling on the post-trial motions. Strategically, the plaintiff should recognize that a suspended appeal deadline only delays resolution. She should press for briefing and a hearing on the motions as soon as possible. The post-trial process can be slow and cumbersome unless the plaintiff pushes for swift rulings. Conversely, defense counsel who has lost a jury verdict can take one of two approaches upon a verdict for the plaintiff in which defense counsel plans to file post-trial motions. First, counsel can ask the court to suspend entry of a final judgment order so that no deadlines begin. Even if the judge agrees, the attorney would do well to check with the court regularly to ensure that no orders have been entered. Courts have been known to enter judgment orders on verdicts even after telling counsel they would withhold a judgment order. Although counsel should receive a copy of the order mailed from the court, clerks inadvertently fail to mail orders from time to time.[1] Second, if the judge will not withhold entry of a final judgment, then defense counsel should file her post-trial motions within the deadline in her jurisdiction. The process of briefing motions, conducting a hearing, and reaching a decision will likely take at least a couple of months. If she is in the great majority of jurisdictions in which post-trial motions for judgments notwithstanding the verdict and/or for a new trial automatically suspend any requirement of filing a notice of appeal, the defendant can plan for the appeal in the event the post-trial motions are unsuccessful. Because a losing defendant will be the appellant, and have responsibility for ordering a transcript and preparing an appendix of materials selected from the record, such a jump-start may be worthwhile.

C. Overview of Applicable Law

This section has three parts. The first will discuss how to recognize when a final judgment has been entered. The initial section also addresses the deadlines triggered by a final judgment (and how to avoid losing a client's right to appeal while post-trial motions are pending). The second part will consider the most common post-trial motions—motions for judgment notwithstanding the verdict and motions for a new trial, along with the tools of additur and remittitur, which have become intertwined with the topic of new trials. The final section will briefly note a final type of post-trial motion, similar to that allowed under Federal Rule of Civil Procedure 60, seeking relief from a judgment based upon extraordinary grounds.

Entry of Judgment and Deadlines to Watch

One of the most fundamental points when handling a case at this stage of litigation is to know when judgment has been entered. Without knowing that, a lawyer cannot keep

---

1. Thus some states have a provision for allowing at least an appeal from a final order that was not sent to counsel, but these provisions put an outside limit on the time within which a party may rely on them. *See* Am. Jur. 2d *Judgments* § 105 (2009); *see, e.g.*, Ind. R. Trial P. 72(E).

track of deadlines for filing post-trial motions or for filing a notice of appeal. Needless to say, failing to know these matters exposes one to malpractice liability.

The first point that counsel must realize is that neither a verdict nor a decision by the court in a non-jury trial is the same as the entry of a judgment. 46 AM. JUR. 2d *Judgments* § 101 (2009). The judge renders a decision and announces it in open court or receives a jury verdict, but these do not represent the *entry* of a judgment. *Id.* §§ 59, 101. Instead, the majority rule provides that entry of judgment occurs upon its notation in the official record of the court. *Id.* § 94; *see* Appendix 12-1 (states approaches to rule on determining date of judgment); *see, e.g.,* COLO. R. CIV. P. 58 ("The court shall promptly prepare, date, and sign a written judgment and the clerk shall enter it on the register of actions."). Only when the court formally *enters* a judgment will the time periods for filing post-trial motions and notices of appeal begin to run. Appendix 12-1; 46 AM. JUR. 2d *Judgments* § 5 (2009).

Although the overarching concept is the same, jurisdictions differ slightly on the proceedings and practice regarding *entry* of a judgment. *Id.* § 94. Because the deadlines for filing post-trial motions and a notice of appeal typically run from the entry of the judgment, counsel must research her jurisdiction's statutes and rules to be sure she knows: (1) how to determine a final judgment, especially when the order may not call itself that but still qualifies as a final judgment; and (2) when key post-trial motion deadlines and appeal deadlines expire.

The jurisdictions that model themsleves on the Federal Rules of Civil Procedure closely follow Federal Rule 58, which embodies the "separate document" requirement. The separate document rule provides that a judgment is only effective when it is set out in a separate document and entered on the docket by the clerk of the court. Appendix 12-1 (most jurisdictions follow Federal Rule of Civil Procedure 58's approach of requiring some form of separate document or action, aside from a ruling or verdict, to signify the date of a final judgment); *see, e.g.,* MASS. R. CIV. P. 58 ("Every judgment shall be set forth on a separate document.... A judgment is effective only when so set forth ... and when entered."). Under this requirement, the date of a verdict or decision of the court (*e.g.,* an opinion granting summary judgment and ending the case) is not the date from which any post-trial deadlines are calculated because these actions do not constitute formal entry of the judgment. Instead, the date that a separate document—often called "Judgment in a Civil Case"—is entered will form the date from which all post-trial deadlines run. Appendix 12-1; 46 AM. JUR. 2d *Judgments* § 109 (2009); *see, e.g.,* FED. R. CIV. P. Form 70.

Some states do not mandate that the judgment be set forth in a separate document, but these states provide specific procedures by which entry is perfected. 46 AM. JUR. 2d *Judgments* § 94 (2009); *see, e.g.,* COLO. R. CIV. P. 58 ("The effective date of entry of judgment shall be the actual date of the signing of the written judgment."). The judgment is usually deemed effective from the date the clerk enters it into the court's record system, which could be a civil docket, judgment roll or index, or separately maintained bench notes. 46 AM. JUR. 2d *Judgments* § 94 (2009). In Alabama, the judgment is deemed entered on the date that the clerk puts the judgment into the State Judicial Information System. ALA. R. CIV. P. 58(c). In Kansas, a judgment is effective when the clerk of the court files a journal entry or judgment form signed by the judge. KAN. STAT. ANN. § 60-258 (2008). Louisiana's Code of Civil Procedure states that the judgment must be signed by the judge and filed into the record before it is considered final, such that an appeal can be taken. LA. CODE CIV. PROC. ANN. art. 1911 (2008). Each of these approaches has the same effect as a separate document rule. Only when the judgment is "entered" on the docket or whatever the state specifies the verdict must be written into, will it become appealable. 46 AM. JUR. 2d *Judgments* § 94 (2009).

If you know the date a final judgment has been entered, you can also determine the date from which post-trial motion deadlines run. However, a lawyer's job goes beyond watching post-trial motion deadlines; she must also keep an eye on the deadline for filing a notice of appeal. What if you not only want to file a post-trial motion, such as a motion challenging the verdict or for new trial, but also a notice of appeal if necessary? Again, most states follow, if not the exact language of the Federal Rules of Civil Procedure and Federal Rule of Appellate Procedure 4, at least the principles underlying these rules. Federal Rule of Appellate Procedure 4, concerning the timing and requirements of a notice of appeal, provides that the timely filing of certain specified motions—including a motion for judgment notwithstanding the verdict and a motion for a new trial—automatically suspend the necessity to file a notice of appeal. 5 AM. JUR. 2d *Appellate Review* § 271 (2009); *see, e.g.*, MASS. R. APP. P. 4(a). Instead, the full time allotted for a notice of appeal (*e.g.*, 30 days) will run from the date of the order deciding post-trial motion(s). *See, e.g.*, KAN. STAT. ANN. § 60-2103 (2008). States that follow this approach may not state these principles in exactly the same manner as Federal Rule of Appellate Procedure 4. However, they achieve the same result—varying, of course, according to the state, both on the deadline for the filing of post-trial motions, and on the full time allotted for a notice of appeal to be filed. *See, e.g.*, MINN. R. CIV. APP. P. 104.01 (an appeal may be taken within 60 days of entry of judgment and if a timely post-trial motion was filed, and the time for appeal begins to run from the time parties are served with the notice of the filing of the order disposing of the last post-trial motion).

Lawyers should understand the interrelationship of their jurisdiction's rule or statute on appeal deadlines and the effect (or lack thereof) on post-trial motions. By so doing, lawyers can avoid missing post-judgment deadlines, especially an appeal deadline. Some states apply different deadlines within which post-trial motions must be filed (the Federal Rules' period had for many years been 10 days, but as of December 1, 2009, it became 28 days),[2] but some states shorten, or more often extend, the amount of time to file such motions. *See, e.g.*, COLO. R. CIV. P. 59 (party may move for post-trial relief within 15 days of entry of judgment). *But see* KY. R. CIV. P. 50.02 (post-trial motions must be filed not later than 10 days after the entry of judgment). Likewise, many states allow periods different from Federal Rule of Appellate Procedure 4 to file a notice of appeal (30 days under the Federal Rule, but as long as 60 days in some states). *See, e.g.*, LA. CODE CIV. PROC. ANN. art. 2088 (2008) (allowing 60 days to take an appeal); KAN. STAT. ANN. § 60-258 (2008) (providing 30 days to appeal from entry of judgment). Nevertheless, despite the variance among states concerning the amount of time to meet the post-trial motion deadline and the notice-of-appeal deadline, most states generally follow the principle that the filing of a post-trial motion suspends the time for a notice of appeal. 5 AM. JUR. 2d *Appellate Review* § 270 (2009). In these circumstances, the deadline for a notice of appeal would be "reset"—*i.e.*, it would run from the date of the court's order ruling on the post-trial motion. *See, e.g.*, KAN. STAT. ANN. § 60-258 (2008). If a post-trial motion is not timely filed, the deadline for filing

---

2. As part of a comprehensive set of changes to timing in the Federal Rules of Civil Procedure, renewed motions for judgment as a matter of law under Rule 50 (otherwise referred to as JNOV motions), and motions for a new trial under Rule 59, will no longer be 10 days, but rather will be 28 days from entry of judgment. *See* AMENDMENTS TO FED. R. CIV. P., *available at* http://www.uscourts.gov/rules/Supreme%20Court%202008/2008-CV-Clean_Rules.pdf (last visited Aug. 27, 2009).

an appeal is not tolled. 5 Am. Jur. 2d *Appellate Review* § 275 (2009). Therefore, if a party files a motion for a new trial one day late, the deadline for filing a notice of appeal will run from the date the judgment was entered. *Id.*

Before turning to those jurisdictions with more challenging post-trial procedural hurdles, counsel in the jurisdictions where post-trial motions automatically suspend the time for filing a notice of appeal should be aware of a major trap. Ten days is not a long period of time. Thus, as one might expect, plenty of lawyers have sought extensions on the ten-day deadline to file a motion to set aside the verdict or motion for a new trial. If the court grants such a motion, one may be pleased to have more time. However, beware the effect of the motion for extension of time to file post-trial motions (such as motion for judgment notwithstanding the verdict or motion for a new trial, which clearly suspend the appeal deadline). Many decisions have held that such a motion to extend post-trial deadlines does not extend the deadline for a notice of appeal. *See* Charles Alan Wright et al., Federal Practice & Procedure § 3905.4 (2009) (collecting cases considering such extension motions as motions for reconsideration, rather than a motion under Fed. R. Civ. P. 59, and thus not suspending the 30-day appeal deadline, which continued to run).

A few jurisdictions that do not follow the Federal Rules' approach present particularly dangerous traps of which counsel must be aware. Instead of having a post-trial motion automatically suspend the appeal deadline, the deadline for a notice of appeal continues to run in these states from the date the judgment is entered. 4 C.J.S. *Appeal and Error* § 371 (2009). With such jurisdictions, both the trial court and counsel can mistakenly believe that the appeal deadline has been suspended, when in fact it has not, by (a) a trial court's statement of willingness to entertain post-trial motions after entry of judgment or (b) filing of a post-trial motion. *See* N.M. Stat. Ann. § 12-503 (West 2009); Va. S. Ct. R. 1:1. In such jurisdictions, it is crucial for counsel to take *additional action* that is required under the state's rules of procedure in order to suspend the previous final judgment so that the court can timely entertain post-trial motions. N.M. Stat. Ann. § 12-503 (West 2009); Va. S. Ct. R. 1:1; 5:9. In New Mexico and Virginia, for instance, an attorney should have the trial court enter an order suspending or vacating the final judgment order, pending the resolution of post-trial motions. *Id.* In other words, neither state provides for automatic tolling of a time period for filing an appeal via filing of post-trial motions. N.M. Stat. Ann. § 12-503 (West 2009); Va. S. Ct. R. 1:1; 5:9. After final judgment is entered, a trial court loses jurisdiction in New Mexico after 30 days and, in Virginia, after 21 days. N.M. Stat. Ann. § 39-1-1 (West 2009); Va. S. Ct. R. 1:1. Because a party seeking to appeal has only 30 days in which to appeal in both states, the only way to ensure that the trial court can rule safely on post-trial motions is to (1) ensure the trial court withholds entry of final judgment, and (2) if the trial court has entered a final judgment, have a separate order vacate entry of final judgment pending its ruling on post-trial motions.

In states such as New Mexico and Virginia, both trial judges and lawyers regularly fail to take actions to have the trial court retain jurisdiction so that it can rule on post-trial motions. What then happens? As already suggested, a plaintiff who wants the verdict to stand will, upon entry of a final judgment, gladly allow the date to pass upon which the trial court loses jurisdiction. If the trial court continues and even grants a defendant's motion after such date, such an action will be void. In *Super Fresh Food Markets of Virginia, Inc. v. Ruffin*, 263 Va. 555, 561 S.E.2d 734 (2002), for instance, the court entered judgment on a jury verdict. Within a week after that, the court told counsel on a conference call that the court would entertain and rule on the defendant's post-trial motions, but never entered an order vacating the final judgment. Several months later, the judge denied the post-trial motions and defendant appealed within 30 days of the order denying the post-trial motions. Plaintiff moved to dismiss the appeal, and the court granted the motion on the ground that the defendant had not filed a notice of appeal within 30 days of the initial judgment order. All of the activity after that judgment had been a nullity because neither the trial court nor the defendant took the step of vacating the final judgment order.

In short, counsel in these scenarios commits malpractice because she (1) fails to recognize that her jurisdiction requires more than filing a post-trial motion for the trial court to retain jurisdiction and for the notice-of-appeal deadline to be suspended, and (2) fails to file a notice of appeal within the required deadline after entry of final judgment.

Louisiana presents yet another example of the kind of unique rules that can entrap the unwary lawyer. Final judgment has to be entered before appeal may be taken, and the deadline in which to timely file a notice of appeal is tolled upon the filing of post-trial motions. A party ordinarily has 60 days to "take an appeal" from the entry of the judgment. LA. CODE CIV. PROC. ANN. art. 2088 (2008). However, a motion for a new trial must be filed within 7 days of final judgment. *Id.* art. 1911. The 7-day deadline in which to file a motion for a new trial begins to run the day after either the clerk mails or the sheriff serves the notice of judgment. *Id.* art. 1974. Additionally, if a party timely files a post-trial motion, the time period for filing a notice of appeal begins to run when the trial court mails the denial of the motion. *Id.* art. 2088(A)(2). If no timely post-trial motion is filed, the time period begins to run the day after the clerk mails the notice of judgment. *Id.* art. 2088(A)(1).

As the above discussion should make clear, counsel should have a firm grasp on the rules in her jurisdiction for a trial court's entry of final judgment and for filing post-trial motions. A lawyer should give thanks if she practices in a jurisdiction where a post-trial motion automatically suspends the deadline for filing a notice of appeal. Nevertheless, she should be sure that the post-trial motion she files is one that clearly falls within the classification of motions that suspend the appeal deadline. If you are so unfortunate as to practice in a jurisdiction where filing a post-trial motion is not enough, you must determine the additional action necessary to vacate the final judgment so as to preserve the right to appeal.

Follow-Up Questions

1. Can a final judgment order be entered in a document that does not refer to itself as a "final judgment"?

2. What are the criteria in your jurisdiction for defining a final judgment? Why is it important for you to know these criteria?

3. If you are confident a final judgment has been entered, and you are in a jurisdiction in which the clock for filing a notice of appeal will automatically be suspended upon filing a motion for judgment notwithstanding the verdict, a motion for a new trial, or both, what is the deadline by which you must file such a motion?

4. If you are in a jurisdiction that does not follow the Federal Rules model, and in which the trial court loses jurisdiction a certain amount of time after a final judgment, what order would you need to present to the court, and in what time frame, so as to ensure both the opportunity to have the trial court entertain post-trial motions and, afterward, to appeal?

Professional Identity Question

Suppose the jury renders a verdict against your client and the court enters a final judgment. You advise your client that you see no winning arguments on which to file a motion for judgment notwithstanding the verdict or for a new trial. If your client asks you to file a motion anyway to "buy time," would you do so? Would you require at least some basis supporting an argument for a new trial (*e.g.*, erroneous ruling on evidence) to file the motion?

Practice Problems

Practice Problem 12-1

Betty Bade sues Gas-Em-Up, Inc., a natural gas company, after an accident involving one of its trucks driven by Fearless Freddy. During the trial, Gas-Em-Up moves for a directed verdict on the ground that Betty failed to put on sufficient evidence that Fearless Freddy was acting within the scope of his employment at the time of the accident, a prerequisite for recovery against it under principles of vicarious liability. The jury returned a verdict for Betty and the judge entered, on April 1, a short order in the court's file noting the jury's verdict, the date, and that he took the verdict and dismissed the jurors. If Gas-Em-Up wants to move for judgment notwithstanding the verdict, by what date must it file its motion? In your jurisdiction, would that suspend the deadline for filing a notice of appeal until the court ruled on the motion?

Practice Problem 12-2

On March 2, after a jury verdict, the court entered a judgment for Paul Plaintiff against Defendant Dan in the amount of $85,700. On March 16 the highest court in the jurisdiction handed down an opinion. Defendant Dan's counsel read this opinion as supporting his view that the trial court erred in admitting certain evidence offered by the plaintiff—evidence that was essential to support the judgment of March 2. The opinion came to the attention of Ms. Justice in the late afternoon of March 12. Dan Defendant's counsel, after unsuccessfully attempting to contact the plaintiff's attorney, met with the trial court, explained the problem, and asked for leave to file a motion for a new trial. The trial court entered the following order on March 12:

"For good cause shown, it is hereby ORDERED that the time by which Defendant Dan may file a motion based on the recent opinion on admissibility of the disputed evidence is hereby extended to and including March 22."

Defendant Dan, by his attorney Ms. Justice, filed such a motion, giving notice to the attorney for the plaintiff and after a hearing thereon, the trial court entered an order on April 10 vacating the judgment of March 2, and granting the defendant a new trial. After a new trial on the merits, the trial court, again sitting without a jury, entered judgment for Defendant Dan. Paul Plaintiff filed a notice of appeal, his sole argument being that the trial court was without authority to enter the orders of March 12 and April 10. He asked the appellate court to reinstate the order of March 2, which had granted him judgment. How should the appellate court rule? Explain your answer fully.

Motions for Judgment Notwithstanding the Verdict or, Alternatively, for a New Trial

Motions for Judgment Notwithstanding the Verdict

To understand a motion for judgment notwithstanding the verdict (JNOV), one needs to recall the procedures and standards for directed verdicts discussed in Chapter 11 on pages 256–57. Although the timing of a JNOV motion differs from a directed verdict motion, the standard applied by the court is the same. As explained in Chapter 11, a party may move for a directed verdict at any time before a case is surrendered to the jury for deliberation. 75A Am. Jur. 2d *Trial* § 809 (2009). For sake of terminology, states differ in what they call this motion. Some call it a directed verdict, a motion for judgment on the evidence, or an instructed verdict. *Id.*; *see* Tex. R. Civ. P. 268. A motion for a directed verdict challenges the legal sufficiency of the evidence. 75A Am. Jur. 2d *Trial* § 782 (2009). If, after all of the evidence has been presented at trial, the court determines that there is insufficient evidence on a material issue such that reasonable jurors could not disagree, then the court may take the case from the jury and enter judgment accordingly. *Id.*; Appendix 11-1 (majority of states have such motions).

Most states have statutes or rules of court that closely follow Federal Rule of Civil Procedure 50 concerning entry of a JNOV. Appendix 12-2 (majority of states have motions for JNOV, governed by the same standard as Fed. R. Civ. P. 50); 46 Am. Jur. 2d *Judgments* § 307 (2009); *see, e.g.*, Ala. R. Civ. P. 50. A party may move for JNOV after the jury returns a verdict and ask the court to set aside the verdict. The court may vacate the jury verdict if the court finds that there was insufficient evidence to support the verdict. 46 Am. Jur. 2d *Judgments* § 309 (2009).

A motion for JNOV is simply a renewed motion for a directed verdict. *Id.* § 308. It is governed by the same rules as those of a directed verdict because it raises the same issue regarding the sufficiency of the evidence. *Id.* As such, most jurisdictions require, as a prerequisite for a JNOV motion, that a party has moved for a directed verdict during trial. *Id.* § 88; *see, e.g.*, Ky. R. Civ. P. 50.02. When a party moves for JNOV, she asks the court to set aside the jury's verdict and enter judgment in her favor consistent with her motion for a directed verdict. 46 Am. Jur. 2d *Judgments* § 317. If the trial judge enters a JNOV, she is essentially saying that she has reconsidered the prior motion for a directed verdict and realizes she should have granted that motion before the verdict. *Id.* In a minority of states, a defendant must move for a directed verdict both at the close of the plaintiff's case *and* at the close of all of the evidence in order for the court to consider a motion for JNOV. *See, e.g.*, W. Va. R. Civ. P. 50(b). In such states, if the party so preserves the opportunity for a JNOV, and the trial judge grants it, she is still effectively saying that she should have granted the directed verdict at least by the end of the trial and before verdict.

The Federal Rules of Civil Procedure, and those states that have modeled their rules on the Federal Rules, provide that a motion for a JNOV must be made within 10 days[3]

---

3. As part of a comprehensive set of changes to timing in the Federal Rules of Civil Procedure, renewed motions for judgment as a matter of law under Rule 50 (formerly referred to as "JNOV motions" in federal practice), and motions for a new trial under Rule 59, will no longer be 10 days, but rather will be 28 days from entry of judgment. *See* Amendments To Fed. R. Civ. P., *available at* http://www.uscourts.gov/rules/Supreme%20Court%202008/2008-CV-Clean_Rules.pdf (last visited Aug. 27, 2009).

after entry of judgment. Appendix 12-2 (states follow JNOV with some variety of deadlines after trial, but same standard as Fed. R. Civ. P. 50); *see, e.g.*, Ky. R. Civ. P. 50.02. Even in states that do not replicate the Federal Rules of Civil Procedure, their approach to requiring a JNOV motion mirrors the Federal Rules—*i.e.*, they require the motion to be filed within a specified number of days from the entry of a judgment. *See, e.g.*, Ala. R. Civ. P. 50 (requiring that the motion be made within 30 days of the entry of judgment). An attorney must carefully follow the procedural rule of the forum state and move for JNOV within the prescribed time period after the jury returns a verdict. *See* E. H. Schopler, *Practice and Procedure with Respect to Motions for Judgment Notwithstanding or in Default of Verdict under Federal Civil Procedure Rule 50(b) or Like State Provisions*, 69 A.L.R. 2d 449 (1960).

Follow-Up Questions

1. What is the deadline in your jurisdiction for filing a motion for JNOV?

2. What are the instances in which a motion for JNOV is most likely to be successful?

3. If the judge denied a directed verdict motion during trial, and/or a renewed directed verdict motion at the close of the trial, should you take that as a signal on how the court will rule on a motion for JNOV? Why or why not?

4. If you are making a motion for JNOV, what are the kinds of arguments most likely to persuade a judge that reasonable jurors could not disagree over an element of a claim?

5. If you are opposing a motion for JNOV, what arguments are most likely to convince the court to let the jury verdict stand?

Practice Problem

Practice Problem 12-3

Pete Plaintiff worked the night shift as a plant operator for an asphalt company. To make the asphalt, a large wheel loader went up a gradual incline to some bins in which it dumped materials that were then mixed and, when ready, were picked up by a front-end loader to be loaded on trucks. One night Pete went up to the top of the bins for some reason—perhaps to check something—although he cannot recall what he was going to check. He was later found three quarters of the way down the ramp with one leg missing. He cannot recall anything other than a vague memory of going down the ramp. The front-end loader operator could not recall anything other than the loader slowing down on one trip down the incline. The plant owner did find a piece of Pete's pants in the loader's wheel. Pete sued the front-end loader manufacturer on the basis that the loader was defectively designed because the lighting on the loader did not cast a broad enough area of light so as to allow the operator to see someone and stop before running over the person. Pete offered expert testimony that broader lighting was both possible and desirable to avoid accidents. The manufacturer challenged the reliability of the experts, the scientific basis for their opinions, and particularly their conclusion that in this case the alleged defect had caused the injuries to Pete when no evidence showed exactly what had happened. The judge denied the defendant's motion for directed verdict at the close of the plaintiff's case in chief and again at the close of all of the evidence. When the jury returned a verdict for plaintiff for $15 million, the defendant filed a motion for JNOV or, alternatively, for a new trial. Can the judge reconsider his decision to allow the expert testimony during trial? Can the judge, notwithstanding the prior denials of the directed verdict motions, grant a JNOV motion here? Should she?

Motions for New Trial

Even when there is sufficient evidence to support a verdict, the court may disagree with the jury's decision and believe it is against the great weight of the evidence. 58 AM. JUR. 2d *New Trial* § 294 (2009). A verdict is against the great weight of the evidence when it is not substantiated or supported by the evidence. *Id.* The standard for measuring whether a verdict is against the great weight of the evidence is whether a group of reasonable jurors could have arrived at the same decision. *Id.* § 297. All jurisdictions permit a motion for a new trial, GENE R. SHREVE & PETER RAVEN-HANSEN, UNDERSTANDING CIVIL PROCEDURE § 12.09(2)(a) (4th ed. 2009), but they also tend to restrict its availability to a short period—only 10 days in jurisdictions that follow federal court rule FED. R. CIV. P. 59(b),[4] but as long as 30 in other jurisdictions. *See, e.g.*, ALA. R. CIV. P. 59(b); TEX. R. CIV. P. 329(a). When ruling on a motion for a new trial, a court can consider the credibility of the witnesses, the weight of the evidence, and other criteria that are forbidden to be considered on a motion for summary judgment, motion for directed verdict, or JNOV motion. The power of the court to order a new trial is not unconstitutional. Rather, the court's ability to order a new trial ensures that party's right to a fair jury trial is protected. 58 AM. JUR. 2d *New Trial* § 8 (2009).

In addition to a verdict being against the great weight of the evidence, the trial court can grant a new trial on other grounds. If the court believes an error occurred that is serious enough to affect the verdict, a new trial is the appropriate remedy. 58 AM. JUR. 2d *New Trial* § 61 (2009). Some states' rules list the grounds for a new trial. *Id.* § 64; *see, e.g.*, COLO. R. CIV. P. 59(d), MINN. R. CIV. P. 59.01. However, FED. R. CIV. P. 59(b) and most states' rules permit a new trial for any reason that it might have been granted in the past at common law. Appendix 12-3 (showing most states have a version of the new trial rule such as Fed. R. Civ. P. 59); *see, e.g.*, ALA. R. CIV. P. 59(a). Any of the bases for granting a mistrial, including those discussed in Chapter 11, would also constitute grounds for granting a new trial. In other words, the granting of a new trial generally falls into one of two categories. First, if the trial judge believes the verdict is against the great weight of the evidence, the trial court can, rather than entering judgment as a matter of law, take the less intrusive approach of ordering a new trial—a new trial that will occur before a different jury but still honor the notion that factual disputes should be typi-

---

4. As part of a comprehensive set of changes to timing in the Federal Rules of Civil Procedure, renewed motions for judgment as a matter of law under Rule 50 (otherwise referred to as JNOV motions), and motions for a new trial under Rule 59, will no longer be 10 days, but rather will be 28 days from entry of judgment. *See* AMENDMENTS TO FED. R. CIV. P., *available at* http://www.uscourts.gov/rules/Supreme%20Court%202008/2008-CV-Clean_Rules.pdf (last visited Aug. 27, 2009). It remains to be seen whether states that have modeled their rules on the Federal Rules will follow the change in timing being implemented by these federal amendments.

cally resolved by juries, not judges. 58 Am. Jur. 2d *New Trial* § 262 (2009). Second, a trial judge should grant a new trial if she believes there was an error in the trial process — whether the error included events that could have led to a mistrial, admission of inadmissible evidence, giving a jury instruction that was erroneous, or failure of the jury to follow the judge's instructions. *Id.* §§ 284, 292. In many instances, an objection or argument that counsel made during trial to a perceived error may have been overruled, but when the trial judge has more time to consider the matter, she can grant a new trial even though she had previously ruled against the moving party. Again, however, it bears repeating: when a judge grants a new trial, she does not determine who wins — that will be left up to a jury, which will be a *new* jury. *See* Jack H. Friedenthal, Mary Jay Kane & Arthur R. Miller, Civil Procedure § 12.4, at 594 (West 4th ed. 1999) (thus, the litigant is not deprived of a jury; in fact, he is afforded "too much jury trial, not too little.").

If, after the jury returns the verdict (and upon a proper motion for a new trial), the judge believes that the verdict in favor of a party should be increased, the judge may order a reduction in the damages award (called "additur") to the parties. *See* 58 Am. Jur. 2d *New Trial* § 459 (2009); *see, e.g.,* Ten. Code Ann. § 20-10-101(a)(1) (West 2009). If the defendant still refuses to pay the reduced amount, or the plaintiff still considers the verdict inadequate, the judge may award a new trial. *See, e.g.,* Tenn. Code Ann. § 20-10-101(a)(2) (West 2009). Conversely, the judge may order a reduction of a jury award, called a "remittitur." 58 Am. Jur. 2d *New Trial* § 451 (2009). Remittitur should be used when the verdict is so excessive that it shocks the conscience of the court. *Id.* § 272. If either the party against whom the verdict was rendered or the party for whom the jury returned a favorable verdict disagrees with the remittitur, the alternative is to proceed to a new trial. 66 C.J.S. *New Trial* § 271 (2009); *see, e.g.,* Tenn. Code Ann. § 20-10-101 (West 2009); Vt. R. Civ. P. 59. Ideally, addittur and remittitur should be used sparingly because their primary purpose is to avoid the expense of a new trial. 66 C.J.S. *New Trial* § 271 (2009). However, in reality, judges use remittitur frequently.

Remittitur often puts parties in positions in which they must make difficult decisions as to whether to reject or take a reduced verdict. If the defendant rejects the reduced amount, the new trial may produce a larger verdict in which the court does not remit as much. If the plaintiff rejects the remittitur, she may have a new trial and recover less than the first trial. Additionally, a plaintiff's acceptance of a reduced award of damages usually serves as a waiver of the plaintiff's right to appeal the amount of damages. 5 Am. Jur. 2d *Appellate Review* § 593 (2009). In either case, a new trial will add time and expense for both parties.

In a minority of jurisdictions, parties may appeal an additur or remittitur decision, thus removing some of their difficulty in deciding how to deal with the decision. *See, e.g.,* Va. Code Ann. § 8.01-383.1 (2009). In these cases, however, the appellate route typically requires a party to accept the additur/remittitur decision "under protest" and then file a notice of appeal. *Id.* Then, the appellate court may review the issue of the amount of damages and rule on the trial court's judgment. *See, e.g.,* Vt. R. Civ. P. 59(a) ("A party may accept a remission of a portion of the damages awarded, or an addition to the verdict, conditioned on the outcome of an appeal from the decision of the court that the damages were excessive or inadequate."). Indeed, the appellate court has the power to change the amount of the additur decision or the remittitur decision on its own in these circumstances and to enter judgment according to its decision. 5 Am. Jur. 2d *Appellate Review* § 789 (2009).

In *Dimick v. Schiedt*, 293 U.S. 474 (1935), the U.S. Supreme Court held that in federal court cases additur is unconstitutional and infringes on the right to trial by jury. The Seventh Amendment provides in pertinent part, "[T]he right of trial by jury shall be preserved, and no fact tried by a jury shall be otherwise re-examined in any Court of the United States." U.S. Const. amend. VII. The words "shall not be re-examined" prohibit a judge from changing the amount of damages in a jury verdict. Therefore, in federal court, additur is unconstitutional. Remittitur, however, is still allowed in the federal system. 66 C.J.S. *New Trial* § 271 (2009). The Court has held that remittitur is constitutional because, procedurally, the plaintiff is always given the choice of whether to accept the reduced amount of damages, or to be given a new trial. *See* Charles Alan Wright et al., 11 Federal Practice & Procedure—Civil 2d § 2815 (2009). Therefore, the plaintiff's right to a jury trial is not disrupted by the use of remittitur.

Most states permit additur and remittitur, but these states do not have a phrase in their constitutions prohibiting re-examination of the decision that is reached by a jury. *See, e.g.*, Cal. Const. art. 1 § 16 (amended 1998). Oregon and West Virginia do not permit remittitur or additur at all, but these states have clauses in their constitutions that mirror the clause in the Seventh Amendment. *See* Or. Const. art. VII, § 3 ("The right of trial by jury shall be preserved, and no fact tried by a jury shall be otherwise re-examined in any court of this state."); W. Va. Const. art. 3-13 ("No fact tried by a jury shall be otherwise reexamined in any case than according to the rule of court or law.").

Follow-Up Questions

1. Is a new trial motion easier for a trial judge to grant than a JNOV motion? Why or why not?

2. What can a trial judge consider on a new trial motion that she cannot on a JNOV motion?

3. How can one put "meat" on the somewhat slippery standard for a new trial if it is "against the great weight of the evidence"? An argument is more likely to persuade the judge if it focuses on specifics of *how* a verdict is against the great weight of the evidence rather than general arguments. How can you be specific? If you are the defendant and the plaintiff has several elements to her claim, each of which must be proved, might you choose the one or two elements where you see the greatest chance of success?

Professional Identity Question

What if the trial is not going as well as you or your client had hoped? Indeed, say that you realize you need an expert to contradict the opposing party's expert but did not retain one. Your client, who has not yet testified, tells you she wants a mistrial so that she will have a second chance. She asks you what she can do when she is on the stand—without getting you into trouble—that would require the court to declare a mistrial and, thus, a new trial. How would you respond?

Practice Problems

Practice Problem 12-4

Wyatt Earp brought action against Clampett Van Lines, Inc. in a court of general jurisdiction to recover damages in the sum of $500,000 for serious injuries sustained by plaintiff when his car was involved in an accident with the defendant's van. At the close of evidence and instructions from the court, counsel proceeds with closing arguments. In the course of her argument, plaintiff's counsel says to the jury: "All Wyatt Earp asks members of the jury to do is, when you retire to your jury room, to apply the Golden Rule: Do unto others as you wish others would do to you and award an amount you would want." Defense counsel promptly objected to that part of the closing argument and, when the judge called counsel up to the bench, defense counsel moved for a mistrial or at least an instruction to the jury to disregard the argument. The court denied the motion for a mistrial and, alternatively, for a curative instruction. The jury returned a verdict for the plaintiff in the sum of $150,000. Shortly thereafter, defense counsel moved for a JNOV or, alternatively, for a new trial. In support, counsel argued that the court should have granted a mistrial or at the least a cautionary instruction. The trial court denied all post-trial motions. Defendant appealed. The only error argued was the trial court's failure to grant a mistrial or a cautionary instruction. How should the appellate court rule?

Practice Problem 12-5

The jurisdiction in question permits recovery for intentional infliction of emotional distress so long as the plaintiff exhibits physical symptoms corroborating the emotional distress. Jerry Joker tells Pam Plaintiff that Pam's husband, Harry Husband, has been in an accident and is seriously injured. In fact, Harry is fine, and Jerry was playing a practical joke on Pam. However, Jerry does not inform Pam he is joking for a couple of hours. Pam believes Jerry and becomes ill, throwing up and having a severe depressive episode. Once Harry returns home, and Pam sees that he is in fact fine, she improves.

Pam brings suit against Jerry for intentional infliction of emotional distress. The applicable jurisdiction requires, as elements of the tort, intentional conduct that is outrageous in the extreme that causes severe emotional distress. Pam's proof of actual medical expenses were limited (a discussion with a psychiatrist the day of the accident and a temporary supply of a medication that helps offset depression and anxiety). Her expenses were the one doctor visit and the prescription. She missed no work as a result of Jerry's conduct. The jury finds for Pam and awards her $1 million in compensatory damages and $5 million in punitive damages.

Jerry timely brings a JMOL motion and, alternatively, a motion for a new trial. The trial judge issues a decision finding that the jury's verdict on damages was so excessive that it shocks the conscience of the court. The court exercised remittitur on both the compensatory and punitive damages. The court determined that the most that could be awarded for compensatory damages, accounting for intangibles such as pain and suffering, was $5,000. The court further determined that a punitive award had to be in proportion to the amount of compensatory damages such that it was not so great as to violate principles of due process and, thus, reduced the punitive damages award to $50,000. In its decision, the court held that if the plaintiff did not agree to the remitted awards, then a new trial would be necessary, limited to the issue of damages. If you were advising Pam as her counsel, what would you recommend?

Motions for Relief from Judgment for Extraordinary Reasons

If a party fails to make a timely motion for JNOV, or timely motion for a new trial, she may seek extraordinary relief in the form of a motion to set aside judgment after the verdict has been rendered. GENE R. SHREVE & PETER RAVEN-HANSEN, UNDERSTANDING CIVIL PROCEDURE § 12.11(2)(b) (4th ed. 1999). Most jurisdictions permit such a motion. Appendix 12-4. These motions fall into two categories. The first category includes relief from a judgment for a variety of reasons revolving around the inability of the defendant to have responded to the suit, such as surprise or excusable neglect. *Id.* For example, a party may show that it was not aware of the suit or that the party was not represented by counsel. *See id.*; *see also* CHARLES ALAN WRIGHT ET AL., FEDERAL PRACTICE & PROCEDURE § 2858 (2009). Second, where the party against whom the judgment was entered can show fraud in a party's obtaining the judgment, the void nature of the judgment, or similar scenarios where enforcement of the judgment would be unjust, a party can obtain relief. *See* GENE R. SHREVE & PETER RAVEN-HANSEN, UNDERSTANDING CIVIL PROCEDURE § 12.11(2)(b) (4th ed. 2009); *see also* CHARLES ALAN WRIGHT ET AL., FEDERAL PRACTICE & PROCEDURE § 2864 (2009).

Motions such as those described above are similar to motions under Federal Rule of Civil Procedure 60. Like the fate of most Rule 60 motions, motions such as these in state court are difficult to win. *See, e.g.*, SHREVE, § 12.11(2)(b) ("It is not easy to obtain relief under [Federal Rule of Civil Procedure 60]...."). In state courts, parties will have the same level of difficulty. In Texas, for instance, the applicable rule of procedure provides that a judgment cannot be set aside "except by bill of review for sufficient cause," another way of saying that the relief will be difficult to obtain. TEX. R. CIV. P. 329(f).

Follow-Up Questions

If motions other than those one can bring shortly after judgment (*e.g.*, motion for JNOV or new trial motion), such as those discussed above, are so difficult to obtain, why do jurisdictions allow for these motions? What policy reasons support such a "safety net"?

Professional Identity Question

Assume you represent a nonresident corporation as a defendant. The defendant asks you to move to set aside a jury verdict. The request is made after the deadline for motions for JNOV or new trials (*i.e.*, for extraordinary causes, such as for surprise or excusable neglect). The defendant told you that it had not received any notice and to move for relief on that basis. However you check the court's file and find a return of service showing personal service on the president of the corporate defendant. How would you handle this situation? Would you show the return to the client before filing? Would you file the motion regardless of the client's response, based on the rationale that the president of the company is likely busy and may have misplaced the process?

Practice Problem

Practice Problem 12-6

A plaintiff is injured by a product that has "ACME" stamped on it. You mistakenly believe the defendant is ACME, Inc. in California, file suit against that company, and serve that defendant through the secretary of state. The defendant does not respond and judgment is entered. Actually, the product is not made by ACME, Inc., but rather is made by ACME Corp. in Minnesota. The defendant files a motion, more than 10 days after judgment, asserting surprise and excusable neglect because when it received the process it knew that it did not make any such products, called the plaintiff and left a message on his answering machine to that effect, and assumed the case had been dropped. ACME, Inc. argues in its motion that it would be unjust to enforce a judgment against a company that does not even make the product over which the plaintiff sued, especially in light of its alerting the plaintiff by the telephone message. Should the court grant relief from the judgment in these circumstances?

D. Methods to Reinforce and Integrate Topics Covered in This Chapter

Draw a timeline beginning with the entry of final judgment as a succeeding point, followed by the deadlines in your jurisdiction for post-trial motions.

Entry of Final Judgment	Post-Trial Motions
_____	_____
_____	_____
_____	_____
_____	_____

In the blank lines provided under "Entry of Final Judgment," list the criteria that courts in your jurisdiction consider determinative of when a final judgment has been entered, even if it is not labeled as such (*e.g.*, grants all relief requested, does not mention retaining jurisdiction). In the blanks under the box labeled "Post-Trial Motions," list the key motions that a party in your jurisdiction can make after entry of final judgment, such as a JNOV motion or motion for new trial, and the deadlines for these.

Finally note the following: (1) what the time period is for an appeal; (2) whether it is suspended by filing post-trial motions; and (3) what kind of post-trial motions must be filed to achieve suspension of the clearly suspend the appeal deadline.

E. Written Assignments

1. Write an argument for the City of Arcadia and HorsePower, Inc. seeking remit-titur of the compensatory damages awards against them and, in the case of Ar-cadia, arguing for remittitur of the punitive damages award.

2. Write an argument for Sally opposing the arguments you made for the City and for HorsePower, Inc. and seeking to maintain both the compensatory and the puni-tive damages award.

Appendices

Table of Contents

Appendix 2-1
Rule for Calculation of Time

Majority Approach	*Minority Approach*	*Nonconforming States*
Alabama		
Alaska		
Arizona		
Arkansas		
California		
Connecticut		
Colorado		
Delaware		
District of Columbia		
Florida		
Georgia		
Hawaii		
Idaho		
Illinois		
Indiana		
Iowa		
Kansas		
Kentucky		
Louisiana		
Maine		
Maryland		
Massachusetts		
Michigan		
Minnesota		
Mississippi		
Missouri		
Montana		
Nebraska		
Nevada		
New Hampshire		
New Jersey		
New Mexico		
New York		
North Carolina		
North Dakota		
Ohio		
Oklahoma		
Oregon		
Pennsylvania		
Rhode Island		
South Carolin		
South Dakota		
Tennessee		
Texas		
Utah		
Vermont		
Virginia		
Washington		
West Virginia		
Wisconsin		
Wyoming		

The overwhelming majority of states follow the same approach to calculating deadlines as is stated in Federal Rule of Civil Procedure 6. Thus, for instance, when a deadline is stated in terms of days, the approach followed is to start counting the deadline on the day after the event specified. For instance, if a notice of appeal must be filed 30 days after final judgment, the date of the final judgment is not counted; rather the day after final judgment is Day 1. Counting in this fashion to 30 days after the judgment, one can determine one's deadline. Moreover, all states allow for the deadline to carry over if the last day of a calculated deadline falls on a weekend or holiday recognized statutorily in that state. Because holidays vary from state to state, the practitioner would need to determine which holidays apply.

Appendix 3-1
Long Arm Statutes[1]

"To the Limits" of Due Process Statutes or Rules	*Enumerated Acts Statutes or Rules with a "Catch All" Provision*	*"True" Enumerated Acts Statutes or Rules*
ARIZONA *See* ARIZ. R. CIV. P. 4.2 (2003)	ALABAMA *See* ALA. R. CIV. P. 4.2(b)	ALASKA[2] *See* ALASKA STAT. § 09.05.015(c) (2009)
ARKANSAS *See* ARK. CODE ANN. 16-4-101 (2009)	ILLINOIS *See* 735 ILL. COMP. STAT. ANN. 5/2-209(c) (LexisNexis 2009)	COLORADO *See* COLO. REV. STAT. 13-1-124 (2009); *Safari Outfitters v.* *Superior Ct.*, 448 P.2d 783, 784 (Colo. 1968)
CALIFORNIA *See* CAL. CIV. PROC. CODE 410.10 (Deering 2009)	INDIANA *See* IND. R. TRIAL P. 4.4(A)(8)	CONNECTICUT *See* CONN. GEN. STAT. 52-59b (2008); *Knipple v. Viking* *Communications*, 674 A.2d 426, 428–29 (Conn. 1996).
IOWA *See* IOWA R. CIV. P. 1.306	KANSAS *See* KAN. STAT. ANN. § 60-308 (2008); *Woodring v. Hall*, 438 P.2d 135, 141 (Kan. 1968) (interpreting Kansas Long-Arm to extend to limits of due process)	DELAWARE *See* DEL. CODE ANN. tit. 10, § 3104 (2009); *Hercules, Inc. v.* *Leu Trust & Banking*, 611 A.2d 476, 480 (Del. 1992)
NEVADA *See* NEV. REV. STAT. ANN. § 14.065 (LexisNexis 2009)	LOUISIANA *See* LA. REV. STAT. ANN. § 13:3201 (2009); *Drilling Eng'g,* *Inc. v. Indep. Indonesian Am.* *Petroleum Co.*, 283 So. 2d 687, 689 (La. 1973)	DISTRICT OF COLUMBIA *See* D.C. Code § 13-423 (2003)
NEW JERSEY *See* N.J. CT. R. 4:4-4	MAINE *See* ME. REV. STAT. ANN. tit. 14, § 704-A(2)(I) (2009)	FLORIDA *See* FLA. STAT. ANN. § 48.193 (2009); *Garrett v. Garrett*, 668 So. 2d 991, 993–94 (Fla. 1996)
OKLAHOMA *See* 12 OKLA. STAT. § 2004(F) (2009)	NEBRASKA *See* NEB. REV. STAT. ANN. § 25-536 (LexisNexis 2009)	GEORGIA *See* GA. CODE ANN. § 9-10-91 (2009); *ETS Payphone, Inc. v.* *TK Indus.*, 513 S.E.2d 257, 258 (Ga. 1999)

---

1. For an excellent analysis of variations among state long arm statutes, see Douglas M. McFarland, *Dictum Run Wild: How Long-Arm Statutes Extended to the Limits of Due Process*, 84 B.U.L. RCV. 401 (2004). Although this Appendix does not classify many states in the same fashion as in Dean McFarland's article, his analysis offered insights into the difference among states' long arm statutes. Moreover, his article's having been written over six years ago likely accounts for differences between our classifications. Nevertheless, one would benefit from reading his article while researching one's state to reach one's own judgment, at present, as to what kind of long arm statute one's state has adopted by legislation, by rule, and/or by judicial interpretation of these.

2. The law of Alaska, antedating this section, subjected foreign corporations to Alaska process to "the outer limits of the due process clause of the federal constitution." This section cannot be broader than that, and it is not seriously contended that this section is narrower. Jones Enters., Inc. v. Atlas Serv. Corp., 442 F.2d 1136 (9th Cir. 1971). Since this section has been construed by the Alaska Supreme Court to establish jurisdiction to the maximum extent permitted by due process, federal court needs only consider whether asserting jurisdiction over the defendant would violate the Due Process Clause of the Fourteenth Amendment. Insurance Co. of N. Am. v. Marina Salina Cruz, 649 F.2d 1266 (9th Cir. 1981).

RHODE ISLAND
See R.I. Gen. Laws
§ 9-5-33(a) (2009).

UTAH
See Utah Code Ann.
§ 78B-3-201 (2009)

VERMONT
See Vt. Stat. Ann. tit. 12,
§ 913 (2009)

WYOMING
See Wyo. Stat. Ann.
§ 5-1-107(a) (2009)

OREGON
See Ore. R. Civ. P. 4(L)

PENNSYLVANIA
See 42 Pa. Cons. Stat.
5322 (2009)

SOUTH DAKOTA
See S.D. Codified Laws
§ 15-7-2 (2009)

TENNESSEE
See Tenn. Code Ann.
§ 20-2-214(a) (2009)

HAWAII
See Haw. Rev. Stat. § 634-35
(2009); *Shaw v. N. Am. Title Co.*,
876 P.2d 1291, 1295–96
(Haw. 1994)

IDAHO
See Idaho Code Ann. § 5-514
(Michie 2009); *Beco Corp. v.
Roberts & Sons Constr. Co.*, 760
P.2d 1120, 1123 (Idaho 1988).

KENTUCKY
See Ky. Rev. Stat. Ann.
§ 454.210 (2009); *Franklin
Roofing v. Eagle Roofing &
Sheet Metal*, 61 S.W.3d 239,
241 (Ky. Ct. App. 2001)

MARYLAND
See Md. Code Ann., Cts. &
Jud. Proc. § 6-103
(LexisNexis 2009); *Geelhoed
v. Jensen*, 352 A.2d 818,
821 (Md. 1976)

MASSACHUSETTS
See Mass. Ann. Laws.
ch. 223A, § 3 (LexisNexis 2009);
*Good Hope Indus., Inc.
v. Ryder Scott Co.*, 389
N.E.2d 76, 79 (Mass. 1979)

MICHIGAN
See Mich. Comp. Laws Serv.
§ 600.705 (LexisNexis 2009);
Green v. Wilson, 565 N.W.2d
813, 815 (Mich. 1997).

MINNESOTA
See Minn. Stat. § 543.19 (2008)

MISSISSIPPI
See Miss. Code Ann.
§ 13-3-57 (2009); *Wilkinson v.
Mercantile Nat'l Bank*, 529 So.
2d 616, 618–19 (Miss. 1988)

MISSOURI
See Mo. Rev. Stat.
§ 506.500 (2009); *Chromalloy
Am. Corp. v. Elyria Foundry Co.*,
955 S.W.2d 1, 4 (Mo. 1997)

MONTANA
See Mont. R. Civ. P. 4B;
Petrik v. Colby, 730 P.2d 1167,
1167–68 (Mont. 1986)

NEW HAMPSHIRE
See N.H. Rev. Stat. Ann.
§ 510:4 (LexisNexis 2009);
*Roy v. N. Am. Newspaper
Alliance, Inc.*, 205 A.2d 844,
845 (N.H. 1964)

NEW MEXICO

See N.M. Stat. Ann.
§ 38-1-16 (LexisNexis 2009);
Sanchez v. Church of Scientology,
857 P.2d 771, 773 (N.M. 1993)

NEW YORK

See N.Y. C.P.L.R. 302
(Consol. 2009); *Ingraham v.
Carroll*, 687 N.E.2d 1293,
1294–95 (N.Y. 1997)

NORTH CAROLINA

See N.C. Gen. Stat.
§ 1-75.4 (2009); *Tom Togs, Inc.
v. Ben Elias Indus. Corp.*, 348
S.E.2d 782, 785–86 (N.C. 1986)

NORTH DAKOTA

See N.D. R. Civ. P. 4;
*Hebron Brick Co. v. Robinson
Brick & Tile Co.*, 234 N.W.2d
250, 255–56 (N.D. 1975).

OHIO

See Ohio Rev. Code Ann.
§ 2307.382 (LexisNexis 2009);
Ohio R. Civ. P. 4.3; *Goldstein v.
Christiansen*, 638 N.E.2d 541,
545 n.1 (Ohio 1994)

SOUTH CAROLINA

See S.C. Code Ann.
§ 36-2-803 (2008); *Triplett v.
R.M. Wade & Co.*, 200
S.E.2d 375, 376 (S.C. 1973)

TEXAS

See Tex. Civ. Prac. & Rem.
Code Ann. § 17.042 (2009);
*BMC Software Belg., N.V. v.
Marchand*, 83 S.W.3d 789,
795 (Tex. 2002)

VIRGINIA

See Va. Code Ann. § 8.01-328.1
(2009); *Carmichael v. Snyder*,
164 S.E.2d 703, 707 (Va. 1968)

WASHINGTON

See Wash. Rev. Code Ann.
§ 4.28.185 (LexisNexis 2009);
*Tyee Constr. Co. v. Dulien
Steel Prods., Inc.*, 381 P.2d
245, 247 (Wash. 1963)

WEST VIRGINIA

See W. Va. Code Ann.
§ 56-3-33 (LexisNexis 2009);
*Abbott v. Owens-Corning
Fiberglas Corp.*, 444 S.E.2d
285, 292–93 (W. Va. 1994)

WISCONSIN

See Wis. Stat. § 801.05 (2009)

Appendix 4-1
Standard for Pleading

Majority Approach	*Minority Approach*	*Nonconforming States*
Alabama	Arkansas	New Hampshire
Alaska	California	Wisconsin
Arizona	Connecticut	
Colorado	Louisiana	
Delaware	Maryland	
District of Columbia	Michigan	
Florida	Missouri	
Georgia	Oregon	
Hawaii	Pennsylvania	
Idaho		
Illinois		
Indiana		
Iowa		
Kansas		
Kentucky		
Maine		
Massachusetts		
Minnesota		
Mississippi		
Montana		
Nebraska		
Nevada		
New Jersey		
New Mexico		
New York		
North Carolina		
North Dakota		
Ohio		
Oklahoma		
Rhode Island		
South Carolina		
South Dakota		
Tennessee		
Texas		
Utah		
Vermont		
Virginia		
Washington		
West Virginia		
Wyoming		

These findings are not comprehensive analyses of states' rule for general pleadings. Rather, the chart reflects whether the states fit within the essential criteria of Federal Rule of Civil Procedure 8. One should always reference her state's rules for the specific requirements in that state.

Majority Approach: A majority of states follow Federal Rule of Civil Procedure 8. Notice pleading governs the sufficiency of a complaint. Most states do not require a statement of grounds for jurisdiction because state courts, unlike federal courts, deal far less with subject matter jurisdiction. If a plaintiff has sued in a court of general jurisdiction and the case is obviously one that fits within the broad scope of such court's jurisdiction, parties rarely if ever have to plead subject matter jurisdiction.

Minority Approach: Minority states require more than a "short and plain statement." These states require a more detailed statement of facts in the pleadings.

Nonconforming Approach: Pleading requirements for states classified under the Nonconforming Approach category vary in their approach. For example, in New Hampshire the court may require a detailed "statement" of the grounds for an action and/or a defense. In Wisconsin, the short and plain statement requires the transaction(s)/occurrence(s) and the relief sought.

Appendix 4-2
Standard for Pleading Matters with Particularity

Majority Approach	*Minority Approach*	*Nonconforming States*
Alabama	Arkansas	California
Alaska	*(+ duress & undue influence)*	Connecticut
Arizona	Delaware	Illinois
Colorado	*(+ negligence)*	Iowa
District of Columbia	Idaho	Maryland
Florida	*(violation of civil or constitutional rights)*	New Hampshire
Georgia	Massachusetts	Oregon
Hawaii	*(+ duress, undue influence)*	Texas
Indiana	Nebraska	
Kansas	*(+ undue influence)*	
Kentucky	New Jersey	
Louisiana	*(+ undue influence, breach of*	
Maine	*trust, willful default)*	
Michigan	New York	
Minnesota	*(+ undue influence, breach of*	
Mississippi	*trust, willful default)*	
Missouri		
Montana		
New Mexico		
Nevada		
North Carolina		
North Dakota		
Ohio		
Oklahoma		
Pennsylvania		
Rhode Island		
South Carolina		
South Dakota		
Tennessee		
Utah		
Vermont		
Virginia		
Washington		
West Virginia		
Wisconsin		
Wyoming		

These findings are not comprehensive analyses of states' rules for pleading special matters. Rather, the chart captures the extent to which states fit within the essential criteria of Federal Rule of Civil Procedure 9. One should always refer to her state's rule for the specific requirements in that state.

Majority Approach: A majority of states follow the approach of Federal Rule of Civil Procedure 9 by requiring that the circumstances constituting fraud and/or mistake be pled with particularity, and not generally.

Minority Approach: States classified in the Minority Approach category actually require the particularity demanded of those in the Majority approach, but include additional matters that must be pled with particularity. For example, states in this category alternately require more specific pleading for the following claims: negligence, duress, undue influence, violations of civil/constitutional rights, breach of trust, and/or willful default. Some of these specialized areas are listed above with the state under the Minority column.

Nonconforming Approach: Nonconforming Approach states either do not provide for matters that must be pled with particularity or use vague language in their rules that leave room for debate in different cases about whether the pleadings require a high level of particularity (*e.g.*, pleading with enough particularity for fairness to the defendant).

Appendix 4-3
Good Faith Basis for Pleadings

Majority Approach	Minority Approach	Nonconforming States
Alabama	California	Connecticut
Alaska	Delaware	Florida
Arizona	District of Columbia	Iowa
Arkansas	Hawaii	Louisiana
Colorado	Indiana	Massachusetts
Georgia	Minnesota	New Hampshire
Idaho	Montana	
Illinois	Nevada	
Kansas	New Jersey	
Kentucky	New York	
Maine	North Dakota	
Maryland	Oklahoma	
Michigan	Oregon	
Mississippi	South Dakota	
Missouri	Tennessee	
Nevada	Utah	
New Mexico	Vermont	
North Carolina	West Virginia	
Ohio	Wisconsin	
Pennsylvania	Wyoming	
Rhode Island		
South Carolina		
Texas		
Virginia		
Washington		

These findings are not comprehensive analyses of states' rule for signing pleadings, motions, and other papers; representations to the court; and/or sanctions. Rather, the chart indicates the extent to which states follow the essential criteria of Federal Rule of Civil Procedure 11. One should always reference her states rule for the specific requirements in that state.

Majority Approach: Majority states tend to follow the Federal approach as it existed after the 1983 Amendments to Federal Rule of Civil Procedure 11 ("1993 Amendments"). The 1983 Amendments created a series of certification requirements for a lawyer, when she signs a pleading or appears in court to argue a motion based on a pleading. Under the 1993 Amendments, the lawyer must certify that she is making a representation that the allegations have a good faith basis in law and fact and that the allegations are not interposed for any improper purpose such as to harass or delay. These amendments gave Rule 11 "teeth." The 1983 Amendments allowed the opposing party to file a Rule 11 motion whenever that party believed any of these certifications had been breached. Moreover, the court was required to impose sanctions if a party or lawyer violated Rule 11.

Minority Approach: States follow the Minority Approach if their rule captures the essence of the 1993 Amendments to Federal Rule 11 ("1993 Amendments"). Adopted ten years after the amendments described above, these amendments were designed to cut down on Rule 1l motions. Under the 1993 Amendments a party, before filing a Rule 11 motion, must serve a notice on the opponent who can then withdraw the allegations, thus providing the opponent a so-called "safe-harbor provision." The party is also allowed to allege facts for which he or she did not have supporting evidence at the outset as long as these were identified in the pleading, and the pleader stated that "after an opportunity for further investigation and discovery" the pleader expected to have support.

Nonconforming Approach: Nonconforming states stray from both the 1983 and 1993 Amendments to Rule 11. These states have either not adopted the 1983 or 1993 amendments. Nor have they adopted key provisions of Rule 11 in general.

Appendix 4-4
Joinder of Claims and Remedies

Majority Approach	*Minority Approach*	*Nonconforming States*
Alabama		California
Alaska		Connecticut
Arizona		Louisiana
Arkansas		New Hampshire
Colorado		Virginia
Delaware		
District of Columbia		
Florida		
Georgia		
Hawaii		
Idaho		
Illinois		
Indiana		
Iowa		
Kansas		
Kentucky		
Maine		
Maryland		
Massachusetts		
Michigan		
Minnesota		
Mississippi		
Missouri		
Montana		
Nebraska		
Nevada		
New Jersey		
New Mexico		
New York		
North Carolina		
North Dakota		
Ohio		
Oklahoma		
Oregon		
Pennsylvania		
Rhode Island		
South Carolina		
South Dakota		
Tennessee		
Texas		
Utah		
Vermont		
Washington		
West Virginia		
Wisconsin		
Wyoming		

These findings are not comprehensive analyses of states' rule for joinder of claims and remedies. Rather, the chart identifies whether states follow the essential criteria of Federal Rule of Civil Procedure 18. One should always reference her state's requirements for joinder of claims and remedies.

Majority Approach: States following the Majority Approach to joinder of claims and remedies apply the same criteria as Federal Rule of Civil Procedure 18. That rule is so broad that it allows joinder of any claims that a party has against another, regardless of whether they are transactionally related. Also, the legal theory does not matter. A party may join tort, contract, property, etc. claims together.

Minority Approach: There is no significant Minority Approach. Instead, the states that depart from the majority rule do so in ways different enough that they cannot be classified as a group. Thus, they are included in the Nonconforming Approach category.

Nonconforming Approach: Nonconforming states do not follow the Federal Rule approach to joinder of claims and remedies, and they do not form a significant minority approach. For example, the Virginia joinder rule takes a narrower approach than the majority model. To be joined, claims must arise from the same transaction and occurrence, a requirement not found in the majority approach. Va. Code Ann. §8.01-272; *Powers v. Cherin*, 249 Va. 33, 452 S.E.2d 666 (1995). Connecticut, by contrast, allows parties to include different types of claims, seeking diverse relief, but provides further: "but, if several causes of action are united in the same complaint, they shall be brought to recover, either (1) upon contract, express or implied, or (2) for injuries, with or without force, to person or property, or either, including a conversion of property to the defendant's use, or (3) for injuries to character, or (4) upon claims to recover real property, with our without damages for the withholding thereof, and the rents and profits of same, or (5) upon claims to recover personal property specifically, with or without damages for the withholding thereof, or (6) claims arising by virtue of contract or by operation of law in favor of or against a party in some representative or fiduciary capacity, or (7) upon claims, whether in tort or contract or both, arising from the same transaction or transactions connected with the subject...." Conn. Gen. Stat. Ann. §10-21. Although parties in civil suits may effectively in Connecticut be able to achieve joinder of claims close to the breadth permitted under the Majority Rule, the detailed nature of the statute requiring one to confirm satisfaction of one of the conditions makes it, in the author's opinion, one fit for the Nonconforming Approach category. Most joinder rules or statutes are far simpler.

Appendix 4-5
Joinder of Parties

Majority Approach	*Minority Approach*	*Nonconforming States*
Alabama	California	Louisiana
Alaska	Connecticut	New Hampshire
Arizona	Illinois	Virginia
Arkansas	Missouri	
Colorado	Oklahoma	
Delaware		
District of Columbia		
Florida		
Georgia		
Hawaii		
Idaho		
Indiana		
Iowa		
Kansas		
Kentucky		
Maine		
Maryland		
Massachusetts		
Michigan		
Minnesota		
Mississippi		
Montana		
Nebraska		
Nevada		
New Jersey		
New Mexico		
New York		
North Carolina		
North Dakota		
Ohio		
Oregon		
Pennsylvania		
Rhode Island		
South Carolina		
South Dakota		
Tennessee		
Texas		
Utah		
Vermont		
Washington		
West Virginia		
Wisconsin		
Wyoming		

These findings are not comprehensive analyses of states' rules for joinder of parties. Rather, the chart identifies whether states follow the essential criteria of Federal Rules of Civil Procedure 19 and 20. One should always refer to her state's joinder rule for a more detailed approach to joinder of parties.

Majority Approach: States follow the Majority Approach to permissible joinder of parties if their joinder rule captures the essence of Federal Rule 20 by: (1) requiring that claims against the original party and the one sought to be added arise from the same transaction or occurrence, and (2) also requiring that the claim against the party sought to be joined involves a question of law or fact in common with the claim against the original party. The majority also tends to follow Federal Rule of Civil Procedure 19 regarding parties indispensable to litigation.

Minority Approach: The Minority Approach states tend to follow the Majority. However, these states allow permissible joinder of parties with *either* the same transaction or occurrence requirement, *or* the common question of law or fact requirement.

Nonconforming Approach: Nonconforming states stray from both the Majority Approach and Minority Approach. For example, the Louisiana permissive joinder rule follows the cumulation of actions rule. The joinder of plaintiffs or defendants or both in the same suit is considered the joining of plural actions in the same suit for actions that are asserted separately against each defendant by each plaintiff. *See* LA. CODE CIV. PROC. ANN. art. 647. Therefore, the joinder of parties is regulated by the rules that Louisiana has adopted regarding the cumulation of actions.

Appendix 4-6
Counterclaims and Cross-claims

Majority Approach	*Minority Approach 1*	*Nonconforming States*
Alabama	Alaska	California
Arizona	Illinois	Georgia
Arkansas	New York	Louisiana
Colorado	Oregon	Michigan
Connecticut	Wisconsin	New Jersey
Delaware		South Dakota
District of Columbia	*Minority Approach 2*	Tennessee
Florida	Maryland	Texas
Hawaii	Nebraska	
Idaho	Virginia	
Indiana		
Iowa		
Kansas		
Kentucky		
Maine		
Massachusetts		
Minnesota		
Mississippi		
Missouri		
Montana		
Nevada		
New Hampshire		
New Mexico		
North Carolina		
North Dakota		
Ohio		
Oklahoma		
Rhode Island		
South Carolina		
Utah		
Vermont		
Washington		
West Virginia		
Wyoming		

These findings are not comprehensive analyses of states' rule for counterclaims and cross-claims. Rather, the chart identifies the degrees to which states follow the essential criteria of Federal Rule of Civil Procedure 13. One should always refer to her state's requirements for the specifics of requirements for counterclaims and cross-claims.

Majority Approach: States follow the Majority Approach to counterclaims and cross-claims if their rule captures the essence of Federal Rule 13. For counterclaims, that means that the pleader (1) must assert a compulsory counterclaim if the opposing party sued and has a claim arising from the same transaction or occurrence that is the subject matter of the opposing party's claim, and (2) may assert a permissive counterclaim if the party that has been sued can assert a counterclaim against whomever has sued that party even if not compulsory. As in the federal system, cross-claims are always permissive but must relate to the same transaction or occurrence as the original claim brought by the plaintiff against defendants.

Minority Approach: Minority Approach states tend to follow the Majority Approach to counterclaims with the following variations. Minority Approach 1 states allow a party to file as a counterclaim any claim against the opposing party regardless of whether arising out of the transaction or occurrence that is the subject matter of the opposing party's claim. Minority Approach 2 states do not require compulsory counterclaims. Therefore, in Minority Approach 2 only permissive counterclaims are asserted against the opposing party—though of course, if they qualified as what one would ordinarily consider a compulsory counterclaim, one has permission to assert such a counterclaim. It simply is not mandatory. As with the Majority Approach, however, the minority states make in making cross-claims permissive but require them to arise from the same transaction or occurrence as the main claim.

Nonconforming Approach: States in the Nonconforming Approach stray from the Majority and Minority in idiosyncratic ways. For example, in Tennessee, with regards to compulsory counterclaims, tort claims are excluded. California follows the compulsory counterclaim rule by requiring a party against whom a claim has been asserted to assert a claim arising from the same subject matter. However, the state uses "cross-complaint" as its term for such a claim (not to be confused with cross claim). For this reason, the State has been separated for special treatment, so as to highlight potential confusion due to terminology. New Jersey, unlike most states, has an "entire controversy doctrine provision" that effectively makes both counterclaims and cross-claims that could be asserted in an action mandatory. *See* N.J. Ct. Rules 4:30(a).

Appendix 4-7
Impleader of Third-party Claims

Majority Approach	*Minority Approach*	*Nonconforming States*
Alabama		California
Alaska		New Hampshire
Arizona		New York
Arkansas		
Colorado		
Connecticut		
Delaware		
District of Columbia		
Florida		
Georgia		
Hawaii		
Idaho		
Illinois		
Indiana		
Iowa		
Kansas		
Kentucky		
Louisiana		
Maine		
Maryland		
Massachusetts		
Michigan		
Minnesota		
Mississippi		
Missouri		
Montana		
Nebraska		
Nevada		
New Jersey		
New Mexico		
North Carolina		
North Dakota		
Ohio		
Oklahoma		
Oregon		
Pennsylvania		
Rhode Island		
South Carolina		
South Dakota		
Tennessee		
Texas		
Utah		
Vermont		
Virginia		
Washington		
West Virginia		
Wisconsin		
Wyoming		

These findings are not comprehensive analyses of states' rule for impleader or third-party practice. Rather, the chart shows the extent to which states follow the essential criteria of Federal Rule of Civil Procedure 14. One should always refer to her state's requirements for asserting an impleader claim and for any nuances to third-party practice in her state.

Majority Approach: States follow the Majority Approach to impleader or third-party practice if their third-party joinder rule captures the following essential characteristics of Federal Rule of Civil Procedure 14. First, a party that has been sued may bring suit against a "nonparty" if that nonparty is or may be liable to the party in the suit. This always means there will be an indemnity claim (that is to say, the third party has express or an implied contractual duty to indemnify) or contribution liability (joint tortfeasor) liability. Second, the majority rule, like Federal Rule 14, also allows all parties, once a new party is brought in, to assert claims against the new party, and allows the new party to assert claims against all other parties.

Minority Approach: None of the states forms a significant Minority Approach to impleader or third-party practice.

Nonconforming Approach: Nonconforming Approach states stray from the majority model and do not form a significant minority approach. Generally, each of these states approaches impleader somewhat differently by adding additional requirements for specific types of claims, or by achieving the same result as impleader but by a different means (*e.g.*, in New Hampshire moving to add a third party).

Appendix 4-8
Amended Pleadings

Majority Approach	Minority Approach 1	Nonconforming States
Alabama	Indiana	Arkansas
Alaska	Mississippi	California
Arizona	Missouri	Connecticut
Colorado	Nebraska	Illinois
Delaware	North Carolina	Iowa
District of Columbia	South Carolina	Louisiana
Hawaii		Maryland
Idaho	*Minority Approach 2*	Michigan
Kansas	Florida	New Hampshire
Kentucky		New York
Maine	*Minority Approach 3*	Pennsylvania
Massachusetts	Georgia	Texas
Minnesota	Tennessee	Wisconsin
Montana		Wyoming
Nevada	*Minority Approach 4*	
New Mexico	New Jersey	
North Dakota		
Ohio		
Oklahoma		
Oregon		
Rhode Island		
South Dakota		
Utah		
Vermont		
Virginia		
Washington		
West Virginia		

These findings are not comprehensive analyses of each state's rule for amendments to pleadings. Rather, the chart reflects the extent to which states follow the essential criteria of Federal Rule of Civil Procedure 15. A lawyer should always refer to her state's rule for the specific requirements of her state.

Majority Approach: States follow the Majority Approach to amendments to pleadings if their amendment rule captures the following essential criteria of Federal Rule 15: (1) allowing a party an amendment of right to the complaint without leave of court before the answer filed or to the answer if it is amended within 21 days; (2) allowing an amendment requiring leave of court (which is freely given as justice so requires) between the "of right" stage above and the beginning of trial; (3) allowing amendments to pleadings at trial by leave of the court to conform to the evidence (if the evidence offered varies from what has been pled) "freely" when (a) doing so aids in the presentation of the merits, and (b) the objecting party fails to show prejudice; and (4) providing that an amendment, after the complaint is filed, will relate back to the date of the filing of the original complaint if the amended pleading relates to a claim or defense that arose from the same transaction or occurrence as the original complaint.

Minority Approach: Minority states tend to follow the Majority Approach to a great extent. However, three Minority positions allow different amounts of time for parties to amend as a matter of course. Minority Approach 1 states allow a 30-day window to amend as matter of course. Minority Approach 2 allows a 20-day window to amend as matter of course. Minority Approach 3 states allow a 15-day window to amend as a matter of course. Minority Approach 4 (New Jersey's) allows the longest period—90 days from service of the answer.

Nonconforming Approach: Nonconforming Approach states stray from the majority and minority approaches. Generally, each of these states approaches amendments to pleadings uniquely and omits one or more of the four requirements of Federal Rule 15. Perhaps the most striking example is Maryland, in which a party may file amended pleadings as of right up until trial, and the party opposing the amendment has the burden to show the amended pleading is not warranted. *See* MD. RULES 2-341.

Appendix 5-1
Service of Process

Majority Approach	*Minority Approach*	*Nonconforming States*
Alabama	California	Connecticut
Alaska	Illinois	Kansas
Arizona	Maryland	Kentucky
Arkansas	Mississippi	Louisiana
Colorado	New Mexico	Michigan
Delaware	Texas	Missouri
District of Columbia	Wisconsin	New Hampshire
Florida		New Jersey
Georgia		Ohio
Hawaii		Pennsylvania
Idaho		
Indiana		
Iowa		
Maine		
Massachusetts		
Minnesota		
Montana		
Nebraska		
Nevada		
New York		
North Carolina		
North Dakota		
Oklahoma		
Oregon		
Rhode Island		
South Carolina		
South Dakota		
Tennessee		
Utah		
Vermont		
Virginia		
Washington		
West Virginia		
Wyoming		

These findings are not comprehensive analyses of states' rule for service of process. Rather, the chart shows the degree to which states follow the essential criteria of Federal Rule of Civil Procedure 4. A lawyer should always refer to her state's service of process rule for the details of requirements in her state.

Majority Approach: States follow the Majority Approach to service of process if their service rule captures the following essential criteria of Federal Rule 4: (1) process includes both a summons and complaint; (2) the rule specifies who may serve process; (3) process may be served in a number of ways, in no particular order (*i.e.*, in a non-hierarchical fashion); and (4) the provisions identify those upon whom process may be served on behalf of a corporation.

Minority Approach: States in the Minority Approach tend to follow the Majority Approach with the following caveat. These states, unlike the majority, do rank methods of service — at least as to individuals — hierarchically. All of these states prefer that the defendant be personally served before other methods of "substituted service" are used. These states differ as to whether service by certified mail or service on an appropriate resident at the defendant's usual place of abode is the next-most-favored method.

Nonconforming Approach: States in the Nonconforming Approach category stray from both the Majority and Minority Approaches. For example, the New Jersey service rule takes a majority-minority hybrid approach. Defendants may be served personally, by leaving process with an appropriate adult at the defendant's usual place of abode, or through the defendant's agent; however, defendants may also be served by mail, but only if the defendant answers or appears in court. N.J. Cт. R. 4:4-4(a)(1), (c). Thus, the process is hierarchical, but only in a limited circumstance. Defendants in Missouri should be particularly wary. That state is among the only that explicitly provides by statute that process servers may carry a firearm. Mo. Ann. Sat. § 506.145 (West 2010).

Appendix 6-1
Responsive Pleadings and Defenses

Majority Approach	*Minority Approach 1*	*Nonconforming States*
Alabama	Mississippi	Illinois
Alaska	Nebraska	Louisiana
Arizona	New Jersey	Michigan
Arkansas	Oregon	New York
Colorado	Wisconsin	Pennsylvania
Delaware		Texas
District of Columbia	*Minority Approach 2*	
Florida	California	
Georgia	Connecticut	
Hawaii	New Hampshire	
Idaho	Virginia	
Indiana		
Iowa		
Kansas		
Kentucky		
Maine		
Maryland		
Massachusetts		
Minnesota		
Missouri		
Montana		
Nevada		
New Mexico		
North Carolina		
North Dakota		
Ohio		
Oklahoma		
Rhode Island		
South Carolina		
South Dakota		
Tennessee		
Utah		
Vermont		
Washington		
West Virginia		
Wyoming		

These findings are not comprehensive analyses of states' rules on responsive pleadings. Rather, the chart identifies the degree to which states follow the essential criteria of Federal Rule of Civil Procedure 12. One should always refer to her state's rules or statutes addressing responsive pleadings to ensure full compliance with these.

Majority Approach: States follow the majority approach to responsive pleadings if their rules capture the following essential criteria of Federal Rule 12: (1) defendant's response may be an answer or a pre-answer motion challenging the complaint on any number of grounds; (2) the applicable provision states that the four easily waivable defenses (insufficient process, insufficient service of process, lack of personal jurisdiction, and improper venue) are waived if not raised in either the answer or a motion to dismiss (whichever is filed first); (3) the applicable provision allows for other defenses to be raised by motion or by answer, such as failure to state a claim upon which relief can be granted, failure to join an indispensable party, etc.; and (4) the defendant may raise defenses other than lack of personal jurisdiction with that defense and doing so will not operate as a general appearance—*i.e.*, a waiver of the personal jurisdiction defense.

Minority Approach 1: States in the first Minority Approach tend to follow the Majority Approach. However, they do not include improper venue as one of the waivable defenses.

Minority Approach 2: States in the second Minority Approach tend to follow the Majority Approach. However, these states allow a "demurrer" (the historical antecedent to Federal Rule of Civil Procedure 12(b)(6) motion to dismiss for failure to state a claim upon which relief can be granted) as a responsive pleading.

Nonconforming Approach: Nonconforming Approach states stray from both the Majority and Minority Approaches. Although these states allow most of the same types of challenges included in the Majority and Minority Approaches, they tend to use different terminology and include their own order of priority for certain defenses, in some circumstances.

Note: In December 2009, Federal Rule of Civil Procedure 12's timing requirement was amended. Under the amendment, a defendant has 21 days (not 20 days, the deadline in this Rule for many years). States vary in the length of time permitted to respond. That was true before the amendment to Federal Rule 12 and remains true.

Appendix 6-2
Answers to Complaints

Majority Approach	*Minority Approach*	*Nonconforming States*
Alabama		
Alaska		
Arizona		
Arkansas		
California		
Colorado		
Connecticut		
Delaware		
District of Columbia		
Florida		
Georgia		
Hawaii		
Idaho		
Illinois		
Indiana		
Iowa		
Kansas		
Kentucky		
Louisiana		
Maine		
Maryland		
Massachusetts		
Michigan		
Minnesota		
Mississippi		
Missouri		
Montana		
Nebraska		
Nevada		
New Hampshire		
New Jersey		
New Mexico		
New York		
North Carolina		
North Dakota		
Ohio		
Oklahoma		
Oregon		
Pennsylvania		
Rhode Island		
South Carolina		
South Dakota		
Tennessee		
Texas		
Utah		
Vermont		
Virginia		
Washington		
West Virginia		
Wisconsin		
Wyoming		

These findings are not comprehensive analyses of each state's rule for answers to complaints. Rather, the chart captures the extent to which states follow the essential criteria of Federal Rule of Civil Procedure 8(b). One should always refer to her state's rule(s) for more detailed requirements on answers in her state.

Majority Approach: States follow the Majority Approach to answers to complaints if their rule(s) capture the following essential criteria of Federal Rule of Civil Procedure 8(b): (1) The answer must admit, deny, or state that the party answering lacks sufficient basis to admit or deny the allegations against the party; (2) claiming insufficient knowledge to form a belief about the truth of an allegation operates as a denial; and (3) affirmative defenses must be included in the answer.

Minority Approach: None of the states follows an approach that varies significant from that of Federal Rule 8(b).

Nonconforming Approach: None of the states follows an approach that may be considered "nonconforming" to the essential criteria of Fed. R. Civ. P. 8(b).

Appendix 7-1
Default Judgments

Majority Approach	Minority Approach	Nonconforming States
Alabama	Arkansas	Connecticut
Alaska	Colorado	Florida
Arizona	Illinois	Georgia
California	Indiana	Louisiana
Delaware	Kentucky	Maryland
District of Columbia	Mississippi	Oklahoma
Hawaii	Missouri	Texas
Idaho	Nebraska	Virginia
Iowa	New Hampshire	
Kansas	New Mexico	
Maine	Ohio	
Massachusetts	South Dakota	
Michigan	Tennessee	
Minnesota	Washington	
Montana		
Nevada		
New Jersey		
New York		
North Carolina		
North Dakota		
Oregon		
Pennsylvania		
Rhode Island		
South Carolina		
Utah		
Vermont		
West Virginia		
Wisconsin		
Wyoming		

These findings are not comprehensive analyses of states' rules for default judgments. Rather, the chart seeks to depict whether states follow the essential criteria of Federal Rule of Civil Procedure 55. A lawyer should always refer to her state's rule(s) to determine the nuances of default judgments in that state.

Majority Approach: States follow the Majority Approach to default judgments if their rule(s) contain the following essential criteria of Federal Rule of Civil Procedure 55: (1) a default must first occur, and does occur when the party against whom relief is sought fails to plead or otherwise defend within the time specified for responsive pleadings; (2) if the sum sought by the party seeking relief is a sum certain, the clerk may enter a default judgment against the defaulting party; and (3) if the sum sought by the party seeking relief is not a sum certain, the party must apply to the court for default judgment, and the court may order a hearing on, among other things, the amount of damages to be awarded to the relief-seeking party.

Minority Approach: Minority Approach states take an approach similar to the Majority Approach in two distinct ways: (1) they require a failure on the part of the party against whom relief is sought (*i.e.*, a failure to plead, appear, respond, or otherwise defend) for a party to be deemed in default; and (2) they generally require proof, in testimony or in the form of an affidavits, of the opposing party's default and/or proof of damages or entitlement to relief. If these two requirements are met, states in the minority category generally allow a default judgment to be entered against the defaulting party in the amount of damages the party seeking relief appears to have sustained or has originally demanded. However, many if not most of these states require a judge, not the clerk, to enter an order of default. States in the minority category vary from the Majority Approach in other ways too. For example, many states require that the defaulting party receive notice of the default and/or default judgment entered against him, or the states may only require that the defaulting party receive notice in certain situations (*e.g.*, if the defaulting party appears). Additionally, many states have specific requirements crafted specifically for entry of defaults and/or default judgments against a party who is a service member or who has been served by publication.

Nonconforming Approach: The states listed in the Nonconforming Approach category generally follow the same approach to default judgments as the Majority and Minority Approaches. However, these states' procedures pursuing default judgments are sufficiently different that they have been classified separately. For instance, Florida requires "well-pleaded facts" from the plaintiff for a court to enter a default judgment — essentially allowing the defendant to contest liability even if in default in some cases. See Fl. R. Civ. P. 1,500.

Appendix 7-2
Voluntary Dismissals

Majority Approach	*Minority Approach*	*Nonconforming States*
Alabama	Arkansas	New Hampshire
Alaska	California	Pennsylvania
Arizona	Connecticut	
Colorado	Florida	
Delaware	Iowa	
District of Columbia	Louisiana	
Georgia	Missouri	
Hawaii	Nebraska	
Idaho	Oklahoma	
Illinois	Tennessee	
Indiana	Texas	
Kansas	Virginia	
Kentucky		
Maine		
Maryland		
Massachusetts		
Michigan		
Minnesota		
Mississippi		
Montana		
Nevada		
New Jersey		
New Mexico		
New York		
North Carolina		
North Dakota		
Ohio		
Oregon		
Rhode Island		
South Carolina		
South Dakota		
Utah		
Vermont		
Washington		
West Virginia		
Wisconsin		
Wyoming		

These findings are not comprehensive analyses of states' rule for dismissal of actions. Rather, the chart seeks to capture the extent to which states follow the essential criteria of Federal Rule of Civil Procedure 41. One should always refer to her state's rules for the specific requirements in that state.

Majority Approach: Majority Approach states follow the approach of Federal Rule 41. Voluntary dismissal may be done with and without a court order. A plaintiff may dismiss an action without a court order by filing either (1) a notice of dismissal before the opposing party serves either an answer or a motion for summary judgment, or (2) a stipulation of dismissal signed by all parties who have appeared. If a plaintiff fulfills one of the above requirements, the dismissal is generally without prejudice. If a plaintiff does not meet any of the above requirements, an action may be dismissed at the plaintiff's request only by court order, on terms that the court considers proper.

Minority Approach: Minority Approach states' rules generally allow for dismissal of an action at different times from states following the Majority Approach. The time requirements vary. The time may expire, depending on the state, before submission to the jury; before a hearing on the merits; before pretrial; before plaintiff has introduced all her evidence (with notice to parties); and/or before the action is submitted to the court. Note that these requirements may combine other requirements and may use different exceptions regarding notice, stipulation, and the court's ability to grant the motion. Some states do not include any provisions for stipulations among the parties to dismiss an action. Moreover, states tend to use different terminology for voluntary dismissals, including notice of dismissal, notice of withdrawal, and/or notice of discontinuance.

Nonconforming Approach: Nonconforming Approach states stray from the Majority and Minority Approaches. New Hampshire has no rule akin to Federal Rule 41, but does allow settlement and/or alternative dispute resolution upon meeting the notice requirements. Pennsylvania allows for a "discontinuance" only if all parties give written consent. Such a conclusion is Pennsylvania's only method of voluntarily discontinuing of a suit. *See e.g.*, Pa. R. Civ. Proc. 229 (2010).

Appendix 8-1
General Discovery Rules

Majority Approach	*Minority Approach*	*Nonconforming States*
Alabama	Arkansas	Alaska
Arizona	Florida	Colorado
California	Illinois	Utah
Connecticut	Louisiana	Wyoming
Delaware	Missouri	
District of Columbia	Nebraska	
Georgia	New York	
Hawaii	Ohio	
Idaho	Pennsylvania	
Indiana	South Carolina	
Iowa	South Dakota	
Kansas	Wisconsin	
Kentucky		
Maine		
Maryland		
Massachusetts		
Michigan		
Minnesota		
Mississippi		
Montana		
Nevada		
New Hampshire		
New Jersey		
New Mexico		
North Carolina		
North Dakota		
Oklahoma		
Oregon		
Rhode Island		
Tennessee		
Texas		
Vermont		
Virginia		
Washington		
West Virginia		

These findings are not comprehensive analyses of states' rule(s) for discovery. Rather, the chart seeks to identify the extent to which states adhere to the essential components of Federal Rule of Civil Procedure 26. One should always refer to her state's discovery rule(s) for a more detailed approach.

Majority Approach: Most states follow the Federal Rule approach to general provisions regarding discovery. However, unlike Federal Rule 26, these states *do not* require automatic initial disclosures at the outset of a case. The scope of discovery is relevance to any claim or defense. Work Product privileges are included and allow, as in the Federal Rule, for a discovering party to overcome the privilege by showing a substantial need and an inability to obtain a substantial equivalent to the privileged information. Provisions regarding objections to discovery requests and protective orders are set forth. Also, provisions concerning sanctions for certain certification/discovery violations are described.

Minority Approach: These states follow much of the majority approach above, including the *lack* of automatic initial disclosures at the outset of a case. The main difference that qualifies these states as among the minority is that their general discovery rule includes no provisions regarding sanctions for certification/discovery violations. Needless to say, other sources in the state likely support courts' ability to sanction for misconduct in discovery.

Nonconforming Approach: These states follow the current Federal Rule 26, including the provision for automatic initial disclosure requirements at the outset of the case. However, these states may also have certain state exemptions to the automatic initial disclosure requirements.

Appendix 8-2
Request for Production of Documents

Majority Approach	*Minority Approach*	*Nonconforming States*
Alabama	Iowa	California
Alaska	*(d/f has 60 days to respond)*	*(more specific in request form for*
Arizona	Louisiana	*production as well as response)*
Arkansas	*(15 days and 30 days*	Connecticut
California	*for defendant)*	*(more specific requests*
Colorado	Michigan	*required-clearly designate)*
Delaware	*(28 days and 42 days for d/f)*	Illinois
District of Columbia	New Jersey	*(requires affidavit from*
Florida	*(35 days and d/f has 50)*	*responding party that*
Georgia	New York	*requests responded to)*
Hawaii	*(20 days to respond)*	New Hampshire
Idaho	Oregon	*(governed by written*
Indiana	*(no e-discovery provision)*	*interrogatories and no*
Kansas	Pennsylvania	*e-discovery provision)*
Kentucky	*(no e-discovery provision)*	
Maine	Virginia	
Maryland	*(21 days to respond)*	
Massachusetts	Wisconsin	
Minnesota	*(no e-discovery provision)*	
Mississippi		
Missouri		
Montana		
Nebraska		
Nevada		
New Mexico		
North Carolina		
North Dakota		
Ohio		
Oklahoma		
Rhode Island		
South Carolina		
South Dakota		
Tennessee		
Texas		
Utah		
Vermont		
Washington		
West Virginia		
Wyoming		

These findings are not comprehensive analyses of states' rule for request for production of documents. Rather, the chart seeks to reflect the extent to which the states have modeled their rules on the essential components of Federal Rule of Civil Procedure 34. One should always reference her state's request for production of documents rule for a more detailed approach.

Majority Approach: States in the majority follow Federal Rule of Civil Procedure 34 closely.

Minority Approach: States in the minority category have rules that substantially follow Federal Rule of Civil Procedure 34, but they depart from Rule 34 in one of two ways. First, a state qualifies as a minority state if its rule provides deadlines for responding to requests for production of documents significantly different from the 30 days permitted by Federal Rule 34. Second, states qualify as Minority Approach states if their rules do not include a provision for electronic discovery.

Nonconforming Approach: States in the Nonconforming Approach category have requirements different from Federal Rule of Civil Procedure 34, such as requirements governing the manner in which the request or response must be made.

Appendix 8-3
Subpoenas and Subpoenas Duces Tecum

Majority Approach	*Minority Approach*	*Nonconforming States*
Alabama	Illinois	
Alaska	Iowa	
Arizona	Louisiana	
Arkansas	Maryland	
California	Michigan	
Connecticut	New Hampshire	
Colorado	New Mexico	
Delaware	Pennsylvania	
District of Columbia		
Florida		
Georgia		
Hawaii		
Idaho		
Indiana		
Kansas		
Kentucky		
Maine		
Massachusetts		
Minnesota		
Mississippi		
Missouri		
Montana		
Nebraska		
Nevada		
New Jersey		
New York		
North Carolina		
North Dakota		
Ohio		
Oklahoma		
Oregon		
Rhode Island		
South Carolina		
South Dakota		
Tennessee		
Texas		
Utah		
Vermont		
Virginia		
Washington		
West Virginia		
Wisconsin		
Wyoming		

These findings are not comprehensive analyses of states' rule for subpoenas. Rather, the chart seeks to identify whether states follow the essential components of Federal Rule of Civil Procedure 45. One should always refer to her state's subpoena rule for the requirements of her state.

Majority Approach: States following the Majority Approach conform to the provisions of Federal Rule of Civil Procedure 45 in virtually every respect, thus allowing attorneys to issue supbpoenas for both the production of documents by nonparties and for the attendance of nonparties at depositions, hearings, or trials. As in Federal Rule 45, nonparties have the ability to move to quash the subpoena in whole or in part.

Minority Approach: States following the Minority Approach also conform substantially to the provisions of Federal Rule of Civil Procedure 45. However, these states require a judge, or more often the court clerk, to issue the subpoena.

Nonconforming Approach: No states follow a nonconforming approach to subpoenas and subpoenas duces tecum.

Appendix 8-4
Interrogatories

Majority Approach	Minority Approach 1	Nonconforming States
Alabama	District of Columbia	Louisiana
Alaska	Georgia	Oregon
California	Hawaii	
Colorado	Idaho	
Florida	Minnesota	
Illinois	Montana	
Iowa	Nevada	
Kentucky	New Hampshire	
Maine	New Mexico	
Maryland	North Carolina	
Massachusetts	Ohio	
Mississippi	West Virginia	
Montana		
New Jersey	***Minority Approach 2***	
Oklahoma	Arizona	
Rhode Island	Arkansas	
Utah	Connecticut	
Virginia	Delaware	
Wyoming	Indiana	
	Kansas	
	Michigan	
	New York	
	North Carolina	
	North Dakota	
	Pennsylvania	
	South Carolina	
	South Dakota	
	Tennessee	
	Texas	
	Vermont	
	Washington	
	Wisconsin	

These findings are not comprehensive analyses of states' rule for interrogatories. Rather, the chart seeks to reflect the degree to which states follow the essential components of Federal Rule of Civil Procedure 33. One should always reference her state's interrogatories rule for the requirements of her state.

Majority Approach: States in the majority follow the criteria of Federal Rule of Civil Procedure 33 closely and, although some allow more than the 25 interrogatories including parts and subparts, none listed here allows more than 30 interrogatories.

Minority Approach 1: Although the states listed under the significant minority approach follow Federal Rule 33 in substance, they allow significantly more interrogatories than the 25 interrogatories permitted by the Federal Rule. Minority Approach 1 states allow interrogatories ranging from 40 to 60 in number.

Minority Approach 2: The states categorized as Minority Approach 2 place no limits on the number of interrogatories. Presumably, the opposing party could seek relief by objection or motion for a protective order, but these states' rules as written are quite broad.

Nonconforming Approach: Oregon is a truly nonconforming state. It has no rule on interrogatories. Indeed, the state is known for being averse to interrogatory practice. *See* Kerry J. Shepherd, *Civil Litigation in Oregon: Tips for the Out-of-State Attorney: Volume 1*, July 2003, *available at* http://www.markowitzherbold.com/showarticles.asp? Show=153 (last checked November 29, 2009).

Louisiana is the only other nonconforming state, though it still permits interrogatories. The limit is 35 interrogatories including subparts. In addition, the applicable statute does not contain an equivalent to Federal Rule 33's option to produce business records as a means to answer an interrogatory.

Appendix 8-5
Requests for Admission

Federal Rules Approach	*Minority Approach 1*	*Nonconforming States*
Alabama	Illinois	New York
Alaska	Louisiana	New Hampshire
Arizona	Michigan	
Arkansas	Virginia	
Connecticut		
Colorado	*Minority Approach 2*	
Delaware	California	
District of Columbia	Florida	
Georgia	Iowa	
Hawaii	Oregon	
Idaho		
Indiana		
Kansas		
Kentucky		
Maine		
Maryland		
Massachusetts		
Minnesota		
Mississippi		
Missouri		
Montana		
Nebraska		
Nevada		
New Jersey		
New Mexico		
North Carolina		
North Dakota		
Ohio		
Oklahoma		
Pennsylvania		
Rhode Island		
South Carolina		
South Dakota		
Tennessee		
Texas		
Utah		
Vermont		
Washington		
West Virginia		
Wisconsin		
Wyoming		

These findings are not comprehensive analyses of states' rule for requests for admission. Rather, the chart seeks to show the extent to which state rules mirror the essential components of Federal Rule of Civil Procedure 36. One should always refer to her state's requests for admission rule for that state's particular requirements.

Majority Approach: States in the majority approach follow Federal Rule of Civil Procedure 36 in all material respects.

Minority Approach: States in the minority fall into two categories. Minority Approach 1 states provide less than the 30 days allowed by Federal Rule 36 for a party to respond to a Request for Admission before the request is deemed admitted. The shorter time frames range from 15 days to 28 days.

Minority Approach 2 states place a limit on the number of Requests for Admissions that may be propounded.

Nonconforming States: Although the nonconforming states share many similarities with Federal Rule 36, the provisions in the states provide additional criteria that an attorney propounding Request for Admissions must certify in order to pursue the requests. Although these criteria are not overly demanding, *e.g.*, certifying that the matter sought is not subject to substantial dispute, the requirement is an extra step not required by Federal Rule 36.

Appendix 8-6
Depositions

Majority Approach	*Minority Approach*	*Nonconforming States*
Alabama	California	Illinois
Alaska	Maryland	
Arizona	Missouri	
Arkansas	New Jersey	
Colorado	New York	
Connecticut	Virginia	
Delaware		
District of Columbia		
Florida		
Georgia		
Hawaii		
Idaho		
Iowa		
Indiana		
Kansas		
Kentucky		
Louisiana		
Maine		
Massachusetts		
Michigan		
Minnesota		
Mississippi		
Montana		
Nebraska		
Nevada		
New Hampshire		
New Mexico		
North Carolina		
North Dakota		
Ohio		
Oklahoma		
Oregon		
Pennsylvania		
Rhode Island		
South Carolina		
South Dakota		
Tennessee		
Texas		
Utah		
Vermont		
Washington		
West Virginia		
Wisconsin		
Wyoming		

These findings are not comprehensive analyses of states' rule for depositions. Rather, the chart seeks to reflect the extent to which states incorporate the essential components of Federal Rule of Civil Procedure 30. One should always refer to her state's depositions rule for the requirements in that state.

Majority Approach: States following the Majority Approach include those that substantially follow the requirements of Federal Rule of Civil Procedure 30.

Minority Approach: States following the Minority Approach include those that follow most of the requirements of Federal Rule 30. However, rather than allowing for depositions to be noticed a "reasonable time" before the deposition, these states specify time limits within which notices must be issued prior to a deposition.

Nonconforming Approach: Unlike Federal Rule 30 and most states, Illinois requires the party noticing the deposition to specify whether the deposition is to be used as evidence at trial (as, for instance, for witnesses beyond the subpoena power of the court), on one hand, or to be used solely as a discovery deposition, on the other.

Appendix 8-7
Motions to Compel and Discovery Sanctions

Majority Approach	*Minority Approach*	*Nonconforming States*
Alabama	Illinois	California
Alaska	Maryland	Connecticut
Arizona	Missouri	
Arkansas	New Hampshire	
Colorado	New York	
Delaware	Pennsylvania	
District of Columbia		
Florida		
Georgia		
Hawaii		
Idaho		
Indiana		
Iowa		
Kansas		
Kentucky		
Louisiana		
Maine		
Massachusetts		
Michigan		
Minnesota		
Mississippi		
Montana		
Nebraska		
Nevada		
New Jersey		
New Mexico		
North Carolina		
North Dakota		
Ohio		
Oklahoma		
Oregon		
Rhode Island		
South Carolina		
South Dakota		
Tennessee		
Texas		
Utah		
Vermont		
Virginia		
Washington		
West Virginia		
Wisconsin		
Wyoming		

These findings are not comprehensive analyses of states' rule for motions to compel and discovery sanctions. Rather, the chart seeks to reflect the extent to which states incorporate the essential components of Federal Rule of Civil Procedure 37. One should always reference her state's rule(s) on motions to compel and discovery sanctions for that state's requirements.

Majority Approach: States following the Majority Approach follow Federal Rule of Civil Procedure 37 in the two-tier approach to sanctions set forth there. First, a moving party who maintains that discovery responses were deficient in part, but not completely, must bring a motion to compel for a partial failure and obtain a court order compelling a response to the deficiencies. Only then can the moving party receive sanctions. Second, a party seeking discovery may seek sanctions immediately for failing to respond at all to a discovery request (*e.g.*, a party's failure to attend a noticed deposition, failure to respond to any interrogatories)

Minority Approach: States in the minority also follow Federal Rule 37, but they vary the requirements of that Rule either by not requiring an initial motion to compel before receiving sanctions, by omitting the part of the Rule dealing with complete failures to produce discovery (presumably believing these are encompassed in the description of any failure to produce), or by simply streamlining the Rule. Illinois' Supreme Court, for instance, held that the state's "discovery rules... contemplate that discovery will proceed without judicial intervention." *Williams v. A.E. Staley Mfg.*, 416 N.E.2d 252, 254 (Il. 1981). Sanctions can thus follow if the responding party lacked "substantial justification" for her failure to respond. IL Sup. Ct. R. 219.

Nonconforming Approach: California adds a requirement to its motions to compel. A "separate statement" must be filed with the request to compel or for sanctions that "set[] forth all of the information necessary to understand each discovery request and all the responses to it that are at issue." Edward K. Esping & Susan L. Thomas, California Jurisprudence 3rd, *Discovery and Depositions* § 310 (2009). Connecticut has a similar requirement.

Appendix 9-1
Summary Judgment

Majority Approach	Minority Approach	Nonconforming States
Arkansas	Alabama	New York
California	Alaska	Virginia
Colorado	Arizona	
Delaware	Connecticut	
District of Columbia	Iowa	
Florida	Massachusetts	
Georgia	Missouri	
Hawaii	Nevada	
Idaho	New Mexico	
Illinois	Oklahoma	
Indiana	South Dakota	
Kansas	Tennessee	
Kentucky	Utah	
Louisiana	Vermont	
Maine		
Maryland		
Michigan		
Minnesota		
Mississippi		
Montana		
Nebraska		
New Hampshire		
New Jersey		
North Carolina		
North Dakota		
Ohio		
Oregon		
Pennsylvania		
Rhode Island		
South Carolina		
Texas		
Washington		
West Virginia		
Wisconsin		
Wyoming		

These findings are not comprehensive analyses of states' rules for summary judgment. Rather, the chart seeks to identify the extent to which states follow the essential components of Federal Rule of Civil Procedure 56. One should always refer to her state's summary judgment rule for the detailed requirements of that state.

Majority Approach: States in the Majority follow most, if not all, of the procedures in Federal Rule of Civil Procedure 56.

Minority Approach: States in the Minority follow the Majority Approach but require some additional submission, beyond the affidavits, discovery, or other materials relied on to support the summary judgment motion. The additional submission (often referred to as a narrative, statement, or summary) is independent of the original materials relied on to support summary judgment and designed to demonstrate to the court how affidavits, discovery, or other materials justify summary judgment.

Nonconforming Approach: Nonconforming states vary from both the Majority and Minority Approaches to a greater or lesser extent. For example, Virginia's summary judgment rules stray greatly from the Majority and Minority Approaches. By prohibiting the use of depositions to support summary judgment motions absent agreement of the parties, the rule limits the effectiveness of pretrial summary judgment significantly. Conversely, New York includes everything in Rule 56, but contains a number of other notable provisions. For instance, the New York summary judgment statute provides certain provisions that accelerate the hearing of, and limit the ability to, argue discovery that has not been had in certain classes of cases. *See* McKinney's Cons. Laws of N.Y. Ann. § 3212 (h) (cases involving public petition and participation); *id.* § 3212(i) (cases against architects, engineers, land surveyors, land architects).

Appendix 10-1
Pretrial Conferences

Majority Approach	Minority Approach	Nonconforming States
Alabama	Arkansas	California
Alaska	Connecticut	Louisiana
Arizona	Florida	New Hampshire
Colorado	Georgia	North Carolina
Delaware	Illinois	Oklahoma
District of Columbia	Maryland	Oregon
Hawaii	Michigan	Virginia
Idaho	Mississippi	Wisconsin
Indiana	Nebraska	
Iowa	New Jersey	
Kansas	New York	
Kentucky	Pennsylvania	
Maine	Texas	
Massachusetts		
Minnesota		
Missouri		
Montana		
Nevada		
New Mexico		
North Dakota		
Ohio		
Rhode Island		
South Carolina		
South Dakota		
Tennessee		
Utah		
Vermont		
Washington		
West Virginia		
Wyoming		

These findings are not comprehensive analyses of states' rule for pretrial conferences. Rather, the chart compares state approaches to the essential components of Federal Rule of Civil Procedure 16. One should always refer to her state's rule for that state's requirements on pretrial conferences.

Majority Approach: States in the majority follow the federal approach to pretrial conferences if their rule includes the essential criteria of Federal Rule 16 providing for: (1) a conference to schedule a trial date, (2) discovery cut-offs, etc.; and (3) final pretrial conferences to be held as close to trial as possible for formulating a trial plan that often deals with exhibits, ruling on motions, etc.

Minority Approach: States in the minority tend to loosely follow the majority approach. These states do not include all of the criteria noted above. In particular, these states do not include the requirement that final pretrial conferences are to be held as close to trial as possible.

Nonconforming Approach: Nonconforming states stray from both the majority and minority approaches. In general, the provisions allow wide discretion to trial courts to set up whatever schedule the court deems appropriate.

Appendix 11-1
Trial Motions for Judgment as a Matter of Law

Majority Approach	*Minority Approach*	*Nonconforming States*
Alabama		Oklahoma
Alaska		Pennsylvania
Arizona		Virginia
Arkansas		
California		
Colorado		
Connecticut		
Delaware		
District of Columbia		
Florida		
Georgia		
Hawaii		
Idaho		
Illinois		
Indiana		
Iowa		
Kansas		
Kentucky		
Louisiana		
Maine		
Maryland		
Massachusetts		
Michigan		
Minnesota		
Mississippi		
Missouri		
Montana		
Nebraska		
Nevada		
New Hampshire		
New Jersey		
New Mexico		
New York		
North Carolina		
North Dakota		
Ohio		
Oregon		
Rhode Island		
South Carolina		
South Dakota		
Tennessee		
Texas		
Utah		
Vermont		
Washington		
West Virginia		
Wisconsin		
Wyoming		

These findings are not comprehensive analyses of states' rule for trial motions for judgment as a matter of law (JNOV). Rather, the chart seeks to identify the extent to which states follow the essential components of Federal Rule of Civil Procedure 50(a). One should always refer to her state's rule for the specific requirements of a particular state.

Majority Approach: States follow the Majority Approach to trial motions for JNOV if their rule captures the following essential criteria of Federal Rule 50(a): (1) that reasonable jurors could not, based on the evidence presented, find for the party with the burden of proof; and (2) that allowing such a motion at any time before the case is submitted to the jury (including a motion at the close of the plaintiff's evidence and/or at the close of the trial).

Minority Approach: None of the states forms a significant Minority Approach to Federal Rule 50(a).

Nonconforming Approach: Nonconforming states stray from the norm. Generally, each of these states approaches JNOV by including additional provisions limiting the availability of this rule. For instance, the difference between the Majority Approach and that adopted by Oklahoma is one of time. In Oklahoma, the motion for "directed verdict" is made at the end of the trial after all the evidence has been presented.

Appendix 12-1
Rule on Determining Date of Final Judgment

Majority Approach	*Minority Approach*	*Nonconforming States*
Alabama	Connecticut	
Alaska	*(clerk must mail notice*	
Arizona	*of judgment to parties)*	
Arkansas		
California		
Colorado		
Delaware		
District of Columbia		
Florida		
Georgia		
Hawaii		
Idaho		
Illinois		
Indiana		
Iowa		
Kansas		
Kentucky		
Louisiana		
Maine		
Maryland		
Massachusetts		
Michigan		
Minnesota		
Mississippi		
Missouri		
Montana		
Nebraska		
Nevada		
New Hampshire		
New Jersey		
New Mexico		
New York		
North Carolina		
North Dakota		
Ohio		
Oklahoma		
Oregon		
Pennsylvania		
Rhode Island		
South Carolina		
South Dakota		
Tennessee		
Texas		
Utah		
Vermont		
Virginia		
Washington		
West Virginia		
Wisconsin		
Wyoming		

These findings are not comprehensive analyses of states' rule for entering judgment. Rather, the chart seeks to reflect states' conformity to (or procedures similar to) the essential components of Federal Rule of Civil Procedure 58. One should always refer to her state's statutes, rules, and/or case law for the specific requirements of determining what is a final judgment.

Majority Approach: States in the majority follow the approach of Federal Rule 58 (closely or loosely) by employing some method to signify judgment that has been entered and is final so that the necessary deadlines will be triggered. Such methods include, *inter alia*: separate document to be filed/entered into the civil docket (as in Federal Rule 58); notation in the docket by the court clerk; or providing that the date an order is signed by the judge will, if it disposes of the case, be a final judgment. Note that some states included in the majority do *not* require, as can happen often in the federal system, two documents—a ruling and/or verdict, followed by a separate order. That is, as long as some final written order is entered, that will satisfy the final judgment rule. Of course, it may also happen in a federal trial that a judge announces a decision from the bench in a judge trial, and that only one order—the one then entered disposing of the case—represents the final judgment order.

Minority Approach: In Connecticut, the court clerk must mail/deliver copies of the judgment to the parties.

Nonconforming Approach: No states stray from either the majority or minority approaches.

Appendix 12-2
Post-trial Motions for Judgment as a Matter of Law

Majority Approach	*Minority Approach*	*Nonconforming States*
Alaska	Alabama	Minnesota
Arkansas	Arizona	Virginia
California	Delaware	
Colorado	District of Columbia	
Connecticut	Hawaii	
Florida	Kansas	
Georgia	Maine	
Idaho	Montana	
Illinois	Nevada	
Indiana	New Mexico	
Iowa	New York	
Kentucky	North Dakota	
Louisiana	Rhode Island	
Maryland	South Dakota	
Massachusetts	Vermont	
Michigan	Washington	
Mississippi	West Virginia	
Missouri	Wyoming	
Nebraska		
New Hampshire		
New Jersey		
North Carolina		
Ohio		
Oklahoma		
Oregon		
Pennsylvania		
South Carolina		
Tennessee		
Texas		
Utah		
Wisconsin		

These findings are not comprehensive analyses of states' rule for post-trial motions for judgment as a matter of law. Rather, the chart seeks to identify the degree to which states follow the essential components of Federal Rule of Civil Procedure 50(b). One should always refer to her state's provisions on post-trial motions for judgment as a matter of law for the specific requirements of that state.

Majority Approach: The states in the majority continue to follow the directed verdict/JNOV (Judgment Notwithstanding the Verdict) language. A defendant must move for a directed verdict (also called "Judgment as a Matter of Law" or "JMOL") both at the close of the plaintiff's case in chief, and at the close of all of the evidence, to seek to have the court set aside an adverse verdict on grounds of insufficient evidence. If the defendant fails to make these motions at trial, the post-trial motion is waived.

Minority Approach: A minority of states follow the newer approach of Federal Rule 50(b). If the court does not grant the motion to strike/motion for JMOL made during trial (usually at the close of all the evidence), the movant may file a renewed motion for JMOL within a stated time period. Further, the movant may make a motion to request a new trial or alternatively join such request with a motion for a new trial under Rule 59. The court may then either: allow judgment on the verdict; order a new trial; or direct entry of JMOL.

Nonconforming Approach: Nonconforming states' rules include a "motion to strike plaintiff's evidence" during trial. However, these states allow a party to bring a motion to set aside the verdict (challenging the sufficiency of the evidence to support a verdict) *even if* the party did not make the motion to strike at trial. In other words, these states allow a challenge to the sufficiency of the evidence even though the challenge or motion was not raised at trial.

Appendix 12-3
Motions for a New Trial

Majority Approach	*Minority Approach*	*Nonconforming States*
Alaska	Alabama	Indiana
Connecticut	Arizona	Louisiana
Delaware	Arkansas	Oklahoma
District of Columbia	California	
Florida	Colorado	
Hawaii	Georgia	
Iowa	Idaho	
Kansas	Illinois	
Kentucky	Michigan	
Maine	Minnesota	
Maryland	Missouri	
Massachusetts	New Hampshire	
Mississippi	New Jersey	
Montana	New York	
Nebraska	North Carolina	
Nevada	North Dakota	
New Mexico	Ohio	
Oregon	Tennessee	
Pennsylvania	Texas	
Rhode Island	Virginia	
South Carolina	Wisconsin	
South Dakota		
Utah		
Vermont		
Washington		
West Virginia		
Wyoming		

These findings are not comprehensive analyses of states' rule for motions for a new trial and altering or amending a judgment. Rather, the chart seeks to explain the extent to which states the essential components of Federal Rule of Civil Procedure 59. One should always refer to her state's rule for its particular approach to new trials and altering or amending a judgment.

Majority Approach: States in the majority follow the Federal Rule of Civil Procedure 59. The court may grant a motion for a new trial on some or all of the issues. These states, however, still use the timing rule requiring a motion for a new trial to be made within *10 days* after the entry of the judgment. This timing differs from the newer approach in the federal system (28 days to file motion for new trial under amended version of Federal Rule 59). Note that the filing period for appeal(s) differs among the states. One must not only check (1) one's deadlines for filing the motion for a new trial and for a notice of appeal, but also (2) that one's post-trial motion suspends the deadline for filing a notice of appeal. If one is uncertain, she should ask the court to vacate any order that may be a final judgment so as to avoid missing a deadline.

Minority Approach: States in the minority follow the majority approach procedurally, but have different timing rules that *exceed* the old timing deadline of 10 days to file a motion for a new trial. Nevertheless, most of these states do not use the amended 28-day timing deadline that the federal rule has recently adopted. A statement of grounds for a new trial may also need to be included in the motion for a new trial.

Nonconforming Approach: States in the Nonconforming Approach category differ from either the majority or minority approaches above. Indiana calls its motion a "Motion to Correct Error," but gives the moving party 30 days to file. Louisiana requires a 7-day "delay" to file the motion, requires the grounds be stated, and the court must decide the motion within 10 days. Oklahoma requires the grounds be stated in the motion and allows 90 days to file it.

Appendix 12-4
Other Post-trial Motions

Majority Approach	*Minority Approach*	*Nonconforming States*
Alabama*	Connecticut	Georgia
Alaska	Illinois	
Arizona*	Pennsylvania	
Arkansas**	Texas	
California* **		
Colorado* **		
Delaware*		
District of Columbia		
Florida		
Hawaii		
Idaho*		
Indiana**		
Iowa**		
Kansas		
Kentucky**		
Louisiana**		
Maine		
Maryland**		
Massachusetts		
Michigan		
Minnesota		
Mississippi*		
Missouri**		
Montana*		
Nebraska* **		
Nevada*		
New Hampshire**		
New Jersey		
New Mexico		
New York* **		
North Carolina		
North Dakota		
Ohio**		
Oklahoma*		
Oregon		
Rhode Island		
South Carolina		
South Dakota		
Tennessee**		
Utah*		
Vermont		
Virginia* **		
Washington**		
West Virginia		
Wisconsin**		
Wyoming		

These findings are not comprehensive analyses of states' rule for relief from a judgment or order. Rather, this Appendix seeks to document the extent to which states model thier rules on the essential components of Federal Rule of Civil Procedure 60. One should always refer to her state's rule for the particular requirements in that state for seeking relief from a judgment or order.

Majority Approach: Theses states follow the approach of Federal Rule 60 for motions to set aside a judgment. They permit the motion in a one-year time period for specific reasons such as those in Federal Rule 60 (*e.g.*, mistake, inadvertence, surprise, excusable neglect, newly discovered evidence, and/or fraud). Motions to set aside a judgment or order for other reasons do not have a time limit (*e.g.*, judgment is void or has been satisfied/discharged, etc.). These states may have certain minimal differences regarding grounds and/or timing. The following key is used in the chart to signify these differences:

   *   timing differs from the one-year time limit for certain grounds
   **   grounds are added or excluded to/from those of the federal rule

Minority Approach: Minority Approach states allow a motion to set aside a judgment or order and require the grounds be stated, but no particular grounds are set forth as examples in these states' rules. Nor is a time period set forth in which to make the motion.

Nonconforming Approach: Georgia allows more than a one-year time period to bring a motion to set aside a judgment or order for grounds that, in other states, would typically require a motion within a year.

Index